DEREK

FOUNDATIONS

FOR

CHRISTIAN

LIVING

DPM

Derek Prince Ministries-UK
Baldock, Herfordshire

FOUNDATIONS FOR CHRISTIAN LIVING

Copyright © 1993 Derek Prince Ministries-International

This edition first published by Derek Prince Ministries–UK 2004.

This printing 2009.

This book was previously published by Word UK under the title *The Spirit-Filled Believer's Handbook,* 1994.

Previous DPM edition published 1998 under the title of *Foundations For Righteous Living.*

ISBN: 1-901144-25-9

Unless otherwise indicated, Scripture quotations are from the New King James Version of the Bible, copyright © 1979, 1980, 1982 by Thomas Nelson Inc., Publishers. Used by permission.

Scripture quotations marked KJV are from the King James Version of the Bible.

Scripture quotations marked NIV are from the Holy Bible, New International Version, copyright © 1973, 1978, 1984 International Bible Society. Used by permission.

Cover Design by Ronna Fu

Printed in China.

1 2 3 4 5 6 7 8 9 10 / 07 06 05 04

Derek Prince Ministries
www.dpmuk.org

FOR NO OTHER FOUNDATION CAN
ANYONE LAY THAN THAT WHICH IS LAID,
WHICH IS JESUS CHRIST.

1 CORINTHIANS 3:11

GENERAL CONTENTS

CONTENTS

PART II: REPENT AND BELIEVE

PART III: NEW TESTAMENT BAPTISMS

PART IV: PURPOSES OF PENTECOST

SECTION A: THE SPIRIT-FILLED BELIEVER

SECTION B: THE SPIRIT-FILLED CONGREGATION

SECTION C: THE SPIRIT-FILLED PREACHER

PART V: LAYING ON OF HANDS

PART VI: RESURRECTION OF THE DEAD

PART VII: ETERNAL JUDGEMENT

ABOUT THE AUTHOR

Derek Prince (1915–2003) was born in India of British parents. He was educated as a scholar of Greek and Latin at Eton College and King's College, Cambridge in England. Upon graduation he held a fellowship (equivalent to a professorship) in Ancient and Modern Philosophy at King's College. Derek also studied Hebrew, Aramaic, and modern languages at Cambridge and the Hebrew University in Jerusalem. As a student, he was a philosopher and an agnostic.

While in the British Medical Corps during World War II, Derek began to study the Bible as a philosophical work. Converted through a powerful encounter with Jesus Christ, he was baptized in the Holy Spirit a few days later. Out of this encounter, he formed two conclusions: first, that Jesus Christ is alive; second, that the Bible is a true, relevant, up-to-date book. These conclusions altered the whole course of his life, which he then devoted to studying and teaching the Bible as the Word of God.

Discharged from the army in Jerusalem in 1945, Derek married Lydia Christensen, founder of a children's home there. Upon their marriage, he immediately became father to Lydia's eight adopted daughters—six Jewish, one Palestinian Arab, and one English. Together, the family saw the rebirth of the state of Israel in 1948. In the late 1950s, they adopted another daughter while he was serving as principal of a teacher training college in Kenya.

In 1963, the Princes immigrated to the United States and pastored a church in Seattle. In 1973, Derek became one of the founders of Intercessors for America. His book, *Shaping History through Prayer and Fasting*, has awakened Christians around the world to their responsibility to pray for their governments. Many consider underground translations of the book as instrumental in the fall of communist regimes in the USSR, East Germany, and Czechoslovakia.

Lydia Prince died in 1975, and Derek married Ruth Baker (a single mother to three adopted children) in 1978. He met his second wife, like his first wife, while she was serving the Lord in Jerusalem. Ruth died in December 1998 in Jerusalem, where they had lived since 1981.

Until a few years before his own death in 2003 at the age of 88, Derek persisted in the ministry God had called him to as he travelled the world, imparting God's revealed truth, praying for the sick and afflicted, and sharing his prophetic insights into world events in the light of Scripture. Internationally recognized as a Bible scholar and spiritual patriarch, Derek Prince established a teaching ministry that spanned six continents and more than 60 years. He is the author of more than 50 books, 600 audio teachings, and 100 video teachings, many of which have been translated and published in more than 100 languages. He pioneered teaching on such groundbreaking themes as generational curses, the biblical significance of Israel, and demonology.

Derek's radio program, which began in 1979, has been translated into more than a dozen languages and continues to touch lives. His main gift of explaining the Bible and its teaching in a clear and simple way has helped build a foundation of faith in millions of lives. His nondenominational, nonsectarian approach has made his teaching equally relevant and helpful to people from all racial and religious backgrounds, and his teaching is estimated to have reached more than half the globe.

In 2002, he said, "It is my desire—and I believe the Lord's desire—that this ministry continue the work, which God began through me over 60 years ago, until Jesus returns."

Derek Prince Ministries continues to distribute Derek's teachings and to train missionaries, church leaders, and congregations through the outreaches of more than thirty Derek Prince offices around the world, including primary work in Australia, Canada, China, France, Germany, the Netherlands, New Zealand, Norway, Russia, South Africa, Switzerland, the United Kingdom, and the United States. For current information about these and other worldwide locations, visit www.derekprince.com.

INTRODUCTION

For fifty years I have been teaching, counselling and praying for Christians from a multitude of national and denominational backgrounds. The problems in their lives have been as varied as their backgrounds, but underneath them all I have continually discerned one basic deficiency: They have never laid a sound doctrinal foundation. Consequently, they have never been able to build a stable, successful Christian life.

I picture such Christians as people who have purchased a lot for the purpose of building a home for themselves. On this, over the years, they have assembled a mass of materials, acquired from attending various churches, conferences, seminars or even Bible colleges. Yet, in spite of all this, no house has ever been built. All they have to show for their activity is an ever-growing pile of things they have acquired – building materials, furnishings, appliances and so on.

From time to time they attend yet another conference and return with some special item for the house – perhaps a marble bath or an oak front door. Yet the house never takes shape. The reason is simple: They have never laid the necessary foundation.

Does this description perhaps apply to you – or to someone whom you are trying to counsel?

In this book you will be confronted – possibly for the first time in your life – with the fact that there is a specific foundation of biblical doctrines which you must lay before you can build a successful Christian life. You will discover that the Bible reveals six such doctrines (see Heb. 6:1-2). If you work carefully through the book, you will be thoroughly grounded in all six of them. You will also discover how they fit into the total revelation of Scripture.

Once you have mastered these foundational doctrines and learned how to apply them practically in your life, you will be in a position to make use of all that material you have been piling up through the years – even the marble bath and the oak front door!

This is not a dream or mere wishful thinking. It is something extremely real and practical. It works!

I have proved this in two ways. First, it has worked in my own life. I have been able to build a life of successful Christian service which has stood the test of more than fifty difficult and strenuous years.

Second, it has produced similar results in the lives of countless others to whom I have ministered. I hardly ever attend a church or a conference in any nation where I am not approached by some grateful Christian who says, "Brother Prince, I want to thank you that your teaching has given me a solid foundation on which I have been building for many years."

The material for this book was developed for my first radio programme, "*The Study Hour*," which was broadcast once a week during 1963 and 1964. I continued the programme for a year, resulting in fifty-two separate studies. Transcripts were eventually produced and compiled into seven books. A dozen years later I revised and edited all of the material, which was then published in Great Britain as a single volume.

The present volume has been subjected to further scrutiny and revision. In each case the purpose has been to make the contents as accurate and as easy to read as possible.

This material has been translated – either wholly or in part – into at least twenty languages, which include Arabic, Albanian, Chinese, Hebrew, Hungarian, Indonesian, Mongolian, Russian and Serbo-Croatian.

It has not been possible to keep an exact record of all the copies that have been distributed, but they total tens of thousands.

A comprehensive correspondence course titled Christian Foundations was developed in 1983 for in-depth, personal study of this book.

Students – both ministers and lay people – have been enrolled from every continent.

Though the material has had a global impact, it has never been printed as a single volume in the United States, nor has it been easily available through Christian bookstores in the U.S. I am delighted that this single-volume American edition has finally become a reality. It also contains an expanded topical index and a completely new Scripture index (particularly helpful for pastors and teachers).

In closing, let me offer a word of counsel to each reader: Try to approach these studies with an open heart and mind. Do your best to lay aside any personal prejudices or preconceptions you may have – whether intellectual or religious. Let God speak directly to you in His own words. He has much to say to you – and all of it is for your good.

Derek Prince
Fort Lauderdale, Florida
January 8, 1993

HOW TO USE
"FOUNDATIONS FOR
CHRISTIAN LIVING"

Foundations for Christian Living is designed to help you lay a solid foundation on which to build your Christian faith. Its special features and study helps include:

Table of Contents
The table of contents is expanded to list all the headings within each chapter. This will help you locate the information you are seeking and provide you with a helpful framework for reading the entire section.

Scripture Index
This index will help you locate commentary on specific verses and includes every passage quoted here, with page numbers to the right of each entry.

Topical Index
To help you find answers to the most basic questions of the Christian faith, the entire volume has been analysed exhaustively to provide a thorough listing. Page numbers are included to the right of each entry.

PART I

FOUNDATION FOR FAITH

WHOEVER COMES TO ME, AND HEARS
MY SAYINGS AND DOES THEM, I WILL SHOW
YOU WHOM HE IS LIKE: HE IS LIKE A MAN
BUILDING A HOUSE, WHO DUG DEEP AND LAID
THE FOUNDATION ON THE ROCK.

LUKE 6:47-48

INTRODUCTION TO PART I

ABOUT THE BIBLE

Adherents to the Christian faith throughout the world today number at least one billion persons. This total includes Christians from all sections of the church, in all areas of the earth and from a multitude of racial backgrounds. Not all these are actively practising their faith, but all are recognised as adherents. As such, they constitute one of the largest and most significant elements in the world's population.

Virtually all these Christians recognise the Bible as the authoritative basis of their faith and practice. The Bible also plays a significant role in two other major world religions: Judaism and Islam. By all objective standards it is the most widely read and influential book in the history of the human race. Year after year it consistently heads the list of the best-selling books of the world. It is obvious, therefore, that any person who desires a good general education cannot afford to omit the study of the Bible.

The Bible, as we have it today, is divided into two major sections. The first section, the Old Testament, contains thirty-nine books. It was written primarily in Hebrew – although a few portions were written in a sister Semitic language called Aramaic. The second section, the New

Testament, contains twenty-seven books. The oldest extant manuscripts are in Greek.

The Old Testament describes briefly the creation of the world and, in particular, of Adam. It relates how Adam and his wife, Eve, disobeyed God and thereby brought a series of evil consequences upon themselves, their descendants and the entire environment in which God had placed them. It then goes on to trace in outline the history of the first generations descended from Adam.

After eleven chapters, the Old Testament focuses on Abraham, a man chosen by God to be the father of a special people, through whom God purposed to provide redemption for the entire human race. It records the origin and history of this special people, to whom God gave the name Israel. Altogether, the Old Testament records the dealings of God with Abraham and his descendants over a period of about two thousand years.

The Old Testament reveals various important aspects of God's character and His dealings both with individuals and with nations. Included in this revelation are God's justice and His judgements; His wisdom and His power; His mercy and His faithfulness. The Old Testament particularly emphasises God's faithfulness to keep the covenants and promises He makes, whether with individuals or with nations.

Central to God's special purpose for Israel was His promise, sealed by His covenant, that He would send them a deliverer with the God-given task of redeeming mankind from all the consequences of his rebellion and restoring him to God's favour. The Hebrew title of this deliverer was Messiah – which means literally "anointed one."

The New Testament records the outworking of this promise in the Person of Jesus of Nazareth. This is indicated by the title given Him: Christ. This title is derived from a Greek word – *Christos* – which means precisely the same as the Hebrew title Messiah – that is, "anointed one." Jesus came to Israel as the anointed One whom God had promised in the Old Testament. He fulfilled everything that the Old Testament had foretold about His coming. Viewed from this perspective, the Old Testament and the New Testament are linked together to form a single, harmonious revelation of God and His purposes for man.

1
THE FOUNDATION OF
THE CHRISTIAN FAITH

In various places the Bible compares the life of a believer to the construction of a building. For instance, the epistle of Jude says: "Building yourselves up on your most holy faith" (v. 20).

The apostle Paul also uses the same picture in various places:

> You are God's building . . . as a wise master builder I have laid the foundation (1 Cor. 3:9-10).

> You also are being built together for a habitation of God in the Spirit (Eph. 2:22).

> I commend you . . . to the word of His grace, which is able to build you up (Acts 20:32).

In all these passages the believer's life is compared to the construction of a building.

Now, in the natural order, the first and most important feature of any permanent structure is its foundation. The foundation necessarily sets a limit to the weight and height of the building to be erected upon it. A weak foundation can support only a small building. A strong foundation can support a large building. There is a fixed relationship between the foundation and the building.

In the city of Jerusalem I once lived in a house that had been built by an Assyrian. This man had obtained from the municipality a licence to build a house of two stories, and the foundation was laid accordingly. However, in order to increase his income from renting the building, this Assyrian had built on a third story without obtaining permission to do so. The result was that, while we were actually living in the house, the whole building began to settle down on one corner and eventually went right out of perpendicular. What was the reason for this? The foundation was not strong enough to support the house which that man tried to erect upon it.

Even so, in the spiritual order the same thing happens in the lives of many professing Christians. They set out with every intention of raising a fine, imposing edifice of Christianity in their lives. But, alas, before long their fine edifice begins to sink, to sag, to get out of true. It leans grotesquely. Sometimes it collapses completely and leaves nothing but a ruined heap of vows and prayers and good intentions that have gone unfulfilled.

Beneath this mass of ruins the reason for the failure lies buried. It was the foundation. Never properly laid, it was unable to support the fine edifice which had been planned.

Christ the Rock

What, then, is God's appointed foundation for the Christian life? The answer is clearly given by the apostle Paul: "For no other foundation can anyone lay than that which is laid, which is Jesus Christ" (1 Cor. 3:11).

This is confirmed also by Peter as he speaks of Jesus Christ: "Therefore it is also contained in the Scripture, 'Behold, I lay in Zion a chief cornerstone, elect, precious' " (1 Pet. 2:6).

Here Peter is referring to the passage in Isaiah which reads: "Therefore thus says the Lord God: 'Behold, I lay in Zion a stone for a foundation' " (Is. 28:16). Thus Old Testament and New Testament alike agree in this vital fact: The true foundation of the Christian life is Jesus Christ Himself – nothing else, and no one else. It is not a creed, a church, a denomination, an ordinance or a ceremony. It is Jesus Christ Himself – and "no other foundation can anyone lay."

Consider the words of Jesus.

When Jesus came into the region of Caesarea Philippi, He
asked His disciples, saying, "Who do men say that I, the Son
of Man, am?" So they said, "Some say John the Baptist, some
Elijah, and others Jeremiah or one of the prophets." He said
to them, "But who do you say that I am?" And Simon Peter
answered and said, "You are the Christ, the Son of the living
God." Jesus answered and said to him, "Blessed are you,
Simon Bar-Jonah, for flesh and blood has not revealed this to
you, but My Father who is in heaven. And I also say to you
that you are Peter, and on this rock I will build My church,
and the gates of Hades shall not prevail against it" (Matt.
16:13-18).

It has sometimes been suggested that these words of Jesus mean that
Peter is the rock upon which the Christian church is to be built, and thus
that Peter is in some sense the foundation of Christianity rather than
Christ Himself. This question is of such vital and far-reaching importance that it is imperative to examine the words of Jesus very carefully
to ascertain their proper meaning.

In the original Greek of the New Testament there is, in Christ's
answer to Peter, a deliberate play upon words. In Greek, the name
"Peter" is *Petros;* the word for "rock" is *petra.* Playing upon this
similarity in sound, Jesus says, "You are Peter [*Petros*], and on this rock
[*petra*] I will build My church" (Matt. 16:18).

Though there is a similarity in sound between these two words, their
meaning is quite different. *Petros* means a small stone or a pebble. *Petra*
means a large rock. The idea of building a church upon a pebble would
obviously be ridiculous and therefore could not be Christ's real meaning.

Jesus uses this play on words to bring out the truth He is seeking to
impart. He is not identifying Peter with the rock; on the contrary, He is
contrasting Peter with the rock. He is pointing out how small and
insignificant the little stone, Peter, is in comparison to the great rock
upon which the church is to be built.

Common sense and Scripture alike confirm this fact. If the church of
Christ were really founded upon the apostle Peter, it would surely be the
most insecure and unstable edifice in the world. Later in the same
chapter of Matthew's Gospel we read that Jesus began to forewarn His
disciples of His impending rejection and crucifixion. The account then
continues:

Then Peter took Him aside and began to rebuke Him, saying,

"Far be it from You, Lord; this shall not happen to You!" But
He turned and said to Peter, "Get behind Me, Satan! You are
an offence to Me, for you are not mindful of the things of
God, but the things of men" (Matt. 16:22-23).

Here Christ directly charges Peter with being influenced by the
opinions of men, and even by the promptings of Satan himself. How
could such a man be the foundation of the entire Christian church?

Later on in the Gospels we read that, rather than confess Christ before
a serving maid, Peter publicly denied his Lord three times.

Even after the resurrection and the day of Pentecost, Paul tells us that
Peter was influenced by fear of his countrymen to compromise at one
point concerning the truth of the gospel (see Gal. 2:11-14).

Surely, then, Peter was no rock. He was loveable, impetuous, a born
leader – but a man just like the rest, with all the inherent weaknesses of
humanity. The only rock upon which Christian faith can be based is
Christ Himself.

Confirmation of this vital fact is found also in the Old Testament.

The psalmist David, prophetically inspired by the Holy Spirit, says
this:

> The Lord is my rock . . . in whom I will trust;
> My shield and the horn of my salvation, my stronghold (Ps.
>   18:2).

In Psalm 62 David makes a similar confession of faith.

> Truly my soul silently waits for God;
> From Him comes my salvation.
> He only is my rock and my salvation;
> He is my defence;
> I shall not be greatly moved.

> My soul, wait silently for God alone . . .
> . . . He only is my rock and my salvation;
> He is my defence;
> I shall not be moved.
> In God is my salvation and my glory;
> The rock of my strength,
> And my refuge, is in God (Ps. 62:1-2, 5-7).

Nothing could be plainer than that. The word *rock* occurs three times, and the word *salvation* occurs four times. That is to say, the words *rock* and *salvation* are by the Scripture intimately and inseparably joined. Each is found only in one person, and that Person is the Lord Himself. This is emphasised by the repetition of the word *only*.

If anyone should require yet further confirmation of this, we may turn to the words of Peter himself. Speaking to the people of Israel concerning Jesus, Peter says:

> Nor is there salvation in any other, for there is no other name under heaven given among men by which we must be saved (Acts 4:12).

The Lord Jesus Christ, therefore, is the true rock, the rock of ages, in whom there is salvation. The person who builds upon this foundation can say, like David:

> He only is my rock and my salvation;
> He is my defence;
> I shall not be moved (Ps. 62:6).

Confrontation

How, then, does a person build upon this rock, which is Christ?

Let us turn back again to that dramatic moment when Christ and Peter stood face-to-face and Peter said, "You are the Christ, the Son of the living God" (Matt. 16:16). We have seen that Christ is the rock. But it is not Christ in isolation or abstraction. Peter had a definite personal experience. There were four successive stages in this experience.

1. A direct, personal confrontation of Peter by Christ. Christ and Peter stood face-to-face. There was no mediator between them. No other human being played any part at all in the experience.
2. A direct, personal revelation granted to Peter. Jesus said to Peter, "Flesh and blood has not revealed this to you, but My Father who is in heaven" (Matt. 16:17). This was not the outcome of natural reasoning or intellectual understanding. It was the outcome of a direct spiritual revelation to Peter by God the Father Himself.
3. A personal acknowledgement by Peter of the truth which

had thus been revealed to him.
4. An open and public confession by Peter of the truth which he acknowledged.

In these four successive stages we see what it means to build upon the rock. There is nothing abstract, intellectual or theoretical about the whole thing. Each stage involves a definite, individual experience.

The first stage is a direct, personal confrontation of Christ. The second stage is a direct, spiritual revelation of Christ. The third stage is a personal acknowledgement of Christ. The fourth stage is an open and personal confession of Christ.

Through these four experiences, Christ becomes for each individual believer the rock upon which his faith is built.

Revelation

The question arises: Can a person today come to know Christ in the same direct, personal way that Peter came to know Him?

The answer is yes, for the following two reasons: First, it was not Christ in His purely human nature who was revealed to Peter: Peter already knew Jesus of Nazareth, the carpenter's son. The One who was now revealed to Peter was the divine, eternal, unchanging Son of God. This is the same Christ who now lives exalted in heaven at the Father's right hand. In the passage of nearly two thousand years there has been no change in Him at all. It is still Jesus Christ, the same yesterday, today and forever. As He was revealed to Peter, He can still be revealed today to those who sincerely seek Him.

Second, the revelation did not come by "flesh and blood" – by any physical or sensory means. It was a spiritual revelation, the work of the Holy Spirit. The same Spirit who gave this revelation to Peter is still at work in all the world, revealing the same Christ. Jesus Himself promised His disciples:

> When He, the Spirit of truth, has come, He will guide you into all truth; for He will not speak on His own authority, but whatever He hears He will speak; and He will tell you things to come. He will glorify Me, for He will take of what is Mine and declare it to you (John 16:13-14).

Since spiritual revelation is in the eternal, spiritual realm, it is not limited by material or physical factors, such as the passage of time or the

change of language, customs, clothing or circumstances.
This personal experience of Jesus Christ the Son of God – by the Holy
Spirit revealed, acknowledged and confessed – remains the one
unchanging rock, the one immovable foundation, upon which all true
Christian faith must be based. Creeds and opinions, churches and
denominations – all these may change, but this one true rock of God's
salvation by personal faith in Christ remains eternal and unchanging.
Upon it a person may build his faith for time and for eternity with a
confidence that nothing can ever overthrow.

Acknowledgement

Nothing is more striking in the writings and testimony of the early
Christians than their serenity and confidence concerning their faith in
Christ. Jesus says:

> And this is eternal life, that they may know You, the only true
> God, and Jesus Christ whom You have sent (John 17:3).

This is not merely to know God in a general way through nature or
conscience as Creator or Judge. This is to know Him revealed personally
in Jesus Christ. Neither is it to know about Jesus Christ merely as a
historical character or a great teacher. It is to know Christ Himself,
directly and personally, and God in Him. The apostle John writes:

> These things I have written to you who believe in the name of
> the Son of God, that you may know that you have eternal life
> (1 John 5:13).

The early Christians not only believed, but they also knew. They had
an experiential faith which produced a definite knowledge of that which
they believed.
A little further on in the same chapter John writes again:

> We know that the Son of God has come and has given us an
> understanding, that we may know Him who is true; and we
> are in Him who is true, in His Son Jesus Christ (v. 20).

Note the humble, yet serene, confidence of these words. Their basis is
knowledge of a person, and that Person is Jesus Christ Himself. Paul
gave the same kind of personal testimony when he said:

I know whom I have believed and am persuaded that He is
able to keep what I have committed to Him until that Day
(2 Tim. 1:12).

Notice that Paul did not say, "I know what I have believed." He said,
"I know whom I have believed." His faith was not founded upon a creed
or a church, but upon a Person whom he knew by direct acquaintance –
Jesus Christ. As a result of this personal acquaintance with Christ, he
had a serene confidence concerning the well-being of his soul, which
nothing in time or eternity could overthrow.

Confession

For a number of years I conducted regular street meetings in London,
England. At the close of the meetings I would sometimes approach
people who had listened to the message and ask them this simple
question: "Are you a Christian?" Many times I would receive answers
such as, "I think so," or "I hope so," or "I try to be," or "I don't know."
All who give answers like these betray plainly one fact: Their faith is not
built upon the one sure foundation of a direct, personal knowledge of
Jesus Christ.

Suppose I were to put that same question to you: Are you a Christian?
What kind of answer would you be able to give?

One final word of advice from Job:

Now acquaint yourself with Him, and be at peace;
Thereby good will come to you (Job 22:21).

2
HOW TO BUILD ON THE FOUNDATION

Once we have laid in our own lives the foundation of a personal encounter with Christ, how can we continue to build upon this foundation?

The answer to this question is found in the well-known parable about the wise man and the foolish man, each of whom built a house.

> Therefore whoever hears these sayings of Mine, and does them, I will liken him to a wise man who built his house on the rock: and the rain descended, the floods came, and the winds blew and beat on that house; and it did not fall, for it was founded on the rock. Now everyone who hears these sayings of Mine, and does not do them, will be like a foolish man who built his house on the sand: and the rain descended, the floods came, and the winds blew and beat on that house; and it fell. And great was its fall (Matt. 7:24-27).

Notice that the difference between these men did not lie in the tests to which their houses were subjected. Each man's house had to endure the storm – the wind, the rain, the floods. Christianity has never offered anyone a storm-free passage to heaven. On the contrary, we are warned that "we must through many tribulations enter the kingdom of God" (Acts 14:22).

Any road sign posted "To Heaven" which bypasses tribulation is a deception. It will not lead to the promised destination.

What, then, was the real difference between the two men and their houses? The wise man built upon a foundation of rock, the foolish man upon a foundation of sand. The wise man built in such a way that his house survived the storm unmoved and secure; the foolish man built in such a way that his house could not weather the storm.

The Bible – Foundation of Faith

Just what are we to understand by this metaphor of building upon a rock? What does it mean for each of us as Christians? Christ Himself makes this very clear.

> Whoever hears these sayings of Mine, and does them, I will liken him to a wise man who built his house on the rock (Matt. 7:24).

Thus, building on the rock means hearing and doing the words of Christ.

Once the foundation – Christ the Rock – has been laid in our lives, we build on that foundation by hearing and doing the Word of God; diligently studying and applying in our lives the teaching of God's Word. This is why Paul told the elders of the church at Ephesus:

> And now, brethren, I commend you to God and to the word of His grace, which is able to build you up (Acts 20:32).

It is God's Word, and God's Word alone – as we hear it and do it, as we study it and apply it – that is able to build up within us a strong, secure edifice of faith, laid upon the foundation of Christ Himself.

This brings us to a subject of supreme importance in the Christian faith: the relationship between Christ and the Bible, and, hence, the relationship of each Christian to the Bible.

Throughout its pages the Bible declares itself to be the "Word of God." On the other hand, in a number of passages the same title – "the Word" or "the Word of God" – is given to Jesus Christ Himself.

For example:

> In the beginning was the Word, and the Word was with God,
> and the Word was God (John 1:1).

> And the Word became flesh and dwelt among us, and we
> beheld His glory, the glory as of the only begotten of the
> Father (John 1:14).

> He [Christ] was clothed with a robe dipped in blood, and His
> name is called The Word of God (Rev. 19:13).

This identity of name reveals an identity of nature. The Bible is the
Word of God, and Christ is the Word of God. Each alike is a divine,
authoritative, perfect revelation of God. Each agrees perfectly with the
other. The Bible perfectly reveals Christ; Christ perfectly fulfils the
Bible. The Bible is the written Word of God; Christ is the personal Word
of God. Before His incarnation Christ was the eternal Word with the
Father. In His incarnation Christ is the Word made flesh. The same Holy
Spirit that reveals God through His written Word also reveals God in the
Word made flesh, Jesus of Nazareth.

Proof of Discipleship

If Christ is in this sense perfectly one with the Bible, then it follows
that the relationship of the believer to the Bible must be the same as his
relationship to Christ. To this fact the Scriptures bear testimony in many
places.

Let us turn first to John 14. In this chapter Jesus warns His disciples
that He is about to be taken from them in bodily presence and that thereafter there must be a new kind of relationship between Him and them.
The disciples are unable and unwilling to accept this impending change.
In particular they are unable to understand how, if Christ is about to go
away from them, they will still be able to see Him or have communion
with Him. Christ tells them:

> A little while longer and the world will see Me no more, but
> you will see Me (John 14:19).

The final phrase of that verse might also be rendered, "but you will
continue to see Me." Because of this statement, Judas (not Iscariot, but

the other Judas) asks:

> Lord, how is it that You will manifest Yourself to us, and not
> to the world? (John 14:22).

In other words: "Lord, if You are going away, and if the world will see
You no more, how can You still manifest Yourself to us, Your disciples,
but not to those who are not Your disciples? What kind of communication will You maintain with us, which will not be open to the world?"
Jesus answers:

> If anyone loves Me, he will keep My word; and My Father
> will love him, and We will come to him and make Our home
> with him (John 14:23).

The key to understanding this answer is found in the phrase "he will
keep My word." The distinguishing mark between a true disciple and a
person of the world is that a true disciple keeps Christ's word.

Revealed in Christ's answer are four facts of vital importance for
every person who sincerely desires to be a Christian.

For the sake of clarity, let me first repeat the answer of Jesus:

> If anyone loves Me, he will keep My word; and My Father
> will love him, and We will come to him and make Our home
> with him (John 14:23).

Here, then, are the four vital facts:

1. Keeping God's Word is the supreme feature which distin-
    guishes the disciple of Christ from the rest of the world.
2. Keeping God's Word is the supreme test of the disciple's
    love for God and the supreme cause of God's favour
    toward the disciple.
3. Christ manifests Himself to the disciple through God's
    Word, as it is kept and obeyed.
4. The Father and the Son come into the life of the disciple
    and establish their enduring home with him through
    God's Word.

Test of Love

Side by side with this answer of Christ's, let me set the words of the apostle John.

> He who says, "I know Him," and does not keep His commandments, is a liar, and the truth is not in him. But whoever keeps His word, truly the love of God is perfected in him. By this we know that we are in Him (1 John 2:4-5).

We see from these two passages that it is impossible to overemphasise the importance of God's Word in the believer's life.

To summarise, the keeping of God's Word distinguishes you as a disciple of Christ. It is the test of your love for God. It is the cause of God's special favour toward you. It is the medium through which Christ manifests Himself to you, and through which God the Father and the Son come into your life and make Their home with you.

Let me put it to you in this way.

Your attitude toward God's Word is your attitude toward God Himself. You do not love God more than You love His Word. You do not obey God more than you obey His Word. You do not honour God more than you honour His Word. You do not have more room in your heart and life for God than you have for His Word.

Do you want to know how much God means to you? Just ask yourself, How much does God's Word mean to me? The answer to the second question is the answer also to the first. God means as much to you as His Word means to you – just that much, and no more.

Means of Revelation

There is today a general and ever-increasing awareness among the Christian church that we have entered into the period of time foretold in Acts 2:17.

> And it shall come to pass in the last days, says God, that I will pour out of My Spirit on all flesh; your sons and your daughters shall prophesy, your young men shall see visions, your old men shall dream dreams.

I am humbly grateful to God that in recent years I have been privi-leged to experience and observe firsthand outpourings of the Spirit in five different continents – Africa, Asia, Europe, America and Australia – in which every detail of this prophecy has been enacted and repeated many times over. As a consequence, I believe firmly in the scriptural manifestation in these days of all nine gifts of the Holy Spirit; I believe that God speaks to His believing people through prophecies, visions, dreams and other forms of supernatural revelation.

Nevertheless, I hold most firmly that the Scriptures are the supreme, authoritative means by which God speaks to His people, reveals Himself to His people, guides and directs His people. I hold that all other forms of revelation must be carefully proved by reference to the Scriptures and accepted only insofar as they accord with the doctrines, precepts, practices and examples set forth in the Scriptures. We are told:

> Do not quench the Spirit. Do not despise prophecies. Test all things; hold fast what is good (1 Thess. 5:19-21).

It is wrong, therefore, to quench any genuine manifestation of the Holy Spirit. It is wrong to despise any prophecy given through the Holy Spirit. On the other hand, it is vitally necessary to test any manifestation of the Spirit, or any prophecy, by reference to the standard of the Scriptures and thereafter to hold fast – to accept, to retain – only those manifestations or prophecies which are in full accord with this divine standard. Again, in Isaiah we are warned:

> To the law and to the testimony! If they do not speak according to this word, it is because there is no light in them (Is. 8:20).

Thus the Scripture – the Word of God – is the supreme standard by which all else must be judged and tested. No doctrine, no practice, no prophecy, no revelation is to be accepted if it is not in full accord with the Word of God. No person, no group, no organisation, no church has authority to change, override or depart from the Word of God. In whatever respect or whatever degree any person, group, organisation or church departs from the Word of God, in that respect and in that degree they are in darkness. *There is no light in them.*

We are living in a time when it is increasingly necessary to emphasise the supremacy of the Scripture over every other source of revelation or doctrine. We have already made reference to the great world-wide outpouring of the Holy Spirit in the last days and to the various supernatural manifestations which will accompany this outpouring.

However, the Scripture also warns us that, side by side with this increased activity and manifestation of the Holy Spirit, there will be a parallel increase in the activity of demonic forces, which always seek to oppose God's people and God's purposes in the earth.

Speaking about this same period of time, Christ Himself warns us:

> Then if anyone says to you, "Look, here is the Christ!" or "There!" do not believe it. For false christs and false prophets will arise and show great signs and wonders, so as to deceive, if possible, even the elect. See, I have told you beforehand (Matt. 24:23-25).

In the same way, the apostle Paul warns us:

> Now the Spirit expressly says that in latter times some will depart from the faith, giving heed to deceiving spirits and doctrines of demons, speaking lies in hypocrisy, having their own conscience seared with a hot iron, forbidding to marry, and commanding to abstain from foods which God created to be received with thanksgiving by those who believe and know the truth (1 Tim. 4:1-3).

Paul here warns us that in these days there will be a great increase in the propagation of false doctrines and cults and that the unseen cause behind this will be the activity of deceiving spirits and demons. As examples, he mentions religious doctrines and practices which impose unnatural and unscriptural forms of asceticism in regard to diet and to the normal marriage relationship. Paul indicates that the safeguard against being deceived by these forms of religious error is to *believe and know the truth* – that is, the truth of God's Word.

By this divine standard of truth we are enabled to detect and to reject all forms of satanic error and deception. But for the people who profess religion, without sound faith and knowledge of what the Scripture teaches, these are indeed perilous days.

We need to lay hold upon one great guiding principle which is established in the Scripture. It is this: God's Word and God's Spirit should always work together in perfect unity and harmony. We should never divorce the Word from the Spirit or the Spirit from the Word. It is not God's plan that the Word should ever work apart from the Spirit or the Spirit apart from the Word.

> By the word of the Lord the heavens were made,
> And all the host of them by the breath of His mouth
>   (Ps. 33:6).

The word here translated "breath" is actually the normal Hebrew word for "spirit." However, the use of the word "breath" suggests a beautiful picture of the working of God's Spirit. As God's Word goes out of His mouth, so His Spirit – which is His breath – goes with it.

On our human level, each time we open our mouths to speak a word, our breath necessarily goes out together with the word. So it is also with God. As God's Word goes forth, His breath – that is, His Spirit – goes with it. In this way God's Word and God's Spirit are always together, perfectly united in one single divine operation.

We see this fact illustrated, as the psalmist reminds us, in the account of creation. In Genesis we read:

> The Spirit of God was hovering over the face of the waters
> (Gen. 1:2).

In the next verse Gen. 1:3 we read:

> Then God said, "Let there be light."

That is, God's Word went forth; God pronounced the word *light.* And as the Word and the Spirit of God were thus united, creation took place, light came into being, and God's purpose was fulfilled.

What was true of that great act of creation is true also of the life of each individual. God's Word and God's Spirit united in our lives contain all the creative authority and power of God Himself. Through them God will supply every need and will work out His perfect will and plan for us. But if we divorce these two from one another – seeking the Spirit without the Word, or studying the Word apart from the Spirit – we go astray and miss God's plan.

To seek the manifestations of the Spirit apart from the Word will always end in foolishness, fanaticism and error. To profess the Word without the quickening of the Spirit results only in dead, powerless orthodoxy and religious formalism.

3
THE AUTHORITY OF GOD'S WORD

In our study of this subject, let us turn first to the words of Christ Himself. He is here speaking to the Jews and is justifying the claim which He has made, and which the Jews had contested, that He is the Son of God. In support of His claim, Christ quotes from the Psalms in the Old Testament, which He designates by the phrase "your law." Here is what He says:

> Jesus answered them, "Is it not written in your law, 'I said, "You are gods" ' ? If He called them gods, to whom the word of God came (and the Scripture cannot be broken), do you say of Him whom the Father sanctified and sent into the world, 'You are blaspheming,' because I said, 'I am the Son of God'?" (John 10:34-36).

In this reply Jesus makes use of the two titles which have ever since been used more than all others by His followers to designate the Bible. The first of these titles is "the Word of God"; the second is "the Scripture." It will be profitable to consider what each of these two main titles has to tell us about the nature of the Bible.

When Jesus called the Bible "the Word of God," He indicated that the truths revealed in it do not have their origin with men, but with God. Though many different men have been used in various ways to make the Bible available to the world, they are all merely instruments or channels. In no case did the message or the revelation of the Bible originate with men, but always and only with God Himself.

The Bible – God's Written Word

On the other hand, when Jesus used the second title, "the Scripture," He indicated a divinely appointed limitation of the Bible. The phrase "the Scripture" means literally "that which is written." The Bible does not contain the entire knowledge or purpose of almighty God in every aspect or detail. It does not even contain all the divinely inspired messages that God has ever given through human instruments. This is proved by the fact that the Bible itself refers in many places to the utterances of prophets whose words are not recorded in the Bible.

We see, therefore, that the Bible, though completely true and authoritative, is also highly selective. Its message is intended primarily for the human race. It is expressed in words which human beings can understand. Its central theme and purpose are the spiritual welfare of man. It reveals primarily the nature and consequences of sin and the way of deliverance from sin and its consequences through faith in Christ.

Let us now take one more brief look at the words of Jesus in John 10:35. Not merely does He set His personal seal of approval upon the Bible's two main titles – "the Word of God" and "the Scripture" – He also sets His seal of approval quite clearly upon the Bible's claim to complete authority, for He says, " . . . and the Scripture cannot be broken."

This short phrase, "cannot be broken," contains within it every claim for supreme and divine authority that can ever be made on behalf of the Bible. Volumes of controversy may be written either for or against the Bible, but in the last resort Jesus has said all that is necessary in five simple words: "the Scripture cannot be broken."

When we give proper weight to the Bible's claim that the men associated with it were in every case merely instruments or channels and that every message and revelation in it has its origin with God Himself, there remains no logical or reasonable ground for rejecting the Bible's claim to complete authority. We are living in days when men can launch satellites into space and then, by means of invisible forces such as radio, radar or electronics, control the course of these satellites at distances of thousands or millions of miles, can maintain communication with them and can receive communication from them.

If men can achieve such results as these, then only blind prejudice – and that of a most unscientific character – would deny the possibility that God could create human beings with mental and spiritual faculties such that He could control or direct them, maintain communication with them and receive communication from them. The Bible asserts that this is in fact what God has done and still continues to do.

The discoveries and inventions of modern science, so far from discrediting the claims of the Bible, make it easier for honest and open-minded people to picture the kind of relationship between God and men which made the Bible possible.

Inspired by the Holy Spirit

The Bible indicates plainly that there is one supreme, invisible influence by which God did in fact control, direct and communicate with the spirits and minds of the men by whom the Bible was written. This invisible influence is the Holy Spirit – God's own Spirit. For example, the apostle Paul says:

> All Scripture is given by inspiration of God, and is profitable for doctrine, for reproof, for correction, for instruction in righteousness (2 Tim. 3:16).

The word here translated "by inspiration" means literally "inbreathed of God" and is directly connected with the word *Spirit*. In other words, the Spirit of God – the Holy Spirit – was the invisible, but inerrant, influence which controlled and directed all those who wrote the various books of the Bible.

This is stated perhaps more plainly still by the apostle Peter.

> Knowing this first, that no prophecy of Scripture is of any private interpretation (2 Pet. 1:20).

In other words, as we have already explained, in no case does the message or revelation of the Bible originate with man, but always with God.

Then Peter goes on to explain just how this took place.

For prophecy never came by the will of man, but holy men of God spoke as they were moved by the Holy Spirit (2 Pet. 1:21).

The Greek word translated "moved by" means more literally "borne along by," or we might say, "directed in their course by." In other words, just as men today control the course of their satellites in space by the interplay of radio and electronics, so God controlled the men who wrote the Bible by the interplay of His divine Spirit with the spiritual and mental faculties of man. In the face of contemporary scientific evidence, to deny the possibility of God's doing this is merely to give expression to prejudice.

In the Old Testament the same truth of divine inspiration is presented to us in another picture, taken from an activity which goes much further back into human history than the contemporary launching of satellites into space. The psalmist David says:

The words of the Lord are pure words,
Like silver tried in a furnace of earth,
Purified seven times (Ps. 12:6).

The picture is taken from the process of purifying silver in a furnace or oven built of clay. (Such clay ovens are still used for various purposes among the Arabs today.) The clay furnace represents the human element; the silver represents the divine message which is to be conveyed through the human channel; the fire which ensures the absolute purity of the silver, that is, the absolute accuracy of the message, represents the Holy Spirit. The phrase "seven times" indicates – as the number seven does in many passages of the Bible – the absolute perfection of the Holy Spirit's work.

Thus, the whole picture assures us that the complete accuracy of the divine message in the Scriptures is due to the perfect operation of the Holy Spirit, over-ruling all the frailty of human clay and purging all the dross of human error from the flawless silver of God's message to man.

Eternal, Authoritative

Probably no character in the Old Testament had a clearer understanding than the psalmist David of the truth and authority of God's Word. David writes:

Forever, O Lord,
Your word is settled in heaven (Ps. 119:89).

Here David emphasises that the Bible is not the product of time but of eternity. It contains the eternal mind and counsel of God, formed before the beginning of time or the foundation of the world. Out of eternity it has been projected through human channels into this world of time, but when time and the world pass away, the mind and counsel of God revealed through Scripture will still stand unmoved and unchanged. The same thought is expressed by Christ Himself.

Heaven and earth will pass away, but My words will by no means pass away (Matt. 24:35).

Again, David says:

The entirety of Your word is truth,
And every one of Your righteous judgements endures forever (Ps. 119:160).

In the last century or two persistent criticism and attack have been directed against the Bible, both Old and New Testaments. However, by far the greatest part of this attack has always been focused on the book of Genesis and the next four books which follow it. These first five books of the Bible, known as the Pentateuch or Torah, are attributed to the authorship of Moses.

It is remarkable, therefore, that nearly three thousand years before these attacks against the Pentateuch were conceived in the minds of men, David had already given the Holy Spirit's testimony to the faith of God's believing people throughout all ages.

The entirety of Your word is truth (Ps. 119:160).

In other words, the Bible is true from Genesis 1:1 right on through to the very last verse of Revelation.

Christ and His apostles, like all believing Jews of their time, accepted the absolute truth and authority of all the Old Testament Scriptures, including the five books of the Pentateuch.

In the account of Christ's temptation by Satan in the wilderness, we read that Christ answered each temptation of Satan by direct quotation from the Old Testament Scriptures (see Matt. 4:1-10). Three times He commenced His answer with the phrase "It is written . . ." Each time He was quoting directly from the fifth book of the Pentateuch, Deuteronomy. It is a remarkable fact that not only Christ, but also Satan, accepted the absolute authority of this book.

In the Sermon on the Mount Christ said:

> Do not think that I came to destroy the Law or the Prophets. [This phrase 'the Law or the Prophets' was generally used to designate the Old Testament Scriptures as a whole.] I did not come to destroy but to fulfil. For assuredly, I say to you, till heaven and earth pass away, one jot or one tittle will by no means pass from the law till all is fulfilled (Matt. 5:17-18).

The word *jot* is the English form of the name of the smallest letter in the Hebrew alphabet, roughly corresponding in size and shape to an inverted comma in modern English script. The word *tittle* indicates a little curl or horn, smaller in size than a comma, added at the corner of certain letters in the Hebrew alphabet to distinguish them from other letters very similar in shape.

Thus, what Christ is saying, in effect, is that the original text of the Hebrew Scriptures is so accurate and authoritative that not even one portion of the script smaller in size than a comma can be altered or removed. It is scarcely possible to conceive how Christ could have used any form of speech which would have more thoroughly endorsed the absolute accuracy and authority of the Old Testament Scriptures.

Consistently throughout His earthly teaching ministry He maintained the same attitude toward the Old Testament Scriptures. For instance, we read that when the Pharisees raised a question about marriage and divorce, Christ answered by referring them to the opening chapters of Genesis (see Matt. 19:3-9). He introduced His answer by the question:

> Have you not read that He who made them at the beginning "made them male and female"? (v. 4).

The phrase "at the beginning" constituted a direct reference to the book of Genesis since this is its Hebrew title.

Again, when the Sadducees raised a question about the resurrection from the dead, Christ answered them by referring to the account of Moses at the burning bush in the book of Exodus (see Matt. 22:31-32). As with the Pharisees, He replied in the form of a question:

Have you not read what was spoken to you by God, saying,
"I am the God of Abraham, the God of Isaac, and the God of
Jacob"? (Matt. 22:32).

Christ here quotes from Exodus 3:6. But in quoting these words
recorded by Moses nearly fifteen centuries earlier, Christ said to the
Sadducees of His own day, "Have you not read what was spoken to you
by God?" Note that phrase "spoken to you by God." Christ did not
regard these writings of Moses as merely a historical document of the
past, but rather as a living, up-to-date, authoritative message direct from
God to the people of His own day. The passage of fifteen centuries had
not deprived the record of Moses of its vitality, its accuracy or its
authority.

Not merely did Christ accept the absolute accuracy of the Old
Testament Scriptures in all His teaching, He also acknowledged their
absolute authority and control over the whole course of His own earthly
life. From His birth to His death and resurrection there was one supreme,
controlling principle which was expressed in the phrase "that it might be
fulfilled." That which was to be fulfilled was in every case some relevant
Scripture passage of the Old Testament. For example, the Bible specifically records that each of the following incidents in the earthly life of
Jesus took place in fulfilment of Old Testament Scriptures:

His birth of a virgin; His birth at Bethlehem; His flight into
Egypt; His dwelling at Nazareth; His anointing by the Holy
Spirit; His ministry in Galilee; His healing of the sick; the
rejection of His teaching and His miracles by the Jews; His
use of parables; His betrayal by a friend; His being forsaken
by His disciples; His being hated without a cause; His being
condemned with criminals; His garments being parted and
divided by lot; His being offered vinegar for His thirst; His
body being pierced without His bones being broken; His
burial in a rich man's tomb; His rising from the dead on the
third day.

The entire earthly life of Jesus was directed in every aspect by the
absolute authority of the Old Testament Scriptures. When we set this fact
side by side with His own unquestioning acceptance of the Old
Testament Scriptures in all His teaching, we are left with only one
logical conclusion: If the Old Testament Scriptures are not an absolutely
accurate and authoritative revelation from God, then Jesus Christ

Himself was either deceived or He was a deceiver.

Coherent, Complete, All-sufficient

Let us now consider the authority claimed for the New Testament.

We must first observe the remarkable fact that, so far as we know, Christ Himself never set down a single word in writing – with the exception of one occasion when He wrote on the ground in the presence of a woman taken in adultery.

Nevertheless, He explicitly commanded His disciples to transmit the record of His ministry and His teaching to all nations on earth.

> Go therefore and make disciples of all the nations, baptising them in the name of the Father and of the Son and of the Holy Spirit, teaching them to observe all things that I have commanded you (Matt. 28:19-20).

Previously He had said:

> Therefore, indeed, I send you prophets, wise men, and scribes (Matt. 23:34).

The word *scribes* means "writers," that is, those who set down religious teaching in written form. It is therefore clear that Jesus intended the record of His ministry and teaching to be set down by His disciples in permanent form.

Furthermore, Jesus made all necessary provisions for the absolute accuracy of all that He intended His disciples to put down in writing, for He promised to send the Holy Spirit to them for this purpose.

> But the Helper, the Holy Spirit, whom the Father will send in My name, He will teach you all things, and bring to your remembrance all things that I said to you (John 14:26).

A further, similar promise is contained in John 16:13-15. Notice that in these words Christ made provision both for past and for future; that is, both for the accurate recording of those things which the disciples had already seen and heard and also for the accurate imparting of the new truths which the Holy Spirit would thereafter reveal to them. The past is provided for in the phrase "He will . . . bring to your remembrance all things that I said to you" (John 14:26). The future is provided for in the phrase "He will teach you all things" (v. 26) and again, in John 16:13, "He will guide you into all truth."

We see, therefore, that the accuracy and authority of the New Testament, like that of the Old Testament, depend not upon human observation, memory or understanding, but upon the teaching, guidance and control of the Holy Spirit. For this reason, the apostle Paul says, "All scripture [Old Testament and New Testament alike] is given by inspiration of God" (2 Tim. 3:16).

We find that the apostles themselves clearly understood this and laid claim to this authority in their writings. For example, Peter writes:

> Beloved, I now write to you this second epistle . . . that you may be mindful of the words which were spoken before by the holy prophets, and of the commandment of us the apostles of the Lord and Saviour (2 Pet. 3:1-2).

Here Peter sets the Scriptures of the Old Testament prophets and the written commandments of Christ's apostles side by side, as being of precisely equal authority. Peter also acknowledges the divine authority of the writings of Paul, for he says:

> And consider that the long-suffering of our Lord is salvation – as also our beloved brother Paul, according to the wisdom given to him, has written to you, as also in all his epistles, speaking in them of these things, in which are some things hard to understand, which untaught and unstable people twist to their own destruction, as they do also the rest of the Scriptures (2 Pet. 3:15-16).

The phrase "the rest of the Scriptures" indicates that even in the lifetime of Paul the other apostles acknowledged that his epistles possessed the full authority of Scripture. Yet Paul himself had never known Jesus in His earthly ministry. Therefore, the accuracy and authority of Paul's teaching depended solely upon the supernatural inspiration and revelation of the Holy Spirit.

The same applies to Luke, who never received the title of apostle. Nevertheless, in the preamble to his Gospel, he states that he "had perfect understanding of all things from the very first" (Luke 1:3). The Greek word translated "from the very first" means literally "from above."

In John 3:3, where Jesus speaks of being "born again," it is the same

Greek word which is translated "again" or "from above." In each of these passages the word indicates the direct, supernatural intervention and operation of the Holy Spirit.

Thus we find, on careful examination, that the claim to absolute accuracy and authority of both Old and New Testaments alike depends not on the variable and fallible faculties of human beings, but on the divine, supernatural guidance, revelation and control of the Holy Spirit. Interpreted together in this way, the Old and New Testaments confirm and complement each other and constitute a coherent, complete and all-sufficient revelation of God.

We have also seen that there is nothing in this total view of the Scriptures which is inconsistent with logic, science or common sense. On the contrary, there is much in all three to confirm such a view and render it easy to believe.

4
INITIAL EFFECTS OF GOD'S WORD

We shall now examine the practical effects which the Bible claims to produce in those who receive it. In Hebrews 4:12 we are told that "the word of God is living and powerful."

The Greek word translated "powerful" is the one from which we obtain the English word *energetic*. The picture conveyed to us is one of intense, vibrant energy and activity.

Similarly, Jesus Himself says, "The words that I speak to you are spirit, and they are life" (John 6:63).

Again, the apostle Paul tells the Christians in Thessalonica:

> For this reason we also thank God without ceasing, because when you received the word of God which you heard from us, you welcomed it not as the word of men, but as it is in truth, the word of God, which also effectively works in you who believe (1 Thess. 2:13).

Thus we see that God's Word cannot be reduced merely to sounds in the air or marks on a sheet of paper. On the contrary, God's Word is life;

it is Spirit; it is alive; it is active; it is energetic; it works effectively in those who believe it.

Response Determines Effect

However, the Bible also makes it plain that the manner and the degree in which it works in any given instance are decided by the response of those who hear it. For this reason James says:

> Therefore lay aside all filthiness and overflow of wickedness [naughtiness], and receive with meekness the implanted word, which is able to save your souls (James 1:21).

Before the Word of God can be received into the soul with saving effect, there are certain things which must be laid aside. The two things James specifies are "filthiness" and "wickedness," or naughtiness. Filthiness denotes a perverse delight in that which is licentious and impure. This attitude closes the mind and heart against the saving influence of God's Word.

On the other hand, naughtiness particularly suggests the bad behaviour of a child. We call a child "naughty" when he refuses to accept instruction or correction from his senior but argues and answers back. This attitude is often found in the unregenerate soul toward God. Several passages of Scripture refer to this attitude.

> But indeed, O man, who are you to reply against God? (Rom. 9:20).

> Shall the one who contends with the Almighty correct Him?
> He who rebukes God, let him answer it (Job 40:2).

This attitude, like that of filthiness, closes the heart and mind to the beneficial effects of God's Word.

The opposite of filthiness and naughtiness is described by James as meekness. Meekness carries with it the ideas of quietness, humility, sincerity, patience, openness of heart and mind. These characteristics are often associated with what the Bible calls "the fear of the Lord"; that is, an attitude of reverence and respect toward God. Thus we read the following description in Psalms of the man who is able to receive benefit and blessing from the instruction of God through His Word.

> Good and upright is the Lord;
> Therefore He teaches sinners in the way.
> The humble He guides in justice,
> And the humble He teaches His way . . .
> Who is the man that fears the Lord?
> Him shall He teach in the way He chooses . . .
> The secret of the Lord is with those who fear Him,
> And He will show them His covenant (Ps. 25:8-9,12,14).

We see here that meekness and the fear of the Lord are the two attitudes necessary in those who desire to receive instruction and blessing from God through His Word. These two attitudes are the opposites of those which James describes as "filthiness" and "naughtiness."

Thus we find that God's Word can produce quite different effects in different people and that these effects are decided by the reactions of those who hear it. For this reason we read in Hebrews 4:12 not merely that God's Word is "alive" and "active," but also that it "is a discerner of the thoughts and intents of the heart." In other words, God's Word brings out into the open the inward nature and character of those who hear it and distinguishes sharply between the different types of hearers.

In like manner Paul describes the dividing and revealing character of the gospel.

> For the message of the cross is foolishness to those who are perishing, but to us who are being saved it is the power of God (1 Cor. 1:18).

There is no difference in the message preached; the message is the same to all men. The difference lies in the reaction of those who hear. For those who react in one way, the message appears to be mere foolishness; for those who react in the opposite way, the message becomes the saving power of God actually experienced in their lives.

This leads us to yet another fact about the Word of God which is stated in that key verse Hebrews 4:12. Not only is the Word of God alive and active; not only is it a discerner or revealer of the thoughts and intents of the heart; it is also "sharper than any two-edged sword." That is, it divides all those who hear into two classes – those who reject it and call it foolishness, and those who receive it and find in it the saving power of God.

It was in this sense that Christ said:

Do not think that I came to bring peace on earth. I did not come to bring peace but a sword. For I have come to "set a man against his father, a daughter against her mother, and a daughter-in-law against her mother-in-law" (Matt. 10:34-35).

The sword which Christ came to send upon earth is that which John saw proceeding out of Christ's mouth – the sharp, two-edged sword of God's Word (see Rev. 1:16). This sword, as it goes forth through the earth, divides even between members of the same household, severing the closest of earthly bonds, its effect determined by the response of each individual.

Faith

Turning now to those who receive God's Word with meekness and sincerity, with openness of heart and mind, let us examine in order the various effects it produces.

The first of these effects is faith.

So then faith comes by hearing, and hearing by the word of God (Rom. 10:17).

There are three successive stages in the spiritual process here described: 1) God's Word, 2) hearing, 3) faith. God's Word does not immediately produce faith, but only hearing. Hearing may be described as an attitude of aroused interest and attention, a sincere desire to receive and to understand the message presented. Then out of hearing there develops faith.

It is important to see that the hearing of God's Word initiates a process in the soul out of which faith develops and that this process requires a minimum period of time. This explains why there is so little faith to be found among so many professing Christians today. They never devote enough time to the hearing of God's Word to allow it to produce in them any substantial proportion of faith. If they ever devote any time at all to private devotions and the study of God's Word, the whole thing is conducted in such a hurried and haphazard way that it is all over before faith has had time to develop.

As we study how faith is produced, we also come to understand much more clearly how scriptural faith should be defined. In general conversation we use the word *faith* very freely. We speak of having faith in a doctor or faith in a medicine or faith in a newspaper or faith in a politician or political party. In scriptural terms, however, the word *faith* must be much more strictly defined. Since faith comes only from hearing God's Word, faith is always directly related to God's Word. Scriptural faith does not consist in believing anything that we ourselves may wish or please or fancy. Scriptural faith may be defined as believing that God means what He has said in His Word – that God will do what He has promised in His Word to do.

For example, David exercised this scriptural kind of faith when he said to the Lord:

> And now, O Lord, the word which You have spoken concerning Your servant and concerning his house, let it be established forever, and do as You have said (1 Chron. 17:23).

Scriptural faith is expressed in those five short words: "do as You have said."

Likewise, the virgin Mary exercised the same kind of scriptural faith when the angel Gabriel brought her a message of promise from God, and she replied:

> Let it be to me according to your word (Luke 1:38).

That is the secret of scriptural faith – *according to Your word.* Scriptural faith is produced within the soul by the hearing of God's Word and is expressed by the active response of claiming the fulfilment of that which God has said.

We have emphasised that faith is the first effect produced in the soul by God's Word because faith of this kind is basic to any positive transaction between God and any human soul.

> But without faith it is impossible to please Him, for he who comes to God must believe that He is, and that He is a rewarder of those who diligently seek Him (Heb. 11:6).

We see that faith is the first and indispensable response of the human soul in its approach to God.

> He who comes to God must believe (Heb. 11:6).

The New Birth

After faith, the next great effect produced by God's Word within the soul is that spiritual experience which is called in Scripture "the new birth" or "being born again." Thus James says concerning God:

> Of His own will He brought us forth by the word of truth, that we might be a kind of firstfruits of His creatures (James 1:18).

The born-again Christian possesses a new kind of spiritual life brought forth within him by the Word of God received by faith in his soul.

Similarly, the apostle Peter describes Christians as being "born again, not of corruptible seed but incorruptible, through the word of God which lives and abides forever" (1 Pet. 1:23).

It is a principle, both in nature and in Scripture, that the type of seed determines the type of life which is produced from the seed. A corn seed produces corn; a barley seed produces barley; an orange seed produces an orange.

So it is also in the new birth. The seed is the divine, incorruptible, eternal Word of God. The life which this produces, when received by faith into the heart of the believer, is like the seed – divine, incorruptible, eternal.

It is, in fact, the very life of God Himself coming into a human soul through His Word.

John writes:

> Whoever has been born of God does not sin, for His seed remains in him; and he cannot sin, because he has been born of God (1 John 3:9).

John here directly relates the victorious life of the overcoming Christian to the nature of the seed which produced that life within him – that is, God's own seed – the incorruptible seed of God's Word. Because the seed is incorruptible, the life it produces is also incorruptible; that is, absolutely pure and holy.

However, this Scripture does not assert that a born-again Christian can never commit sin. Within every born-again Christian a completely new nature has come into being. Paul calls this new nature "the new man" and contrasts it with "the old man" – the old, corrupt, depraved, fallen nature which dominates every person who has never been born again (see Eph. 4:22-24).

There is a complete contrast between these two: The "new man" is righteous and holy; the "old man" is depraved and corrupt. The "new man," being born of God, cannot commit sin; the "old man," being the product of man's rebellion and fall, cannot help committing sin.

The kind of life which any born-again Christian leads is the outcome of the interplay within him of these two natures. So long as the "old man" is kept in subjection and the "new man" exercises his proper control, there is unsullied righteousness, victory and peace. But whenever the "old man" is allowed to reassert himself and regain his control, the inevitable consequence is failure, defeat and sin.

We may sum up the contrast in this way: The true Christian who has been born again of the incorruptible seed of God's Word has within him the possibility of leading a life of complete victory over sin. The unregenerate man who has never been born again has no alternative but to commit sin. He is inevitably the slave of his own corrupt, fallen nature.

Spiritual Nourishment

We have said that the new birth through God's Word produces within the soul a completely new nature – a new kind of life. This leads us to consider the next main effect which God's Word produces.

In every realm of life there is one unchanging law: As soon as a new life is born, the first and greatest need of that new life is nourishment to sustain it. For example, when a human baby is born, that baby may be sound and healthy in every respect; but unless it quickly receives nourishment, it will pine away and die.

The same is true in the spiritual realm. When a person is born again, the new spiritual nature produced within that person immediately requires spiritual nourishment, both to maintain life and to promote growth. The spiritual nourishment which God has provided for all His born-again children is found in His own Word. God's Word is so rich and varied that it contains nourishment adapted to every stage of spiritual development.

God's provision for the first stages of spiritual growth is described in the first epistle of Peter. Immediately after Peter has spoken in chapter 1 about being born again of the incorruptible seed of God's Word, he goes on to say in chapter 2:

> Therefore, laying aside all malice, all guile, hypocrisy, envy, and all evil speaking, as new-born babes, desire the pure milk of the word, that you may grow thereby (1 Pet. 2:1-2).

For new-born spiritual babes in Christ, God's appointed nourishment is the pure milk of His own Word. This milk is a necessary condition of continued life and growth.

However, there is a warning attached. In the natural order, no matter how pure and fresh milk may be, it easily becomes contaminated and spoiled if it is brought into contact with anything that is sour or rancid. The same is true spiritually. For new-born Christians to receive proper nourishment from the pure milk of God's Word, their hearts must first be thoroughly cleansed from all that is sour or rancid.

For this reason Peter warns us that we must lay aside all malice, all guile, all hypocrisy, all envy and all evil speaking. These are the sour and rancid elements of the old life which, if not purged from our hearts, will frustrate the beneficial effects of God's Word within us and hinder our spiritual health and growth.

However, it is not the will of God that Christians should continue in spiritual infancy too long. As they begin to grow up, God's Word offers them more substantial food. When Christ was tempted by Satan to turn stones into bread, He replied:

> It is written, "Man shall not live by bread alone, but by every word that proceeds from the mouth of God" (Matt. 4:4).

Christ here indicates that God's Word is the spiritual counterpart of bread in man's natural diet. In other words, it is the main item of diet and source of strength.

It is significant that Christ said with emphasis, "every word that proceeds from the mouth of God." In other words, Christians who wish to mature spiritually must learn to study the whole Bible, not just a few of the more familiar portions.

It is said of George Müller that he regularly read the Bible through several times each year. This explains in large measure the triumphs of his faith and the fruitfulness of his ministry. Yet there are many professing Christians and church members who scarcely know where to find in their Bibles such books as Ezra and Nehemiah or some of the minor prophets. Far less have they ever studied for themselves the messages of such books.

No wonder they continue forever in a kind of spiritual infancy. They are, in fact, sad examples of retarded development due to inadequate diet.

Beyond milk and bread, God's Word also provides solid food. The writer of Hebrews rebuked the Hebrew believers of his day on the grounds that they had been familiar for many years with the Scriptures but had never learned to make any proper study or application of their teaching. Consequently, they were still spiritually immature and unable to help others who stood in need of spiritual teaching. This is what the writer says:

> For though by this time you ought to be teachers, you need someone to teach you again the first principles [or elements] of the oracles of God; and you have come to need milk and not solid food. For everyone who partakes only of milk is unskilled in the word of righteousness, for he is a babe. But solid food belongs to those who are of full age, that is, those who by reason of use have their senses exercised to discern both good and evil (Heb. 5:12-14).

What a picture of a great mass of professing Christians and church members today! They have owned a Bible and attended church for many years. Yet how little they know of what the Bible teaches! How weak and immature they are in their own spiritual experience; how little able to counsel a sinner or instruct a new convert! After so many years they are still spiritual babes, unable to digest any kind of teaching that goes beyond milk!

However, it is not necessary to remain in this condition. The writer of Hebrews tells us the remedy. It is to have our senses exercised by reason of use. The regular, systematic study of the whole of God's Word will develop and mature our spiritual faculties.

5
PHYSICAL AND MENTAL EFFECTS OF GOD'S WORD

In the previous study we discovered the following three effects of God's Word:

1. God's Word produces faith, and faith, in turn, is directly related to God's Word because faith is believing and acting upon what God has said in His Word.
2. God's Word, received as incorruptible seed into a believer's heart, produces the new birth – a new spiritual nature created within the believer and called in the Scriptures "the new man."
3. God's Word is the divinely appointed spiritual nourishment with which the believer must regularly feed the new nature within him if he is to grow into a healthy, strong, mature Christian.

Physical Healing

God's Word is so varied and wonderful in its working that it provides

not only spiritual health and strength for the soul but also physical health
and strength for the body. Let us turn first to Psalms.

> Fools, because of their transgression,
> And because of their iniquities, were afflicted.
> Their soul abhorred all manner of food,
> And they drew near to the gates of death.
> Then they cried out to the Lord in their trouble,
> And He saved them out of their distresses.
> He sent His word and healed them,
> And delivered them from their destructions (Ps. 107:17-20).

The psalmist gives us a picture of men so desperately sick that they
have lost all appetite for food and are lying right at death's door. In their
extremity they cry out to the Lord, and He sends them that which they
cry for – healing and deliverance. By what means does He send these?
By His Word. For the psalmist says:

> He sent His word and healed them,
> And delivered them from their destructions (Ps. 107:20).

Side by side with this passage in Psalm 107 we may set the passage
in Isaiah 55:11 where God says:

> So shall My word be that goes forth from My mouth;
> It shall not return to Me void,
> But it shall accomplish what I please,
> And it shall prosper in the thing for which I sent it.

In Psalm 107:20 we read that God sent His Word to heal and deliver;
in Isaiah 55:11 God says that His Word will accomplish the thing for
which He sent it. Thus God guarantees that He will provide healing
through His Word.

This truth of physical healing through God's Word is even more fully
stated in Proverbs, where God says:

> My son, give attention to my words;
> Incline your ear to my sayings.
> Do not let them depart from your eyes:
> Keep them in the midst of your heart;
> For they are life to those who find them,

And health to all their flesh (Prov. 4:20-22).

What promise of physical healing could be more all-inclusive than that? "Health to all their flesh." Every part of our physical frame is included in this phrase. Nothing is omitted. Furthermore, in the margin of the 1611 edition of the King James Version, the alternative reading for "health" is "medicine." The same Hebrew word includes both shades of meaning. Thus God has committed Himself to providing complete physical healing and health.

Notice the introductory phrase at the beginning of verse 20: "My son." This indicates that God is speaking to His own believing children. When a Syro-Phoenician woman came to Christ to plead for the healing of her daughter, Christ replied to her request by saying:

> It is not good to take the children's bread and throw it to the little dogs (Matt. 15:26).

By these words Christ indicated that healing is the children's bread; in other words, it is part of God's appointed daily portion for all His children. It is not a luxury for which they have to make special pleas and which may or may not be granted them. No, it is their "bread," part of their daily provision from their heavenly Father. This agrees exactly with the passage we read in Proverbs 4, where God's promise of perfect healing and health is addressed to every believing child of God. Both in Psalm 107 and in Proverbs 4 the means by which God provides healing is His Word. This is one further example of the vital truth which we stressed earlier in this series: that God Himself is in His Word and that it is through His Word that He comes into our lives.

As we consider the claim made in Proverbs 4:20-22 that God's Word is medicine for all our flesh, we might call these three verses God's great "medicine bottle." They contain a medicine such as was never compounded on earth – one medicine guaranteed to cure all diseases.

However, when a doctor prescribes a medicine, he normally ensures that the directions for taking it are written clearly on the bottle. This implies that no cure can be expected unless the medicine is taken regularly, according to the directions. The same is true with God's "medicine" in Proverbs. The directions are "on the bottle," and no cure is guaranteed if the directions are not followed.

What are these directions? They are fourfold.

1. "Give attention to my words."

2. "Incline your ear."
3. "Do not let them depart from your eyes."
4. "Keep them in the midst of your heart."

Let us analyse these directions a little more closely. The first direction is "give attention to my words." As we read God's Word, we need to give it close and careful attention. We need to focus our understanding upon it. We need to give it free, unhindered access to our whole inward being. So often we read God's Word with divided attention. Half our mind is occupied with what we read; the other half is occupied with those things which Jesus called "the cares of this life." We read some verses, or perhaps even a chapter or two, but at the end we have no clear impression of what we have read. Our attention has wandered.

Taken in this way, God's Word will not produce the effects God intended. When reading the Bible, it is well to do what Jesus recommended when He spoke of prayer; that is, to enter our closet and shut the door. We must shut ourselves in with God and shut out the things of the world.

The second direction on God's medicine bottle is "incline your ear." The inclined ear indicates humility. It is the opposite of being proud and stiff-necked. We must be teachable. We must be willing to let God teach us. In Psalm 78:41 the psalmist speaks of Israel's conduct as they wandered through the wilderness from Egypt to Canaan, and he brings this charge against them: They limited the Holy One of Israel.

By their stubbornness and unbelief they set limits to what they would allow God to do for them. Many professing Christians do just the same today. They do not approach the Bible with an open mind or a teachable spirit. They are full of prejudices or preconceptions – very often instilled by the particular sect or denomination with which they are associated – and they are not willing to accept any revelation or teaching from the Scriptures which goes beyond, or contrary to, their own set thoughts. Jesus charged the religious leaders of His day with this fault.

> Thus you have made the commandment of God of no effect
> by your tradition . . . And in vain they worship me, teaching
> as doctrines the commandments of men (Matt. 15:6,9).

The apostle Paul had been a prisoner of religious prejudices and traditions, but through the revelation of Christ on the Damascus road he was set free from them. Thereafter we find him saying in Romans 3:4:

Let God be true but every man a liar.

If we wish to receive the full benefit of God's Word, we must learn to take the same attitude.

The third direction on God's medicine bottle is "do not let them depart from your eyes," with the word *them* referring to God's words and sayings. The late evangelist Smith Wigglesworth once said, "The trouble with many Christians is that they have a spiritual squint: with one eye they are looking at the promises of the Lord, and with the other eye they are looking in some other direction."

In order to receive the benefits of physical healing promised in God's Word, it is necessary to keep both eyes fixed unwaveringly on the Lord's promises. One mistake many Christians make is to look away from God's promises to the case of some other Christian who has failed to receive healing. As they do this, their own faith wavers, and they, too, fail to receive healing.

> He who doubts is like a wave of the sea driven and tossed by the wind. For let not that man suppose that he will receive anything from the Lord; he is a double-minded man, unstable in all his ways (James 1:6-8).

A helpful verse to remember in such a situation is this one:

> The secret things belong to the Lord our God, but those things which are revealed belong to us and to our children forever, that we may do all the words of this law (Deut. 29:29).

The reason why some Christians fail to receive healing remains a secret, known only to God and not revealed to man. We do not need to be concerned with such secrets as this. Rather we need to concern ourselves with those things which are revealed: the clear statements and promises of God given to us in His Word. The things thus revealed in God's Word belong to us and to our children forever; they are our heritage as believers; they are our inalienable right. And they belong to us "that we may do them"; that is, that we may act upon them in faith. When we do, we prove them true in our experience.

The first direction spoke of "attending"; the second spoke of the "inclined ear"; the third spoke of the "focused eyes." The fourth direction on God's medicine bottle concerns the heart, the inward centre of the human personality, for it says "keep them in the midst of your heart." Proverbs emphasises the decisive influence of the heart in human experience.

> Keep your heart with all diligence,
> For out of it spring the issues of life (Prov. 4:23).

In other words, what is in our hearts controls the whole course of our lives and all that we experience.

If we receive God's words with careful attention – if we admit them regularly through both the ear and the eye so that they occupy and control our hearts – then we find them to be exactly what God has promised: both life to our souls and health to our flesh.

During World War II, while working with the medical services in North Africa, I became sick with a condition of the skin and nerves for which medical science, in that climate and those conditions, could provide no cure. I spent more than one year in the hospital, receiving every kind of treatment available. For more than four months at a stretch I was confined to bed. Eventually, I was discharged from the hospital at my own request, uncured.

I decided to seek no further medical treatment but to put the promises of God in Proverbs 4:20-22 to the test in my own case. Three times a day I went apart by myself, shut myself in with God and His Word, prayed and asked God to make His Word to me what He had promised it should be – medicine to all my flesh.

The climate, the diet and all other external circumstances were as unfavourable as they could be. Indeed, many healthy men all around me were falling sick. Nevertheless, through God's Word alone, without recourse to any other means of any kind, I received within a short time a complete and permanent cure.

Let me add that I am in no sense criticising or belittling medical science. I am grateful for all the good that medical science accomplishes. Indeed, I myself was working with the medical services. But the power of medical science is limited; the power of God's Word is unlimited.

Many Christians of different denominational backgrounds have testimonies similar to mine. I received a letter from a Presbyterian lady who was asked to give a word of testimony in a service in which there were a number of sick people to be prayed for. While this lady was testifying and actually quoting the words of Proverbs 4:20-22, another lady in the seat next to hers, who had been suffering excruciating pain from a crushed disc in her neck, was instantly healed – without any prayer being offered – simply through listening with faith to God's Word.

Later, I devoted a week on my radio Bible teaching programme to this theme of God's medicine bottle. A lady listener suffering from chronic eczema decided to take the medicine according to the "directions." Three months later she wrote to tell me that for the first time in twenty-five years her skin was completely free from eczema. The words of Psalm 107:20 are still being fulfilled today.

> He sent His word and healed them,
> And delivered them from their destructions.

Christians who testify today of the healing power of God's Word can say, as Christ Himself said to Nicodemus:

> Most assuredly, I say to you, We speak what We know and testify what We have seen (John 3:11).

For those who need healing and deliverance:

> Oh, taste and see that the Lord is good;
> Blessed is the man who trusts in Him! (Ps. 34:8).

Taste this medicine of God's Word for yourself! See how it works! It is not like so many earthly medicines, bitter and unpalatable. Nor does it work, like so many modern drugs, bringing relief to one organ of the body but causing a reaction which impairs some other organ. No, God's Word is altogether good, altogether beneficial. When received according to His direction, it brings life and health to our whole being.

Mental Illumination

In the area of the mind, also, the effect of God's Word is unique.

> The entrance of Your words gives light;
> It gives understanding to the simple (Ps. 119:130).

The psalmist speaks of two effects produced in the mind by God's Word: "light" and "understanding."

In the world today education is probably more highly prized and more universally sought after than at any previous period in man's history. Nevertheless, secular education is not the same as "light" or "under-standing." Nor is it any substitute for them. Indeed, there is no substitute for light. Nothing in the whole universe can do what light does.

So it is with God's Word in the human mind. Nothing else can do in the human mind what God's Word does, and nothing else can take the place of God's Word.

Secular education is a good thing, but it can be misused. A highly educated mind is a fine instrument – just like a sharp knife. But a knife can be misused. One man can take a sharp knife and use it to cut up food for his family. Another man may take a similar knife and use it to kill a fellow human being.

So it is with secular education. It is a wonderful thing, but it can be misused. Divorced from the illumination of God's Word, it can become extremely dangerous. A nation or civilisation which concentrates on secular education but gives no place to God's Word is simply forging instruments for its own destruction. The history of recent developments in the technique of nuclear fission is one among many historical examples of this fact.

On the other hand, God's Word reveals to man those things which he can never discover by his own intellect: the reality of God the Creator and Redeemer; the true purpose of existence; man's own inner nature; his origin and his destiny. In the light of this revelation, life takes on an entirely new meaning. With a mind thus illuminated, a man sees himself as part of a single comprehensive plan that spans the universe. Finding his place in this divine plan, he achieves a sense of self-worth and personal fulfilment that satisfies his deepest longings.

The effect of God's Word upon the mind, no less than its effect upon the body, has been made real for me in personal experience. I was privileged to receive the highest form of education that Britain had to offer in my generation. This climaxed with seven years at Cambridge University, studying philosophy, both ancient and modern. Always I was seeking something that would give real meaning and purpose to life. Academically I was successful, but inwardly I was still frustrated and unfulfilled.

Finally, as a last resort, I started to study the Bible simply as a work of philosophy. I studied it sceptically, as one who had rejected all forms of religion. Yet before many months, and before I had even reached the New Testament, the entrance of God's Word had imparted to me the light of salvation, the assurance of sins forgiven, the consciousness of inward peace and eternal life. I had found what I had been seeking: the real meaning and purpose of life.

It is appropriate to close this section by returning to Hebrews 4:12.

For the word of God is living and powerful [or energetic], and sharper than any two-edged sword, piercing even to the division of soul and spirit, and of joints and marrow, and is a discerner of the thoughts and intents of the heart.

This confirms and sums up the conclusions we have reached concerning God's Word. There is no area of the human personality which God's Word does not penetrate. It reaches right down into the spirit and soul, the heart and the mind, and even into the innermost core of our physical body, the joints and the marrow.

In perfect accord with this, we have seen in this and in the previous chapter that God's Word, implanted as a seed in the heart, brings forth eternal life. Thereafter it provides spiritual nourishment for the new life thus brought forth. Received into our bodies it produces perfect health, and received into our minds it produces mental illumination and understanding.

6
VICTORIOUS EFFECTS OF GOD'S WORD

Victory Over Sin

We have already remarked that probably no character in the Old Testament had a clearer vision of the authority and power of God's Word than the psalmist David. For an introduction to our present subject, victory over sin and Satan, we may turn once again to the words of David.

> Your word I have hidden in my heart,
> That I might not sin against You (Ps. 119:11).

The Hebrew word here translated "hidden" means, more exactly, "to store up as a treasure." David did not mean he had hidden God's Word away so that its presence could never be detected. Rather he meant he had stored up God's Word in the safest place, reserved for things he treasured most, so he might have it available for immediate use in every time of need.

In Psalm 17:4 David again expresses the keeping power of God's Word.

Concerning the works of men,
By the word of Your lips,
I have kept myself from the paths of the destroyer.

Here is a word of direction concerning our participation in "the works of men" – human activities and social interaction. Some of these activities are safe, wholesome, acceptable to God; others are dangerous to the soul and contain the hidden snares of the destroyer. ("The destroyer" is one of many names in Scripture for the devil.) How are we to distinguish between those which are safe and wholesome and those which are spiritually dangerous? The answer is, by the application of God's Word.

One often hears questions such as these: Is it right for a Christian to dance? to smoke? to gamble? and so on. The answer to all such questions must be decided not by accepted social practice, nor by accepted church tradition, but by the application of God's Word.

For instance, I remember that a group of Christian African women students once asked me, as a Christian minister, if there was any harm in their attending dances at the college where they were being trained as teachers. In reply I did not offer them my own personal opinion or the regulations laid down by a mission board. Instead I asked them to turn with me to two passages in the Bible.

Therefore, whether you eat or drink, or whatever you do, do all to the glory of God (1 Cor. 10:31).

And whatever you do in word or deed, do all in the name of the Lord Jesus, giving thanks to God the Father through Him (Col. 3:17).

I pointed out that these two passages of Scripture contain two great principles which are to decide and direct all that we do as Christians. First, we must do all things to the glory of God. Second, we must do all things in the name of the Lord Jesus, giving thanks to God by Him. Therefore, anything that we can do to the glory of God and in the name of the Lord Jesus is good and acceptable; anything that we cannot do to the glory of God and in the name of the Lord Jesus is wrong and harmful.

I then applied these principles to the question they had asked me. I said, "If you can attend those dances to the glory of God, and if you can freely give thanks to God in the name of the Lord Jesus while you are dancing, then it is perfectly all right for you to dance. But if you cannot do your dancing in this way and upon these conditions, then it is wrong for you to dance."

It was my responsibility, as I saw it, to give those young women basic scriptural principles. Thereafter it was their responsibility, not mine, to apply those principles to their particular situation.

Medical research has brought to light one very definite way in which many modern Christians, like David of old, have been kept from the paths of the destroyer by the application of God's Word.

The Scriptures teach very plainly that the body of the Christian, having been redeemed from the dominion of Satan by the blood of Christ, is a temple for the Holy Spirit to dwell in and is therefore to be kept clean and holy. For example, Paul says:

> Do you not know that you are the temple of God and that the Spirit of God dwells in you? If anyone defiles the temple of God, God will destroy him. For the temple of God is holy, which temple you are (1 Cor. 3:16-17).

> Or do you not know that your body is the temple of the Holy Spirit who is in you, whom you have from God, and you are not your own? For you were bought at a price; therefore glorify God in your body and in your spirit, which are God's (1 Cor. 6:19-20).

> For this is the will of God, your sanctification . . . that each of you should know how to possess his own vessel [that is, the earthen vessel of his physical body] in sanctification and honour (1 Thess. 4:3-4).

On the basis of these and other similar passages, many Christians have refrained from using tobacco in any form. Until fairly recently it was often suggested by unbelievers that this refusal by Christians to indulge in tobacco was merely a kind of foolish, old-fashioned fad, akin to fanaticism. However, modern medical research has demonstrated, beyond all possibility of doubt, that smoking – particularly of cigarettes – is a direct contributory cause of lung cancer. The medical associations of both the United States and Great Britain have endorsed this conclusion. In the United States this year there will be an estimated 146,000 deaths from lung cancer (American Cancer Society). Another undisputed fact, proved by experience and endorsed by medical science, is that death through lung cancer is usually lingering and painful.

In the face of facts such as these, the refusal of Christians to smoke can no longer be dismissed as foolishness or fanaticism. If foolishness can be charged to anyone today, it is certainly not to the Christian but to the person who regularly wastes substantial sums of money to gratify a lust which greatly increases the possibility of a painful death through lung cancer. And if foolishness can be charged to the victims of this lust, surely nothing short of wickedness can be charged to those who, by every means of persuasion and modern publicity, wilfully seek, for the sake of their own financial profit, to bring their fellow human beings under the cruel bondage of this degrading and destroying habit.

Almost exactly the same that has been said about tobacco smoking applies equally to excessive indulgence in alcohol.

Again, a majority of sincere Christians have through the years refrained from this kind of indulgence on the basis of the Bible's warnings against it. It is a well-established fact that excessive indulgence in alcohol is a major contributing factor in many kinds of mental and physical disease and also in the modern toll of traffic accidents.

Here again, as in the case of smoking, millions of Christians have been preserved from harm and disaster by their practical application of the Bible's teaching.

A new, "modern" plague – AIDS – came upon the world in the 1980s. Christians who practice monogamy and refrain from immorality protect themselves and their children from the devastation of that disease. On the other hand, homosexuality, so often touted as an "alternative life-style," has proved to be an alternative death-style. Christians who have been protected from these evils can surely echo, with deep thankfulness, the words of David.

> Concerning the works of men,
> By the word of Your lips,
> I have kept myself from the paths of the destroyer (Ps. 17:4).

Victory Over Satan

Not merely does God's Word, applied in this way, give victory over sin. It is also the divinely appointed weapon that gives victory over Satan himself. The apostle Paul commands:

> And take . . . the sword of the Spirit, which is the word of God (Eph. 6:17).

Thus, God's Word is an indispensable weapon in the Christian warfare. All the other items of the Christian armour listed in Ephesians 6 – the girdle, the breastplate, the shoes, the shield and the helmet – are intended for defence. The only weapon of attack is the Spirit's sword, the Word of God.

Without a thorough knowledge of God's Word and how to apply it, a Christian has no weapon of attack, no weapon with which he can assault Satan and the powers of darkness and put them to flight. In view of this, it is not surprising that Satan has throughout the history of the Christian church used every means and device within his power to keep Christians ignorant of the true nature, authority and power of God's Word.

In the use of God's Word as a weapon, the Lord Jesus Christ Himself is the Christian's supreme example. Satan brought three main temptations against Jesus, and Jesus met and defeated each temptation of Satan with the same weapon – the sword of God's written Word (see Luke 4:1-13). For in each case Jesus began His answer with the phrase "It is written" and then quoted directly from the Scriptures.

There is significance in the two different phrases which Luke uses in this account of Satan's temptation of Christ and its consequences. In Luke 4:1 he says:

Then Jesus, being filled with the Holy Spirit . . . was led by the Spirit into the wilderness.

But at the end of the temptations, in Luke 4:14, we read:

Then Jesus returned in the power of the Spirit to Galilee.

Before His encounter with Satan, Jesus was already "filled with the Holy Spirit." But it was only after Jesus had encountered and defeated Satan with the sword of God's Word that He was able to commence His God-appointed ministry "in the power of the Spirit." There is a distinction therefore between being filled with the Spirit and being able to minister in the power of the Spirit. Jesus only entered into the power of the Spirit after He had first used the sword of God's Word to defeat Satan's attempt to turn Him aside from the exercise of His Spirit-empowered ministry.

This is a lesson which needs to be learned by Christians today. Many Christians who have experienced a perfectly scriptural infilling of the Holy Spirit never go on to serve God in the power of the Spirit. The reason is that they have failed to follow the example of Christ. They have never learned to wield the sword of God's Word in such a way as to defeat Satan and repulse his opposition to the exercise of the ministry for which God actually filled them with the Holy Spirit.

It may safely be said that no person has a greater and more urgent need to study the Word of God than the Christian who has newly been filled with the Holy Spirit. Yet, sad to say, such Christians often seem to imagine that being filled with the Spirit is somehow a substitute for the diligent study and application of God's Word. In reality, the very opposite is true.

No other item of a soldier's armour is any substitute for his sword, and no matter how thoroughly he may be armed at all other points, a soldier without his sword is in grave danger. So it is with the Christian. No other spiritual equipment or experience is any substitute for a thorough knowledge of God's Word, and no matter how thoroughly he may be equipped in all other respects, a Christian without the sword of God's Word is always in grave danger.

The early Christians of the apostolic age, though often simple and uneducated, certainly followed the example of their Lord in learning to know and use God's Word as a weapon of offence in the intense spiritual conflict brought upon them by their profession of faith in Christ. For example, the apostle John in his advanced years wrote to the young Christian men who had grown up under his instruction:

> I have written to you, young men, because you are strong, and the word of God abides in you, and you have overcome the wicked one (1 John 2:14).

John makes three statements about these young men: 1) they are strong, 2) they have God's Word abiding in them, 3) they have overcome the wicked one (Satan). The second of these two statements is related to the first and the third, as cause is related to effect. The reason why these young Christian men were strong and able to overcome Satan was that they had God's Word abiding in them. It was God's Word within them that gave them their spiritual strength.

We need to ask ourselves this question: How many of the young Christian people in our churches today are strong and have overcome the devil? If we do not see many young Christian people today who manifest this kind of spiritual strength and victory, the reason is not in doubt. It is simply this: The cause which produces these effects is not there.

The only source of such strength and victory is a thorough, abiding knowledge of God's Word. Christian young people who are not thoroughly instructed in God's Word can never be really strong and overcoming in their experience.

We are today in grave danger of underrating the spiritual capacity of young people and treating them in a manner that is altogether too childish. There is even a tendency to create in young people today the impression that God has provided for them some special kind of Christianity with lesser demands and lower standards than those which God imposes upon adults. In this connection Solomon made a very relevant and penetrating remark.

> For childhood and youth are vanity (Eccl. 11:10).

In other words, childhood and youth are merely fleeting, external appearances which in no way alter the abiding spiritual realities that concern all souls alike.

William Booth's daughter, Catherine Booth-Clibborn, expressed a similar thought when she said, "There is no sex in soul." The deep, abiding spiritual realities upon which Christianity is based are in no way affected by differences of age or sex. Christianity is based upon such qualities as repentance, faith, obedience, self-sacrifice, devotion. These qualities are the same for men and women, boys and girls alike.

It is sometimes suggested that the way to meet this need of thorough scriptural teaching for Christian young people is to send them to Bible colleges. However, this proposed remedy can be accepted only with two qualifications. First, it must be stated that there is an increasing tendency at present, even among evangelical or full-gospel Bible colleges, to devote less and less time to the actual study of the Bible and more and more time to other secular studies. Paul warned the Colossians:

> Beware lest anyone cheat you through philosophy and empty deceit, according to the tradition of men (Col. 2:8).

Paul also warned Timothy:

> O Timothy! Guard what was committed to your trust [that is, the truth of God's Word], avoiding the profane and vain babblings and contradictions of what is falsely called knowledge – by professing it, some have strayed concerning the faith (1 Tim. 6:20-21).

These warnings need to be repeated today. In many cases, it is possible for a young person to complete a course at a modern Bible college and come away with an inadequate knowledge of the Bible's teachings and how to apply them in a practical way.

The second qualification we must make is that no Bible college course, however sound and thorough it may be, can ever exonerate the pastors of local churches from their duty to provide all the members of their congregations with regular, systematic training in God's Word.

The local church is the central point in the whole New Testament plan for scriptural instruction, and no other institution can ever usurp the local church's function. The apostles and Christians of the New Testament had no other institution for giving scriptural instruction except the local church. Yet they were more successful in their task than we are today.

Other institutions, such as Bible colleges, may provide special instruction to supplement the teaching done in the local churches, but they can never take their place. The most desperate need of the great majority of local churches today is not more organisation or better programmes or more activities. It is simply this: thorough, practical, regular instruction in the basic truths of God's Word and how to apply them in every aspect of Christian life.

Only by this means can the church of Christ, as a whole, rise up in strength, administer in Christ's name the victory of Calvary and accomplish the task committed to her by her Lord and Master.

This accords with the picture in Revelation of a victorious church at the close of this age.

> And they [the Christians] overcame him [Satan] by the blood
> of the Lamb and by the word of their testimony (Rev. 12:11).

Here are revealed the three elements of victory: the blood, the Word, our testimony. The blood is the token and seal of Christ's finished work upon the cross and of all that this makes available to us of blessing and power and victory. Through the Word we come to know and understand all that Christ's blood has purchased for us. Finally, through testifying to that which the Word reveals concerning the blood, we make Christ's victory over Satan real and effectual in our personal experience.

As we study this divine programme of victory over Satan, we see once again that the Word occupies a central position. Without proper knowledge of the Word, we cannot understand the true merits and power of Christ's blood, and thus our testimony as Christians lacks real conviction and authority. The whole of God's programme for His people centres around the knowledge of His Word and the ability to apply it.

Without this knowledge, the church finds herself today in the same condition as Israel in Hosea's day, concerning whom the Lord declared:

> My people are destroyed for lack of knowledge. Because you have rejected knowledge, I also will reject you (Hos. 4:6).

A church that rejects the knowledge of God's Word faces the certainty of rejection by God Himself and of destruction at the hands of her great adversary, the devil.

7
PURIFYING EFFECTS OF
GOD'S WORD

Cleansing

The seventh great effect of God's Word is that of cleansing and sanctification. The key text for this is Ephesians 5:25-27.

> Christ also loved the church and gave Himself for it, that He
> might sanctify and cleanse it with the washing of water by the
> word, that He might present it to Himself a glorious church,
> not having spot or wrinkle or any such thing, but that it should
> be holy and without blemish.

There are a number of important points in this passage which deserve
attention.

Notice, first, that the two processes of cleansing and sanctifying are
closely joined together. However, although these two processes are
closely related, they are not identical.

The distinction between them is this: That which is truly sanctified
must of necessity be absolutely pure and clean; but that which is pure

and clean need not necessarily be in the fullest sense sanctified. In other words it is possible to have purity, or cleanness, without sanctification, but it is not possible to have sanctification without purity, or cleanness.

Thus cleansing is an essential part of sanctification but not the whole of it. Later in this study we shall examine more closely the exact meaning of the word *sanctification.*

Turning again to Ephesians 5 we notice, second, that one main, definite purpose for which Christ redeemed the church is "that He might sanctify and cleanse it" (v. 26).

Thus the purpose of Christ's atoning death for the church as a whole, and for each individual Christian in particular, is not fulfilled until those who are redeemed by His death have gone through a subsequent process of cleansing and sanctifying. Paul makes it plain that only those Christians who have gone through this process will be in the condition necessary for their final presentation to Christ as His bride – and the condition which he specifies is that of a glorious church, "not having spot or wrinkle or any such thing . . . holy and without blemish" (v. 27).

The third point to notice in this passage is that the means which Christ uses to cleanse and sanctify the church is "the washing of water by the word" (v. 26). It is God's Word which is the means of sanctifying and cleansing; in this respect the operation of God's Word is compared to the washing of pure water.

Even before Christ's atoning death upon the cross had actually been consummated, He had already assured His disciples of the cleansing power of His Word which He had spoken to them.

> You are already clean because of the word which I have spoken to you (John 15:3).

We see, therefore, that the Word of God is a divine agent of spiritual cleansing, compared in its operation to the washing of pure water.

Side by side with the Word, we must also set the other great agent of spiritual cleansing referred to by the apostle John.

> But if we walk in the light as He is in the light, we have fellowship with one another, and the blood of Jesus Christ His Son cleanses us from all sin (1 John 1:7).

Here John speaks of the cleansing power of Christ's blood, shed upon the cross, to redeem us from sin.

God's provision for spiritual cleansing always includes these two divine agents – the blood of Christ shed upon the cross and the washing with water by His Word. Neither is complete without the other. Christ redeemed us by His blood so that He might cleanse and sanctify us by His Word.

John places these two great operations of Christ in the closest possible connection with each other. Speaking of Christ, he says:

> This is He who came by water and blood – Jesus Christ; not only by water, but by water and blood. And it is the Spirit who bears witness, because the Spirit is truth (1 John 5:6).

John declares that Christ is not only the great Teacher who came to expound God's truth to men; He is also the great Saviour who came to shed His blood to redeem men from their sin. In each case it is the Holy Spirit who bears testimony to Christ's work – to the truth and authority of His Word and to the merits and power of His blood.

John teaches us, therefore, that we must never separate these two aspects of Christ's work. We must never separate the Teacher from the Saviour, nor the Saviour from the Teacher.

It is not enough to accept Christ's teaching through the Word without also accepting and experiencing the power of His blood to redeem and cleanse us from sin. On the other hand, those who claim redemption through Christ's blood must thereafter submit themselves to the regular, inward washing of His Word.

There are various passages concerning the ordinances of the Old Testament sacrifices which set forth, in type, the close association between the cleansing by Christ's blood and the cleansing by His Word. For instance, in the ordinances of the tabernacle of Moses we read how God ordained that a laver of bronze containing clean water was to be placed close to the sacrificial altar of bronze and was to be used regularly in conjunction with it.

> Then the Lord spoke to Moses, saying: "You shall also make a laver of bronze, with its base also of bronze, for washing. You shall put it between the tabernacle of meeting and the altar. And you shall put water in it, for Aaron and his sons shall wash their hands and their feet in water from it. When they go into the tabernacle of meeting, or when they come near the altar to minister, to burn an offering made by fire to the Lord, they shall wash with water, lest they die. So they shall wash their hands and their feet, lest they die. And it shall

be a statute forever to them – to him and his descendants throughout their generations" (Ex. 30:17-21).

If we apply this picture to the New Testament, the sacrifice upon the bronze altar speaks of Christ's blood shed upon the cross for redemption from sin; the water in the laver speaks of the regular spiritual cleansing which we can receive only through God's Word. Each alike is essential to the eternal welfare of our souls. Like Aaron and his sons, we must regularly receive the benefits of both, "lest we die."

Sanctification

Having thus noted the process of cleansing through God's Word, let us now go on to consider the further process of sanctification.

First we must consider briefly the meaning of this word *sanctification*. The ending of the word – *ification* – occurs in many English words and always denotes an active process of doing or making something. For example, clarification means "making clear"; rectification means "making right or straight"; purification means "making pure," and so on. The first part of the word *sanctification* is directly connected with the word *saint* – in fact, it is simply another way of writing the same word. *Saint* in turn is simply an alternative way of translating the word which is more normally translated "holy."

Thus, the simple, literal meaning of sanctification is "making saintly," or "making holy."

The New Testament mentions five distinct agents in connection with sanctification: 1) the Spirit of God, 2) the Word of God, 3) the altar, 4) the blood of Christ, 5) our faith. Following are the main passages which mention these various agents of sanctification:

> God from the beginning chose you for salvation through sanctification by the Spirit and belief in the truth (2 Thess. 2:13).

Peter tells Christians that they are

> elect according to the foreknowledge of God the Father, in sanctification of the Spirit, for obedience and sprinkling of the blood of Jesus Christ (1 Pet. 1:2).

Thus, both Paul and Peter mention "sanctification of [or by] the Holy

Spirit" as an element of Christian experience.

Sanctification through the Word of God was referred to by Christ Himself when He prayed to the Father for His disciples.

> Sanctify them by Your truth. Your word is truth (John 17:17).

Here we see that sanctification comes through the truth of God's Word.

Sanctification through the altar is likewise referred to by Christ. He told the Pharisees:

> Fools and blind! For which is greater, the gift or the altar that sanctifies the gift? (Matt. 23:19).

Here Christ endorses that which had already been taught in the Old Testament – that the gift which was offered in sacrifice to God was sanctified, made holy, set apart, by being placed upon God's altar. In the New Testament, as we shall see, the nature of the gift and of the altar is changed, but the principle still remains true that it is "the altar that sanctifies the gift."

Sanctification through the blood of Christ is referred to in Hebrews 10:29. Here the author considers the case of the apostate – the person who has known all the blessings of salvation but has deliberately and openly rejected the Saviour. Concerning such a person he asks:

> Of how much worse punishment, do you suppose, will he be thought worthy who has trampled the Son of God underfoot, counted the blood of the covenant by which he was sanctified a common thing, and insulted the Spirit of grace?

This passage shows that the true believer who continues in the faith is sanctified by the blood of the new covenant which he has accepted – that is, by Christ's own blood.

Sanctification through faith is referred to by Christ Himself, as quoted by Paul as he related the commission which he received from Christ to preach the gospel to the Gentiles.

> To open their eyes and to turn them from darkness to light, and from the power of Satan to God, that they may receive forgiveness of sins and an inheritance among those who are sanctified by faith in Me (Acts 26:18).

Here we see that sanctification is through faith in Christ. Summing up these passages, we arrive at this conclusion: Sanctification, according to the New Testament, is through five great means or agencies: 1) the Holy Spirit, 2) the truth of God's Word, 3) the altar of sacrifice, 4) the blood of Christ and 5) faith in Christ.

The process thus unfolded may be briefly outlined as follows: The Holy Spirit initiates the work of sanctification in the heart and mind of each one whom God has chosen in His eternal purposes. Through the truth of God's Word, as it is received in the heart and mind, the Holy Spirit speaks, reveals the altar of sacrifice, separates the believer from all that holds him back from God and draws him to place himself in surrender and consecration upon that altar. There the believer is sanctified and set apart to God both by the contact with the altar and by the cleansing and purifying power of the blood that was shed upon the altar.

However, the exact extent to which each of these four sanctifying agents – the Spirit, the Word, the altar and the blood – accomplish their sanctifying work in each believer is decided by the fifth factor in the process; that is, by the individual faith of each believer. In the work of sanctification, God does not violate the one great law which governs all His works of grace in each believer – the law of faith.

As you have believed, so let it be done for you (Matt. 8:13).

Let us now examine a little more closely the part played by God's Word in this process of sanctification. First we must note that there are two aspects to sanctification – one negative and the other positive. The negative aspect consists in being separated from sin and the world and from all that is unclean and impure. The positive aspect consists in being made partaker of God's holy nature.

In much preaching, both on this and on other related subjects, there is a general tendency to overemphasise the negative at the expense of the positive. As Christians we tend to speak much more about the "do nots" in God's Word than about the "dos." For example, in Ephesians 5:18 we usually lay much more stress upon the negative "do not be drunk with wine" than we do upon the positive "be filled with the Spirit." However, this is an inaccurate and unsatisfactory way to present God's Word.

With regard to holiness, the Scriptures make it plain that this is something much more than a negative attitude of abstaining from sin and uncleanness. For example, in Hebrews 12:10 we are told that God, as a heavenly Father, chastens us, His children, for our profit that we may be partakers of His holiness. Again, in 1 Peter 1:15-16 we read:

> But as He who called you is holy, you also be holy in all your
> conduct, because it is written, "Be holy, for I am holy."

We see that holiness is a part of God's eternal, unchanging nature.
God was holy before sin ever entered into the universe, and God will still
be holy when sin has once again been banished forever. We, as God's
people, are to be partakers of this part of His eternal nature. Separation
from sin, just like cleansing from sin, is a stage in this process, but it is
not the whole process. The final, positive result which God desires in us
goes beyond both cleansing and separation.

God's Word plays its part both in the negative and in the positive
aspects of sanctification. Paul describes the negative aspect in Romans
12:1-2.

> I beseech you therefore, brethren, by the mercies of God, that
> you present your bodies a living sacrifice, holy, acceptable to
> God, which is your reasonable service. And do not be
> conformed to this world, but be transformed by the renewing
> of your mind, that you may prove what is that good and
> acceptable and perfect will of God.

There are four successive stages in the process which Paul here
describes.

1. *Presenting our bodies as living sacrifices upon God's
   altar.* We have already seen that the altar sanctifies that
   which is presented upon it.
2. *Not being conformed to the world* – that is, being
   separated from its vanity and sin.
3. *Being transformed by the renewing of our minds* – that is,
   learning to think in entirely new terms and values.
4. *Getting to know God's will personally for our lives.* This
   revelation of God's will is granted only to the renewed
   mind. The old, carnal, unrenewed mind can never know
   or understand God's perfect will.

It is here, in the renewing of the mind, that the influence of God's
Word is felt. As we read, study and meditate in God's Word, it changes
our whole way of thinking. It both cleanses us with its inward washing

and separates us from all that is unclean and ungodly. We learn to think about things – to estimate them, to evaluate them – as God Himself thinks about things.

In learning to think differently, of necessity, we also act differently. Our outward lives are changed in harmony with our new inward processes of thought. We are no longer conformed to the world because we no longer think like the world. We are transformed by the renewing of our minds.

However, not to be conformed to the world is merely negative. It is not a positive end in itself. If we are not to be conformed to the world, to what then are we to be conformed? The answer is plainly stated by Paul.

> For whom He [God] foreknew, He also predestined to be conformed to the image of His Son, that He might be the firstborn among many brethren (Rom. 8:29).

Here is the positive end of sanctification: to be conformed to the image of Christ. It is not enough that we are not conformed to the world – that we do not think and say and do the things that the world does. This is merely negative. Instead of all this, we must be conformed to Christ – we must think and say and do the things that Christ would do.

Paul dismisses the negative type of holiness as quite inadequate.

> Therefore, if you died with Christ from the basic principles of the world, why, as though living in the world, do you subject yourselves to regulations – "Do not touch, do not taste, do not handle," which all concern things which perish with the using? (Col. 2:20-22).

True sanctification goes far beyond this barren, legalistic, negative attitude. It is a positive conforming to the image of Christ Himself; a positive partaking of God's own holiness.

This positive aspect of sanctification, and the part played in it by God's Word, is beautifully summed up by Peter.

> His [God's] divine power has given to us all things that pertain to life and godliness, through the knowledge of Him who called us by glory and virtue, by which have been given to us exceedingly great and precious promises, that through

these you may be partakers of the divine nature, having escaped the corruption that is in the world through lust (2 Pet. 1:3-4).

There are three main points to notice here.

1. God's power has already provided us with all that we need for life and godliness. The provision is already made. We do not need to ask God to give us more than He has already given. We merely need to avail ourselves to the full of that which God has already provided.
2. This complete provision of God is given to us through the exceedingly great and precious promises of His own Word. The promises of God already contain within them all that we shall ever need for life and godliness. All that remains for us now to do is to appropriate and to apply these promises by active, personal faith.
3. The result of appropriating and applying God's promises is twofold, both negative and positive. Negatively, we escape the corruption that is in the world through lust; positively, we are made partakers of the divine nature. Here is the complete process of sanctification that we have described: both the negative escape from the world's corruption, and the positive partaking of God's own nature, of God's own holiness.

All this – both the negative and the positive – is made available to us through the promises of God's Word. It is in measure as we appropriate and apply the promises of God's Word that we experience true, scriptural sanctification.

Jacob once dreamed of a ladder reaching from earth to heaven. For the Christian, the counterpart to that ladder is found in God's Word. Its foot is set on earth, but its head reaches heaven – the plane of God's being. Each rung in that ladder is a promise. As we lay hold by the hands and feet of faith upon the promises of God's Word, we lift ourselves up by them out of the earthly realm and closer to the heavenly realm. Each promise of God's Word, as we claim it, lifts us higher above earth's corruption and imparts to us a further measure of God's nature.

Sanctification is by faith. But that faith is not merely negative or passive. The faith that truly sanctifies consists in a continual, active appropriating and applying of the promises of God's Word. It was for this reason that Jesus prayed to the Father:

Sanctify them by Your truth. Your word is truth (John 17:17).

8
REVELATORY EFFECTS OF
GOD'S WORD

In the last four chapters we have examined seven practical effects God's Word produces in us as, with faith and obedience, we receive and apply its teaching. These seven effects are:

1. Faith
2. The new birth
3. Complete spiritual nourishment
4. Healing and health for our physical bodies
5. Mental illumination and understanding
6. Victory over sin and Satan
7. Cleansing and sanctification

Now let us examine two further ways in which the Bible, as God's Word, works in the believer.

Our Mirror

The first of these is that the Bible provides us with a *mirror of spiritual revelation.* This operation of God's Word is described in James 1:23-25. In the two preceding verses James has already warned that for God's Word to produce its proper effects in us, there are two basic conditions: 1) we must "receive [it] with meekness" (v. 21) – that is, with the proper attitude of heart and mind; 2) we must be "doers of the word, and not hearers only" (v. 22) – that is, we must immediately apply it in a practical way in our daily lives.

If we fail to do this, James warns that we shall be deceiving ourselves; we may be calling ourselves Christians or disciples or Bible students, but we will not be experiencing any of the practical blessings and benefits of which the Bible speaks. We might sum this up by saying that the Bible works practically in those who apply it practically.

After this warning, James continues in the next three verses as follows.

> For if anyone is a hearer of the word and not a doer, he is like a man observing his natural face in a mirror; for he observes himself, goes away, and immediately forgets what kind of man he was. But he who looks into the perfect law of liberty and continues in it, and is not a forgetful hearer but a doer of the word, this one will be blessed in what he does (James 1:23-25).

James likens God's Word to a mirror. The only difference is that a normal mirror shows us only what James calls our "natural face" – our external, physical features and appearance. The mirror of God's Word, as we look into it, reveals not our external, physical features, but our inward spiritual nature and condition. It reveals to us those things about ourselves which no material mirror and no work of human wisdom can reveal – things which we can never come to know in any other way.

Someone has summed this up by saying: "Remember that while you are reading your Bible, your Bible is also reading you."

I can still recall, after the lapse of many years, how vividly I proved this in my own experience. I first began to study the Bible as a sceptic and an unbeliever – with the background of a student and teacher of philosophy. I approached it as being merely one among many systems of philosophy in the world. However, as I continued to study it, I became conscious, even against my own will, of certain strange and deep-seated changes taking place within me. My attitude of intellectual superiority, my sense of self-confidence and self-sufficiency began to crumble.

I had adopted the attitude of the ancient Greek philosopher who said,

"Man is the measure of all things." I had assumed that by my own intellectual and critical faculties I was capable of measuring any book or system of wisdom that I cared to study. But now to my own surprise, as I studied the Bible, even though I could not fully understand it, I became conscious that I was being measured by some standard that was not my own nor that of any human being. Like Belshazzar in the hour of his feast, there seemed to open up before my unwilling eyes the words "You have been weighed in the balances, and found wanting."

Without any special change of outward circumstance, I became inwardly restless and dissatisfied. Pleasures and activities which had previously attracted and occupied me lost their power to divert or to entertain. I became increasingly conscious of some deep need within my own being which I could neither define nor satisfy. I did not clearly understand it, but through the mirror of His Word, God was showing me the truth concerning my own inner need and emptiness.

After several months this revelation of my need caused me, even in my spiritual ignorance and blindness, to seek God with humility and sincerity. Finding Him in this way, I discovered that He who had thus revealed my need through His written Word was able also to satisfy it completely through the Person of His living Word, the Lord Jesus Christ.

Yes, the Bible is a mirror of the soul. But in this, as in its other operations, the result it produces in us depends to a large extent upon our reaction to it.

In the natural order, when we look in a mirror, we normally do it with the intention of acting upon anything which the mirror may reveal to us. If we see that our hair is untidy, we brush it; if we see that our face is dirty, we wash it; if our clothes are in disorder, we adjust them; if we see the evidence of some infection, we consult the doctor for suitable treatment.

To receive the benefits of the mirror of God's Word, we must act in a similar way. If the mirror reveals a condition of spiritual uncleanness, we must without delay seek the cleansing which comes to us through the blood of Christ. If the mirror reveals some spiritual infection, we must consult the Great Physician of our souls, the One "who forgives all your iniquities, who heals all your diseases" (Ps. 103:3).

Only by acting practically and without delay upon that which the mirror of God's Word reveals to us can we receive the forgiveness, cleansing and healing and all the other blessings God has provided for us.

It is just at this point that many people fail to make proper use of God's mirror, to their own spiritual and eternal loss. Through the hearing or the reading of God's Word and the moving of God's Spirit, they come under conviction concerning those things in their hearts and lives which are unclean, harmful and unpleasing to God. Looking thus into the mirror of God's Word, they see their own spiritual condition just as God sees it.

Their immediate reaction is one of sorrow and remorse. They realise their need and their danger. They may even go forward to the altar at some church, pray and shed tears. But their reaction goes no further than this. There is no real effectual change in the way they live. By the next day the impression has begun to wear off. They start to settle down into their old ways.

Very soon such a person forgets *what kind of man he was.* He no longer recalls the unpleasant truths which God's mirror so clearly and faithfully revealed to him. Unmoved and complacent, he continues on a course that takes him further and further from God.

However, the mirror of God's Word can reveal not only the unpleasant but also the pleasant. It can reveal not only what we are in our own fallen condition without Christ, but also what we can become through faith in Christ. It can reveal not only the filthy rags of our own righteousness, but also the spotless garment of salvation and the shining robe of right-eousness which we can receive through faith in Christ. It can reveal not only the corruption and the imperfections of "the old man" without Christ, but also the holiness and the perfections of "the new man" in Christ.

If, when God's mirror first reveals to us the truth of our own sin and uncleanness, we immediately act upon this revelation – if we repent, if we believe and obey the gospel – then the next time we look into the mirror we no longer see our old sinful nature. Instead we see ourselves as God now sees us in Christ: forgiven, cleansed, justified, a new creation. We are made to understand that a miracle has taken place.

The faithful mirror no longer reveals our sins or our failures. Rather it reveals to us:

> If anyone is in Christ, he is a new creation; old things have passed away; behold, all things have become new. Now all things are of God, who has reconciled us to Himself through Jesus Christ (2 Cor. 5:17-18).

Not only have the old things passed away and all things become new, but *all things are of God.* In other words, God Himself accepts respon-sibility for every feature and aspect of the new creation in Christ, as it is here revealed in His own mirror. There is nothing at all in it of man's ways or doings. The whole thing is of God Himself.

A little further on in the same chapter, Paul says again:

> For He made Him [Christ] who knew no sin to be sin for us, that we might become the righteousness of God in Him (v. 21).

Note the completeness of the exchange: Christ was made sin with our sinfulness that we in turn might be made righteous with God's righteousness. What is God's righteousness? It is a righteousness without blemish and without spot; a righteousness which has never known sin. This is the righteousness which is imputed to us in Christ. We need to gaze long and earnestly at this in God's mirror until we see ourselves there as God sees us.

We find the same revelation also in the Old Testament, in the Song of Solomon, where Christ (the Bridegroom) speaks to the church (His bride) and says:

> You are all fair, my love,
> And there is no spot in you (Song 4:7).

Here the flawless mirror reveals a flawless righteousness, which is ours in Christ.

Paul emphasises the need for Christians to look continually in the mirror of God's Word.

> But we all, with unveiled face, beholding as in a mirror the glory of the Lord, are being transformed into the same image from glory to glory, just as by the Spirit of the Lord (2 Cor. 3:18).

Paul, like James, is referring to the mirror of God's Word. He tells us that this mirror reveals to us who believe, not our sins, which have been done away with in Christ never to be remembered anymore; but in their place it reveals the glories of the Lord, which He is waiting to impart to us by faith. Paul emphasises that it is while we are thus looking into the mirror and beholding there the glories of the Lord that the Spirit of God is able to work upon us and to transform us into the very image of those glories which we behold.

In this, as in so many other examples of Scripture, we see that the

Spirit and the Word of God are always ordained to work together in harmony. It is while we look into the mirror of the Word of God that the Spirit works upon us and changes us into the likeness of what the mirror reveals. If we cease to look into the mirror of the Word, then the Spirit is no longer able to work in this way.

In 2 Corinthians Paul returns to the same theme.

> For our light affliction, which is but for a moment, is working for us a far more exceeding and eternal weight of glory, while we do not look at the things which are seen, but at the things which are not seen. For the things which are seen are temporary, but the things which are not seen are eternal (4:17-18).

Here Paul teaches that the faithful, victorious enduring of temporal afflictions can produce in us, as believers, results of great and eternal glory; but he adds the same qualification as in the previous chapter. This working out of spiritual glory within us is only effective

> while we do not look at the things which are seen, but at the things which are not seen (v. 18).

If we once take our eyes off the eternal things, our afflictions no longer produce the same beneficial effects within us. It is in the mirror of God's Word that we behold these eternal things. Therefore, it is in this mirror that we must continue steadfastly to look.

For example, notice how Moses endured forty years of exile in the wilderness after he fled from Egypt.

> By faith he forsook Egypt, not fearing the wrath of the king;
> for he endured as seeing Him who is invisible (Heb. 11:27).

Note the source of Moses' power to endure affliction: "he endured as seeing Him who is invisible." It was Moses' vision of the eternal, invisible God and Saviour of his people that gave him faith and courage to endure and to triumph over all his afflictions. The same vision can give the same faith and courage to us today. Where shall we find this continuing vision of God in our daily needs and testings? In the wonderful spiritual mirror which He has given us for this very purpose – that is, the mirror of His own Word. The secret both of transforming grace and of victorious living lies here – in the use that we make of

God's mirror. While we use the mirror aright, God's Spirit works out these effects in our lives.

Our Judge

Finally, God's Word is also our judge. Throughout the entire Bible it is emphasised that by sovereign eternal right, the office of judge belongs to God alone. This theme runs through the entire Old Testament. For instance, Abraham says to the Lord, "Shall not the Judge of all the earth do right?" (Gen. 18:25). Jephthah said, "May the Lord, the Judge, render judgement this day" (Judg. 11:27). The psalmist wrote, "Surely He is God who judges in the earth" (Ps. 58:11). And Isaiah said, "For the Lord is our Judge" (Is. 33:22).

As we move on into the New Testament, we enter into a fuller revelation of the motives and methods of God's judgement. Christ says:

> For God did not send His Son into the world to condemn the world, but that the world through Him might be saved (John 3:17).

Again we read in 2 Peter 3:9:

> The Lord is not slack concerning His promise, as some count slackness, but is long-suffering toward us, not willing that any should perish but that all should come to repentance.

These verses – and many others like them – reveal that God delights to administer mercy and salvation, but He is reluctant to administer wrath and judgement.

This reluctance of God to administer judgement finds expression in the way in which, as the New Testament reveals, God's judgement will ultimately be carried out. In the first instance, by sovereign eternal right, judgement belongs to God the Father. Peter speaks of "the Father, who without partiality judges according to each one's work" (1 Pet. 1:17).

Here judgement of all men is plainly stated to be the office of God the Father. However, Christ reveals that the Father has chosen in His sovereign wisdom to commit all judgement to the Son.

> For the Father judges no one, but has committed all judgement to the Son, that all should honour the Son just as they honour the Father (John 5:22-23).

Again, Christ says:

> For as the Father has life in Himself, so He has granted the
> Son to have life in Himself, and has given Him authority to
> execute judgement also, because He is the Son of Man (John
> 5:26-27).

Here we see that the office of judgement has been transferred from the
Father to the Son.

Two reasons are given for this. First, because with the office of judge
goes also the honour due to the judge, and in this way all men will be
obliged to show the same honour toward God the Son as they would
toward God the Father. Second, because Christ is also the Son of Man,
as well as the Son of God – that is, He partakes of the human as well as
of the divine nature, and thus in His judgement He is able to make
allowance, from His own experience, for all the infirmities and temptations of human flesh.

However, such is the grace and the mercy of the divine nature in the
Son, as in the Father, that Christ, too, is unwilling to administer
judgement. For this reason He, in turn, has transferred the final authority
of judgement from His own Person to the Word of God.

> And if anyone hears My words and does not believe, I do not
> judge him; for I did not come to judge the world but to save
> the world. He who rejects Me, and does not receive My
> words, has that which judges him – the word that I have
> spoken will judge him in the last day (John 12:47-48).

This reveals that the final authority of all judgement is vested in the
Word of God. This is the impartial, unchanging standard of judgement
to which all men must one day answer.

In Isaiah 66:2 the Lord says:

> But on this one will I look:
> On him who is poor
> and of a contrite spirit
> And who trembles at My word.

In the light of the New Testament revelation, we can well understand
why a man should tremble at God's Word. For as we read its pages and
hear its teaching, we find ourselves, by anticipation, standing before the

judgement bar of almighty God. Here, already revealed to those who will receive them, are unfolded the principles and standards of divine judgement for the whole human race. Christ described God's judgement this way:

> Till heaven and earth pass away, one jot or one tittle will by no means pass from the law till all is fulfilled (Matt. 5:18).

> Heaven and earth will pass away, but My words will by no means pass away (Matt. 24:35).

In the closing chapters of the Bible, the veil of the future is drawn aside to reveal what will transpire when, in fulfilment of Christ's words, heaven and earth pass away, and God's throne is set for the last great judgement.

> And I saw a great white throne, and him that sat on it, from whose face the earth and the heaven fled away; and there was found no place for them. And I saw the dead, small and great, stand before God . . . and the dead were judged . . . every man according to their works (Rev. 20:11-13).

At this last great scene Christ has assured us there will be one, and only one, standard of judgement: the eternal, unchanging Word of God. This will be the fulfilment of Psalm 119:160:

> The entirety of Your word is truth,
> And every one of Your righteous judgements endures forever.

Here will be unfolded, in their absolute completeness, every one of the righteous judgements of God's unchanging Word.

If we can but see it, this revelation that all judgement will be according to God's Word is a provision of God's grace and mercy, since it enables us here, in this present life, to anticipate God's judgement upon ourselves and thus to escape from it. For this reason Paul says:

> For if we would judge ourselves, we would not be judged (1 Cor. 11:31).

How may we judge ourselves? By applying to every aspect and detail of our lives the judgements of God's Word. If we do this, and then by repentance and faith accept God's provision of forgiveness and mercy, God Himself will never bring judgement upon us. Christ assures us of this.

> Most assuredly, I say to you, he who hears My word and believes in Him who sent Me has everlasting life, and shall not come into judgement, but has passed from death into life (John 5:24).

This assurance is repeated in Romans 8:1.

> There is therefore now no condemnation to those who are in Christ Jesus.

What must we do to escape God's condemnation? We must hear His Word. In humility and repentance we must accept every one of its righteous judgements as applied to our lives. In faith we must accept its record that Christ took our condemnation and suffered our punishment. Accepting these truths of God's Word, we are acquitted, we are justified, we pass out from under condemnation and death into pardon and everlasting life.

All this is through God's Word. Refused and rejected, it will be our judge at the last day. Accepted and obeyed, it assures us already of perfect pardon and full salvation through a righteousness which is not ours, but the righteousness of God Himself.

REPENT AND BELIEVE

REPENT, AND BELIEVE
IN THE GOSPEL.

MARK 1:15

INTRODUCTION TO PART II

THE BASIC DOCTRINES

When we set out to study the Bible in detail, is there some easy way to identify the basic and most important doctrines that should be studied first?

This is a reasonable question, and, like all such questions related to the study of the Bible, an answer to it may be found within the pages of the Bible itself. The Bible does clearly state that certain of its doctrines are more important than the rest and should therefore be studied first. In fact, the Bible gives a list of six such basic, or foundational, doctrines.

> Therefore, leaving the discussion of the elementary principles of Christ, let us go on to perfection, not laying again the foundation of repentance from dead works and of faith toward God, of the doctrine of baptisms, of laying on of hands, of resurrection of the dead, and of eternal judgement (Heb. 6:1-2).

In the margin of the 1611 edition of the King James Version, the alternative reading suggested for the elementary principles of Christ is "the word of the beginning of Christ." This brings out the point that we are here dealing with the doctrines which should constitute the beginning – the starting-off point – in our study of Christ and His teaching as a whole.

This point is further emphasised by the use, in the same verse, of the phrase "the foundation." The writer of Hebrews is setting two thoughts side by side: 1) the laying of the right doctrinal foundation; 2) going on after this to perfection – that is, to a completed edifice of Christian doctrine and conduct. The purpose of his exhortation is that we should go on to perfection, to the completed edifice. But he makes it plain that we cannot hope to do this unless we have first laid a complete and stable foundation of the basic doctrines.

In speaking of this foundation, the writer lists in order the following six successive doctrines: 1) repentance from dead works, 2) faith toward God, 3) the doctrine of baptisms, 4) laying on of hands, 5) resurrection of the dead, 6) eternal judgement.

We need to note one particularly important feature of this inspired outline of basic doctrines. If we follow it through in the order given, it spans the entire gamut of Christian experience. It starts – in time – from the sinner's initial response: repentance. It takes us on, by a logical succession, to the climax – in eternity – of all Christian experience: resurrection and final judgement.

While it is important to study carefully each of these individual doctrines, we must never lose the vision of the single divine and perfect plan that runs through them all. In particular, we must never become so occupied with the things of time that we lose the vision of eternity. Otherwise, we may suffer the tragedy described by Paul in 1 Corinthians 15:19.

> If in this life only we have hope in Christ, we are of all men the most pitiable.

The studies that follow in this section focus on the first two of these doctrines: repentance and faith.

9
REPENTANCE

Explained From Greek and Hebrew

First of all, we need a clear understanding of the meaning of the word *repentance* as used in the Scripture.

In the New Testament the English verb "to repent" is normally used to translate the Greek verb *metanoein*. This Greek verb *metanoein* has one definite meaning throughout the history of the Greek language, right through classical Greek down into New Testament Greek. Its basic meaning is always the same: "to change one's mind." Thus, "repentance" in the New Testament is not an emotion but a decision.

Knowing this fact serves to dispel many false impressions and ideas connected with repentance. Many people associate repentance with emotion – with the shedding of tears and so on. It is possible, however, for a person to feel great emotion and to shed many tears and yet never repent in the scriptural sense. Other people associate repentance with the carrying out of special religious rites or ordinances – with what is called "doing penance." But here, too, the same applies: It is possible to go through many religious rites and ordinances and yet never repent in the scriptural sense.

True repentance is a firm, inward decision; a change of mind.

If we turn back to the Old Testament, we find that the word most commonly translated "to repent" means literally "to turn," "to return," "to turn back." This harmonises perfectly with the meaning of repentance in the New Testament. The New Testament word denotes the inner decision, the inner change of mind; the Old Testament word denotes the outward action which is the expression of the inward change of mind – the act of turning back, of turning around.

Thus, the New Testament emphasises the inward nature of true repentance; the Old Testament emphasises the outward expression in action of the inner change. Putting the two together, we form this complete definition of repentance: Repentance is an inner change of mind resulting in an outward turning back, or turning around; to face and to move in a completely new direction.

The Sinner's First Response to God

The perfect example of true repentance, defined in this way, is found in the parable of the prodigal son (see Luke 15:11-32). Here we read how the prodigal turned his back on father and home and went off into a distant land, there to waste all that he had in sin and dissipation. Eventually he came to himself, hungry, lonely and in rags, sitting among the swine, longing for something to fill his stomach. At this point he made a decision. He said, "I will arise and go to my father" (v. 18).

He immediately carried out his decision: "And he arose and came to his father" (v. 20). This is true repentance: first, the inward decision; then the outward act of that decision – the act of turning back to father and home.

In his own unregenerate, sinful condition, every man that was ever born has turned his back on God, his Father, and on heaven, his home. Each step he takes is a step away from God and from heaven. As he walks this way, the light is behind him, and the shadows are before him. The farther he goes, the longer and darker the shadows become. Each step he takes is one step nearer the end – one step nearer the grave, nearer hell, nearer the endless darkness of a lost eternity.

For every man who takes this course, there is one essential act he must make. He must stop, change his mind, change his direction, face the opposite way, turn his back to the shadows and face toward the light.

This first, essential act is called repentance in the Scriptures. It is the first move any sinner must make who desires to be reconciled with God.

Distinguished From Remorse

Of course, there are some passages in some translations where the verb "to repent" is used in a different sense, but when we examine these passages carefully, we find that the English word "to repent" is used to translate some other word in the original language. For example, in the 1611 King James Version we read in Matthew 27:3-4 that when Judas Iscariot saw that Christ had been condemned to death, afterward he "repented" of betraying Christ for money.

> Then Judas, which had betrayed him, when he saw that he was condemned, repented himself, and brought again the thirty pieces of silver to the chief priests and elders, saying, I have sinned in that I have betrayed the innocent blood. And they said, What is that to us? See thou to that.

Here we read that Judas "repented himself." But the Greek word used in the original is not the word *metanoein* defined earlier. The Greek word used of Judas, *metamelein,* denotes that which people often wrongly interpret as repentance: remorse, anguish. There is no doubt that at this moment Judas experienced intense anguish and remorse. Nevertheless, he did not experience true, scriptural repentance; he did not change his mind, his course, his direction.

On the contrary, the very next verse says he went and hanged himself; in Acts 1:25 this is expressed by the words:

> Judas by transgression fell, that he might go to his own place.

Certainly Judas experienced emotion – strong emotion, bitter anguish and remorse. But he did not experience true repentance; he did not change his mind or his course. The truth is that he could not change his course; he had already gone too far. In spite of the Saviour's warning, he had deliberately committed himself to a course from which there could be no return. He had passed "the place of repentance."

What a terrible and solemn lesson this is! It is possible for a man, by stubborn and wilful continuance in his own way, to come to a place of no turning back – a place where the door of repentance has, by his own wilfulness, been forever slammed shut behind him.

Another man who made this same tragic error was Esau, who for one morsel of food sold his birthright.

For you know that afterward, when he wanted to inherit the blessing, he was rejected, for he found no place for repentance, though he sought it diligently with tears (Heb. 12:17).

In a foolish, careless moment Esau sold his birthright to his brother Jacob in exchange for a bowl of soup. Genesis records: "Thus Esau despised his birthright" (Gen. 25:34). We must remember that in despising his birthright, he despised all the blessings and the promises of God that were associated with the birthright. Later, Esau regretted what he had done. He sought to regain the birthright and the blessing, but he was rejected. Why? Because he found no place of repentance. (In the margin of the 1611 King James Version the alternative translation is: "He found no way to change his mind" Heb. 12:17).

Here is further evidence that strong emotion is not necessarily proof of repentance. Esau cried aloud and shed bitter tears. But in spite of all this, he found no place of repentance. By a trivial, impetuous act he had decided the whole course of his life and his destiny both for time and for eternity. He had committed himself to a course from which afterward he could find no way of return.

How many men today do just the same as Esau! For a few moments of sensual pleasure or carnal indulgence, they despise all the blessings and promises of almighty God. Later, when they feel their mistake, when they cry out for those spiritual and eternal blessings which they had despised, to their dismay they find themselves rejected. Why? Because they find no place of repentance, no way to change their minds.

The Only Way to True Faith

The New Testament is unanimous on this one point: True repentance must always go before true faith. Without true repentance there can never be true faith.

The call to repentance begins at the very introduction to the New Testament with the ministry of John the Baptist.

> The voice of one crying in the wilderness:
> "Prepare the way of the Lord,
> Make His paths straight."
> John came baptising in the wilderness and preaching a baptism of repentance for the remission of sins (Mark 1:3-4).

John the Baptist's call to repentance was a necessary preparation for the revelation of the Messiah to Israel. Until Israel had been called back to God in repentance, their long-awaited Messiah could not be revealed among them.

A little further on we read the first message that Christ Himself preached after John had prepared the way before Him.

> Now after John was put in prison, Jesus came to Galilee, preaching the gospel . . . and saying, "The time is fulfilled, and the kingdom of God is at hand. Repent, and believe in the gospel" (Mark 1:14-15).

The first commandment that ever fell from the lips of Christ was not to believe but to repent. First repent, then believe.

After His death and resurrection, when Christ commissioned His apostles to go out to all nations with the gospel, once again the first word in His message was "repentance."

> Then He said to them, "Thus it is written, and thus it was necessary for the Christ to suffer and to rise from the dead the third day, and that repentance and remission of sins should be preached in His name to all nations, beginning at Jerusalem" (Luke 24:46-47).

Here again it is repentance first, and after that, remission of sins.

Shortly after the resurrection, the apostles, through their spokesman Peter, began to fulfil this commission of Christ. After the Holy Spirit's coming on the day of Pentecost, the convicted (but still unconverted) multitude asked: "Men and brethren, what shall we do?" (Acts 2:37). To this inquiry there came an immediate and definite answer.

> Then Peter said to them, "Repent, and let every one of you be baptised in the name of Jesus Christ for the remission of sins; and you shall receive the gift of the Holy Spirit" (Acts 2:38).

Here again it is repentance first; after that, baptism and remission of sins.

When Paul spoke to the elders of the church at Ephesus, he outlined the gospel message which he had preached to them.

> I kept back nothing that was helpful, but proclaimed it to you, and taught you publicly and from house to house, testifying

to Jews, and also to Greeks, repentance toward God and faith toward our Lord Jesus Christ (Acts 20:20-21).

The order of Paul's message is the same: first repentance, then faith.

Finally, as we have already seen in Hebrews 6:1-2, the order of the basic foundation doctrines of the Christian faith is first repentance from dead works, then faith, baptisms and so on.

Without exception, throughout the entire New Testament, repentance is the first response to the gospel that God demands. Nothing else can come before it, and nothing else can take its place.

True repentance must always precede true faith. Without such repentance, faith alone is an empty profession. This is one reason why the experience of so many Christians today is so unstable and insecure. They are seeking to build without the first of the great foundation doctrines. They are professing faith but they have never practised true repentance. As a result, the faith which they profess procures for them neither the favour of God nor the respect of the world.

In many places today the simplification of the gospel message has been taken one step too far. The message often preached today is "Only believe." But that is not the message of Christ. Christ and His apostles preached "Repent and believe." Any preacher who leaves out the call to repentance is misleading sinners and misrepresenting God. For Paul tells us that it is God Himself who "commands all men everywhere to repent" (Acts 17:30). That is the general edict of God to the entire human race: "All men everywhere must repent."

In Hebrews 6:1 repentance is defined as "repentance from dead works"; in Acts 20:21 it is defined as "repentance toward God." This means that, in the act of repentance, we turn away from our dead works and face toward God, ready to hear and obey His next command.

The phrase "dead works" includes all acts and activities that are not based upon repentance and faith. It includes even the acts and activities of religion – even of professing Christianity – if they are not built on this basis. It is in this sense that Isaiah cries out:

And all our righteousnesses are like filthy rags (Is. 64:6).

There is no reference here to acts of open sin and wickedness. Even those acts which are done in the name of religion and morality, if they are not based on repentance and faith, are not acceptable to God. Charity, prayers, church attendance, every kind of religious rite and ordinance – if they are not based on repentance and faith – are merely "dead works" and "filthy rags"!

There is one other fact about scriptural repentance which must be emphasised. True repentance begins with God and not with man. It originates not in the will of man but in the free and sovereign grace of God. Apart from the working of God's grace and the moving of God's Spirit, man left to himself is incapable of repentance. For this reason the psalmist cries out for restoration.

Restore us, O God . . . and we shall be saved! (Ps. 80:3,7).

The word translated "restore us" means literally "cause us to turn back." Jeremiah uses the same word in Lamentations 5:21.

Turn us back to You, O Lord, and we will be restored.

Unless God first moves man toward Himself, man cannot of his own unaided will turn to God and be saved. The first move is always made by God.

In the New Testament Christ expressed the same truth.

No one can come to Me unless the Father who sent Me draws him (John 6:44).

The supreme crisis of every human life comes at the moment of the Spirit's drawing to repentance. Accepted, this drawing leads us to saving faith and eternal life; rejected, it leaves the sinner to continue on his way to the grave and the unending darkness of an eternity apart from God. The Scripture makes it plain that even in this life it is possible for a man to pass "the place of repentance" – to come to a point where the Spirit of God will never again draw him to repentance, and where all hope is lost even before he enters the portals of eternity.

It is fitting to close this study with the words of Christ in Luke 13:3 (which are also repeated in verse 5).

Unless you repent you will all likewise perish.

Christ was speaking of men who died in the very act of performing a religious rite; that is, a company of Galileans whose blood Pilate had mingled with their own sacrifices. While carrying out their sacrifices in the temple, these men had been executed by order of the Roman governor, and their blood had been mingled on the temple floor with that of their sacrifices.

Yet Christ tells us that these men perished; they went to a lost eternity. Even their religious act of sacrifice in the temple could not save their souls, because it was not based on true repentance.

The same is true of the religious ceremonies of many professing Christians today. None of these religious activities is any substitute for true repentance. Without such repentance, Christ Himself said, " . . . you will all likewise perish" (Luke 13:3).

10
THE NATURE OF FAITH

Outside the Scriptures the word *faith* has many different meanings, but in our present study we do not need to concern ourselves with these. Within the Scriptures there are two definite, distinguishing features of faith. First, faith always originates directly in God's Word; second, it is always directly related to God's Word.

Faith is one of comparatively few words actually defined in the Bible. This definition is found in Hebrews 11:1.

> Now faith is the substance of things hoped for, the evidence
> of things not seen.

This verse might also be translated: "Now faith is the ground, or confidence, of things hoped for, a sure persuasion, or conviction, concerning things not seen."

Distinguished From Hope

This important verse brings out various facts about faith. First of all, it indicates a distinction between faith and hope. There are two main ways in which faith differs from hope. The first is that hope is directed toward the future, but faith is established in the present. Hope is an attitude of expectancy concerning things that are yet to be, but faith is a substance – a confidence, something real and definite within us – that we possess here and now.

The second main difference between faith and hope is that hope is anchored in the realm of the mind; faith is anchored in the realm of the heart. This is very strikingly brought out in Paul's description of scriptural armour required by the Christian soldier.

> But let us who are of the day be sober, putting on the breast-plate of faith and love, and as a helmet the hope of salvation (1 Thess. 5:8).

Notice that faith – together with love – is found in the region of the breast; that is, the region of the heart. But hope is pictured as a helmet, in the region of the head, or mind. Thus, hope is a mental attitude of expectancy concerning the future; faith is a condition of the heart, producing within us here and now something so real that it can be described by the word *substance*.

In Romans Paul again directly associates the heart with the exercise of faith, or believing.

> With the heart one believes unto [literally, *into*]* right-eousness (Rom. 10:10).

Many people make a profession of faith in Christ and the Bible, but their faith is only in the realm of the mind. It is an intellectual acceptance of certain facts and doctrines. This is not true, scriptural faith, and it does not produce any vital change in the lives of those who profess it.

On the other hand, heart faith always produces a definite change in those who profess it. When associated with the heart, the verb "to believe" becomes a verb of motion. Hence Paul says, "With the heart one believes [into] righteousness" – not merely "unto righteousness," but "into righteousness." It is one thing to believe with the mind "unto right-eousness," merely as an abstract theory or ideal. It is quite another thing to believe with the heart "into righteousness"; that is, to believe in a way that produces a transformation of habits, character and life.

---

* The Greek preposition used here is *eis*, which is regularly translated "into."

In the words of Christ, the verb phrase "to believe" is regularly followed by the preposition *into,* to express change or motion. For instance, He says:

> You believe in [literally, *into*] God, believe also in [literally, *into*] Me (John 14:1).

This brings out the fact that the verb phrase "to believe" is associated with a process of change or motion. It is not enough to believe "in" Christ with mere mental acceptance of the facts of His life or the truths of His teaching. We must believe "into" Christ – we must be moved by heartfelt faith out of ourselves and into Christ, out of our sin and into His righteousness, out of our weakness and into His power, out of our failure and into His victory, out of our limitations and into His omnipotence. This scriptural faith of the heart always produces change. It is always believing *into* Christ and *into* righteousness; and the result is always something definite, experienced here and now, not something merely hoped for in the future.

For this reason, in John 6:47 Christ uses the present and not the future tense. He says, "He who believes . . . has everlasting life" – not *shall have,* but already *has,* everlasting life. Scriptural faith into Christ produces everlasting life here and now within the believer. It is not something that we hope to have in the next world after death. It is something that we already possess, something that we already enjoy, a reality, a substance within us.

So many people have a religion which they hope will somehow do them good when they reach the threshold of eternity. But true Bible faith gives the believer a here-and-now experience and an assurance of everlasting life already within him. His faith is a real substance within him. Because of this present faith he also has a serene hope, a sure confidence concerning the future. A hope that is based on this kind of faith will stand the test of death and eternity; but a hope that lacks this present substance of faith is mere wishful thinking, doomed to final, bitter disillusionment.

Based Solely on God's Word

Let us turn back now to the definition of faith given in Hebrews 11:1 and note one other important fact about faith.

Faith is "the evidence of things not seen," or a sure conviction concerning things not seen. This shows that faith deals with *things not seen.*

Faith is not based on the evidence of our physical senses but on the eternal, invisible truths and realities revealed by God's Word. Paul brings out this contrast between the objects of faith and the objects of sense perception when he says, "For we walk by faith, not by sight" (2 Cor. 5:7).

Faith is here contrasted with sight. Sight, along with the other physical senses, is related to the objects of the physical world. Faith is related to the truths revealed in God's Word. Our senses deal with things that are material, temporary and changeable. Faith deals with the revealed truths of God which are invisible, eternal and unchanging.

If we are carnally minded, we can accept only that which our senses reveal to us. But if we are spiritually minded, our faith makes the truths of God's Word more real than anything which our senses may reveal to us. We do not base our faith on that which we see or experience; we base our faith on God's Word. Thereafter, that which we see or experience is the outcome of that which we have already believed. In spiritual experience sight comes after faith, not before it.

David says:

> I would have lost heart, unless I had believed
> That I would see the goodness of the Lord
> In the land of the living (Ps. 27:13).

David did not see first and then believe. He believed first, and then he saw. Notice also that the experience which faith produced for him was not merely something after death, in the next world, but here and now, in the land of the living.

This same lesson is brought out in the conversation between Jesus and Martha outside the tomb of Lazarus.

> Jesus said, "Take away the stone." Martha, the sister of him who was dead, said to Him, "Lord, by this time there is a stench, for he has been dead four days." Jesus said to her, "Did I not say to you that if you would believe you would see the glory of God?" (John 11:39-40).

Here Jesus makes it plain that faith consists in believing first, then seeing – not the other way around. Most carnally minded people reverse this order. They say, "I only believe in what I can see." But this is incorrect. When we actually see a thing, we do not need to exercise faith for it. It is when we cannot see that we need to exercise faith. As Paul says, faith and sight are opposite in their nature.

Quite often in our experience we find an apparent conflict between the evidence of our senses and the revelation of God's Word. For instance, we may see and feel within our bodies all the evidence of physical sickness. Yet the Bible reveals that Jesus "Himself took our infirmities and bore our sicknesses" (Matt. 8:17) and "by whose stripes you were healed" (1 Pet. 2:24).

Here is an apparent conflict. Our senses tell us we are sick. The Bible tells us we are healed. This conflict between the testimony of our senses and the testimony of God's Word confronts us, as believers, with the possibility of two alternative reactions.

On the one hand, we may accept the testimony of our senses and thus accept our physical sickness. In this way we become the slaves of our carnal mind. On the other hand, we may hold firmly to the testimony of God's Word that we are healed.

If we do this with genuine, active faith, the testimony of our senses will in due course be brought into line with the testimony of God's Word, and we shall then be able to say we are healed, not merely on the basis of faith in God's Word, but also on the basis of actual physical experience and the testimony of our senses.

At this point, however, it is necessary to re-emphasise that the kind of faith that produces these results is faith in the heart, not in the mind. We must recognise that mere mental acceptance of the Bible's statements concerning healing and health lacks the power to make them real in our physical experience. The words of Paul in Ephesians 2:8 concerning faith for salvation apply equally to faith for healing. Thus we may say:

> For by grace you have been saved [healed] through faith, and that [faith] not of yourselves; it is the gift of God, not of works, lest anyone should boast.

The faith that brings healing is a gift of God's sovereign grace. It cannot be produced by any kind of mental gymnastics or psychological techniques. This kind of faith can be apprehended only by the spiritual mind. To the carnal mind it appears foolish. The carnal mind accepts the testimony of the senses in all circumstances and is thus ruled by the senses. The spiritual mind accepts the testimony of God's Word as invariably and unchangeably true and then accepts the testimony of the senses only insofar as it agrees with the testimony of God's Word. Thus, the attitude of the spiritual mind toward the testimony of God's Word is summed up by David.

> I cling to Your testimonies;
> O Lord, do not put me to shame! (Ps. 119:31).

> Concerning Your testimonies,
> I have known of old that You have founded them forever (Ps. 119:152).

The scriptural pattern of this kind of faith is found in the experience of Abraham (see Rom. 4:17-21). Paul tells us that Abraham's faith was directed toward God . . .

> . . . who gives life to the dead and calls those things which do not exist as though they did (Rom. 4:17).

This statement that God "calls those things which do not exist as though they did" means that as soon as God has declared a thing to be true, faith immediately reckons that thing to be true, even though no evidence of its truth may be manifested to the senses.

Thus, God called Abraham "a father of many nations," and from that moment forward Abraham reckoned himself as being what God had called him, "a father of many nations," even though at that time he had not even one son born to Sarah and himself.

Abraham did not wait until he saw evidence being worked out in his physical experience before he would accept God's statement as true. On the contrary, he accepted God's statement as true first, and later his physical experience was brought into line with what God had declared.

In the next verse Paul tells us that Abraham, "contrary to hope, in hope believed" (Rom. 4:18).

This phrase "in hope believed" tells us that at this time Abraham had both faith and hope – hope concerning the future and faith in the present – and that his hope concerning the future was the outcome of his faith in the present.

> [Abraham] did not consider his own body, already dead (since he was about a hundred years old), and the deadness of Sarah's womb (Rom. 4:19).

Abraham refused to accept the testimony of his senses. The testimony of his senses undoubtedly told him that it was no longer possible for him and Sarah to have a child. But Abraham did not accept this testimony because it did not agree with what God had said. Abraham turned a deaf ear to the testimony of his senses; he refused to consider it.

> He [Abraham] did not waver at the promise of God through unbelief . . . being fully convinced that what He [God] had promised He was also able to perform (Rom 4:20-21).

This shows clearly the object upon which Abraham's faith was focused: God's promise. Thus, faith is based on the promises and statements of God's Word and accepts the testimony of the senses only insofar as they agree with the statements of God's Word.

A little earlier in Romans 4 Paul calls Abraham "the father of all those who believe" (v. 11), and in the next verse he speaks of those "who also walk in the steps of the faith which our father Abraham had" (v. 12).

This shows that scriptural faith consists in acting like Abraham and in following the steps of his faith. In analysing the nature of Abraham's faith, we have seen that there were three successive steps or stages.

1. Abraham accepted God's promise as being true from the moment it was uttered.
2. Abraham refused to accept the testimony of his senses as long as it did not agree with the statement of God.
3. Because Abraham held fast to what God had promised, his physical experience and the testimony of his senses were brought into line with the statement of God.

Thus, the thing which he had first accepted in naked faith, contrary to the testimony of his senses, became reality in his own physical experience, confirmed by the testimony of his senses.

By many, this attitude of accepting God's Word as true in defiance of the testimony of our senses would be dismissed as mere foolishness or fanaticism. Yet the remarkable thing is that philosophers and psychologists of many different ages and backgrounds have agreed in declaring that the testimony of our physical senses is variable, subjective and unreliable.

If, then, the testimony of our senses cannot be accepted by itself as true and reliable, where can we find the correct standard of truth and reality by which the testimony of the senses must be judged? To this question neither philosophy nor psychology has ever been able to offer any satisfactory answer.

Indeed, all through the centuries, philosophers and psychologists have echoed the question asked by Pilate as he sat in his judgement hall: "What is truth?" (John 18:38). For the Christian believer, however, the answer is found in the words of Christ to His Father: "Your Word is truth" (John 17:17).

The ultimate, unchanging standard of all truth and reality is found in God's Word. Faith consists in hearing, believing and acting upon this truth.

In considering the relationship between faith and our physical senses, it is necessary to make a clear distinction between true, scriptural faith on the one hand and such teachings as mind-over-matter or Christian Science (falsely so-called) on the other hand.

The two main points of difference are as follows: First, teachings such as mind-over-matter or Christian Science tend to magnify and exalt the purely human element – such things as man's mind, or reason, or willpower. Thus, these teachings are essentially man-centred. On the other hand, true, scriptural faith is essentially God-centred. It abases all that is human and magnifies only God and God's truth and power.

Second, teachings such as mind-over-matter or Christian Science are not based directly, or even mainly, upon the Word of God. Many of the things they assert and seek to make real by the exercise of the human will are not in accordance with the teaching of God's Word. In fact, in certain respects, they are contrary to God's Word. On the other hand, scriptural faith, by its very nature and definition, is confined within the limits of God's Word.

We need also to distinguish between faith and presumption. The line that divides these two is very fine, but it marks the boundary between success and disaster.

Presumption contains an element of human arrogance and self-glorification. It is the assertion of man's will, even if it is cloaked in spiritual language. Faith, on the other hand, is totally dependent on God, and its outworking will always glorify God. It never takes the initiative away from God.

We come back to the words of Paul: Such faith is "not of yourselves; it is the gift of God, not of works, lest anyone should boast" (Eph. 2:8-9). Its attitude is summed up by John the Baptist.

A man can receive nothing unless it has been given to him from heaven (John 3:27).

Very simply stated, faith *receives,* and presumption *grabs.*

Expressed by Confession

We come now to another important feature of scriptural faith. We have already considered the words of Paul in the first half of Romans 10:10.

> With the heart one believes to righteousness.

In the second half of this verse, Paul adds:

> And with the mouth confession is made to salvation.

Paul here brings out the direct connection between faith in the heart and confession with the mouth.

This connection between the heart and the mouth is one of the great basic principles of Scripture. Christ Himself says:

> For out of the abundance of the heart the mouth speaks (Matt. 12:34).

We might express this in modern phraseology by saying: "When the heart is full, it overflows through the mouth." It follows, therefore, that when our hearts are full of faith in Christ, this faith will find its proper expression as we confess Christ openly with our mouths. A faith that is held back in silence, without any open confession, is an incomplete faith which will not bring the results and the blessings that we desire.

Paul refers to this connection between believing and speaking when he says:

> But since we have the same spirit of faith, according to what
> is written, "I believed and therefore I spoke," we also believe
> and therefore speak (2 Cor. 4:13).

Note the logical connection indicated by the word *therefore*: "we also believe and therefore speak." Paul here speaks about the "spirit of faith." Mere intellectual faith in the mind may perhaps keep silent; but faith that is spiritual – faith that is in the spirit and the heart of man – must speak. It must be expressed in confession with the mouth.

Actually this truth follows logically from the very meaning of the word *confession.* The English word *confession* – just like the Greek word *homologia* of which it is a translation – means literally "saying the same as." Thus, confession, for Christians, means that we say the same thing with our mouths as God Himself has already said in His Word. Or, more briefly, the words of our mouths agree with the Word of God.

Thus, confession, in this sense, is the natural expression of heart faith. We believe in our hearts what God has said in His Word – this is faith. Thereafter we naturally say the same with our mouths as we believe in our hearts – this is confession. Faith and confession centre in one and the same thing – the truth of God's Word.

There is a revelation of Christ in Hebrews which further emphasises the importance of confession in relation to faith. Christ is called "the High Priest of our confession" (Heb. 3:1).

This means that Christ in heaven serves as our Advocate and Representative in respect of every truth of God's Word to which we on earth confess with our mouth. But whenever we fail to confess our faith on earth, we give Christ no opportunity to act on our behalf in heaven. By closing our lips on earth, we also close the lips of our Advocate in heaven. The extent of Christ's high-priestly ministry on our behalf in heaven is determined by the extent of our confession on earth.

What, then, are the main features of faith as defined and described in the Bible?

- Scriptural faith is a condition of the heart, not the mind.
- It is in the present, not the future.
- It produces a positive change in our behaviour and experience.
- It is based solely on God's Word and accepts the testimony of the senses only when this agrees with the testimony of God's Word.
- It is expressed by confession with the mouth.

11
THE UNIQUENESS
OF FAITH

We have already considered the definition of faith given in Hebrews 11:1. The writer goes on to describe the part played by faith in man's approach to God.

> But without faith it is impossible to please Him [God], for he who comes to God must believe that He is, and that He is a rewarder of those who diligently seek Him (Heb. 11:6).

Notice the two phrases: "without faith it is impossible to please God," and "he who comes to God *must believe*." We see from these that faith is the indispensable condition for approaching God and for pleasing God.

The negative aspect of this truth is that "whatever is not from faith is sin" (Rom. 14:23). This means that anything a person may do at any time, if it is not based on faith, is reckoned by God as sinful. This applies even to religious activities, such as church attendance, praying, singing hymns or performing deeds of charity. If these acts are not done in sincere faith toward God, then they are in no way acceptable to Him.

Unless such acts have been preceded by true repentance and unless they are motivated by true faith, they are nothing but "dead works," totally unacceptable to God.

The Basis of All Righteous Living

Perhaps the most all-inclusive statement concerning the relationship between faith and righteousness is found in Habakkuk 2:4.

The just shall live by his faith.

The two English words *just* and *righteous* are two alternative ways of translating one and the same word in the original text. This applies equally to the Hebrew of the Old Testament and to the Greek of the New Testament. In both languages there is only one root word which, as an adjective, can be translated either by "just" or by "righteous," and, as a noun, can be translated either by "justice" or by "righteousness." Whichever translation may be used, there is no difference whatever in the original sense.

Thus, in translating Habakkuk 2:4 we may say either "the just shall live by his faith" or "the righteous shall live by his faith."

This statement of Habakkuk is quoted three times in the New Testament: in Romans 1:17, in Galatians 3:11 and in Hebrews 10:38. In each of these three passages the New King James Version renders it, "The just shall live by faith." It would be difficult to think of any sentence as short and simple as this which has produced as great an impact upon the history of the human race.

In the New King James Version the entire sentence consists of only six or seven words, none of which contains more than one syllable. Yet this sentence provided the basic, scriptural authority for the gospel message preached by the apostolic church. The proclamation of this simple message by a tiny, despised minority changed the course of world history. Within three centuries it brought to his knees the great Caesar himself, the head of the most powerful, the most far-reaching and the most enduring empire that the world had ever seen.

About twelve centuries later this same sentence, quickened by the Holy Spirit to the heart and mind of Martin Luther, provided the scriptural lever that dislodged the power of papal Rome and, through the Protestant Reformation, once again changed the course of history – first in Europe and then, by its outreach, in the world at large.

There is no doubt that, still today, this same simple sentence, when once apprehended and applied by faith, contains within it the power to revolutionise the lives of individuals or the course of nations and empires.

Though so short and so simple, the scope of this sentence, "The just shall live by faith," is immense. The word *live* covers almost every conceivable condition or act of any sentient being. It covers all areas of the human personality and experience in every conceivable aspect – the spiritual, the mental, the physical, the material. It covers the widest possible range of activities – such as breathing, thinking, speaking, eating, sleeping, working and so on.

The Scripture teaches that, for any person to be accepted as righteous by God, all these activities within that person must be motivated and controlled by the one great principle of faith.

Paul actually applies this principle to the familiar act of eating, for he says:

> But he who doubts is condemned if he eats, because he does
> not eat from faith; for whatever is not from faith is sin (Rom.
> 14:23).

This shows that, in the life of righteousness which alone is acceptable to God, even an act so commonplace as eating food must proceed from faith.

Let us therefore consider for a moment: What does it mean to "eat from faith"? What is implied by this?

First, it implies that we acknowledge that God is the One who has provided us with the food we eat. Thus, the provision of nourishing food for our bodies is an example of the principle stated in James 1:16-17.

> Do not be deceived, my beloved brethren. Every good gift
> and every perfect gift is from above, and comes down from
> the Father of lights, with whom there is no variation or
> shadow of turning.

It is also a fulfilment of the promise contained in Philippians 4:19.

> And my God shall supply all your need according to His
> riches in glory by Christ Jesus.

Second, because we acknowledge that God is the One who provides our food, we naturally pause before eating to thank Him for it. In this way, we obey the commandment contained in Colossians 3:17.

> And whatever you do in word or deed, do all in the name of
> the Lord Jesus, giving thanks to God the Father through Him.

In this way, too, we are assured of God's blessing upon the food that we eat, so that we obtain the maximum amount of nourishment and benefit from it. This is explained by Paul.

> For every creature of God is good, and nothing is to be
> refused if it is received with thanksgiving; for it is sanctified
> by the word of God and prayer (1 Tim. 4:4-5).

Thus, through our faith and prayer, the food we eat is blessed and sanctified to us.

Third, eating in faith implies that we acknowledge that the health and strength we receive through our food belong to God and must be used in His service and for His glory.

> Now the body is not for sexual immorality [not for any
> immoral, unclean, foolish or harmful use] but for the Lord,
> and the Lord for the body (1 Cor. 6:13).

Because our bodies are thus by faith and by holy living given over to the Lord, the responsibility for their care and preservation also belongs to the Lord; and we have every right to expect the fulfilment of Paul's prayer:

> And may your whole spirit, soul, and body be preserved
> blameless at the coming of our Lord Jesus Christ (1 Thess.
> 5:23).

All these – and many more besides – are the implications and the outworkings of the principle "The just shall live by faith," as applied to only one simple aspect of our lives – that of eating. And when we thus analyse what is implied by the phrase "to eat from faith," we are forced to the conclusion that the great majority of people, even those who profess Christianity, do not "eat from faith." In the provision, preparation and consumption of their daily food, no thought whatever is given to God.

No doubt this is one main cause of such diseases as indigestion,

ulcers, tumours, cancer, heart disease and many others. The Western
world has enjoyed an unprecedented abundance of both food and money.
Yet countless thousands are misusing and abusing this abundance to
their own physical distress, because by their indifference and unbelief
they have shut God out of their lives. Solomon gives us a picture of the
carnal, sensual man who makes no room for God in his daily life.

> All his days he also eats in darkness, and he has much sorrow
> and sickness and anger (Eccl. 5:17).

This description is still as true today as when Solomon wrote it. Not
to eat in faith is to eat in "darkness," and three consequences that
commonly follow this are "sorrow . . . sickness and anger."

There is another simple act, familiar and essential to us all, in which
the principle of faith can have a decisive influence: the act of sleeping.
In Psalm 127:2 the psalmist says:

> It is vain for you to rise up early,
> To sit up late,
> To eat the bread of sorrows;
> For so He [God] gives His beloved sleep.

Through the continual, restless pursuit of wealth and pleasure,
millions today are losing the ability to enjoy either food or sleep. Who
can count the millions of pain killers, digestive tablets and sleeping
tablets that are consumed each day throughout the Western world – and
often with so little effect? But to God's believing children, to those
whose lives are based on faith in God, sleep comes as a gift of God's
love, a provision of His daily mercy, "for so He gives His beloved sleep."

Someone has said, "Money can buy medicine, but not health; a bed,
but not sleep." It is not only very costly, but it is also very injurious to
our bodies to shut God out of our daily living.

The psalmist David was a man whose way led through many troubles
and dangers, but in the midst of them all his faith in God sustained him
and gave him the assurance of sweet, untroubled sleep. Listen to David's
own testimony of what prayer and faith could do for him.

> I cried to the Lord with my voice,
> And He heard me from His holy hill.
> I lay down and slept;
> I awoke, for the Lord sustained me (Ps. 3:4-5).

I will both lie down in peace, and sleep;
For You alone, O Lord, make me dwell in safety (Ps. 4:8).

This same blessed assurance of calm, untroubled sleep at the close of each day is still available to those who will enter into all the provisions of God's love and mercy contained in that simple phrase: "The just shall live by faith."

At this point I can imagine a reader saying, "You have spoken about simple, familiar acts such as eating and sleeping and the part that faith can play in these. But the problems of our modern world are much greater and more complex than simple things like eating and sleeping. What solution can faith offer to our great national and international problems today?"

Yes, it is certainly true that we are confronted with vast and intricate problems – social, economic, political. We must acknowledge this. But let us take the truth one step further: There is no human mind and no human wisdom that can comprehend all these problems in their entirety, much less work out solutions to them all. If we must depend solely upon human wisdom for the solutions, then the outlook is hopeless.

But faith is always united with humility. True faith causes man to acknowledge his own limitations. True faith distinguishes between those things which are within the province of man and those which are within the province of God.

Someone has stated the relationship between man's part and God's part in the life of faith as follows: "You do the simple thing; God will do the complicated thing. You do the small thing; God will do the great thing. You do the possible thing; God will do the impossible thing."

God's simple plan for living, "The just shall live by faith," still makes sense today. Let man do his part – let man by faith and obedience seek God's guidance and blessing in the simple acts of daily life, in the familiar relationships of home and community. There will come a relief and a release from the strains, the tensions, the physical, mental and moral breakdown of modern life. And in the vast areas of the modern world that are outside man's comprehension and control, God will move in response to man's faith and will overrule the affairs of nations in a way that will amaze us by its effectiveness.

This simple principle, "The just shall live by faith," which has twice changed the course of world history, still contains today the power to revolutionise the life and destiny of any modern nation that will apply it. This is still God's answer to man's problems, God's provision for man's needs: "The just shall live by faith."

Of all man's faculties and capacities, there is only one by which he can solve the problems that confront him today – one human faculty which is potentially greater than all his material and scientific achievements – and that is man's faith in God.

In order to comprehend the latent possibilities of man's faith in God, it is necessary to look at two statements made by the Lord Jesus Christ during His earthly ministry.

> But Jesus looked at them and said to them, "With men this is impossible, but with God all things are possible" (Matt. 19:26).

> Jesus said to him, "If you can believe, all things are possible to him who believes" (Mark 9:23).

Set these two statements side by side: "with God all things are possible," and "all things are possible to him who believes." This means that through faith God's possibilities become ours. Faith is the channel by which God's omnipotence becomes available to man. The limit of what faith can receive is the limit only of what God Himself can do.

Appropriating All of God's Promises

We have spoken hitherto of faith as an experience of the human heart which revolutionises human behaviour and provides a principle by which to direct the whole course of human life. However, it is most important to add that faith is not merely something subjective, something private and personal in the heart of each believer. It is this, but it is also more.

Faith is based on definite, objective facts. What are these facts? It is possible to give a very wide answer to this question. On the other hand, it is possible also to confine our answer within quite narrow limits.

In the widest sense, faith is based upon the entire Bible. Every statement and every promise in the Bible is a potential object of faith. As we have already said, faith comes through hearing the Word of God; and faith is therefore based upon everything that God's Word contains. For the Christian believer there is nothing within the statements and promises of God that is outside the scope of his faith. This is plainly stated by Paul.

> For all the promises of God in Him [Christ] are Yes, and in

Him Amen, to the glory of God through us (2 Cor. 1:20).

Side by side with this we may set Romans 8:32.

> He who did not spare His own Son, but delivered Him up for us all, how shall He not with Him also freely give us all things?

All things that God possesses – all His blessings, all His promises – are made available freely to each person who will receive them through faith in Christ's atoning death and resurrection.

There is a tendency today to base the interpretation of Scripture on a system of dispensations in such a way that only a small proportion of God's blessings and promises are made available to Christians.

According to this system of interpretation, many of God's choicest blessings and promises are relegated either to periods in the past, such as that of the Mosaic covenant or the apostolic church, or to periods in the future, such as the millennium or the dispensation of the fullness of times.

However, this does not tally with Paul's statement in 2 Corinthians 1:20, which we may amplify as follows:

> For all the promises of God [not some of the promises of God, but all the promises of God] in Him [Christ] are [not were nor *will be*, but *are* here and now] Yes, and in Him Amen [not merely *Yes*, but a double affirmative *Yes* and *Amen*], to the glory of God through us [not through various groups in different ages, but through us who receive these words today].

The context makes it plain that "us" includes all true Christian believers.

In the life of any Christian believer, there is no need which is outside the scope of God's promises.

> And my God shall supply all your need according to His riches in glory by Christ Jesus (Phil. 4:19).

For every need that can arise in the life of any Christian, there is somewhere in God's Word a promise that meets that need and which may be claimed through faith in Christ.

Whenever a need arises in the life of a Christian, therefore, there are three steps that he should take.

1.   He should ask the Holy Spirit to direct him to the particular promise or promises that apply to his situation and meet his need.
2.   He should obediently fulfil in his life the particular conditions attached to those promises.
3.   He should positively expect their outworking in his experience.

This is faith in action, and faith of this kind is "the victory that has overcome the world" (1 John 5:4). The secret of this victory lies in knowing and applying the promises of God's Word.

Peter states this same truth very forcefully.

His [God's] divine power has given to us all things that pertain to life and godliness, through the knowledge of Him [Christ] who called us by glory and virtue, by which have been given to us exceedingly great and precious promises (2 Pet. 1:3-4).

Here Peter's message is in perfect agreement with that of Paul. He tells us that God has already provided us with all that we can ever need for life and godliness and that this provision is made available through Christ by the claiming of God's promises.

In the Old Testament, under Joshua, God brought His people into a promised land. In the New Testament, under Jesus, God brings His people into a land of promises. The parallel is made more exact by the fact that Joshua and Jesus are two different forms of the same name.

In the Old Testament God showed Joshua the principle of active, personal, appropriating faith.

Every place that the sole of your foot will tread upon I have given you (Josh. 1:3).

In the New Testament this principle remains the same. God says, in effect, "Every promise that you personally appropriate, I have given you."

However, it is necessary to add one word of warning: The great majority of God's promises, in the Old and New Testament alike, are conditional. There are conditions attached which must be fulfilled before the promise can be claimed. For example:

> Commit your way to the Lord,
> Trust also in Him,
> And He shall bring it to pass (Ps. 37:5).

The promise here is: "And He shall bring it to pass" – that is, "He shall work out the way of the believer for him." The two conditions which are stated first are: "commit your way" and "trust also in Him." The word *commit* denotes a single definite act; the word *trust* denotes a continuing attitude.

Thus, the conditions attached to this promise may be interpreted as follows: 1) make a single, definite act of commitment, 2) thereafter maintain a continuing attitude of trust. When these two conditions have been fulfilled, the believer can then claim the ensuing promise, "He shall bring it to pass," in whatever way is appropriate to his own particular situation.

This kind of active, appropriating faith is the key to victorious Christian living. It must be based on the promises of God's Word, and it must follow the three successive steps: 1) find the appropriate promise, 2) fulfil all the conditions attached, 3) claim the fulfilment of the promise. Subject to these conditions, the scope of the Christian's faith is as wide as the promises of God.

12
FAITH FOR SALVATION

So far we have considered faith in the widest and most general sense as related to all the statements and promises of God in the Bible. However, there is one part of the Bible's message which is of the greatest importance because it decides the eternal destiny of every human soul. This part is called "the gospel," and it reveals the way of salvation from sin and its consequences.

Very often people think of "the gospel" as something of a vague and emotional nature which is impossible to explain in a rational way. Even in the preaching of "the gospel" there is often so much emphasis on an emotional response that the impression is created that the whole of salvation consists of an emotional experience.

Yet this is incorrect and misleading. The actual gospel message, as stated in the Bible, consists of definite facts, and salvation consists of knowing, believing and acting on these facts.

The Four Basic Facts of the Gospel

What are these facts which constitute the gospel? For an answer to this question we may turn to two passages in the writings of Paul: Romans 4:24-25 and 1 Corinthians 15:1-4.

In Romans 4 Paul analyses the main features of the faith of Abraham and sets forth Abraham's faith as an example to be followed by all Christian believers. He points out that according to the Old Testament Scriptures Abraham was not justified before God by his works, but that his faith was imputed to him for righteousness. Then in verses 23-25 Paul directly applies this example of Abraham to us as believers in Christ, for he says:

> Now it was not written for his sake alone that it was imputed to him, but also for us. It shall be imputed to us who believe in Him who raised up Jesus our Lord from the dead, who was delivered up because of our offences, and was raised because of our justification.

The gospel, as here stated by Paul, contains three definite facts: 1) Jesus was delivered to the punishment of death for our offences; 2) God raised Jesus up again from the dead; 3) if we believe this record of the death and resurrection of Jesus on our behalf, we shall be justified or accepted as righteous before God.

In 1 Corinthians 15:1-4 Paul reminds the Christians at Corinth of the gospel message which he had preached to them and through which they had been saved, and he again sets forth for them the basic facts of the message.

> Moreover, brethren, I declare to you the gospel which I preached to you, which also you received and in which you stand, by which also you are saved, if you hold fast that word which I preached to you – unless you believed in vain. For I delivered to you first of all that which I also received: that Christ died for our sins according to the Scriptures, and that He was buried, and that He rose again the third day according to the Scriptures (1 Cor. 15:1-4).

Again we see that the gospel consists of three definite facts: 1) Christ died for our sins, 2) He was buried, 3) He rose again the third day.

Paul also emphasises that the first and most authoritative of all testimonies to the truth of these facts is not the testimony of the men who were eyewitnesses of Christ's death and resurrection, but the testimony of the Old Testament Scriptures, which had prophetically foreshown these events hundreds of years before they actually took place. The testimony of contemporary eyewitnesses is only mentioned later as supporting that of the Old Testament Scriptures.

If we set side by side the teaching of these two passages from Paul's epistles – Romans 4:24-25 and 1 Corinthians 15:1-4 – it is possible to determine the basic facts which constitute the gospel.

These facts all centre exclusively in the Person of Christ Himself – not in His earthly life and teaching, but in His death and resurrection.

Here are the four basic facts: 1) Christ was delivered by God the Father to the punishment of death on account of our sins; 2) Christ was buried; 3) God raised Him from the dead on the third day; 4) righteousness is received from God through believing these facts.

The Simple Act of Appropriation

Let me restate that there is a vital difference between faith in the mind, which is nothing more than the intellectual acceptance of the facts of the gospel, and faith in the heart, which always results in a positive response to the facts. The whole New Testament makes it plain that the experience of salvation comes to each soul only as a result of this personal response to the gospel.

Various different words are used in the New Testament to describe this personal response to the gospel. All the words thus used have one essential point in common: They all denote simple, familiar acts which anybody can understand and carry out.

For example, Paul explains that salvation comes through believing with the heart and confessing with the mouth the truth of the gospel (see Rom. 10:8-9). He concludes his explanation of the way of salvation by saying, "For 'whoever calls upon the name of the Lord shall be saved' " (Rom. 10:13).

Here the simple act which brings with it the experience of salvation is that of calling upon the name of the Lord; that is, asking God out loud for salvation in the name of the Lord Jesus Christ.

In Matthew 11:28 Christ uses the simple word *come* to describe the response which He requires to the gospel invitation, for He says:

Come to Me, all you who labour and are heavy laden, and I will give you rest.

Christ adds to this invitation a very gracious and assuring promise.

The one who comes to Me I will by no means cast out (John 6:37).

Thus the invitation is supported by the promise, and the promise creates the required faith in those who desire to accept the invitation.

Speaking to the Samaritan woman at Jacob's well, Christ uses the simple act of drinking, which was appropriate to that particular situation, to express the necessary response to the gospel. He says:

But whoever drinks of the water that I shall give him will never thirst. But the water that I shall give him will become in him a fountain of water springing up into everlasting life (John 4:14).

Here the act of receiving salvation is compared to that of drinking water. In this instance the promise is given first – he will never thirst – then later in the New Testament the promise is supported by an invitation. Christ says:

If anyone thirsts, let him come to Me and drink (John 7:37).

And the Spirit and the bride say, "Come!" And let him who hears say, "Come!" And let him who thirsts come. And whoever desires, let him take the water of life freely (Rev. 22:17).

In John 1:11-13 the word used by the apostle John to denote this active response to the gospel is *receive.* In these three verses John writes, concerning Christ:

He came to His own, and His own did not receive Him. But as many as received Him, to them He gave the right to become children of God, even to those who believe in His name: who were born, not of blood, nor of the will of the flesh, nor of the will of man, but of God.

Here the key thought is that of personally receiving Christ. The result of this response of faith is described by John as becoming a child of God, or "being born of God." Christ Himself refers to the same experience in John 3:3, where He calls it being born again. He makes it plain that without this definite, personal experience no person can ever hope to enter God's kingdom, for He says:

> Most assuredly, I say to you, unless one is born again, he
> cannot see the kingdom of God.

Once again this challenge to respond to the gospel by personally
receiving Christ is supported by a definite promise from Christ Himself.

> Behold, I stand at the door and knock. If anyone hears My
> voice and opens the door, I will come in to him and dine with
> him, and he with Me (Rev. 3:20).

Here Christ speaks directly to each individual soul who has heard the
gospel and who desires to respond by opening the heart's door and
receiving Christ within.

To each soul who will make this response, Christ gives a clear,
straightforward promise: "I will come in."

We have seen that in each case where the gospel is presented, faith is
required to make a simple, personal response. The word used to describe
this response may vary, but the essential nature of the response is always
the same. In the cases which we have considered, the following words
are used to describe this response: to *call;* to *come;* to *drink;* to *receive.*

As we have pointed out, each of these denotes a simple, familiar act
such as anybody can understand and carry out. There is one other vitally
important feature which is common to all these acts: Each is an act that
the person must do for himself; no one can perform any of these acts on
behalf of another person.

Each person must *call* for himself; each person must *come* for
himself; each person must *drink* for himself; each person must *receive*
for himself. So it is with the response to the gospel. Each person must
make his own response; no person can make the response required from
another.

Each person will be either saved or lost solely by his own response.

It is the duty of every responsible Christian – whether minister or
layman – to be thoroughly acquainted with these simple facts of the
gospel and also with the various ways in which the New Testament
presents the need for a personal response to the gospel from each soul.

The work of Christ's kingdom would be greatly benefited if every
minister would continually incorporate these facts into the sermons he
preaches.

Where sermons are regularly preached without the clear presentation
of these facts, it is questionable whether anything of eternal value will
result.

I never mention this point without recalling an incident that took place in my own experience while I was working as a minister in London, England. The incident concerns a lady whom we may call Mrs. H.

Mrs. H. had been coming regularly to our house for some weeks to give piano lessons to our two youngest daughters. We did not know much about Mrs. H. except that she was a respectable woman who regularly attended a well-known Protestant church near our home. She gave us to understand that she took some active part in the women's missionary organisation in the church.

One day we learned that Mrs. H. had been rushed to the hospital, gravely ill, and was not expected to live. I felt it my duty to visit her in the hospital. When I asked permission to see her, the nurse replied that she was too ill to have any visitors. When I explained that I was a minister, the nurse told me I could see her for five minutes, and not a moment longer. By the time I had introduced myself to Mrs. H. and made sure she knew who I was, almost one minute of the five had already gone. Without further ado, I told her that she might well be on the threshold of eternity and asked whether, in such a condition, she had the assurance that her sins were forgiven and that she was ready to meet God. She replied that she did not.

I then told her very clearly and simply the basic facts of the gospel: that Christ suffered death as the punishment for our sins; that He was buried and rose again the third day; that we may be saved through believing these facts, but that God expects a definite, personal response of faith from each person who desires to be saved.

I asked her if she wished to make this response, and she said that she did.

I asked Mrs. H. to follow me in prayer, and I said out loud a prayer of a few short sentences, repeating the facts of the gospel and claiming God's promise of salvation. Mrs. H. repeated each sentence after me.

I then asked her if she now believed that she was saved, and she said yes.

I concluded by another short prayer, committing her to the Lord and thanking Him for her salvation.

By this time I still had about half a minute left. Thus from the moment I began to deal with Mrs. H. about her soul, it took me less than four minutes to present the gospel to her and to lead her to the assurance of salvation.

In this way Mrs. H. obtained peace in her heart which she had never known in all her previous life. As a direct consequence of obtaining peace in her heart, she made a rapid and unexpected recovery and was soon discharged from the hospital.

A few weeks later Mrs. H. was back at our house again to resume her piano lessons. When the lessons were over, I said, "Do you mind if I ask you a personal question?" She gave her consent.

"Mrs. H.," I said, "I understand that for many years you have faithfully attended your church every week and have even taken an active part in the life of the church. Yet, when the moment of crisis came and you found yourself face-to-face with eternity, you were not at all ready to die or to face God. Do you mind my asking: What kind of subjects does your minister preach about each Sunday?"

"Well," she replied, "he usually preaches about the Christian life and growing in grace."

"But," I replied, "it was no use whatever preaching to you about leading the Christian life or growing in grace because you had never been born again, and so it was quite impossible for you to lead the Christian life or grow in grace. It is impossible for a baby to start growing up before it has ever been born."

"Yes," she replied, "I realise now that that is true. I'm going to speak to my minister about it."

I could not help wondering what would be the outcome of that. However, she was obviously determined, and I saw no reason to dissuade her.

When I saw Mrs. H. again the next week, I asked, "Well, did you speak to your minister?"

"Yes, I did," she replied.

"And what did he preach about last Sunday?" I asked.

"He preached that the most important thing is to know that you are saved."

Oh! If only these words could somehow be impressed upon every person attending every church that professes the Christian faith: "The most important thing is to know that you are saved."

Imagine that this woman, Mrs. H., had regularly attended a Christian church several times a week for many years and had never come to understand the essential facts upon which the gospel is based, nor the personal response she had to make to the gospel in order to be saved. And yet, in a moment of crisis it proved possible, within a space of four minutes, to present these facts to her in such a way that she made the necessary response and entered into a definite experience of salvation.

How much misused time and misapplied effort must lie behind such a story as this! And yet, doubtless, a case such as this could be multiplied millions of times over in professing Christian churches around the world.

Once in East Africa I heard a young African evangelist speaking to a white missionary who was responsible for the direction of a group of churches stretching over a wide area. He made the following statement: "Your churches are only storehouses, storing people for hell."

To some people this might appear a shocking statement, especially coming from a national to a missionary. Yet, knowing the situation as I did, I realised that the young African was speaking the truth.

Most members of those churches had never once had the basic facts of the gospel presented to them and had never been faced with the need to make a personal response to those facts. They had exchanged paganism for a form of Christianity; they had memorised a catechism; they had been through a form of baptism; they had been accepted as church members; many of them had been educated in mission schools – yet of the essential facts of the gospel and the experience of salvation they had no knowledge nor understanding whatever.

Churches such as these – whether in Africa or in America or anywhere else in the world – are just what that young African called them: "storehouses storing people for hell."

The supreme purpose of every true Christian church, the chief duty of every Christian minister, the main responsibility of every Christian layman, is to present to all who may be reached, in the clearest and most forceful way, the basic facts of the gospel of Christ and to urge all who hear to make the definite, personal response to these facts which God requires. To this, the supreme task, every other duty and activity of the church must be secondary and subsidiary.

Let me now state once again these basic facts of the gospel and the response which each person is required to make.

1. Christ was delivered by God the Father to the punishment of death on account of our sins.
2. Christ was buried.
3. God raised Him from the dead on the third day.
4. Righteousness is received from God through believing these facts.

In order to receive salvation, each individual soul must make a direct, personal response to Christ. This response can be described in any of the following ways: calling upon the name of Christ as Lord; coming to Christ; receiving Christ; drinking of the water of life which Christ alone can give.

To every person who has read this far I would ask this question: Have you believed these facts? Have you made this definite, personal response?

If not, I urge you to do it now. Pray with me, just as Mrs. H. prayed there with me in that hospital room. Say these words:

> Lord Jesus Christ, I believe that You died for my sins; that You were buried; that You rose again the third day.
>
> I now repent of my sins and come to You for mercy and forgiveness.
>
> By faith in Your promise, I receive You personally as my Saviour and confess You as my Lord.
>
> Come into my heart, give me eternal life and make me a child of God.
>
> Amen!

13
FAITH AND WORKS

The relation between faith and works is an important subject which is referred to in many different passages of the New Testament. Yet it is one about which remarkably little teaching is given in most Christian circles today. As a result, a good many Christians are left in confusion or partial bondage, halfway between law and grace. Not a few Christians also, through ignorance on this point, are led astray into false teachings which lay unscriptural emphasis on the observance of some particular day or the eating of certain special foods or other similar matters of the law.

What do we mean by "faith" or by "works"? By "faith" we mean "that which we believe," and by "works" we mean "that which we do."

Thus we can express the relationship between faith and works as taught in the New Testament by the following simple contrast: Faith is not based on works, but works are the outcome of faith. Or, in still simpler words: What we believe is not based on what we do, but what we do is the outcome of what we believe.

Salvation by Faith Alone

Let us begin by considering the first part of this statement: Faith is not based on works. In other words, what we believe is not based on what we do. The whole of the New Testament bears consistent testimony to this vital truth. This fact is supported by the account of the final moments of the sufferings of Jesus upon the cross.

> So when Jesus had received the sour wine, He said, "It is finished!" And bowing His head, He gave up His spirit (John 19:30).

The Greek word translated "it is finished" is the most emphatic word that could possibly be used. It is the perfect tense of a verb which itself means to do a thing perfectly. We might perhaps bring this out by translating: "It is perfectly perfect," or "It is completely complete." There remains nothing more whatever to do.

All that ever needed to be done to pay the penalty of men's sins and to purchase salvation for all men has already been accomplished by the sufferings and death of Christ upon the cross. To suggest that any man might ever need to do anything more than Christ has already done would be to reject the testimony of God's Word and to discredit the efficacy of Christ's atonement.

In the light of this, any attempt by any man to earn salvation by his own good works is in effect an insult both to God the Father and to God the Son. It carries the implication that the work of atonement and salvation, planned by the Father and carried out by the Son, is in some sense inadequate or incomplete. This is contrary to the unanimous testimony of the entire New Testament.

Paul continually and emphatically teaches this. For example, in Romans 4:4-5 he says:

> Now to him who works, the wages are not counted as grace but as debt. But to him who does not work but believes on Him who justifies the ungodly, his faith is accounted for righteousness.

Notice the phrase "to him who does not work but believes." In order to obtain salvation by faith, the first thing any man must do is to stop "working" – to stop trying to earn salvation. Salvation comes through faith alone, through doing nothing but believing. So long as a man tries to do anything whatever to earn salvation, he cannot experience the salvation of God which is received by faith alone.

This was the great mistake which Israel made, as Paul – himself an Israelite – explains.

> But Israel, who pursued a law of righteousness, has not attained it. Why not? Because they pursued it not by faith but as if it were by works (Rom. 9:31-32, NIV).

Again Paul says concerning Israel:

> For they being ignorant of God's righteousness, and seeking to establish their own righteousness, have not submitted to the righteousness of God (Rom. 10:3).

Why did Israel fail to obtain the salvation God had prepared for them? Paul gives two reasons, which go very closely together: 1) "they pursued it not by faith but as if it were by works," 2) they sought to "establish their own righteousness."

In other words, they tried to earn salvation by something which they themselves did in their own righteousness. As a result, those who did this never entered into God's salvation.

The same mistake which was made by Israel in Paul's day is being made today by millions of professing Christians around the world.

There are countless sincere, well-meaning people in Christian churches everywhere who feel that they must do something to help earn their salvation. They devote themselves to such things as prayer, penance, fasting, charity, self-denial, the careful observance of church ordinances, but all in vain! They never obtain true peace of heart and assurance of salvation because – like Israel of old – they seek it not by faith but by works.

Such people go about to establish their own righteousness, and in this way they fail to submit to the righteousness of God, which is by faith in Christ alone.

Paul emphasises the same truth when he tells Christian believers:

> For by grace you have been saved through faith, and that not of yourselves; it is the gift of God, not of works, lest anyone should boast (Eph. 2:8-9).

Notice the tense that Paul uses: "You have been [already] saved." This proves that it is possible to be saved in this present life and to know it. Salvation is not something for which we have to wait until the next life. We can be saved here and now.

How can this present assurance of salvation be received? It is the gift of God's grace – that is, God's free, unmerited favour toward the sinful and undeserving. This gift is received through faith – "not of works, lest anyone should boast." If a man could do anything whatever to earn his own salvation, then he could boast of what he himself had done. He would not owe his salvation entirely to God, but would owe it, in part at least, to his own good works, his own efforts. But when a man receives salvation as a free gift of God, simply through faith, he has nothing whatever to boast of.

> Where is boasting then? It is excluded. By what law? Of works? No, but by the law of faith. Therefore we conclude that a man is justified by faith apart from the deeds of the law (Rom. 3:27-28).

In Romans 6:23 Paul again presents the total contrast between that which we earn by our works and that which we receive solely by faith, for he says:

> For the wages of sin is death, but the gift of God is eternal life in Christ Jesus our Lord.

There is a deliberate contrast between the two words *wages* and *gift*. The word *wages* denotes what we have earned by what we have done. On the other hand, the word translated "gift" – in Greek *charisma* – is directly related to the Greek word for "grace," *charis*. Hence, the word denotes explicitly a free, unmerited gift of God's grace or favour.

Thus, each of us is confronted with a choice. On the one hand, we may choose to take our wages; that is, the due reward for our works. But because our own works are sinful and unpleasing to God, the wages due to us for them is death – not merely physical death but also eternal banishment from the presence of God.

On the other hand, we may choose to receive by faith God's free gift. This gift is eternal life, and it is in Jesus Christ. When we receive Jesus Christ as our personal Saviour, in Him we receive the gift of eternal life.

> Not by works of righteousness which we have done, but according to His mercy He [God] saved us, through the

washing of regeneration and renewing of the Holy Spirit (Titus 3:5).

Nothing could be plainer than this: "Not by works of righteousness which we have done, but according to his mercy He saved us . . ." If we desire salvation, it cannot be upon the basis of any works of righteousness which we have done, but solely upon the basis of God's mercy. Our own works must first be excluded, in order that we may receive God's mercy in salvation.

In the second part of this same verse Paul tells us four positive facts about the way God's salvation works in our lives: 1) it is a washing – that is, we are cleansed from all our sin; 2) it is a regeneration – that is, we are born again, we become children of God; 3) it is a renewing – that is, we are made new creatures in Christ; 4) it is of the Holy Spirit – that is, it is a work of God's own Spirit within our hearts and lives.

None of this can be the result of our own works, but all of it is received solely through faith in Christ.

Living Faith vs. Dead Faith

If salvation is not by works but is solely by faith, we may naturally ask, What part, then, do works play in the life of the Christian believer? The clearest answer to this in the New Testament is given by James.

> What does it profit, my brethren, if someone says he has faith but does not have works? Can faith save him? If a brother or sister is naked and destitute of daily food, and one of you says to them, "Depart in peace, be warmed and filled," but you do not give them the things which are needed for the body, what does it profit? Thus also faith by itself, if it does not have works, is dead. But someone will say, "You have faith, and I have works." Show me your faith without your works, and I will show you my faith by my works. You believe that there is one God. You do well. Even the demons believe – and tremble! But do you want to know, O foolish man, that faith without works is dead? Was not Abraham our father justified by works when he offered Isaac his son on the altar? Do you see that faith was working together with his works, and by works faith was made perfect? And the Scripture was fulfilled which says, "Abraham believed God, and it was accounted to him for righteousness." And he was called the friend of God.

> You see then that a man is justified by works, and not by faith only. Likewise, was not Rahab the harlot also justified by works when she received the messengers and sent them out another way? For as the body without the spirit is dead, so faith without works is dead also (2:14-26).

In this passage James gives several examples to illustrate the connection between faith and works. He speaks of a Christian who sends away a fellow believer, hungry and naked, with empty words of comfort but without food or clothing. He speaks of the demons who believe in the existence of the one true God but find no comfort, only fear, in their belief. He speaks of Abraham who offered his son, Isaac, in sacrifice to God. And he speaks of the harlot Rahab in Jericho who received and protected Joshua's messengers.

However, it is in the last verse, verse 26, that James sums up his teaching about the connection between faith and works by the example of the relationship between the body and the spirit. He says, "For as the body without the spirit is dead, so faith without works is dead also."

This reference to *the spirit,* in connection with faith, provides the key to understanding how faith operates in the life of the believer.

In chapter 10 on "The Nature of Faith" we referred to the words of Paul in 2 Corinthians 4:13.

> But since we have the same spirit of faith, according to what is written, "I believed and therefore I spoke," we also believe and therefore speak.

Here Paul states that true, scriptural faith is something spiritual – it is the spirit of faith. Through this we are able to understand James's example of the body and the spirit.

In the natural order, so long as a man is alive, his spirit dwells within his body. Every action of the man's body is an expression of his spirit within him. Thus, the actual existence and character of the spirit within the man, though invisible, are clearly revealed through the behaviour and the actions of the man's body.

When the spirit finally leaves the man's body, the body ceases from all its actions and becomes lifeless. The lifeless inactivity of the body indicates that the spirit no longer dwells within.

So it is with the spirit of faith within the true Christian. This spirit of faith is alive and active. It brings down the very life of God Himself, in Christ, to dwell within the believer's heart.

This life of God within the believer takes control of his whole nature – his desires, his thoughts, his words, his actions. The believer begins to think, speak and act in an entirely new way – a way that is totally different from what he would have done previously. He says and does things which he neither could nor would have done before the life of God came in, through faith, to take control of him. His new way of living – his new "works," as James calls it – is the evidence and the expression of the faith within his heart.

But if the outward actions are not manifested in the man's life – his works do not correspond to the faith he professes – this proves there is no real living faith within him. Without this living faith, expressed in corresponding actions, his profession of Christianity is no better than a dead body after the spirit has left it.

We may briefly consider, in order, each of the four examples which James gives and see how each illustrates this principle.

First, James speaks of the Christian who sees a fellow Christian naked and hungry and says to him, "Depart in peace, be warmed and filled," but nevertheless does not offer him either food or clothing.

Obviously, this man's words were not sincere. If he had really desired to see the other person warmed and fed, he would have given him food and clothing. The fact that he did not do it indicates that he did not really care. His words were an empty profession without any inward reality. So it is when a Christian professes faith but does not act according to that faith. Such faith is insincere, worthless, dead.

Second, James speaks of the demons, who believe in the one true God but tremble. These demons have no doubt whatever about the existence of God, but they know also that they are the unrepentant enemies of God, under His sentence of wrath and judgement. Therefore, their faith brings them no comfort, but only fear.

This shows that true, scriptural faith is always expressed in submission and obedience to God. Faith that continues stubborn and disobedient is dead faith that cannot save one from God's wrath and judgement.

Third, James gives us the same example of faith as that given by Paul in Romans 4 – the example of Abraham. Abraham believed God, and it was "accounted . . . to him for righteousness" (Gen. 15:6).

Living faith in God's Word came into Abraham's heart. Thereafter, this faith was expressed outwardly in a continual walk of submission and obedience to God. Each act of obedience that Abraham performed developed and strengthened his faith and prepared him for the next act.

The final test of Abraham's faith came in Genesis 22, when God asked him to offer up his son, Isaac, in sacrifice (see also Heb. 11).

> By faith Abraham, when he was tested, offered up Isaac . . .
> accounting that God was able to raise him up, even from the
> dead (Heb. 11:17-19).

By this time, through continual exercise in obedience, Abraham's faith had been developed and strengthened even to the place where he really believed that God could raise up and restore his son to him from the dead. This faith in Abraham's heart found its outward expression in his perfect willingness to offer up Isaac, and it was only the direct intervention of God that kept him from actually slaying his son.

Concerning this, James says:

> Faith was working together with his works, and by works
> faith was made perfect (James 2:22).

We may therefore sum up Abraham's experience as follows: His walk with God began with faith in his heart in God's Word. This faith expressed itself outwardly in a life of submission and obedience. Each act of obedience strengthened and developed his faith and made him ready for the next test. Finally, this interworking of faith and works in his life brought him to the climax of his faith – to the point where he was willing even to offer up Isaac.

The fourth example James gives of the relation between faith and works is that of Rahab. The story of Rahab is related in chapters 2 and 6 of the book of Joshua.

Rahab was a sinful Canaanite woman living in the city of Jericho, which was under the sentence of God's wrath and judgement. Having heard of the miraculous way in which God had led Israel out of Egypt, Rahab had come to believe that the God of Israel was the true God and that He would give Canaan and its inhabitants into the hand of His people Israel. However, Rahab also believed that the God of Israel was merciful enough and powerful enough to save her and her family. This was the faith Rahab had in her heart.

This faith found expression in two things that she did.

First, when Joshua sent two men ahead of his army into Jericho, Rahab received these two men into her home, hid them and enabled them to escape again. In doing this, Rahab risked her own life.

Later, in order to claim God's protection upon her home and family, she hung a line of scarlet from her window to distinguish her house from all the others. This was the same window through which Rahab had previously helped the two men to escape.

As a result of these two acts of Rahab, her house and family were saved from the destruction that later came upon all the rest of Jericho. Had Rahab merely believed secretly in her heart in the God of Israel but been unwilling to perform these two decisive acts, her faith would have been a dead faith. It would have had no power to save her from the judgement that came upon Jericho.

The lesson for us as Christians is twofold. First, if we profess faith in Christ, we must be willing to identify ourselves actively with Christ's cause and Christ's messengers, even though it may mean real personal sacrifice, perhaps the risking or laying down of our very lives. Second, we must be willing to make a definite, open confession of our faith, which marks us out from all the unbelievers around us. The scarlet line speaks particularly of openly confessing our faith in the blood of Christ for the remission and cleansing of our sin.

For a final summary of the relation between faith and works we may turn once again to the writings of Paul.

> Work out your own salvation with fear and trembling; for it is God who works in you both to will and to do for His good pleasure (Phil. 2:12-13).

Here the relationship is plain. First, God works in us both to will and to do. Then we work out, in our actions, what God has first worked in us.

The important thing to realise is that faith comes first, then works. We receive salvation from God by faith alone, without works. Once having received salvation in this way, we then work it out actively in our lives by our works – by the things we do. If we do not actively work out our salvation this way, after believing, this shows that the faith which we have professed is merely dead faith, and that we have no real experience of salvation.

We do not receive salvation by works. But our works are the test of whether our faith is real and the means by which our faith is developed. Only real, living faith can make a real, living Christian.

14
LAW AND GRACE

In our previous chapter we came to the following conclusion: According to the New Testament, salvation is received through faith alone – faith in Christ's finished work of atonement – without human works of any kind. But thereafter this faith always issues in appropriate works – actions which correspond with the faith that has been professed. A faith that does not produce these appropriate works is a mere empty profession – a dead faith – incapable of bringing a real experience of salvation.

This conclusion naturally leads us to a further question. What works should we look for in the life of every person who professes faith in Christ for salvation? More specifically, what is the relationship between faith in Christ and the requirements of the law of Moses?

The answer of the New Testament is clear and consistent: Once a person has trusted Christ for salvation, his righteousness no longer depends on observing the law of Moses, either wholly or in part.

This is a subject on which there is a great deal of confused thinking and speaking among Christians. In order to clear up the confusion, we must first recognise certain basic facts about the law.

The Law of Moses: One Single, Complete System

The first great fact is that the law was given complete, once for all, through Moses.

> For the law was given through Moses, but grace and truth
> came through Jesus Christ (John 1:17).

Notice that phrase "the law was given through Moses." Not "some laws," or "part of the law," but *the law* – the whole law, complete and entire in one system – was given at one period in history and through the human instrumentality of one man only, and that man was Moses. Everywhere in Scripture, unless some special qualifying phrase is added to modify or change the meaning, the phrase "the law" denotes the complete system of law given by God through Moses. Confirmation of this is found in Romans.

> For until the law sin was in the world, but sin is not imputed
> when there is no law. Nevertheless death reigned from Adam
> to Moses, even over those who had not sinned according to
> the likeness of the transgression of Adam (5:13-14).

Notice the two phrases indicating a definite period of time: "until the law," and "from Adam to Moses." When God created Adam and placed him in the garden, He gave him not a complete system of law but a single negative commandment.

> You shall not eat . . . the fruit of the tree which is in the midst
> of the garden (Gen. 3:1-3).

When Adam transgressed this commandment, sin entered into the human race and came upon Adam and all his descendants from that time onward. The evidence that sin came upon all men from the time of Adam onward is the fact that all men became liable to death, which is the outcome of sin.

However, from the time that Adam transgressed against that first, single God-given commandment until the time of Moses, there was no God-given, God-enforced system of law revealed and applied to the human race. This explains how the two phrases "until the law" and "from Adam to Moses" denote the same period of human history – the period from Adam's transgression of the single commandment in the garden down to the time when the complete system of divine law was given by God through Moses.

During this period the human race was without any system of God-given, God-enforced law. This is in full accord with the statement already quoted from John 1:17.

> The law was given through Moses.

This law, so given, was a single, complete system of commandments, statutes, ordinances and judgements. All these are contained, in their entirety, within the compass of four books of the Bible – Exodus, Leviticus, Numbers and Deuteronomy.

Before the time of Moses there was no divine system of law given to the human race. Furthermore, after the close of this period, nothing further was ever added to this system of law. That the law was thus given once for all, complete, is made plain by the words of Moses.

> Now, O Israel, listen to the statutes and the judgements which I teach you to observe, that you may live, and go in and possess the land which the Lord God of your fathers is giving you. You shall not add to the word which I command you, nor take anything from it, that you may keep the commandments of the Lord your God which I command you (Deut. 4:1-2).

These words show that the system of law given by God to Israel through Moses was complete and final. Thereafter nothing more was ever to be added to it and nothing was ever to be taken away from it.

This leads us naturally to the next great fact which must be clearly established in relation to the keeping of the law: Every person who comes under the law is thereby obliged to observe the whole system of law in its entirety at all times. There is no question of observing certain parts of the law and omitting certain other parts. Nor is there any question of keeping the law at certain times and failing to keep it at other times. Any person who comes under the law is necessarily obliged to keep the whole law at all times.

> For whoever shall keep the whole law, and yet stumble in one point, he is guilty of all. For He who said, "Do not commit adultery," also said, "Do not murder." Now if you do not commit adultery, but you do murder, you have become a transgressor of the law (James 2:10-11).

This is both clear and logical. A person cannot say, "I consider certain points of the law to be important, so I will observe these; but I consider certain other points of the law to be unimportant, so I will not observe those." Any person under the law must observe all of its requirements at all times. If he breaks only one point, he has broken the whole law.

The law is a single, complete system which cannot be divided up into some points which are applied and others which are not applied. As a means of righteousness, the whole law must be accepted and applied, complete and entire, as a single system, or else it is of no benefit or validity whatever.

> For as many as are of the works of the law are under the curse; for it is written, "Cursed is everyone who does not continue in all things which are written in the book of the law, to do them" (Gal. 3:10).

Notice that phrase "continue in all things." This indicates that a person who is under the law must observe the whole law at all times. A person who at any time breaks any point of the law has transgressed the whole law, and has thus come under the divine curse pronounced upon all transgressors of the law.

Following on from this, we come to the third important point which must be recognised in connection with the law, and this is a matter of actual historical fact: The system of law given by Moses was ordained by God solely for one small section of the human race, and that was the people of Israel after their deliverance from the bondage of Egypt.

Nowhere in the Bible is there any suggestion that God ever intended that the Gentiles, either nationally or individually, should observe the law of Moses, either wholly or in part. The only exception to this is found in the case of a few individual Gentiles who voluntarily decided to associate themselves with Israel and thereby to place themselves under all the legal and religious obligations which God had imposed upon Israel. Such Gentile converts to Judaism are in the New Testament called "proselytes."

Apart from these, the obligations of the law have never been imposed by God upon any Gentile.

Thus we may briefly sum up the three important facts necessary to recognise before we study the relationship of the Christian believer to the law.

1. The law was given once for all, as a single, complete

system, through Moses; thereafter, nothing could ever be
added to it or taken from it.
2. The law must always be observed in its entirety as a
    single, complete system; to break any one point of the
    law is to break the whole law.
3. As a matter of human history, this system of law was
    never ordained by God for Gentiles, but only for Israel.

Christians Are Not Under the Law

Having established these three facts as a basis, let us examine in detail
what the New Testament teaches about the relation between the
Christian believer and the law. This question is referred to in many
different passages of the New Testament, and in every passage the same
clear, definite truth is taught. The righteousness of the Christian believer
does not depend upon observing any part of the law.

Let us look at a number of passages in the New Testament which
make this plain.

First of all, Romans 6:14 is addressed to Christian believers:

> For sin shall not have dominion over you, for you are not
> under law but under grace.

This verse reveals two important truths. First, Christian believers are
not under law but under grace. These are two alternatives which
mutually exclude each other: A person who is under grace is not under
the law. No person can be under both the law and grace at the same time.

Second, the very reason why sin shall not have dominion over
Christian believers is because they are not under the law. So long as a
person is under the law he is also under the dominion of sin. To escape
from the dominion of sin a person must come out from under the law.

> The sting of death is sin, and the strength of sin is the law
> (1 Cor. 15:56).

The law actually strengthens the dominion of sin over those who are
under the law. The harder they strive to keep the law, the more conscious
they become of the power of sin within themselves, exercising dominion
over them, even against their own will, and frustrating every attempt to
live by the law. The only escape from this dominion of sin is to come out
from under the law and to come under grace.

For when we were in the flesh, the passions of sin which were
aroused by the law were at work in our members to bear fruit
to death. But now we have been delivered from the law,
having died to what we were held by, so that we should serve
in the newness of the Spirit and not in the oldness of the letter
(Rom. 7:5-6).

Here Paul says that those who are under the law are subject to the
passions of sin in their fleshly nature, which cause them to bring forth
fruit to death; but that, as Christian believers, "we have been delivered
from the law . . ." that we should serve God, not according to the letter
of the law, but in the newness of spiritual life which we receive through
faith in Christ.

Again, in Romans 10:4 Paul says:

For Christ is the end of the law for righteousness to everyone
who believes.

As soon as a person puts his faith in Christ for salvation, that is the
end of the law for that person as a means of achieving righteousness.
Here Paul is very precise in what he says. He does not say that there is
an end of the law as a part of God's Word. On the contrary, God's Word
"endures forever." There is an end of the law for the believer as a means
of achieving righteousness.

The believer's righteousness is no longer derived from the keeping of
the law, either wholly or in part, but solely from faith in Christ.

Paul states that the law as a means of righteousness came to an end
with the atoning death of Christ upon the cross.

And you, being dead in your trespasses and the uncircum-
cision of your flesh, He has made alive together with Him,
having forgiven you all trespasses, having wiped out the
handwriting of requirements that was against us, which was
contrary to us. And He has taken it out of the way, having
nailed it to the cross (Col. 2:13-14).

Here Paul says that through the death of Christ, God "wiped out the
handwriting of requirements that was against us" and took "it out of the
way . . ." Paul does not speak about the wiping out of sins but about the
wiping out of *requirements*. This word could better be translated
"ordinances."

These ordinances are the ordinances of the law which stood between God and those who had transgressed them, and therefore they had to be taken out of the way before God could bestow mercy and forgiveness upon them. The word *ordinances* here denotes the whole system of law which God had ordained through Moses, including that particular section of the law which we usually call the Ten Commandments.

That this "wiping out" includes the Ten Commandments is confirmed by Paul later in the same chapter.

> Therefore let no one judge you in food or in drink, or regarding a festival or a new moon or sabbaths (Col. 2:16).

The word *therefore* at the opening of this verse indicates a direct connection with what had been stated two verses earlier; that is, the wiping out of the ordinances of the law through the death of Christ.

Again, the mention of "the sabbaths" at the end of the verse indicates that the religious observance of the Sabbath day was included among those ordinances which had been wiped out. Yet the commandment to observe the Sabbath day is the fourth of the Ten Commandments. This indicates that the Ten Commandments are included among the totality of the ordinances of the law that have been wiped out and taken out of the way through the death of Christ.

This confirms what we have established: the law, including the Ten Commandments, is a single, complete system. As a means of achieving righteousness, it was introduced as a single, complete system by Moses; and, as a single, complete system, it was done away with by Christ.

> For He Himself [Christ] is our peace, who has made both one, and has broken down the middle wall of division between us, having abolished in His flesh the enmity, that is, the law of commandments contained in ordinances, so as to create in Himself one new man from the two, thus making peace (Eph. 2:14-15).

Paul here tells us that Christ, through His atoning death on the cross, has abolished (that is, made of no effect) "the law of commandments"; He has thereby taken away the great dividing line of the law of Moses which separated Jews from Gentiles, making it possible for Jews and Gentiles alike, through faith in Christ, to be reconciled both with God and with each other.

The phrase "the law of commandments" indicates as plainly as possible that the entire law of Moses, including the Ten Commandments, was made of no further effect as a means of righteousness by the death of Christ upon the cross.

In 1 Timothy 1:8-10 Paul again discusses the relationship of the Christian believer to the law and reaches the same conclusion.

> But we know that the law is good if one uses it lawfully, knowing this: that the law is not made for a righteous person, but for the lawless and insubordinate, for the ungodly and for sinners, for the unholy and profane, for murderers of fathers and murderers of mothers, for manslayers, for fornicators, for sodomites, for kidnappers, for liars, for perjurers, and if there is any other thing that is contrary to sound doctrine.

Here Paul defines two classes of persons: On the one hand, there is a righteous man; on the other hand, there are those guilty of the various sins enumerated in Paul's list. A person guilty of these sins is not a true, believing Christian; such a person has not been saved from sin by faith in Christ.

A person who trusts Christ for salvation is no longer guilty of such sins; he has been justified, he has been made righteous – not with his own righteousness, but with the righteousness of God *which is through faith in Jesus Christ to all and on all who believe.*

Paul affirms that the law is not made for a righteous man such as this; he is no longer under the dominion of the law.

> For as many as are led by the Spirit of God, these are sons of God (Rom. 8:14).

God's true, believing sons are those who are led by God's Spirit – that is what marks them out as sons of God. Concerning such people, Paul says:

> But if you are led by the Spirit, you are not under the law (Gal. 5:18).

Thus, the very thing which marks out the true, believing sons of God – being led by God's Spirit – also means that such people are not under the law.

We may put it briefly thus: If you are a true child of God by faith in Christ, the evidence is that you are led by the Spirit of God. But if you are led by the Spirit of God, then you are not under the law. Therefore, you cannot be a child of God and under the law at the same time.

God's children are not under the law. We may illustrate this contrast between the law and the Spirit by the example of trying to find the way to a certain place by two different means: one means is to use a map; the other means is to follow a personal guide. The law corresponds to the map; the Holy Spirit corresponds to the guide.

Under the law a person is given a completely accurate and detailed map, and he is told that if he follows every detail of the map faultlessly, it will direct him on the way from earth to heaven. However, no human being has ever succeeded in following the map faultlessly. That is, no human being has ever made the journey from earth to heaven by the faultless observance of the law.

Under grace a person commits himself to Christ as Saviour, and thereafter Christ sends the Holy Spirit to that person to be his personal guide. The Holy Spirit, having come from heaven, already knows the way there and has no need of the map. The believer in Christ who is led by the Holy Spirit needs only to follow this personal guide to reach heaven. He need not depend on the map, which is the law. Such a believer may be absolutely confident of one thing: The Holy Spirit will never lead him to do anything contrary to His own holy nature.

Therefore, the New Testament teaches that those who are under grace are led by God's Spirit and do not depend upon the law.

We conclude, therefore, that God has never actually expected men to achieve true righteousness by the observance of the law, either wholly or in part.

This conclusion raises a very interesting question: If God never expected men to achieve righteousness by the observance of the law, why was the law ever given to men?

We shall deal with this question in the next chapter.

15
THE PURPOSE OF THE LAW

To Reveal Sin

The first main purpose of the law is to show men their sinful condition.

> Now we know that whatever the law says, it says to those who are under the law, that every mouth may be stopped, and all the world may become guilty before God. Therefore by the deeds of the law no flesh will be justified in His sight, for by the law is the knowledge of sin (Rom. 3:19-20).

Notice, first of all, the very emphatic statement "by the deeds of the law no flesh will be justified in His sight" (Rom. 3:20).

In other words, no human being will ever achieve righteousness in God's sight by the observance of the law.

Side by side with this, Paul states twice, in two different phrases, the primary purpose for which the law was given. He says first that "all the world may become guilty before God." An alternative translation is "that all the world may become subject to the judgement of God." Second, he says, "by the law is the knowledge of sin."

We see, therefore, that the law was not given to make men righteous but, on the contrary, to make men conscious that they were sinners and, as such, subject to the judgement of God upon their sin.

> What shall we say then? Is the law sin? Certainly not! On the contrary, I would not have known sin except through the law. For I would not have known covetousness unless the law had said, "You shall not covet" (Rom. 7:7).

> Therefore the law is holy, and the commandment holy and just and good. Has then what is good become death to me? Certainly not! But sin, that it might appear sin, was producing death in me through what is good, so that sin through the commandment might become exceedingly sinful (Rom. 7: 12-13).

Paul uses three different phrases which all bring out the same truth.

> I would not have known sin except through the law (Rom. 7:7).

> But sin, that it might appear sin . . . (Rom. 7:13).

> . . . so that sin through the commandment might become exceedingly sinful (Rom. 7:13).

In other words, the purpose of the law was to bring sin out into the open – to show sin in its true colours as the subtle, destructive, deadly thing that it really is. Thereafter men were left without any excuse for being deceived as to the extreme sinfulness of their condition.

In the practice of medicine, when treating diseases of the human body, there is a certain order which is always followed: first the diagnosis, then the remedy. First of all, the doctor examines the sick man and tries to ascertain the nature and cause of his disease; only after he has done that does he attempt to prescribe a remedy.

God follows the same order in dealing with man's spiritual need. Before prescribing the cure, God first diagnoses the condition. The basic cause of all human need and suffering lies in one condition common to all members of the human race: sin. No satisfactory remedy for human needs can be offered until this condition has been diagnosed.

The Bible is the only book in the world which correctly diagnoses the cause of all humanity's need and suffering. For this reason alone, apart from all else it offers, the Bible is invaluable and irreplaceable.

To Prove Man's Inability to Save Himself

The second main purpose for which the law was given was to show men that, as sinners, they are unable to make themselves righteous by their own efforts. There is a natural tendency in every human being to desire to be independent of God's grace and mercy. This desire to be independent of God is in itself both a result and an evidence of man's sinful condition, although most men do not recognise it as such.

Thus, whenever a man becomes convicted of his sinful condition, his first reaction is to seek some means by which he can cure himself of this condition and make himself righteous by his own efforts, without having to depend on the grace and mercy of God. For this reason, throughout all ages religious laws and observances have always made a strong appeal to the human race, regardless of differences of nationality or background. In practising such laws and observances men have sought to silence the inward voice of their own conscience and to make themselves righteous by their own efforts.

This was precisely the reaction of many religious Israelites to the law of Moses. Paul describes this attempt of Israel to establish their own righteousness.

> For they being ignorant of God's righteousness, and seeking to establish their own righteousness, have not submitted to the righteousness of God (Rom. 10:3).

As a result of attempting to establish their own righteousness, Israel failed to submit to God and to God's way of righteousness. Thus, the basic cause of their error was spiritual pride – a refusal to submit to God, a desire to be independent of God's grace and mercy.

Nevertheless, whenever men are really willing to be honest with themselves, they are always obliged to admit that they can never succeed in making themselves righteous by the observing of religious or moral law. Paul describes this experience in the first person; he himself had at one time striven to make himself righteous by the observance of the law. Here is what he says, as recorded in Romans 7:18-23:

For I know that in me (that is, in my flesh) nothing good
dwells; for to will is present with me, but how to perform
what is good I do not find. For the good that I will to do, I do
not do; but the evil I will not to do, that I practice. Now if I
do what I will not to do, it is no longer I who do it, but sin that
dwells in me. I find then a law, that evil is present with me,
the one who wills to do good. For I delight in the law of God
according to the inward man. But I see another law in my
members, warring against the law of my mind, and bringing
me into captivity to the law of sin which is in my members.

Here Paul speaks as one who sincerely acknowledges the righteousness and desirability of living by the law. The more he struggles,
however, to do what the law commands, the more he becomes conscious
of another law, another power, within his own fleshly nature, continually
warring against the law and frustrating his strongest efforts to make
himself righteous by observing the law.

The central point of this inward conflict is expressed in verse 21.

I find then a law, that evil is present with me, the one who
wills to do good.

This is an apparent paradox, yet it is confirmed by all human
experience. A man never knows how bad he is until he really tries to be
good. Thereafter, every attempt to be good only brings out more clearly
the hopeless, incurable sinfulness of his own fleshly nature, in face of
which all his efforts and good intentions are entirely in vain.

The second main purpose for the law, then, was to show men that not
merely are they sinful, but they are wholly unable to save themselves
from sin and make themselves righteous by their own efforts.

To Foreshadow Christ

The third main purpose for which the law was given was to foretell
and to foreshadow the Saviour who was to come, and through whom
alone it would be possible for man to receive true salvation and righteousness. This was done through the law in two main ways: The Saviour
was foretold through direct prophecy, and He was foreshadowed through
the types and ceremonies of the ordinances of the law.

An example of direct prophecy, within the framework of the law, is
found in Deuteronomy 18:18-19, where the Lord says to Israel through

Moses:

> I will raise up for them a Prophet like you from among their
> brethren, and will put My words in His mouth, and He shall
> speak to them all that I command Him. And it shall be that
> whoever will not hear My words, which He speaks in My
> name, I will require it of him.

Peter later quotes these words of Moses and applies them directly to
Jesus Christ (see Acts 3:22-26). Thus, the prophet foretold by Moses in
the law is fulfilled in the Person of Christ in the New Testament.

In the sacrifices and ordinances of the law many types foreshadow
Jesus Christ as the Saviour who was to come.

For example, in Exodus 12 the ordinance of the Passover lamb
foreshadows salvation through faith in the atoning blood of Jesus Christ,
shed at the Passover season upon the cross at Calvary. Similarly, the
various sacrifices connected with expiation of sin and approach to God,
described in the first seven chapters of Leviticus, all foreshadow various
aspects of the sacrificial, atoning death of Jesus Christ upon the cross.

For this reason, John the Baptist introduced Christ to Israel with these
words:

> Behold! The Lamb of God who takes away the sin of the
> world! (John 1:29).

By the comparison of Christ to a sacrificial lamb, the people of Israel
were directed to see in Christ the One who had been foreshadowed by
all the sacrificial ordinances of the law.

This purpose of the law is summed up in Paul's words in Galatians:

> But the Scripture has confined all under sin, that the promise
> of faith in Jesus Christ might be given to those who believe.
> But before faith came, we were kept under guard by the law,
> kept for the faith which would afterward be revealed.
> Therefore the law was our tutor to bring us to Christ, that we
> might be justified by faith (3:22-24).

The Greek word here translated "tutor" denotes a senior slave in the
household of a wealthy man whose special responsibility it was to give
the first elementary stages of teaching to the wealthy man's children, and
thereafter to escort them each day to the school where they could receive

more advanced instruction.

In a corresponding way, the law gave Israel their first elementary instruction in God's basic requirements concerning righteousness, and thereafter it was a means to direct them to put their faith in Jesus Christ and to learn from Christ the lesson of the true righteousness which is by faith, without the works of the law.

Just as this slave's educational task was complete as soon as he had delivered his master's children into the care of the fully trained teacher in the school, so the law's task was complete once it had brought Israel to their Messiah, Jesus Christ, and had caused them to see their need of salvation through faith in Him. For this reason Paul concludes:

> But after faith has come, we are no longer under a tutor (Gal. 3:25).

That is, we are no longer under the law.

To Preserve Israel

In the words of Paul, there is a phrase which reveals one further important function of the law in connection with Israel. Speaking as an Israelite, Paul says:

> We were kept under guard by the law, kept for the faith which would afterward be revealed (Gal. 3:23).

The law kept Israel as a special nation, set apart from all others, separated out by its distinctive rites and ordinances, preserved for the special purposes for which God had called them. The prophet Balaam, in his God-given vision of Israel's destiny, sets forth God's plan for them.

> A people [Israel] dwelling alone,
> Not reckoning itself among the nations (Num. 23:9).

God's perfect will for Israel was that they should dwell alone, as a unique and separate nation, in their own land. But even when Israel's disobedience frustrated this first purpose of God for them and caused them to be scattered as exiles and wanderers among all nations of the world, God still ordained that they should not be reckoned among the nations.

In the past nineteen centuries of Jewish dispersion among the Gentile nations, this decree of God has been most wonderfully fulfilled. In all the lands and nations whither they have come, the Jews have always remained a distinct and separate element which has never been assimilated or lost its special identity. The main instrument in keeping Israel a separate nation has been continued adherence to the law of Moses.

In conclusion, we may sum up the four main purposes for which the law of Moses was given.

1. The law was given to show men their sinful condition.
2. The law also showed men that, as sinners, they were unable to make themselves righteous by their own efforts.
3. The law served to foretell by prophecy and to foreshadow by types the Saviour who was to come and through whom alone it would be possible for man to receive true salvation and righteousness.
4. The law has served to keep Israel a separate nation throughout the many centuries of their dispersion, so that even now they are still preserved for the special purposes which God is working out for them.

Perfectly Fulfilled by Christ

Our examination of the relationship between the law and the gospel could not be complete without taking into account the words in which Christ Himself sums up His attitude and His relationship to the law.

> Do not think that I came to destroy the Law or the Prophets. I did not come to destroy but to fulfil. For assuredly, I say to you, till heaven and earth pass away, one jot or one tittle will by no means pass from the law till all is fulfilled (Matt. 5:17-18).

In what sense did Christ fulfil the law? First of all, He personally fulfilled it by His own spotless righteousness and by the faultless, consistent observance of every ordinance.

> God sent forth His Son, born of a woman, born under the law, to redeem those who were under the law, that we might receive the adoption as sons (Gal. 4:4-5).

Notice the words "born of a woman, born under the law . . ." By His birth as a man, Jesus Christ was a Jew, subject to all the ordinances and obligations of the law. These He perfectly fulfilled throughout the entire course of His life on earth, without ever deviating one hair's breadth from all that was required of every Jew under the law. In this sense, Jesus Christ alone, of all those who ever came under the law, perfectly fulfilled it.

Second, Jesus Christ fulfilled the law in another sense by His atoning death on the cross.

> Who committed no sin,
> Nor was guile found in His mouth . . .

who Himself bore our sins in His own body on the tree, that we, having died to sins, might live for righteousness (1 Pet. 2:22,24).

Himself without sin, Christ took upon Himself the sins of all those who had been under the law and then paid in full on behalf of them the law's final penalty, which is death. With the full penalty thus paid by Christ, it became possible for God, without compromising His divine justice, to offer full and free pardon to all who by faith accept Christ's atoning death on their behalf.

Thus Christ fulfilled the law first by His life of perfect righteousness and second by His atoning death, through which He satisfied the law's just demand upon all those who had not perfectly observed it.

Third, Christ fulfilled the law by combining in Himself every feature prophetically set forth in the law concerning the Saviour and Messiah whom God had promised to send. Even at the beginning of Christ's earthly ministry we read how Philip said to Nathanael:

We have found Him of whom Moses in the law, and also the prophets, wrote – Jesus of Nazareth, the son of Joseph (John 1:45).

Again, after His death and resurrection, Christ said to His disciples:

These are the words which I spoke to you while I was still with you, that all things must be fulfilled which were written in the Law of Moses and the Prophets and the Psalms concerning Me (Luke 24:44).

We see, then, that Christ fulfilled the law in three ways: 1) by His perfect life, 2) by His redeeming death and resurrection, 3) by fulfilling all that the law foretold and foreshadowed concerning the Saviour and Messiah who was to come.

We thus find ourselves in perfect agreement with the words of Paul:

> Do we then make void the law through faith? Certainly not!
> On the contrary, we establish the law (Rom. 3:31).

The believer who accepts the atoning death of Jesus Christ as the fulfilment of the law on his behalf is thereby enabled to accept, without compromise or qualification, every jot and tittle of the law as being completely and unchangeably true. Faith in Christ for salvation does not set aside the revelation of the law; on the contrary, it fulfils it.

> For Christ is the end of the law for righteousness to everyone
> who believes (Rom. 10:4).

The Greek word here translated "end" has two related meanings: 1) the purpose for which something is done, 2) that which brings something to a close. In both senses, the law ended with Christ.

In the first sense, once the law has successfully brought us to Christ, it is no longer needed in this capacity. In the second sense, Christ by His death put an end to the law as a means of achieving righteousness with God. Faith in Him is now the one, all-sufficient requirement for righteousness.

In every other respect, however, the law still stands, complete and entire, as a part of God's Word, which "endures forever." Its history, its prophecy and its general revelation of the mind and counsel of God – all these remain eternally and unchangeably true.

16
THE TRUE
RIGHTEOUSNESS

A man went to the doctor complaining of a pain in his stomach. After an examination the doctor diagnosed the man's trouble as appendicitis.

"Appendicitis!" said the man. "What's that?"

"Appendicitis," explained the doctor, "is a condition of irritation or inflammation of the appendix."

"Well," the man confessed, "until now I never even knew that I had an appendix to be inflamed!"

In a similar way, many professing Christians are conscious of some deep-seated trouble in their spiritual experience – trouble that finds expression in such symptoms as instability, inconsistency, lack of assurance, lack of peace. If such Christians were to be informed that the root cause of their trouble lay in the failure to understand such basic New Testament teachings as the relationship between faith and works, or between law and grace, these Christians would have to confess, just like the man with appendicitis, "Well, until now we never even knew that the New Testament had anything to say about such things as that!"

Let us briefly outline the conclusions we have reached on these two related topics thus far.

1. The whole New Testament teaches emphatically that salvation is received through faith alone – faith in Christ's finished work of atonement – without human works of any kind.
2. The faith that brings salvation is always expressed thereafter in appropriate works – in corresponding actions.
3. The works by which faith for salvation is expressed are not the works of the law. The righteousness which God requires cannot be achieved by observing the law of Moses.

These conclusions concerning the nature and purpose of the law of Moses naturally lead us on to one further question: If saving faith is not expressed by the observance of the law, then what are the works by which saving faith is expressed? What are the appropriate actions we should expect to see in the life of every person who professes saving faith in Christ?

The answer to this question, as well as the key to understanding the relationship between law and grace, is given by Paul in Romans.

> For what the law could not do in that it was weak through the flesh, God did by sending His own Son in the likeness of sinful flesh, on account of sin: He condemned sin in the flesh, that the righteous requirement of the law might be fulfilled in us who do not walk according to the flesh but according to the Spirit (8:3-4).

The key phrase here is "that the righteous requirement of the law might be fulfilled in us," where "us" denotes Spirit-led Christians. It is not the law itself which is to be fulfilled in Christians but the righteous requirement of the law.

What is meant by this phrase, "the righteous requirement of the law"?

The answer is given most clearly by Jesus Himself, in response to a Jewish lawyer's question concerning the law.

> Then one of them, a lawyer, asked Him a question, testing Him, and saying, "Teacher, which is the great commandment in the law?" Jesus said to him, " 'You shall love the Lord your God with all your heart, with all your soul, and with all your

mind.' This is the first and great commandment. And the second is like it: 'You shall love your neighbour as yourself.' On these two commandments hang all the Law and the Prophets" (Matt. 22:35-40).

The Two Great Commandments

In these words Jesus defines the righteous requirement of the law to which Paul refers. The law of Moses was only given at a certain period in human history to a small section of the human race. But behind this complete system of law there stand the two great, eternal, unchanging laws of God for the whole human race: "You shall love the Lord your God" and "You shall love your neighbour as yourself."

The system of law given through Moses was merely a detailed application and outworking of these two great commands – love for God and love for our neighbour. These two commandments were the basis of the whole legal system of Moses and the entire ministry and message of all the Old Testament prophets. Here, then, is "the righteous requirement of the law" summed up in two all-inclusive commandments: "love God" and "love your neighbour."

This same truth is taught by Paul in 1 Timothy 1:5-7.

Now the purpose of the commandment is love from a pure heart, from a good conscience, and from sincere faith, from which some, having strayed, have turned aside to idle talk, desiring to be teachers of the law, understanding neither what they say nor the things which they affirm.

Notice that illuminating statement: "the purpose of the commandment is love . . ."

The supreme purpose and object for which the whole law was given was to inculcate love – love for God and love for man. Paul goes on to say that all who seek to teach or interpret the law of Moses without understanding this basic purpose of the whole law "have turned aside to idle talk . . . understanding neither what they say nor the things which they affirm."

In other words, such interpreters have completely missed the main point of the law, which is love. This law of love – love for God and man – is the law behind all other laws.

Paul expresses the same truth about this one supreme law of love in Romans 13:8-10:

Owe no one anything except to love one another, for he who loves another has fulfilled the law. For the commandments, "You shall not commit adultery," "You shall not murder," "You shall not steal," "You shall not bear false witness," "You shall not covet," and if there is any other commandment, are all summed up in this saying, namely, "You shall love your neighbour as yourself." Love does no harm to a neighbour; therefore love is the fulfilment of the law.

And again, more succinctly, in Galatians 5:14:

For all the law is fulfilled in one word, even in this: "You shall love your neighbour as yourself."

Thus "the righteous requirement of the law," with all of its complexities and all of its enactments, can be reduced to one word: love.

Love, the Fulfilling of the Law

At this point someone may feel inclined to say: "You tell me that, as a Christian, I am not under the law or the commandments of Moses. Does this mean I am free to break those commandments and do anything I please? Am I free to commit murder or adultery or to steal, if I so desire?"

The answer to this is that, as a Christian, you are free to do anything that you can do with perfect love in your heart toward God and man. But, as a Christian, you are not free to do anything that cannot be done in love.

The man whose heart is filled and controlled by the love of God is free to do whatsoever his heart desires. For this reason, James twice refers to this law of love as the law of liberty.

But he who looks into the perfect law of liberty and continues in it, and is not a forgetful hearer but a doer of the work, this one will be blessed in what he does (James 1:25).

So speak and so do as those who will be judged by the law of liberty (James 2:12).

James calls this law of love "the perfect law of liberty" because the man whose heart is filled and controlled at all times by the love of God has liberty to do exactly what he desires. Whatsoever such a man desires to do will always be in conformity with the will and nature of God, for God Himself is love. The man who lives by this law of love is the only truly free man on the face of the whole earth – the only man who is free to do at all times what he will. Such a man needs no other law to control him.

James also gives this law of love yet another title. He calls it the "royal law."

> If you really fulfil the royal law according to the Scripture, "You shall love your neighbour as yourself," you do well (James 2:8).

Why is this the "royal" law? Because the man who lives according to this law lives indeed as a king. He is subject to no other law. He is free at all times to do whatever his heart dictates. In fulfilling this law, he fulfils all law. In all circumstances, and in every relationship toward God and man, he reigns in life as a king.

This analysis of what is meant by "the righteous requirement of the law" leads us to the following conclusion: There is no conflict or inconsistency between the standard of true righteousness put forward in the Old Testament under the law of Moses and that put forward in the New Testament in the gospel of Jesus Christ. In each case the standard of true righteousness is one and the same. It is summed up in one word: love – love for God and love for man.

The difference between the two dispensations – the dispensation of law under Moses and the dispensation of grace through Jesus Christ – lies not in the end to be achieved but in the means used to achieve that end.

In each case alike, both under law and under grace, the end to be achieved is love. But under the law the means used to that end is an external system of commandments and ordinances imposed upon man from without; under grace the means used is a miraculous and continuing operation of the Holy Spirit within the believer's heart.

The law of Moses failed to achieve its end, not because of anything wrong with the law itself, but because of the inherent weakness and sinfulness of man's fleshly nature. Paul makes this abundantly plain in the latter part of Romans 7.

> Therefore the law is holy, and the commandment holy and just and good (Rom. 7:12).

For we know that the law is spiritual, but I am carnal, sold under sin (Rom. 7:14).

For I delight in the law of God according to the inward man (Rom. 7:22).

But I see another law in my members, warring against the law of my mind, and bringing me into captivity to the law of sin which is in my members (Rom. 7:23).

The law itself is righteous and good. The man who seeks to live by the law may be perfectly sincere in acknowledging the law's standards and in seeking to live by them. But in spite of all this, the power of sin within him and the weakness of his own fleshly nature continually prevent him from living up to those standards.

Under the New Testament, the grace of God in Jesus Christ still directs man to the same end – love for God and love for his neighbour – but puts at man's disposal completely new and different means to attain that end. Grace begins with a miraculous operation of the Holy Spirit within the believer's heart.

The result of this operation is called "being born again" or "being born of the Spirit." This experience is prophetically described in the Old Testament where the Lord says to the children of Israel:

I will give you a new heart and put a new spirit within you; I will take the heart of stone out of your flesh and give you a heart of flesh (Ezek. 36:26).

The effects of this inward change are further described in Jeremiah.

Behold, the days are coming, says the Lord, when I will make a new covenant with the house of Israel and with the house of Judah (Jer. 31:31).

But this is the covenant that I will make with the house of Israel after those days, says the Lord: I will put My law in their minds, and write it on their hearts; and I will be their God, and they shall be My people (Jer. 31:33).

This new covenant here promised by the Lord is the new covenant of grace, through faith in Jesus Christ, which we today call the New

Testament.

Through this new covenant the sinner's nature is completely changed within. The old, stony, unresponsive heart is taken away; in its place a new heart and a new spirit are implanted within. The new nature is in harmony with God's nature and God's laws.

Thus it becomes natural for the man who has been recreated by God's Spirit to walk in God's ways and to do God's will. The sovereign law of love is by the Spirit Himself engraved upon the responsive tablet of the believer's heart, and from thence it is naturally worked out in the believer's new character and conduct.

> For what the law could not do in that it was weak through the flesh, God did by sending His own Son in the likeness of sinful flesh, on account of sin: He condemned sin in the flesh, that the righteous requirement of the law might be fulfilled in us who do not walk according to the flesh but according to the Spirit (Rom. 8:3-4).

The law failed to achieve God's standard of righteousness, not because of any fault in the law, but because of the weakness of man's fleshly nature. Under grace the Spirit of God changes man's fleshly nature and replaces it with a new nature, one capable of receiving and manifesting God's love.

We may sum up the basic difference between the operation of law and the operation of grace in this way: Law depends upon man's own ability and works from without; grace depends upon the miraculous operation of the Holy Spirit and works from within.

The New Testament tells us the human heart can only come under this law of divine and perfect love through the operation of God's Holy Spirit.

> Now hope does not disappoint, because the love of God has been poured out in our hearts by the Holy Spirit who was given to us (Rom. 5:5).

Notice that it is not mere human love in any form or degree, but it is the love of God – God's own love – which the Spirit of God is able to pour out in our hearts.

This love of God poured out in the human heart by God's Spirit produces, in its perfection, the ninefold fruit of the Spirit. This fruit of the Spirit is the love of God manifested in every aspect of human character and conduct. It is described by Paul:

> But the fruit of the Spirit is love, joy, peace, long-suffering, kindness, goodness, faithfulness, gentleness, self-control. Against such there is no law (Gal. 5:22-23).

Once again Paul emphasises that the life in which divine love is perfectly manifested in this ninefold spiritual fruit does not need to be controlled by any other law. Therefore, he says: "Against such there is no law."

This law of love is thus the end of all other laws and commandments. It is the perfect law, the royal law, the law of liberty.

The New Testament Pattern of Obedience

However, we must guard against leaving any impression that the love of God is something vague, indefinite, unrealistic or sentimental. On the contrary, the love of God is always definite and practical. According to the New Testament, love for God and love for man alike are expressed in ways that correspond to God's own love – ways that are definite and practical.

Throughout the whole Bible the supreme test of man's love for God can be expressed in one word: obedience.

In the Old Testament, God stated this truth to His people in Jeremiah 7:23.

> Obey my voice, and I will be your God, and you shall be My people.

True love for God is always expressed by obedience to Him.

In the New Testament, likewise, Jesus, in His parting discourse to His disciples, emphasised above all other requirements this point of obedience. In John 14 He stresses this point three times in succession within the space of a few verses.

> If you love Me, keep My commandments (v. 15).

> He who has My commandments and keeps them, it is he who loves Me (v. 21).

Then He puts the two alternatives of obedience and disobedience very clearly side by side, for He says:

> If anyone loves Me, he will keep My word (v. 23).

And then, on the contrary:

> He who does not love Me does not keep My words (v. 24).

In the light of these words, it is plain that for any Christian to profess love for Christ without obeying the will of Christ revealed in His words and His commandments is mere self-deception.

The supreme commandment of Christ in the New Testament is love. Without love, it is impossible to speak of obedience. But if we go on to examine the nature and the outworking of Christian love, we discover that the New Testament offers us the pattern of a life that is controlled in every aspect by this love.

It covers the believer's own individual and personal life, his relationship both to God and to his fellow man. It directs and controls Christian marriage and the life of the Christian family, including both parents and children. It provides for the life and conduct of the Christian church. It regulates the attitude and the relationship of the believer to secular society and government.

For us to follow this pattern in our lives, first we must prayerfully study and apply every part of the New Testament's teaching. Second, we must continually acknowledge our moment-by-moment dependence on the supernatural grace and power of the Holy Spirit.

In this way we shall prove in our own experience the truth of 1 John 2:5.

> But whoever keeps His word, truly the love of God is perfected in him. By this we know that we are in Him.

PART III

NEW TESTAMENT BAPTISMS

FOR JOHN TRULY BAPTISED WITH WATER,
BUT YOU SHALL BE BAPTISED
WITH THE HOLY SPIRIT.

ACTS 1:5

GO THEREFORE AND MAKE DISCIPLES
OF ALL THE NATIONS, BAPTISING THEM
IN THE NAME OF THE FATHER AND OF
THE SON AND OF THE HOLY SPIRIT.

MATTHEW 28:19

17
THE VERB BAPTISE

We are working our way systematically through the six great foundation doctrines of the Christian faith as stated in Hebrews 6:1-2. The six doctrines listed there as the foundation of the doctrine of Christ are as follows:

1. Repentance from dead works
2. Faith toward God
3. The doctrine of baptisms
4. Laying on of hands
5. Resurrection of the dead
6. Eternal judgement

In Part II of this book we examined the first two of these six doctrines, repentance from dead works and faith toward God – or, more simply, repentance and faith. Now we shall move on to the third of these great foundation doctrines, the doctrine of baptisms.

The logical way to begin this study is to discover, if possible, the correct, original meaning of the word *baptism* – or, more accurately, of the verb phrase "to baptise," from which the noun *baptism* is formed.

Upon examination, this word *baptise* proves to be a most unusual word. Actually it is not an English word at all. It is a Greek word, transliterated into letters of the English alphabet. If we write out the original Greek word in English letters, as accurately as it is possible to do, this gives us *baptizo.* Then, with the change of the final *o* to an *e*, we have the word in the form which has now become familiar – baptise.

At this point someone may reasonably ask: Why was this particular word never translated? Why was it simply written over from Greek to English letters? Was it because the correct meaning of the original Greek word was not known, and therefore the translators did not know by what English word to translate it?

No, this is definitely not the explanation. As we shall see in due course, the Greek word *baptizo* has a definite and well-established meaning.

Root Meaning

By far the best known and most influential of all the English translations of the Bible is the King James Version – the version which was translated and published through the authority of King James of Britain in the early years of the seventeenth century. It is through this translation that the word *baptise* has gained a place in the English language. Through this King James Version the word *baptise* has been carried over into the majority of all subsequent English versions of the Bible, as well as into a great many translations of the Bible into the languages of the world. Yet this word *baptise,* both in its origin and in its form, is in fact completely alien to almost all those languages.

How did this unusual and unnatural form first find its way into the King James Version of the Bible?

The answer lies in the fact that King James, though holding political power as an absolute monarch, was answerable in matters of religion to the bishops of the established Church of England. Now the relationship between James and his bishops was not always too cordial, and James did not wish the new translation of the Bible, published in his name and with his authority, to make his relationship with his bishops any worse.

For this reason he allowed it to be understood that, so far as possible, nothing was to be introduced into the translation which would cause unnecessary offence to the bishops or which would be too obviously contrary to the practices of the established church. Hence, the Greek word *baptizo,* which could easily have become, in translation, a source of controversy, was never translated at all, but was simply written over directly into the English language.

In this connection, it is interesting to remark that the very word *bishop* is another example of precisely the same influences at work. The word *bishop* is no more an English word than the word *baptise*.

Bishop is just another Greek word that has been taken over, without translation, into the English language; but in this case it has come by a slightly less direct route, by way of Latin. If the Greek original of the word *bishop* had been translated everywhere it occurs in the New Testament by its correct translation – which is "overseer" – the resulting version could have been interpreted as a challenge to the hierarchical order of government that existed in the established Church of England. Therefore, in various places, the translators avoided the issue and simply left the Greek word to stand in its anglicised form – bishop.

However, let us now return to the Greek word *baptizo* and its English equivalent, "baptise." This Greek verb *baptizo* is of a special, characteristic form of which there are a good many other examples in the Greek language. The characteristic feature of this verbal form is the insertion of the two letters *-iz* into a more simple, basic root. Thus, the basic root is *bapto*. The insertion into this root of the two extra letters *iz* produces the compound form – *baptizo*.

The insertion of the additional syllable *-iz* into any Greek verb produces a verb that has a special, causative meaning. That is to say, the compound verb thus formed always has the sense of causing something to be or to happen. The precise nature of that which is thus caused to be or to happen is decided by the meaning of the simple root verb, out of which the compound, causative form has been built up.

With this in mind, we can now form a clear and accurate picture of the Greek verb *baptizo*. This is a compound, causative form, built up out of the simple root form *bapto*. Obviously, therefore, to get a proper understanding of *baptizo,* we need to ascertain the meaning of *bapto*.

This simple root form *bapto* occurs three times in the Greek text of the New Testament which formed the basis of the English King James Version. In every one of these three instances the original Greek verb *bapto* is translated by the same English verb "to dip."

The three New Testament passages in which *bapto* occurs are as follows.

First, Luke 16:24. Here the rich man, in the torments of hell fire, cries out to Abraham:

Father Abraham, have mercy on me, and send Lazarus that he

may dip the tip of his finger in water and cool my tongue.

Second, John 13:26. Here, at the Last Supper, Jesus identifies the traitor who is to betray Him by giving His disciples a distinguishing mark.

It is he to whom I shall give a piece of bread when I have dipped it.

Third, Revelation 19:13. Here John describes the Lord Jesus Christ as he sees Him coming in glory, leading the avenging armies of heaven.

He was clothed with a robe dipped in blood.

In all three passages both the English word used by the translators and also the context of each passage make it clear that the Greek verb *bapto* means "to dip something into a fluid and then take it out again."

In that standard work of biblical reference – *Strong's Exhaustive Concordance of the Bible* – the author gives the following as the primary meaning of the verb *bapto*: "to cover wholly with fluid," hence, "to dip." We also find in the New Testament a compound version of the verb *bapto*, formed by prefixing the Greek preposition *en-*, or *em-*, meaning "in." This gives the compound form *embapto*. This compound form, *embapto*, also occurs three times in the Greek text of the New Testament. The three passages are Matthew 26:23, Mark 14:20 and John 13:26. Any student who cares to check for himself will quickly discover that in all three passages this compound form *embapto* is translated (just like the simple form *bapto*) by the English verb "to dip."

We thus arrive at the following conclusion. The Greek verb *bapto* – either in its simple form or with the prefix *em-* meaning "in" – occurs six times in the Greek text of the New Testament, and in every instance in the King James Version it is translated "to dip." In every instance, also, the context plainly indicates that the action described by this verb is that of dipping something into a fluid and then taking it out again.

Having arrived at the correct meaning of the simple verb *bapto*, there is no difficulty whatever in discovering the correct meaning of the causative compound form *baptizo*.

If *bapto* means "to dip something into a fluid and then take it out again," then *baptizo* can have only one possible literal meaning. Logically, it must mean "to cause something to be dipped into a fluid and then taken out again." More briefly, *baptizo* – from which we get the

English word *baptise* – means "to cause something to be dipped."

Historical Usage

This conclusion can be confirmed by tracing the word *baptizo* back into the earlier history of the Greek language.

In the third century before the Christian era, the extensive conquests of Alexander the Great had spread the use of the Greek language far beyond the geographical confines of Greece herself, or even of the Greek cities and communities of Asia Minor. In this way, by the time of the New Testament, the Greek language had become the generally accepted medium of communication for most of the peoples in the lands bordering on the Mediterranean Sea.

It is this form of the Greek language which is found in the New Testament and which traces its origin, linguistically, back to the purer form of classical Greek originally used by the Greek cities and states in the preceding centuries. Thus, most of the words used in New Testament Greek trace their origin and meaning back to the earlier forms of classical Greek.

This is true of the verb *baptizo*. This word can be traced back into the earlier, classical form of the Greek language as far as the fifth century B.C. From then on it has a continuous history in the Greek language right down into the first and second centuries A.D. (that is, throughout the whole period of the New Testament writings). Throughout this period of six or seven centuries, the word retains one unchanging basic meaning, "to dip," "to plunge," "to submerge." In this sense it may be used either literally or metaphorically.

The following are some examples of its use throughout this period.

1. In the fifth or fourth century B.C. *baptizo* is used by Plato of a young man being "overwhelmed" by clever philo-sophical arguments.
2. In the writings of Hippocrates (attributed to the fourth century B.C.) *baptizo* is used of people being "submerged" in water and of sponges being "dipped" in water.
3. In the Septuagint (the Greek version of the Old Testament attributed to the second or first century B.C.) *baptizo* is used to translate the passage in 2 Kings 5:14 where Naaman went down and "dipped himself" seven times in the Jordan. In this passage *baptizo* is used in verse 14, but

a different Greek word is used in verse 10, where the King James Version used "wash." In other words, *baptizo* means specifically to "dip oneself," not merely to "wash," without dipping.

4. Somewhere between 100 B.C. and 100 A.D., *baptizo* is used by Strabo to describe people who cannot swim being "submerged" beneath the surface of water (in contrast to logs of wood, which float on the surface).

5. In the first century A.D. *baptizo* is used metaphorically by Josephus to describe a man "plunging" a sword into his own neck and of the city of Jerusalem being "overwhelmed" or "plunged" to irremediable destruction by internal strife. It is obvious that such metaphorical uses as these would not be possible unless the literal meaning of the word was already clearly established.

6. In the first or second century A.D. *baptizo* is used twice by Plutarch to describe either the body of a person or the figure of an idol being "immersed" in the sea.

From this brief linguistic study it will be seen that the Greek word *baptizo* has always had one clear, definite meaning which has never changed. From classical Greek right down into New Testament Greek it has always retained the same basic meaning: "to cause something to be dipped," "to immerse something beneath the surface of water or some other fluid." In most cases this act of immersion is temporary, not permanent.

This brief analysis of the meaning of the word *baptism* brings out two distinctive features which are found everywhere that this word is used in the New Testament. Every baptism, considered as an experience, is both total and transitional.

It is total in the sense that it involves the whole person and the whole personality of the one being baptised; it is transitional in the sense that, for the person being baptised, it marks a transition – a passing out of one stage or realm of experience into a new stage or realm of experience never previously entered into.

The act of baptism may thus be compared to the opening and closing of a door. The person being baptised passes through a door opened up to him by the act of baptism, out of something old and familiar, into something new and unfamiliar. Thereafter the door is closed behind him, and there is no way of returning back through that closed door into the old ways and the old experiences.

Four Different Baptisms

Bearing in mind this picture of the nature of baptism, let us turn back once again to the passage where baptism is specified as one of the foundation doctrines of the Christian faith – that is, Hebrews 6:2. We observe that the word *baptism* is here used in the plural, not in the singular. It is "the doctrine of baptisms" (plural), not "the doctrine of baptism" (singular). This indicates plainly that the complete doctrine of the Christian faith includes more than one type of baptism.

Following this conclusion through the pages of the New Testament, we discover that there are actually four distinct types of baptism referred to at different points. If we set out these four types of baptism in chronological order, conforming to the order in which they are revealed in the New Testament, we arrive at the following outline.

First, the baptism preached and practised by John the Baptist – a baptism in water – is directly connected with the message and experience of repentance.

> John came baptising in the wilderness and preaching a baptism of repentance for the remission of sins (Mark 1:4).

Second, there is a type of baptism which is not precisely described by any one word in the New Testament, but which we may call "the baptism of suffering." Jesus says:

> But I have a baptism to be baptised with, and how distressed I am till it is accomplished! (Luke 12:50).

It is also referred to in Mark 10:38. This passage records a request made by the sons of Zebedee to have the privilege of sitting with Christ on His right hand and on His left hand in His glory. To this request Jesus replied with the following question:

> You do not know what you ask. Can you drink the cup that I drink, and be baptised with the baptism that I am baptised with?

It is plain that Jesus here refers to the spiritual and physical surrender that lay ahead of Him as He trod the path to the cross – the surrender of His whole being, spirit, soul and body – to the appointed will of the Father that He might take upon Himself the guilt of the world's sin and then pay by His vicarious sufferings the price required to expiate that sin. By these words Jesus indicated to His disciples that the fulfilment of His plan for their lives would in due course demand of them also a like total surrender of their whole being into the hands of God – even, if need be, for the suffering of death.

The third type of baptism revealed in the New Testament is Christian baptism in water. Christ told His disciples:

> Go therefore and make disciples of all nations, baptising them in the name of the Father and of the Son and of the Holy Spirit (Matt. 28:19).

The primary feature which thus distinguishes Christian baptism from the baptism of John the Baptist is that Christian baptism is to be carried out in the full name and authority of the triune God – Father, Son and Holy Spirit. This was not so with John's baptism.

The fourth type of baptism revealed in the New Testament is the baptism in the Holy Spirit. Jesus speaks about this baptism in Acts 1:5 and carefully distinguishes it from baptism in water. He says to His disciples:

> For John truly baptised with water, but you shall be baptised with the Holy Spirit not many days from now.

Although in the New King James Version the preposition used is "with" – baptised "with" the Holy Spirit – in the actual Greek text the preposition used is "in" – baptised "in" the Holy Spirit. Throughout the entire Greek text of the New Testament there are only two prepositions used with the verb phrase "to baptise." These are *in* and *into*. This is in full accord with our conclusion as to the literal meaning of the word *baptise*: "to cause to be dipped or immersed."

Jesus also reveals the basic purpose of the baptism in the Holy Spirit. He says:

> But you shall receive power when the Holy Spirit has come upon you; and you shall be witnesses to Me (Acts 1:8).

Primarily, therefore, the baptism in the Holy Spirit is a supernatural enduement with power from on high to be a witness for Christ.

Of the four types of baptism which we have listed, there is one – the baptism of suffering – which belongs to a more advanced level of spiritual experience than the rest and therefore does not come within the scope of this series of studies, which is deliberately limited to the basic doctrines and experiences of the Christian faith. For this reason we shall say nothing more about this baptism of suffering, but we shall confine our attention to the other three types of baptism. We shall deal with these in the order in which they are unfolded in the record of the New Testament: 1) the baptism of John the Baptist, 2) Christian baptism in water, 3) the baptism in the Holy Spirit.

18
JOHN'S BAPTISM COMPARED TO CHRISTIAN BAPTISM

Many Christians may not be clear as to the difference between the baptism of John the Baptist and Christian baptism. Therefore it is helpful to begin the study of these two forms of baptism by turning to Acts 19:1-5, where these two types of baptism are set side by side and the important difference between them is clearly brought out.

> And it happened, while Apollos was at Corinth, that Paul, having passed through the upper regions, came to Ephesus. And finding some disciples he said to them, "Did you receive the Holy Spirit when you believed?" And they said to him, "We have not so much as heard whether there is a Holy Spirit." And he said to them, "Into what then were you baptised?" So they said, "Into John's baptism." Then Paul said, "John indeed baptised with a baptism of repentance, saying to the people that they should believe on Him who would come after him, that is, on Christ Jesus." When they heard this, they were baptised in the name of the Lord Jesus.

Here in Ephesus Paul encountered a group of people who called themselves "disciples." At first Paul took them to be disciples of Christ – that is, Christians – but on closer examination he discovered they were only disciples of John the Baptist.

They had heard and accepted John's message of repentance and the form of baptism that went with it, but they had heard nothing of the gospel message of Jesus Christ, or of the Christian form of baptism directly connected with the acceptance of the gospel message.

After Paul had explained the message of the gospel to them, these people accepted it and were once again baptised – this time, the Scripture states, in the name of the Lord Jesus.

This incident shows clearly that the baptism of John and Christian baptism are distinct in their nature and their significance and that once John's ministry had closed and the gospel dispensation had been inaugurated, John's baptism was no longer accepted as being equivalent to, or a substitute for, Christian baptism. On the contrary, those who had only received John's baptism were required to be baptised again with full Christian baptism.

John's Baptism – Repentance and Confession

Mark 1:3-5 provides a summary of John's message and ministry with its accompanying form of baptism.

> The voice of one crying in the wilderness:
> Prepare the way of the Lord,
> Make His paths straight.

> John came baptising in the wilderness and preaching a baptism of repentance for the remission of sins. And all the land of Judea, and those from Jerusalem, went out to him and were all baptised by him in the Jordan River, confessing their sins.

In the providence of God, John's message and ministry served two special purposes: 1) They prepared the hearts of the people of Israel for the advent and revelation of their long-awaited Messiah, Jesus Christ. 2) They provided a link between the dispensation of the law and the prophets, which was closed by John's ministry, and the dispensation of the gospel, which was initiated about three years later as a result of the death and resurrection of Jesus Christ.

In fulfilling both these purposes of God, John's ministry was of necessity brief and temporary. It did not constitute in itself a dispensation but merely a period of transition.

In his message and ministry, John made two main demands upon the people: 1) repentance, 2) public confession of sins. Those who were willing to meet these two conditions were baptised by John in the river Jordan as a public testimony that they had repented of their past sins and were committing themselves henceforward to lead better lives.

> John came baptising in the wilderness and preaching a baptism of repentance for the remission of sins (Mark 1:4).

More literally, John preached a baptism of repentance *into* the remission of sins. This agrees with a similarly literal rendering of Matthew 3:11, where John himself uses the two prepositions *in* and *into*.

> I indeed baptise you in water into repentance.

We see, then, that John's baptism was into *repentance* and *into* remission of sins. It is therefore important to establish the meaning of the preposition *into* when used after the verb phrase "to baptise."

Obviously it does not mean that those who were baptised by John only entered into the experience of repentance and forgiveness after they had been baptised. On the contrary, when many of the Pharisees and Sadducees came to John to be baptised, John refused to accept them and demanded that they produce evidence of a real change in their lives before he would baptise them.

> But when he saw many of the Pharisees and Sadducees coming to his baptism, he said to them, "Brood of vipers! Who has warned you to flee from the wrath to come? Therefore bear fruits worthy of repentance" (Matt. 3:7-8).

In other words John demanded of them: "Prove first by your actions that there has been a real change in your lives before you ask me to baptise you."

John demanded that those who came to him for baptism should produce evidence in their lives of repentance and remission of sins before he would baptise them. Plainly, therefore, the phrase "baptism of repentance for the remission of sins" should not be taken as indicating that these two inward experiences of repentance and forgiveness only followed after the outward act of being baptised. Rather it indicates – as the context makes plain – that the outward act of being baptised served as a visible confirmation that those being baptised had already passed through the experiences of repentance and forgiveness.

Thus the act of baptism served as an outward seal, giving assurance of an inward transformation which had already taken place.

Understanding this point is of great importance because the phrase "to baptise into (or unto)" occurs in two subsequent passages of the New Testament, once in connection with Christian baptism in water and once in connection with the baptism in the Holy Spirit. In each case we must follow the same principle of interpretation as that already established in regard to John's baptism. However, we shall leave until later the detailed examination of these two subsequent passages.

To return to John's baptism, we may sum up its effects as follows. Those who sincerely met John's conditions enjoyed a real experience of repentance and forgiveness which was expressed in lives changed for the better. However, these experiences were similar in character to the ministry of John – they were essentially transitional.

Those whom John baptised did not receive abiding, inward peace and victory over sin, made possible only through the full gospel message of Jesus Christ; but their hearts were prepared to receive and respond to the gospel message when it should be proclaimed.

Christian Baptism – Fulfilling All Righteousness

Let us now turn from the transitional to the permanent – from the baptism of John to full Christian baptism ordained by Christ Himself as an integral part of the complete gospel message. The best introduction to Christian baptism is the baptism of Jesus Himself.

> Then Jesus came from Galilee to John at the Jordan to be baptised by him. And John tried to prevent Him, saying, "I have need to be baptised by You, and are You coming to me?" But Jesus answered and said to him, "Permit it to be so now, for thus it is fitting for us to fulfil all righteousness." Then he allowed Him. Then Jesus, when He had been baptised, came up immediately from the water; and behold, the heavens were opened to Him, and He saw the Spirit of God descending like a dove and alighting upon Him. And suddenly a voice came from heaven, saying, "This is My beloved Son, in whom I am well pleased" (Matt. 3:13-17).

Although Jesus was baptised by John the Baptist, the form of baptism through which He passed was not at all on the same level as that of all the other people whom John baptised. As we have already pointed out, John's baptism made two main demands upon the people: repentance and confession of sins.

However, Jesus had never committed any sins which He needed to confess or repent of. Hence, He did not need to be baptised by John in the same way as all the other people who came to John for baptism.

John himself clearly recognised this fact, for he says:

> I have need to be baptised by You, and are You coming to me? (Matt. 3:14).

However, Jesus answers in the next verse:

> Permit it to be so now, for thus it is fitting for us to fulfil all righteousness (Matt. 3:15).

In Jesus' answer we find both the reason why Jesus Himself was baptised and also the true significance of full Christian baptism, as distinct from the temporary form of baptism administered by John. Jesus was not baptised by John as the outward evidence that He had repented of His sins because He had no sins to repent of. On the contrary, as Jesus Himself explained, He was baptised in order that He might fulfil (or complete) all righteousness.

In this – as in many other aspects of His life and ministry – Jesus was deliberately and consciously establishing a standard of behaviour. By being baptised by John, He was setting an example and pattern of the baptism in which He desired Christian believers to follow Him.

This is in full accord with Peter's description of Christ's actions.

> For to this you were called, because Christ also suffered for us, leaving us an example, that you should follow His steps:
>
> > "Who committed no sin,
> > Nor was guile found in His mouth" (1 Pet. 2:21-22).

This confirms what we have already said: Jesus was not baptised by John because He had repented of His sins. On the contrary, as Peter states, Jesus "committed no sin, nor was guile found in His mouth." But in being thus baptised, He left an example for all Christians, that they should follow His steps.

With this in mind, let us turn back to the reason which Jesus Himself gave for being baptised and examine His words in greater detail: "thus it is fitting for us to fulfil all righteousness" (Matt. 3:15).

We may divide this reason into three sections: 1) the word *thus,* 2) the phrase "it is fitting," 3) the concluding section, "to fulfil all righteousness."

First, the word *thus,* or more plainly, "in this manner": By His example Jesus established a pattern for the method of baptism. Jesus was not baptised as an infant. While Jesus was still an infant, His parents "brought Him to Jerusalem to present Him to the Lord," but there is no thought or suggestion here of baptism (see Luke 2:22). Jesus was not baptised until He had come to years of understanding, so that He knew at that time both what He was doing and why He was doing it.

We read in the next verse, Matthew 3:16:

> Then Jesus, when He had been baptised, came up immediately from the water.

By simple logic we deduce from this that in being baptised, Jesus first went down into, and then came up out of, the water. Taken in conjunction with the literal meaning of the verb phrase "to baptise" (which we have already discussed), this leaves no reasonable room to doubt that Jesus permitted Himself to be wholly immersed beneath the waters of the Jordan.

Let us move on now to the second section of the reason given by Jesus for being baptised: "it is fitting." This phrase suggests that, for those who would follow Christ, being baptised is something ordained by God. It is not exactly a legal commandment, such as those imposed upon Israel by the Law of Moses, but it is for Christians a natural expression of sincere and wholehearted discipleship.

By using the plural form "us" – "it is fitting for us" – Jesus by anticipation identified Himself with all those who would subsequently follow Him through this appointed act of faith and obedience.

Finally we come to the concluding section: "to fulfil [or complete] all righteousness." As we have already pointed out, Jesus was not baptised as evidence that He had confessed and repented of His sins. He had never committed any sins; He was always perfectly righteous. This righteousness was, in the first instance, an inward condition of heart which Jesus had always possessed.

However, in allowing Himself to be baptised, Jesus fulfilled – or completed – this inward righteousness by an outward act of obedience to the will of His heavenly Father. It was through this outward act of obedience and dedication to God that He actually entered into the active life of ministry by which He fulfilled the plan of God the Father.

So it is with all true, believing Christians who are baptised. Such believers are not baptised merely because they are sinners who have confessed and repented of their sins. This would place Christian baptism right back on the same level as John's baptism. It is true that Christians have confessed and repented of their sins. Without this, they could not be Christians at all. But they have passed beyond this into something much fuller and greater than was ever possible for those who knew only the message and baptism of John.

> Therefore, having been justified by faith, we have peace with
> God through our Lord Jesus Christ (Rom. 5:1).

True Christians have not merely confessed and repented of their sins. They have done this and more. By faith in the atoning death and resurrection of Jesus Christ, they have been justified; God has imputed to them the righteousness of Christ Himself on the basis of their faith.

This is why they are baptised – not simply as evidence that they have confessed and repented of their sins, but "to fulfil [or complete] all righteousness." By this outward act of obedience they complete the inward righteousness which they have already received in their hearts by faith. This explanation shows us how totally different Christian baptism is from the baptism which John preached. We can now understand why Paul would not accept John's baptism for those who desired to be true Christians. Instead, he first instructed them in the full truth of the gospel centering in Christ's death and resurrection and then insisted on their being baptised once again with full Christian baptism.

In conclusion, Christian baptism is an outward act of obedience by which the believer fulfils, or completes, the inward righteousness he already enjoys in his heart through faith in Christ's atoning death and resurrection.

19
CONDITIONS FOR
CHRISTIAN BAPTISM

We shall now go on to examine the conditions which must be fulfilled by those who desire to receive Christian baptism.

Repenting

The first condition is stated in Acts 2:37-38, which records the reaction of the Jewish multitude to Peter's sermon on the day of Pentecost and the instructions Peter gave them.

> Now when they heard this, they were cut to the heart, and said to Peter and the rest of the apostles, "Men and brethren, what shall we do?" Then Peter said to them, "Repent, and let every one of you be baptised in the name of Jesus Christ for the remission of sins; and you shall receive the gift of the Holy Spirit."

Here, in answer to the question "What shall we do?" Peter gives two commands: first repent, then be baptised.

We have already seen (in Part II) that repentance is the first response God requires from any sinner who desires to be saved. Repentance, therefore, must precede baptism. Thereafter, baptism is the outward seal or affirmation of the inward change produced by repentance.

Believing

Christ Himself states the second condition for Christian baptism.

And He said to them, "Go into all the world and preach the gospel to every creature. He who believes and is baptised will be saved; but he who does not believe will be condemned" (Mark 16:15-16).

Here Christ states that everywhere the gospel is preached, those who desire to be saved are required to do two things: first to believe, then to be baptised. The church of the New Testament took Him at His word. Once a person had believed in Jesus for salvation, he was then immediately baptised.

The experience of the Philippian jailer provides a dramatic example (see Acts 16:25-34). At midnight, in response to the prayers of Paul and Silas, the whole prison was shaken by a supernatural earthquake, and all the doors were opened. The jailer, knowing that he would have to answer with his own life for any prisoners who might escape, prepared to commit suicide. But Paul restrained him, saying, "Do yourself no harm, for we are all here."

Under deep conviction, the jailer then asked, "Sirs, what must I do to be saved?" Paul replied, "Believe on the Lord Jesus Christ, and you will be saved, you and your household."

Paul and Silas then presented the gospel message to the whole household. Obviously they included in the message the requirement of baptism. Responding with faith, the whole household was immediately baptised. They did not even wait for the light of dawn!

The response of the jailer and his family is the standard pattern in the New Testament. Baptism was regarded as an urgent requirement, but it was always preceded by faith.

The first two requirements for baptism, repenting and believing, line up with the first three foundation doctrines presented in Hebrews 6:1-2: 1) repentance, 2) faith, 3) the doctrine of baptisms. In experience, as in doctrine, baptism must be built upon repenting and believing.

A Good Conscience

A third condition for Christian baptism is made clear in the passage where Peter compares the ordinance of Christian baptism in water to the experience of Noah and his family, who were saved from the wrath and judgement of God when they entered by faith into the ark. Then, once within the ark, they passed safely through the waters of the flood. In direct reference to this account, Peter says:

> There is also an antitype which now saves us, namely baptism (not the removal of the filth of the flesh, but the answer of a good conscience toward God), through the resurrection of Jesus Christ (1 Pet. 3:21).

Here Peter first dismisses the crude suggestion that the purpose of Christian baptism is any kind of cleansing or bathing of the physical body. Rather, he says, the essential condition of Christian baptism lies in the inner response of the believer's heart – "the answer of a good conscience toward God." This inner response of a good conscience toward God, Peter indicates, is made possible through faith in the resurrection of Jesus Christ.

We may briefly summarise the grounds upon which a Christian at his baptism may answer to God for his conduct with a good conscience.

1. Such a believer has humbly acknowledged his sins.
2. He has confessed his faith in the death and resurrection of Christ as the necessary propitiation for his sins.
3. By the outward act of obedience in being baptised, he is completing the final requirement of God needed to give him the scriptural assurance of salvation.

Having thus met all of God's requirements for salvation, he is able to answer God with a good conscience.

Becoming a Disciple

The first three conditions for baptism – repenting, believing and a good conscience – are summed up by a fourth requirement: becoming a disciple. Christ commissioned His followers to carry the message of the gospel to all nations.

Go therefore and make disciples of all the nations, baptising them in the name of the Father and of the Son and of the Holy Spirit, teaching them to observe all things that I have commanded you (Matt. 28:19-20).

Here making disciples, which precedes baptising, consists in bringing those who hear the gospel through the first three stages of repenting, believing and a good conscience. This makes new believers eligible for baptism, by which act they commit themselves publicly to a life of discipleship.

After this public act of commitment, those who have been baptised need to receive more thorough and extensive teaching that they may become true disciples – strong, intelligent, responsible Christians.

We may now sum up the scriptural requirements for baptism. The person must first have heard enough of the gospel to understand the nature of his act. He must have repented of his sins; he must confess his faith that Jesus Christ is the Son of God; he must be able to answer God with a good conscience on the grounds that he has fulfilled all of God's requirements for salvation. Finally, he must commit himself to a life of discipleship.

We conclude, therefore, that to be eligible for Christian baptism according to the New Testament standard, a person must be able to meet these four conditions; conversely, any person who is not able to meet these conditions is not eligible for baptism.

Are Infants Eligible?

It will be seen immediately that these four conditions listed above for baptism automatically rule out infants. By its very nature, an infant cannot repent, cannot believe, cannot answer with a good conscience to God and cannot become a disciple. Therefore, an infant cannot be eligible for baptism.

It is sometimes suggested that there are instances in the New Testament where whole families or households were baptised together and that it is probable that infant members of these households were included with the rest in the act of baptism. Since this has an important bearing on the whole nature and purpose of baptism, it is desirable to investigate this suggestion with care.

The two households usually mentioned are the household of Cornelius in Acts 10 and the household of the Philippian jailer in Acts 16.

Let us consider first the household of Cornelius. We are told that Cornelius was "a devout man and one who feared God with all his household" – that is, all the members of his household were God-fearing people (see Acts 10:2). Before Peter began to preach to them Cornelius said:

> Now therefore, we are all present before God, to hear all the things commanded you by God (Acts 10:33).

This indicates that all those present could hear Peter's message.

> While Peter was still speaking these words, the Holy Spirit fell upon all those who heard the word. And those of the circumcision who believed were astonished, as many as came with Peter, because the gift of the Holy Spirit had been poured out on the Gentiles also. For they heard them speak with tongues and magnify God (Acts 10:44-46).

This indicates that all those present could not merely hear Peter's message, but also receive the Holy Spirit by faith as a result of that message and speak with other tongues. In fact, it was upon this very ground that Peter accepted them as being eligible for baptism.

> Then Peter answered, "Can anyone forbid water, that these should not be baptised who have received the Holy Spirit just as we have?" (Acts 10:46-47).

Furthermore, when Peter gave to the apostles and brethren in Jerusalem an account of what had taken place in the house of Cornelius (see Acts 11), he added another important fact concerning all the members of Cornelius's household.

> Moreover these six brethren accompanied me, and we entered the man's house. And he told us how he had seen an angel standing in his house, who said to him, "Send men to Joppa, and call for Simon whose surname is Peter, who will tell you words by which *you and all your household will be saved"* (Acts 11:12-14, italics added).

We learn from this that, as a result of Peter's preaching in the house of Cornelius, every member of the household was saved.

If we now put together the various pieces of information we have gleaned concerning the household of Cornelius, we arrive at the following facts actually stated about them: All of them were God-fearing; all of them heard Peter's message; all of them received the Holy Spirit and spoke with other tongues; all of them were saved. It is clear, therefore, that all of these were people capable of meeting the New Testament conditions for baptism and that there were no infants among them.

Earlier in this chapter we already considered the second passage that describes the baptism of a whole household – that of the Philippian jailer in Acts 16. From this passage we learn the following three facts:

1. Paul and Silas spoke the word of the Lord to the jailer and all who were in his house (v. 32).
2. He and all his family were baptised (v. 33).
3. He and his whole household believed (v. 34).

This shows us that all could meet personally the New Testament conditions for baptism and that there were no infants among them.

Neither in the household of Cornelius nor in the household of the Philippian jailer nor anywhere else in the New Testament is there any suggestion that infants were ever considered eligible for baptism.

Preliminary Instruction

Although it is necessary to emphasise the conditions for Christian baptism, we must also be careful to guard against an overemphasis on the need for teaching, which leads to unscriptural results. In some places – particularly in certain foreign mission fields – it is common to insist that all those who present themselves for baptism are first subjected to a prolonged period of instruction, extending over weeks or months, before they are accepted for baptism. This practice is traced back to the words of Christ in Matthew 28:19-20.

Go therefore and make disciples of all the nations, baptising them in the name of the Father and of the Son and of the Holy Spirit, teaching them to observe all things that I have commanded you.

This emphasis on preliminary teaching is partly due to the fact that in the 1611 King James Version Christ's words are translated: "Go ye

therefore, and teach all nations . . ." However, the modern version, "Go
. . . and make disciples" is more accurate.

Let it be granted, however, that those desiring to be baptised must first
be taught. The question is, How long does this preliminary process of
teaching need to take? Should the time required be measured in months,
in weeks, in days or in hours?

The events of the day of Pentecost concluded this way:

> Then those who gladly received his [Peter's] word were
> baptised; and that day about three thousand souls were added
> to them (Acts 2:41).

The three thousand people whose baptism is here recorded had, a few
hours earlier, been open unbelievers who rejected the claim of Jesus of
Nazareth to be either the Messiah of Israel or the Son of God. From the
end of Peter's sermon to the moment of their being baptised, the time
required by the apostles to give them the necessary instruction could not
have exceeded a few hours.

Let us see how this corresponds with the response of the people of
Samaria to the preaching of Philip.

> But when they believed Philip as he preached the things
> concerning the kingdom of God and the name of Jesus Christ,
> both men and women were baptised (Acts 8:12).

No exact period of time for instruction is specified. As on the day of
Pentecost, it could have been just a few hours. Certainly it could not have
exceeded a few days, or a week or two at the very most.

Philip baptised the Ethiopian eunuch on the very same day that he met
him and preached the gospel to him (see Acts 8:36-39). Here again the
period of instruction could not have exceeded a few hours.

Then there is the case of Ananias, who was directed by God to go to
Saul of Tarsus and lay hands on him and pray for him.

> Immediately there fell from his [Saul's] eyes something like
> scales, and he received his sight at once; and he arose and was
> baptised (Acts 9:18).

Later Paul himself relates that Ananias said to him at this time:

> And now why are you waiting? Arise and be baptised (Acts
> 22:16).

We see, then, that Saul of Tarsus (later Paul) was baptised on what was probably the day of his conversion – certainly within three days of the first revelation of Jesus Christ to him upon the Damascus road.

Peter commanded Cornelius and his household to be baptised on the same day that he preached the gospel to them (see Acts 10:48).

The Lord opened the heart of Lydia, the seller of purple, to the message of the gospel, and she was then baptised with all her household (see Acts 16:14-15). In this case no further details are given, and no exact period of time is specified.

The Philippian jailer and all his household were baptised the very same night in which they first heard the gospel (Acts 16:33).

In these passages we have examined seven instances of the baptism of new converts. In every case some measure of instruction was given first. Thereafter, in the majority of these cases, baptism followed within a few hours of conversion. In no case was baptism ever delayed more than a few days.

We are thus able to arrive at a clear picture of the practice of baptism in the early church. Before baptism they presented the basic facts of the gospel, centring in the life, death and resurrection of Christ, and they related these facts to the act of baptism.

Baptism then followed immediately – normally within a few hours; at most, within a few days.

Finally, after baptism the new converts continued to receive the more detailed instruction which was needed to establish them firmly in the Christian faith. This latter phase of instruction is summed up in Acts 2:42, which immediately follows the account of the baptism of the new converts on the day of Pentecost.

> And they [that is, those who had been baptised] continued
> steadfastly in the apostles' doctrine and fellowship, in the
> breaking of bread, and in prayers.

This is the New Testament pattern for establishing new converts in the faith after they have been baptised.

20
SPIRITUAL SIGNIFICANCE
OF CHRISTIAN BAPTISM

In this chapter we shall complete our examination of Christian baptism by unfolding, from the teaching of the New Testament, the spiritual significance of this ordinance.

How God's Grace Operates

The key text which unlocks this truth is found in Romans:

> What shall we say then? Shall we continue in sin that grace may abound? Certainly not! How shall we who died to sin live any longer in it? Or do you not know that as many of us as were baptised into Christ Jesus were baptised into His death? Therefore we were buried with Him through baptism into death, that just as Christ was raised from the dead by the glory of the Father, even so we also should walk in newness of life. For if we have been united together in the likeness of His death, certainly we also shall be in the likeness of His resurrection, knowing this, that our old man was crucified

with Him, that the body of sin might be done away with, that
we should no longer be slaves of sin. For he who has died has
been freed from sin (6:1-7).

In Romans 5 Paul emphasised the abundance of God's grace toward
the depths of man's sin.

But where sin abounded, grace abounded much more (v. 20).

This leads to the question Paul asks in Romans 6:1: "What shall we
say then? Shall we continue in sin that grace may abound?" In other
words, Paul imagines someone asking: "If God's grace is in proportion
to man's sin, abounding most where sin abounds most, shall we deliberately go on sinning that God's grace may abound toward us all the more?
Is this the way to avail ourselves of God's grace toward sinners?"

Paul's answer to this dangerous suggestion points out that it is based
on a complete misunderstanding of how God's grace operates. In order
for a sinner to avail himself of God's grace there must be a definite,
personal transaction by faith between the sinner and God. The nature of
this transaction is such that it produces a total transformation within the
personality of the sinner.

There are two opposite, but mutually complementary, sides to this
transformation produced by God's grace in the sinner's personality. First
there is a death – a death to sin and the old life. Then there is a new life
– a life lived to God and to righteousness.

In the light of this fact about the way in which God's grace operates
in the sinner and the results which it produces, we are faced with two
alternative, mutually exclusive possibilities: If we have availed ourselves
of God's grace, we are dead to sin; on the other hand, if we are not dead
to sin, then we have not availed ourselves of God's grace. It is therefore
illogical, and impossible, to speak of availing ourselves of God's grace
and at the same time be living in sin. These two things can never go
together. Paul points this out in Romans 6:2: "Certainly not! How shall
we who died to sin live any longer in it?"

Just what are we to understand by the phrase "died to sin"? To form
a picture of this, let us imagine a man who has been an outstanding
sinner. Let us suppose he has been brutal to his wife and children; he has
forbidden all mention of God or religion in his home; he has used foul
language; and he has been a slave of alcohol and tobacco.

Now let us suppose that this man dies suddenly of a heart attack,
sitting in his chair at home. On the table by him is a lighted cigarette and

a glass of whiskey. Neither cigarette nor whisky any longer produces any reaction from the man; there is no inward stirring of desire, no outward motion of his arm toward them. Why not? The man is dead – dead to alcohol and tobacco alike.

A little later his wife and children come back from Sunday evening service at the local Gospel Tabernacle, singing the new gospel choruses they have just learned. There is no reaction from the man – no anger, no blasphemous words. Why not? The man is dead – dead to anger and blasphemy alike. In one short phrase, that man is "dead to sin." Sin no longer has any attraction for him; sin no longer produces any reaction from him; sin no longer has any power over him.

This is the picture that the New Testament paints of the man who has availed himself, by faith, of God's grace. Through the operation of that grace, the man has become dead to sin. Sin no longer has any attraction for him; sin no longer produces any reaction from him; sin no longer has any power over him. Instead, he is alive to God and to righteousness.

Crucified and Resurrected With Christ

This fact, that the true Christian believer is, through God's grace, dead to sin, is stated repeatedly throughout the New Testament.

> Knowing this, that our old man was crucified with Him [Christ], that the body of sin might be done away with, that we should no longer be slaves of sin. For he who has died has been freed [or justified] from sin (Rom. 6:6-7).

The meaning here is plain: For each person who has accepted the atoning death of Christ on his behalf, the old man – the corrupt, sinful nature – is crucified; the body of sin has been done away with; through death, that person has been freed (or justified) from sin. There is no longer any need to be the slave of sin.

A little later in the same chapter Paul repeats this teaching with renewed emphasis.

> Likewise you also, reckon yourselves to be dead indeed to sin, but alive to God in Christ Jesus our Lord. Therefore do not let sin reign in your mortal body, that you should obey it in its lusts . . . For sin shall not have dominion over you, for you are not under law but under grace (Rom. 6:11-12,14).

Again, the meaning is plain: As Christians we are to reckon ourselves as dead to sin through the grace of God in Jesus Christ. As a result, there is no reason why sin should continue to exercise any control or dominion over us. Later in Romans Paul again states the same truth in the clearest and most emphatic way.

> And if Christ is in you, the body is dead because of sin, but the Spirit is life because of righteousness (Rom. 8:10).

The words Paul uses, "if Christ is in you," indicate that this truth applies to every true Christian believer in whose heart Christ dwells by faith. The double consequence of Christ's indwelling the believer is: 1) a death of the old carnal nature; "the body," that is, the body of sin, is dead; 2) a new life to righteousness through the operation of God's Spirit – the Spirit is life because of righteousness.

Peter presents the same truth with equal clarity. Speaking of the purpose of Christ's death upon the cross, he says:

> Who Himself bore our sins in His own body on the tree, that we, having died to sins, might live for righteousness – by whose stripes you were healed (1 Pet. 2:24).

Peter also presents the two complementary aspects of the transformation that takes place within the believer who accepts the atoning death of Christ on his behalf: 1) death to sins, 2) living for righteousness. In fact, Peter states this as being the supreme purpose of Christ's death on the cross: "that we, having died to sins, might live for righteousness."

The condition of being dead to sins and living to righteousness is something far beyond the mere forgiveness of past sins. In fact, it takes the believer into an altogether different realm of spiritual experience. The majority of professing Christians in almost all denominations have some kind of belief that their past sins can be forgiven. In fact, this is probably the main reason why they attend church – for the purpose of confessing and obtaining forgiveness for the sins they have committed.

However, they have no thought or expectation of experiencing any inward transformation of their own nature. The result is that, having confessed their sins, they leave the church unchanged and continue committing the same kind of sins they have been confessing. In due course they are back in church again, confessing the same sins.

This is a man-made religion on the human level to which some of the outward forms of Christianity have been attached. It has little or nothing in common with the salvation God offers to the true believer through faith in Christ's atonement.

God's central purpose in Christ's atonement was not simply that man should be able to receive forgiveness of his past sinful acts, but rather that, once having been forgiven for the past, he should be able to enter into a new realm of spiritual experience. Henceforth he should be dead to sins but alive to God and to righteousness; he should no longer be the slave of sin; sin should no longer have any dominion over him.

This has been made possible because Christ, in His atonement, not merely took upon Himself the guilt of our sinful acts and then paid the full penalty for all those acts. Above and beyond this, Christ made Himself one with our corrupt, fallen, sinful nature; and when He died upon the cross, according to Scripture, that old nature of ours – "our old man," "the body of sin" – died in Him and with Him.

For the believer to enter into this full purpose of Christ's atonement, two conditions must be fulfilled. These two conditions are stated by Paul, in their logical order, in Romans 6.

> Knowing this, that our old man was crucified with Him, that the body of sin might be done away with, that we should no longer be slaves of sin (Rom. 6:6).

Our old man being crucified with Christ was a definite, historical event that occurred at a given moment in past time.

> Likewise you also, reckon yourselves to be dead indeed to sin, but alive to God in Christ Jesus our Lord (Rom. 6:11).

Here the introductory word *likewise* points out the correspondence between the experience of Christ and the experience of the believer. The meaning is: "Just as Christ died, so reckon that you also died with Him." More briefly, "Christ's death was your death."

Here, then, are the two conditions for being dead to sin and living to righteousness and to God: 1) knowing, 2) reckoning. First, we must know what God's Word teaches about the central purpose of Christ's death. Second, we must reckon God's Word to be true in our own particular case; we must apply this truth of God's Word by faith to our own condition. The experience can be ours only when, and only as long as, we thus know and reckon as true what God's Word teaches about the purpose of Christ's atonement.

Concerning this central purpose of Christ's atonement – "that we, having died to sins, might live for righteousness" – we may make two statements which can scarcely be challenged: 1) There is no truth of greater practical importance in the whole New Testament. 2) There is no truth about which greater ignorance, indifference or unbelief prevail among professing Christians.

The root of this miserable condition lies in the word *ignorance*. With good reason we may apply to this situation the words of the Lord in Hosea 4:6: "My people are destroyed for lack of knowledge."

The primary requirement stated by Paul for entering into the central purpose of Christ's atonement is "knowing this." If God's people do not know this truth, they cannot believe it; if they do not believe it, they cannot experience it. Therefore, the first great need is to bring this truth before the church and to keep it continually before the church in the clearest and most emphatic way.

First Burial, Then Resurrection

What is the relationship between this central truth of Christ's atonement and the ordinance of Christian baptism? The answer to this question is simple and practical. In the natural realm, after every death there follows a burial. The same order applies also in the spiritual realm: first death, then burial. Through faith in Christ's atonement we reckon ourselves, according to God's Word, to be dead with Him; we reckon our old man, the body of sin, to be dead. Thereafter, the next act appointed by God's Word is the burial of this old man, this dead body of sin.

The ordinance by which we carry out this burial is the ordinance of Christian baptism. In every service of Christian baptism there are two successive stages: 1) a burial, 2) a resurrection. These two stages of baptism correspond to the two stages of the inner transformation within the believer who accepts Christ's atonement on his behalf: 1) the death to sin, 2) the new life to righteousness and to God.

Christian baptism in water is, first, a burial in a typical grave of water and, second, a resurrection out of that grave into a new life that is lived to God and to righteousness. The burial is the outward expression of the death to sin, the death of the old man; the resurrection is the outward expression of the new life to righteousness and to God. The New Testament declares this to be the purpose of Christian baptism.

> Or do you not know that as many of us as were baptised into Christ Jesus were baptised into His death? Therefore we were buried with Him through baptism into death, that just as

Christ was raised from the dead by the glory of the Father,
even so we also should walk in newness of life (Rom. 6:3-4).

Buried with Him in baptism, in which you also were raised
with Him through faith in the working of God, who raised
Him from the dead (Col. 2:12).

In both these passages the two successive stages of baptism are
clearly set forth: 1) We are buried with Christ by baptism (literally,
immersion) into His death. 2) We are raised up with Him, through faith
in the working of God's power, to walk with Him in newness of life.

Apart from this basic truth of burial and resurrection, there are three
other important facts about baptism contained in these verses.

First, by true Christian baptism we are baptised into Christ Himself –
not into any particular church or sect or denomination. As Paul says:

For as many of you as were baptised into Christ have put on
Christ (Gal. 3:27).

There is no room here for anything less than Christ: Christ in His
atoning death, and Christ in His triumphant resurrection.

Second, the effect of baptism depends upon the personal faith of the
one being baptised; it is through faith in the working of God – more
simply, "through faith in what God does." Without this faith, the mere
ceremony of baptism alone is of no effect or validity whatever.

Third, the believer who is raised up out of the watery grave of baptism
to walk in newness of life does this not in his own power but in the power
of God's glory, the same power which raised Jesus from the grave. Paul
reveals that the power which raised Jesus from the grave was "the Spirit
of holiness"; that is, God's own Holy Spirit (Rom. 1:4). Thus the
believer, through the waters of baptism, commits himself to a new life to
God and to righteousness, which is to be in total dependence upon the
power of the Holy Spirit.

This agrees with what Paul says in Romans 8:10b.

And if Christ is in you, the body is dead because of sin, but
the Spirit is life because of righteousness.

God's Spirit alone can give the baptised believer the power that he
needs for this new life of righteousness.

It is a general principle of educational psychology that children remember approximately 40 percent of what they hear; 60 percent of what they hear and see; 80 percent of what they hear, see and do. In establishing the ordinance of Christian baptism in the church, God has applied this principle of psychology to the teaching of the great central purpose of Christ's atonement – that we, having died to sins, might live for righteousness.

According to the New Testament pattern, each time new believers are added to the church, they act out, through baptism, their identification by faith with Christ – first, in His death and burial to sin; second, in His resurrection to newness of life. In this way, baptism keeps before the whole church the great central purpose of Christ's atonement.

It follows that this vital truth concerning Christ's atonement can never be fully restored in the Christian church until the true method and meaning of Christian baptism are first restored. Christian baptism must become once again, for each believer individually and for the church as a whole, a re-enactment of this double truth: death and burial to sin; resurrection and life to righteousness and to God.

To complete this study, let me point out briefly that true Christian baptism does not produce within the believer this condition of death to sin, but rather it is the outward seal that the believer has already, by faith, entered into this condition. In the verses already quoted from Romans 6, Paul states clearly that we are first dead with Christ to sin; after that we are baptised into Christ's death.

In this respect, Christian baptism is parallel to John's baptism. In John's baptism the person first repented of his sins and afterward was baptised into repentance. In Christian baptism the believer is first, by faith, dead with Christ to sin, and after that he is baptised into Christ's death. In each case the outward act of baptism does not in itself produce the inward spiritual condition; rather it is the seal and affirmation that this inward condition has been produced already, by faith, in the heart of the person baptised.

21
THE BAPTISM IN THE HOLY SPIRIT

S ince the turn of the twentieth century, the subject of the baptism in the Holy Spirit has been arousing keen interest and discussion among ever-widening circles of the Christian church. Today it continues to be a theme of study, of discussion and quite often of controversy in almost all sections of Christendom. In view of this, we shall seek to approach this study in a way that is careful, thorough and scriptural.

Seven New Testament References

First we shall enumerate the passages in the New Testament where the word *baptise* is used in connection with the Holy Spirit. Appropriately enough – since seven is distinctively the number of the Holy Spirit – there are seven such passages.

John the Baptist contrasted his own ministry with the ministry of Christ which was to follow.

> I indeed baptise you with water unto [into] repentance, but He who is coming after me is mightier than I, whose sandals I am

not worthy to carry. He will baptise you with the Holy Spirit
and fire (Matt. 3:11).

Although the New King James Version uses the English preposition
with in conjunction with the verb phrase "to baptise," the actual preposition used in the original Greek is *in*. This usage applies equally to
baptising in water and to baptising in the Holy Spirit. In each case the
Greek preposition used is *in*. In fact, the only prepositions ever used
anywhere in the New Testament in conjunction with the verb phrase "to
baptise" are *in* and *into*. It is unfortunate that the New King James
Version, by using a variety of different prepositional forms, has obscured
the clear teaching of the original text.

In Mark 1:8 the words of John the Baptist concerning Christ are
rendered as follows.

> I indeed baptised you with water, but He will baptise you with
> the Holy Spirit.

In each case the Greek preposition used is *in*. In Luke 3:16 the words
of John the Baptist are rendered as follows.

> John answered, saying to them all, "I indeed baptise you with
> water; but One mightier than I is coming, whose sandal strap
> I am not worthy to loose. He will baptise you with the Holy
> Spirit and with fire."

Here again, the literal translation is "in the Holy Spirit."

In John 1:33 the testimony of John the Baptist concerning Christ is
given as follows.

> I did not know Him, but He who sent me to baptise with water
> said to me, "Upon whom you see the Spirit descending, and
> remaining on Him, this is He who baptises with the Holy
> Spirit."

Again, in each case the Greek preposition used is *in*.

In Acts 1:5, shortly before His ascension into heaven, Jesus says to
His disciples:

> For John truly baptised with water, but you shall be baptised
> with the Holy Spirit not many days from now.

More literally, Jesus says, "You shall be baptised in the Holy Spirit."
In Acts 11:16 Peter is describing the events which took place in the
household of Cornelius. In this connection he quotes the actual words of
Jesus as given in Acts 1:5, for he says:

> Then I remembered the word of the Lord, how He said, "John
> indeed baptised with water, but you shall be baptised with [in]
> the Holy Spirit."

Finally, in 1 Corinthians 12:13 Paul says:

> For by one Spirit we were all baptised into one body –
> whether Jews or Greeks, whether slaves or free – and have all
> been made to drink into one Spirit.

Here the New King James Version used the preposition *by* – "by one
Spirit we were all baptised into one body." However, the preposition
used in the original Greek text is *in* – "in one Spirit we were all baptised
into one body." Thus, Paul's wording in this passage is in perfect
harmony with the wording of the Gospels and the book of Acts.

Unfortunately, the accident that the translators of the King James
Versions – both Old and New – have used the phrase "by one Spirit" in
this particular passage has given rise to some strange doctrines. It has
been suggested that Paul is referring to some special experience,
different from that referred to in the Gospels or the book of Acts, and
that the Holy Spirit is Himself the agent who does the baptising. Had the
authors of these doctrines paused long enough to consult the original
Greek text, they would have found no basis there for any such doctrine.
In fact, the whole teaching of the entire New Testament agrees on this
fact, clearly and emphatically stated: Jesus Christ alone – and no other –
is the One who baptises in the Holy Spirit.

We must also add that Paul's usage here of the phrase "baptised into,"
in connection with the baptism in the Holy Spirit, agrees with the usage
of the same phrase in connection with John's baptism and with Christian
baptism in water. In both these cases we pointed out that the act of
baptism was an outward seal and affirmation of an inward spiritual
condition. The same applies to Paul's statement here about the
relationship between the baptism in the Holy Spirit and membership of
the body of Christ. The baptism in the Holy Spirit does not make a
person a member of the body of Christ. Rather it is a supernatural seal
acknowledging that that person has already, by faith, become a member

of Christ's body.

Let us now briefly summarise the lessons we may learn from the seven New Testament passages where the phrase "to baptise in the Holy Spirit" is used.

In six out of these seven passages the experience of being baptised in the Holy Spirit is both compared and contrasted with being baptised in water.

In two out of the seven passages "fire" is joined with "the Holy Spirit," and the experience is described as "being baptised in the Holy Spirit and fire."

Apart from the verb phrase "to baptise," the only other verb used in these passages in connection with the Holy Spirit is the verb "to drink." In 1 Corinthians 12:13 Paul says: "We . . . have all been made to drink into one Spirit." In modern English we would say more simply: "We have all been given to drink of one Spirit."

The use of the verb "to drink" agrees with what Jesus Himself says concerning the Holy Spirit in John 7:37-39.

> Jesus stood and cried out, saying, "If anyone thirsts, let him come to Me and drink. He who believes in Me, as the Scripture has said, out of his heart will flow rivers of living water." But this He spoke concerning the Spirit, whom those believing in Him would receive; for the Holy Spirit was not yet given, because Jesus was not yet glorified.

Here Jesus likens the gift of the Holy Spirit to the drinking of water.

This in turn harmonises with the passage in Acts 2:4 concerning the disciples in the upper room on the day of Pentecost, where it states that they were all filled with the Holy Spirit.

It agrees also with various passages in the book of Acts which speak about believers receiving the Holy Spirit. For example, concerning the Samaritans converted through the preaching of Philip, we read that Peter and John were later sent down to them from Jerusalem.

> Who, when they had come down, prayed for them that they might receive the Holy Spirit . . . Then they laid hands on them, and they received the Holy Spirit (Acts 8:15,17).

Peter says, concerning the people in the house of Cornelius upon whom the Holy Spirit had just fallen:

Can anyone forbid water, that these should not be baptised
who have received the Holy Spirit just as we have? (Acts
10:47).

Paul asks the disciples whom he meets at Ephesus:

Did you receive the Holy Spirit when you believed? (Acts
19:2).

In all these passages, the use of phrases such as "to drink of the Holy
Spirit," "to be filled with the Holy Spirit" and "to receive the Holy
Spirit" suggests an experience in which the believer receives the fullness
of the Holy Spirit inwardly within himself.

Immersion From Above

We have seen that the literal, root meaning of the verb phrase "to
baptise" is "to cause something to be dipped or immersed." Thus, the
phrase "to be baptised in the Holy Spirit" suggests that the believer's
whole personality is immersed, surrounded and enveloped in the
presence and power of the Holy Spirit, coming down over him from
above and from without.

We need to bear in mind that, in the natural order, there are two
possible ways of being immersed in water. A person may go down
beneath the surface of the water and come up from under it. Or a person
may walk under a waterfall and allow himself to be immersed from
above. This second form of immersion is the spiritual counterpart of the
baptism in the Holy Spirit.

Without exception, in every place in the book of Acts where the
baptism in the Holy Spirit is described, language is used which indicates
that the Holy Spirit comes down over, or is poured out upon, the believer
from above. For example, on the day of Pentecost:

There came a sound from heaven, as of a rushing wind, and it
filled the whole house where they were sitting (Acts 2:2).

These words reveal that the Holy Spirit came down over these
disciples from above and completely immersed and enveloped them,
even to the extent of filling the whole house where they were sitting
(Acts 2:2).

Later Peter twice confirms this interpretation of the experience. First he declares that this experience is the fulfilment of God's promise.

> In the last days . . . I will pour out of My Spirit on all flesh
> (Acts 2:17).

And he says again concerning Christ:

> Therefore being exalted to the right hand of God, and having
> received from the Father the promise of the Holy Spirit, He
> poured out this which you now see and hear (Acts 2:33).

In each case the picture is one of the Holy Spirit being poured out over the believers from above.

In Acts 8:16 the phrase used for the same experience is that of the Holy Spirit "falling upon" the believers. Here again the language depicts the Spirit coming down over them from above.

In Acts 10, concerning the people in the house of Cornelius, both phrases are used one after the other. In verse 44 we read: "the Holy Spirit fell upon all those who heard the word." In verse 45 we read: "the gift of the Holy Spirit had been poured out on the Gentiles also." This shows that the phrases "to fall upon" and "to be poured out on" are used interchangeably in this connection.

Again, when Peter describes the same event in the house of Cornelius, he says:

> The Holy Spirit fell upon them, as upon us at the beginning
> (Acts 11:15).

Here the phrase "as upon us at the beginning" indicates that the experience of Cornelius and his household was exactly parallel to the experience of the disciples in the upper room on the day of Pentecost.

Finally, we read concerning the disciples in Ephesus, after they had been baptised in water:

> And when Paul had laid hands on them, the Holy Spirit came
> upon them (Acts 19:6).

Here the phrase "to come upon" is obviously similar in meaning to the phrase used in previous passages, "to fall upon."

If we now seek to fit together the pictures created by the various phrases used in the New Testament, we arrive at a conclusion which may be summarised as follows.

- The experience of which we are speaking is made up of two distinct but complementary aspects, one outward and the other inward.
- Outwardly, the invisible presence and power of the Holy Spirit comes down from above upon the believer and surrounds, envelops and immerses him.
- Inwardly, the believer, in the likeness of one drinking, receives the presence and power of the Holy Spirit within himself until there comes a point at which the Holy Spirit, thus received, in turn wells up within the believer and flows forth like a river from the inmost depths of his being.

No human language can fully describe a mighty, supernatural experience such as this, but it may perhaps be illuminating to borrow a picture from the Old Testament.

In the days of Noah the whole world was submerged beneath the flood. In bringing about this flood, God used two distinct but complementary processes.

> In the six hundredth year of Noah's life, in the second month, the seventeenth day of the month, on that day all the fountains of the great deep were broken up, and the windows of heaven were opened (Gen. 7:11).

This account reveals that the waters of the flood came from two sources: from within ("the fountains of the great deep were broken up") and from above ("the windows of heaven were opened"), and the rain was poured down.

We must, of course, observe that the flood of Noah's day was a flood of divine wrath and judgement; the flood which immerses the New Testament believer is one of divine mercy and glory and blessing. However, with this qualification, the New Testament believer who receives the fullness of the Holy Spirit exhibits the same two aspects as in the account of Noah's flood: From within, the fountains of the great deep within the believer's own personality are broken up, and there gushes out a mighty flood of blessing and power from his inmost being; from above, the windows of God's mercy are opened upon the believer, and there is poured upon him such a deluge of glory and blessing that his whole personality is immersed in its outpourings.

It must be emphasised that we are not speaking of two separate experiences, but rather of two distinct yet complementary aspects which together make up the fullness of one single experience.

Someone may object that it is difficult to understand how the believer can at one and the same time be filled with the Holy Spirit from within and immersed in the Holy Spirit from without. However, such an objection in reality serves only to illustrate the limitations of human speech and understanding. A similar type of objection might be brought against such statements as those made by Christ Himself, that He is in the Father, and the Father in Him; or again, that Christ is in the believer, and the believer in Christ.

In the last resort, if men persist in caviling at a supernatural experience of this kind on the basis of human limitations of expression or understanding, the best and shortest answer is found in the words of the Scottish preacher who said, "It's better felt than telt!"

The Outward Evidence

Up to this point we have considered the invisible, inward nature of the baptism in the Holy Spirit. We must now go on to consider the outward manifestations which accompany this inward experience.

First of all we must point out that it is perfectly scriptural to use the word *manifestation* in connection with the Holy Spirit. We acknowledge, of course, that the Holy Spirit Himself is, by His very nature, invisible. In this respect He is compared by Jesus to the wind. Jesus says concerning the operation of the Holy Spirit:

> The wind blows where it wishes, and you hear the sound of
> it, but cannot tell where it comes from and where it goes. So
> is everyone who is born of the Spirit (John 3:8).

Although the wind itself is invisible, the effects which the wind produces when it blows can in many cases be both seen and heard. For example, when the wind blows, the dust rises from the streets; the trees all bend in one direction; the leaves rustle; the waves of the sea roar; the clouds blow across the sky. These effects produced by the wind can be seen or heard.

So it is, Jesus says, with the Holy Spirit. The Spirit Himself is invisible. But the effects which the Holy Spirit produces when He begins to work can often be seen or heard. This fact is confirmed by the language of the New Testament in various places.

For example, let us turn to Peter's description of the effects produced by the descent of the Holy Spirit on the day of Pentecost.

> Therefore being exalted to the right hand of God, and having received from the Father the promise of the Holy Spirit, He [Christ] poured out this which you now see and hear (Acts 2:33).

The effects of the descent of the Holy Spirit could be both seen and heard.

Paul describes the work of the Spirit in his own ministry in these words:

> And my speech and my preaching were not with persuasive words of human wisdom, but in demonstration of the Spirit and of power (1 Cor. 2:4).

He also says that the Spirit can have a similar effect in every believer's experience.

> But the manifestation of the Spirit is given to each one for the profit of all (1 Cor. 12:7).

Notice the phrases which Paul uses in connection with the Holy Spirit – the "demonstration of the Spirit" and the "manifestation of the Spirit." These two words, *demonstration* and *manifestation,* show clearly that the presence and operation of the Holy Spirit can produce effects which can be perceived by our physical senses.

With this in mind, let us now turn to the various passages in the New Testament where the baptism in the Holy Spirit is described; that is, where we are told what actually happened to the people who received this experience. Let us see what the outward manifestations are which accompany this operation of the Spirit.

Three places in the New Testament we are told what happened when people were baptised in the Holy Spirit. We shall consider, in order, the actual words used in each report to describe what took place.

First, let us read what happened to the first disciples on the day of Pentecost.

> And suddenly there came a sound from heaven, as of a

rushing mighty wind, and it filled the whole house where they were sitting. Then there appeared to them divided tongues, as of fire, and one sat upon each of them. And they were all filled with the Holy Spirit and began to speak with other tongues, as the Spirit gave them utterance (Acts 2:2-4).

Second, we turn to what happened when Peter first preached the gospel to Cornelius and his household.

While Peter was still speaking these words, the Holy Spirit fell upon all those who heard the word. And those of the circumcision who believed were astonished, as many as came with Peter, because the gift of the Holy Spirit had been poured out on the Gentiles also. For they heard them speak with tongues and magnify God (Acts 10:44-46).

Finally, we see what happened to the first group of converts to whom Paul preached at Ephesus.

And when Paul had laid hands on them, the Holy Spirit came upon them, and they spoke with tongues and prophesied (Acts 19:6).

If we now carefully compare these three passages, we shall find that there is one – and only one – outward manifestation which is common to all three occasions where people received the baptism in the Holy Spirit. In each case the Scripture explicitly states that those who received this experience "spoke with tongues," or "spoke with other tongues."

Other supernatural manifestations are also mentioned, but none is mentioned as having taken place on more than one of the three occasions.

For example, on the day of Pentecost the sound of a rushing wind was heard, and visible tongues of fire were seen. However, these manifestations were not repeated on the other two occasions.

Again, at Ephesus the new converts not only spoke in tongues but also prophesied. However, this manifestation of prophesying is not mentioned as having taken place either on the day of Pentecost or in the house of Cornelius.

The only manifestation which is common to all three occasions is that all those who received the experience spoke with tongues.

Peter and the other Jews who already knew what had taken place on the day of Pentecost went to the house of Cornelius reluctantly, against their own inclinations, under the explicit direction of God. At that time the Jewish believers did not realise the gospel was for the Gentiles or that Gentiles could be saved and become Christians. However, the moment Peter and the other Jews heard the Gentiles speak with tongues, they immediately understood and acknowledged that these Gentiles had received the Holy Spirit just as fully as the Jews themselves. They never asked for any additional evidence.

The Scripture says that they were "astonished . . . because the gift of the Holy Spirit had been poured out on the Gentiles also. For they heard them speak with tongues" (Acts 10:45-46). For Peter and the other Jews, the sole and sufficient evidence that the Gentiles had received the Holy Spirit was that they spoke with tongues.

In Acts 11 Peter was called to account by the other leaders of the church in Jerusalem for visiting and preaching to Gentiles. In his own defence he explained what had taken place in the house of Cornelius.

> And as I began to speak, the Holy Spirit fell upon them, as upon us at the beginning (Acts 11:15).

Thus Peter directly compares the experience which the household of Cornelius received with that which the first disciples received on the day of Pentecost, for he says, ". . . as upon us at the beginning." Yet in the house of Cornelius there was no mention of a mighty rushing wind or tongues of fire. The one sufficient manifestation which set the divine seal upon the experience of Cornelius and his household was that they spoke with tongues.

From this we conclude that the manifestation of speaking with tongues as the Holy Spirit gives utterance is the accepted New Testament evidence that a person has received the baptism in the Holy Spirit. In confirmation of this conclusion, we may make the following statements.

1. This was the evidence which the apostles themselves received in their own experience.
2. This was the evidence which the apostles accepted in the experience of others.
3. The apostles never asked for any other alternative evidence.
4. No other alternative evidence is offered to us anywhere in the New Testament.

In the next chapter we will examine this conclusion further, and we shall consider various criticisms or objections which are commonly raised against it.

22
RECEIVE THE HOLY SPIRIT

A number of objections are often raised against our conclusion that the manifestation of speaking with tongues is the accepted New Testament evidence that a person has received the baptism in the Holy Spirit. For the sake of clarity and thoroughness, therefore, let us consider some of the most common objections.

One standard objection takes the following form: Every Christian automatically received the Holy Spirit at conversion and therefore does not need any further experience or any other evidence to have the assurance of having received the Holy Spirit.

Much confusion and controversy will be avoided once we establish one important, scriptural fact: The New Testament depicts two separate experiences, both of which are described as "receiving the Holy Spirit." This means it is possible for a Christian to have "received the Holy Spirit" in one use of the expression but not in the other.

The Pattern of the Apostles

A simple way to distinguish these two experiences is to compare the events of two Sundays, each uniquely important in the history of the Christian church. The first is resurrection Sunday; the second is Pentecost Sunday.

On resurrection Sunday Jesus appeared to the apostles in a group for the first time after His resurrection.

> He breathed on them, and said to them, "Receive the Holy Spirit" (John 20:22).

Jesus' breathing on the apostles was suited to the words which accompanied it: "Receive the Holy Spirit." In Greek the same word *pneuma* means both "spirit" and "breath." The words of Jesus could therefore be translated, "Receive holy breath." Furthermore, the tense of the imperative form "receive" indicates that the receiving was a single, complete experience which took place as Jesus uttered the word. It is therefore an incontestable, scriptural fact that at that moment the apostles did actually "receive the Holy Spirit."

In this first encounter with the resurrected Christ, the apostles passed from "Old Testament salvation" to "New Testament salvation." Up to that time the believers of the Old Testament had looked forward, by faith, through prophecies and types and shadows to a redemptive act which had not yet taken place. Those who enter into "New Testament salvation," on the other hand, look back to a single historical event: the death and resurrection of Christ. Their salvation is complete.

There are two requirements for receiving this New Testament salvation.

> If you confess with your mouth the Lord Jesus and believe in your heart that God has raised Him from the dead, you will be saved (Rom. 10:9).

The two requirements are to confess Jesus as Lord and to believe that God raised Him from the dead. Prior to resurrection Sunday the apostles had already confessed Jesus as Lord. But now, for the first time, they also believed that God raised Him from the dead. Thus their salvation was completed.

This was the point at which they experienced the new birth. The Holy Spirit, breathed into them by Jesus, imparted to them a totally new kind of life – eternal life – which had triumphed over sin and Satan, over death and the grave.

This experience of the apostles stands as a pattern for all who enter into the new birth. It contains two essential elements: a direct, personal revelation of the resurrected Christ and the receiving of the Holy Spirit as divine, eternal life. This agrees with the words of Paul, "the Spirit is life because of righteousness"; that is, the righteousness imputed to all who believe in Christ's death and resurrection (Rom. 8:10).

Yet even after this wonderful encounter Jesus made it plain to the apostles that their experience of the Holy Spirit was still incomplete. In His final words to them before His ascension He commanded them not to go out and preach immediately, but to go back to Jerusalem and wait there until they were baptised in the Holy Spirit and thus endued with power from on high for effective witness and service.

> Behold, I send the Promise of My Father upon you; but tarry in the city of Jerusalem until you are endued with power from on high (Luke 24:49).

> For John truly baptised with water, but you shall be baptised with the Holy Spirit not many days from now (Acts 1:5).

> But you shall receive power when the Holy Spirit has come upon you; and you shall be witnesses to Me (Acts 1:8).

Almost all interpreters of the Bible agree that this promise of being baptised in the Holy Spirit was fulfilled on Pentecost Sunday.

> And they were all filled with the Holy Spirit and began to speak with other tongues, as the Spirit gave them utterance (Acts 2:4).

It was on resurrection Sunday that the apostles received the inbreathed Spirit from Christ and thus entered into salvation and the new birth. Yet it was not until Pentecost Sunday, seven weeks later, that they were baptised in – or filled with – the Holy Spirit. This shows that salvation, or the new birth, is a distinct and separate experience from the baptism in the Holy Spirit, although each is described as "receiving the Holy Spirit."

Later on Pentecost Sunday Peter explained that it was Christ, after His ascension, who had poured out the Holy Spirit on the waiting disciples.

> Therefore being exalted to the right hand of God, and having received from the Father the promise of the Holy Spirit, He

poured out this which you now see and hear (Acts 2:33).

We can then sum up the differences between the two experiences of receiving the Holy Spirit.
On resurrection Sunday it was:

- the resurrected Christ
- the inbreathed Spirit
- the result: life.

On Pentecost Sunday it was:

- the ascended Christ
- the outpoured Spirit
- the result: power.

The experience of the apostles demonstrates that salvation, or the new birth, and the baptism in the Holy Spirit are two distinct and separate experiences. The apostles received the first of these experiences on resurrection Sunday; the second, seven weeks later on Pentecost Sunday.
Further study in the book of Acts discloses that the two experiences are normally separate. Furthermore, from Pentecost Sunday onward the term "to receive the Holy Spirit" is applied always and only to the second experience – the baptism in the Holy Spirit. It is never again used to describe the new birth.

Further Outpourings of the Spirit

There are three other occasions subsequent to Pentecost where Scripture describes what took place when people were baptised in the Holy Spirit. These were in Samaria, in Ephesus and in the household of Cornelius. We will examine each of these in turn.
The ministry of Philip in Samaria is introduced in Acts 8:5.

Then Philip went down to the city of Samaria and preached Christ to them.

But when they believed Philip as he preached the things concerning the kingdom of God and the name of Jesus Christ, both men and women were baptised (Acts 8:12).

These people had now heard the truth of Christ preached to them by Philip; they had believed; they had been baptised. It would be unreasonable and unscriptural to deny that these people were saved.

Consider the words of Christ as He commissioned His disciples to preach the gospel.

> And He said to them, "Go into all the world and preach the gospel to every creature. He who believes and is baptised will be saved: but he who does not believe will be condemned" (Mark 16:15-16).

The people of Samaria had heard the gospel preached, they had believed, and they had been baptised. Therefore we know, on the authority of Christ's own words, that they were saved. Yet these same people up to this time had not received the Holy Spirit.

> Now when the apostles who were at Jerusalem heard that Samaria had received the word of God, they sent Peter and John to them, who, when they had come down, prayed for them that they might receive the Holy Spirit. For as yet He had fallen upon none of them. They had only been baptised in the name of the Lord Jesus. Then they laid hands on them, and they received the Holy Spirit (Acts 8:14-17).

We see that the people of Samaria received salvation through the ministry of Philip; they received the Holy Spirit through the ministry of Peter and John. Their receiving the Holy Spirit was a separate experience, subsequent to their receiving salvation. Here, then, is a second scriptural example which indicates it is possible for people to have become genuine Christians but not yet to have received the Holy Spirit in the sense in which this phrase is used from Pentecost onward.

It is interesting to notice that, in the passage in Acts 8, we find two different forms of speech used. One speaks of "receiving the Holy Spirit"; the other speaks of "the Holy Spirit falling upon them." However, the context makes it plain that these are not two different experiences but two different aspects of one and the same experience.

When Paul came to Ephesus and met there certain people described as "disciples," the first question he asked was "Did you receive the Holy Spirit when you believed?" (Acts 19:2).

It is plain that Paul had been given the impression that these people were disciples of Christ. Obviously, if they were not Christians at all, there could have been no question of their having received the Holy Spirit, since this is received only through faith in Christ. However, by further questioning Paul discovered they were not disciples of Christ at all but only of John the Baptist, and so he preached to them the full gospel of Christ.

One fact emerges clearly from this incident so far. Obviously, if people always received the Holy Spirit automatically as an immediate consequence of believing in Christ, it would be illogical and foolish for Paul to ask the question: "Did you receive the Holy Spirit when you believed?" The mere fact that Paul asked this question makes it clear that he recognised the possibility of people having become disciples or believers in Christ without having received the Holy Spirit.

This is confirmed by the record of events that occurred after Paul had explained the gospel of Christ to these people.

> When they heard this, they were baptised in the name of the
> Lord Jesus (Acts 19:5).

These people had now heard and believed the gospel, and they had been baptised. As we have already shown in connection with the people of Samaria, on the authority of Christ's own words, people who have fulfilled the two conditions of believing and being baptised are thereby saved. Nevertheless, these people in Ephesus, just like those in Samaria, had not yet received the Holy Spirit. In Ephesus, just as in Samaria, this came as a separate and subsequent experience.

> And when Paul had laid hands on them, the Holy Spirit came
> upon them, and they spoke with tongues and prophesied
> (Acts 19:6).

Here, then, is a third scriptural example which indicates it is possible for people to have been converted to Christ, but not yet to have received the Holy Spirit.

This conclusion drawn from the book of Acts is further confirmed by what Paul says in his epistle to the Ephesians. We must bear in mind that this group of disciples to whom Paul ministered in Ephesus were among the Ephesian Christians to whom he later wrote his epistle.

In his letter Paul reminds these people of the successive stages in which they were originally converted and received the Holy Spirit. Speaking of their coming to believe in Christ, he says:

> In Him you also trusted, after you heard the word of truth, the
> gospel of your salvation; in whom also, having believed, you
> were sealed with the Holy Spirit of promise (Eph. 1:13).

Here Paul indicates that there were three separate, successive stages
in their experience: 1) they heard the gospel; 2) they believed in Christ;
3) they were sealed with the Holy Spirit. This agrees exactly with the
historical record in Acts 19, which states that these people first heard the
gospel, then believed and were baptised. Finally, when Paul laid his
hands upon them, the Holy Spirit came on them.

In both accounts alike – in Acts and in Ephesians – it is absolutely
clear that the people received the Holy Spirit, not simultaneously with
conversion, but as a separate and subsequent experience after
conversion.

For a fourth example, of a different kind, we shall now consider
briefly the sermon Peter preached in the house of Cornelius and its
results (see Acts 10:34-48).

The Scripture seems to indicate that as soon as Cornelius and his
household heard the gospel and put their faith in Christ, they immediately received the Holy Spirit and spoke with tongues. However, we
must add that, although in this instance these two experiences happened
together, they still remain two quite distinct experiences.

Furthermore, the evidence that Cornelius and his household had
received the Holy Spirit was not the fact that they had put their faith in
Christ, but the fact that, under the impulse of the Holy Spirit, they spoke
with tongues.

In the account of what happened in the household of Cornelius, the
following three different phrases are all used to describe the same
experience: "the Holy Spirit fell upon" them; "the gift of the Holy Spirit
had been poured out on" them; and they "received the Holy Spirit."
Where Peter describes the same incident a second time, he uses the
following three phrases: "the Holy Spirit fell upon them"; they were
"baptised with [in] the Holy Spirit"; "God gave them the same gift [of
the Holy Spirit]" (Acts 11:15-17).

Earlier, two similar phrases were used concerning the Samaritans: the
Holy Spirit "had fallen upon none of them"; and "they received the Holy
Spirit" (Acts 8:16-17).

Putting these passages together, we find that a total of five different
phrases are used to describe this one experience: "the Holy Spirit fell
upon" them; "the gift of the Holy Spirit had been poured out on" them;
they "received the Holy Spirit"; they were "baptised with [in] the Holy

Spirit"; and "God gave them the gift" of the Holy Spirit.

Some modern interpreters would suggest that these different phrases refer to different experiences. However, this is not in line with the usage of the apostles in the New Testament. According to the apostles, these different phrases all denote one single experience – although they describe it from different aspects. It is the same thing for a person to receive the Holy Spirit or receive the gift of the Holy Spirit as it is to be baptised in the Holy Spirit, or for the Holy Spirit to fall upon that person, or for the Holy Spirit to be poured out on that person.

We have now carefully considered four different groups of people portrayed in the New Testament: 1) the apostles, 2) the people of Samaria, 3) the disciples at Ephesus, 4) Cornelius and his household. Of these four groups, we have seen clearly that the first three – the apostles, the people of Samaria, the disciples at Ephesus – had all been converted before they received the Holy Spirit. Their receiving the Holy Spirit was a separate and subsequent experience following their conversion.

There is no other instance recorded, apart from Cornelius and his household, in which people received the Holy Spirit at the same time they believed in Christ. We are therefore justified in concluding that the experience of Cornelius and his household is the exception rather than the rule.

On the basis of this careful examination of the New Testament record, we may now set forth the following conclusions.

1. It is normal for a Christian to receive the Holy Spirit as a separate and subsequent experience, following conversion.

2. Even if a person receives the Holy Spirit at conversion, receiving the Holy Spirit still remains, logically, a distinct experience from being converted.

3. Whether a person receives the Holy Spirit at conversion or after conversion, the evidence that that person has received the Holy Spirit still remains the same: The person speaks with tongues as the Holy Spirit gives utterance.

4. The fact that a person has been genuinely converted does not by itself constitute evidence that that person has received the Holy Spirit.

The Teaching of Jesus

This conclusion concerning the relationship between conversion and receiving the Holy Spirit has been based mainly on a study of the book of Acts. However, it is in full accord with the teaching of Jesus Himself in the Gospels. Jesus told His disciples:

> If you then, being evil, know how to give good gifts to your children, how much more will your heavenly Father give the Holy Spirit to those who ask Him! (Luke 11:13).

The teaching of this verse – reinforced by the examples which precede it, of a son asking his father for bread, for a fish and for an egg – is that God, as a heavenly Father, is willing to give the Holy Spirit to His believing children if they will ask for it. However, a person must first put his faith in Christ to become a child of God.

Plainly, therefore, Jesus teaches not that the Holy Spirit is received at conversion, but rather that it is a gift which every converted believer has a right to ask for, as a child from his or her Father. Furthermore, Jesus definitely places an obligation upon the children of God to ask their heavenly Father specifically for this gift of the Holy Spirit. It is therefore not scriptural for a Christian to assume, or to assert, that he automatically received the gift of the Holy Spirit at conversion without asking for it.

Again, in John 7:38 Christ says:

> He who believes in Me, as the Scripture has said, out of his heart will flow rivers of living water.

In the first half of the next verse these "rivers of living water" are interpreted by the writer of the Gospel as referring to the Holy Spirit, for he says:

> But this He spoke concerning the Spirit, whom those believing in Him would receive (John 7:39).

In both these verses it is clear that the gift of the Holy Spirit, bringing forth rivers of living water from within, is to be received by those who are already believers in Christ. It is something which they should go on to receive after believing in Christ.

Christ teaches the same truth again in John 14:15-17, where He says:

If you love Me, keep My commandments. And I will pray the Father, and He will give you another Helper, that He may abide with you forever, even the Spirit of truth, whom the world cannot receive, because it neither sees Him nor knows Him; but you know Him, for He dwells with you and will be in you.

In this passage the Helper and the Spirit of truth are two different designations of the Holy Spirit. Christ teaches here that the gift of the Holy Spirit is not for the unbelieving people of this world, but for Christ's own disciples who love and obey Him. This confirms, therefore, that it is the privilege of God's believing children, Christ's disciples, to go on to receive the gift of the Holy Spirit as they meet God's conditions. These may be summed up in one all-important requirement: loving obedience to Christ.

23
DO ALL SPEAK WITH TONGUES?

We shall now go on to consider some other objections or misunderstandings associated with the experience of speaking in tongues.

The Gift of "Kinds of Tongues"

One common objection or misunderstanding is based on a question Paul asked: "Do all speak with tongues?" (1 Cor. 12:30). A careful examination of the context shows that Paul clearly implies that the answer to his question is: "No – all do not speak with tongues."

Does this mean, then, that there were Christians in the New Testament church who had received the baptism in the Holy Spirit without speaking with tongues?

No, this is not what Paul is saying. Paul is not here speaking about the baptism in the Holy Spirit but about various supernatural manifestations of the Spirit, which can be exercised by the believer in the church subsequent to, and as a result of, the initial experience of being baptised in the Holy Spirit.

This agrees with what Paul says two verses earlier.

> Now you are the body of Christ, and members individually. And God has appointed these in the church: first apostles, second prophets, third teachers, after that miracles, then gifts of healings, helps, administrations, varieties of tongues (1 Cor. 12:27-28).

Paul is speaking of various ministries which may be exercised by different members within the church. Among these he enumerates "varieties of tongues" or, more literally, "kinds of tongues."

Exactly the same expression is used by Paul still earlier in the same chapter when he enumerates nine gifts or manifestations of the Holy Spirit which may be granted to believers who have been baptised in the Holy Spirit. The list is as follows:

> But the manifestation of the Spirit is given to each one for the profit of all: for to one is given the word of wisdom through the Spirit, to another the word of knowledge through the same Spirit, to another faith by the same Spirit, to another gifts of healing by the same Spirit, to another the working of miracles, to another prophecy, to another discerning of spirits, to another different kinds of tongues, to another interpretation of tongues. But one and the same Spirit works all of these things, distributing to each one individually as He wills (1 Cor. 12:7-11).

Paul is speaking about gifts of the Spirit which may be exercised by believers subsequent to their receiving the baptism in the Spirit. This is confirmed by what he says in verse 13: "For by one Spirit we were all baptised into one body."

Or, more literally, "For in one Spirit we were all baptised into one body."

Paul here speaks of the baptism in the Spirit as an experience that has already been received by those to whom he writes. The nine gifts or manifestations of the Spirit which he lists may then be exercised by believers subsequent to, and as a result of, their having been baptised in the Holy Spirit.

Paul indicates that though the baptism in the Holy Spirit is for all believers – "in one Spirit we were all baptised into one body" – thereafter the various gifts of the Spirit are divided up among the believers according to the sovereign will of the Spirit Himself. One believer may receive one gift and another believer may receive another gift. Not all believers receive all the gifts.

Among the nine gifts of the Spirit listed by Paul, the eighth is "different kinds of tongues." The phrase in the original Greek – "kinds of tongues" – is exactly the same as that translated "varieties of tongues" in 1 Corinthians 12:28. In each case Paul is speaking about a specific spiritual gift, not about the baptism in the Holy Spirit.

It is outside the scope of this book to examine the operation of this particular gift. It is sufficient to have established the fact that in 1 Corinthians 12:28, as in verse 10 of the same chapter, Paul is not talking about being baptised in the Holy Spirit but about one of the nine spiritual gifts exercised by some believers (but not by all) following the baptism in the Holy Spirit.

When Paul says, "Do all speak with tongues?" the question he has in mind is not: "Have all at one time spoken in tongues?" – that is, when they were initially baptised in the Holy Spirit (1 Cor. 12:30). On the contrary, he is asking: "Do all believers who have been baptised in the Holy Spirit regularly exercise the gift of 'kinds of tongues'?" To this question the answer – both then and now – is a definite no. In this respect, the experience of modern believers after being baptised in the Spirit is in full accord with the pattern established in the New Testament.

This distinction between the initial gift of the Holy Spirit, attested by the evidence of speaking in tongues, and the subsequent gift of "kinds of tongues" is very carefully preserved by the linguistic usage of the New Testament. The Greek word used for "gift" when it denotes the gift of the Holy Spirit received at the baptism in the Spirit is *dorea*. The Greek word for "gift" when it denotes any of the nine different gifts or manifestations of the Spirit (including the gift of "kinds of tongues") is *charisma*.

These two words are never interchanged in the New Testament. *Charisma* is never used to denote the gift of the Holy Spirit received at the baptism in the Spirit. Conversely, *dorea* is never used to denote any of the nine gifts of the Holy Spirit manifested in the lives of the believers who have received the baptism in the Holy Spirit. The language, teaching and examples of the New Testament all indicate a clear distinction between these two aspects of spiritual experience.

Is Fruit the Evidence?

Those who claim that speaking with tongues is not necessarily the evidence of having received the baptism in the Holy Spirit are obliged by logic to suggest some alternative evidence by which we may know, according to Scripture, that a person has received the baptism in the Holy Spirit.

One such alternative evidence which is commonly proposed is that of spiritual fruit. The suggestion is that unless a person demonstrates in his life the fruit of the Holy Spirit in a full way, that person cannot be considered to have received the baptism in the Holy Spirit.

The complete list of the fruit of the Holy Spirit is given by Paul in Galatians 5:22-23.

> But the fruit of the Spirit is love, joy, peace, long-suffering, kindness, goodness, faithfulness, gentleness, self-control.

This and other passages make it plain that the primary fruit of the Spirit out of which all the rest develop is love.

Only a foolish, shallow-minded Christian would ever deny that spiritual fruit in general, and love in particular, are of supreme importance in the life of every Christian. This does not mean, however, that spiritual fruit is the scriptural evidence of having received the baptism in the Holy Spirit. In fact, this test of spiritual fruit must be rejected as contrary to Scripture on two main grounds: 1) it is not the test which the apostles themselves applied; 2) it overlooks the clear, scriptural distinction between a gift and fruit.

Let us consider first the test which the apostles applied in their own experience. When the 120 disciples on the day of Pentecost received the baptism in the Holy Spirit with the outward evidence of speaking with other tongues, Peter did not wait several weeks or months to see whether this experience would produce in his life and in the lives of the other disciples a much greater measure of spiritual fruit than they had previously enjoyed. On the contrary, he stood up the very same hour and said without any doubts or qualifications:

> But this is what was spoken by the prophet Joel: "And it shall come to pass in the last days," says God, "that I will pour out of My Spirit on all flesh" (Acts 2:16-17).

What evidence did Peter have for making this statement? Nothing but the fact that they all began to speak with other tongues. No further evidence besides this was required.

Again, after many people in Samaria had been converted through the preaching of Philip, Peter and John went down to pray for them that they might receive the Holy Spirit.

> Now when the apostles who were at Jerusalem heard that
> Samaria had received the word of God, they sent Peter and
> John to them, who, when they had come down, prayed for
> them that they might receive the Holy Spirit. For as yet He
> had fallen upon none of them. They had only been baptised in
> the name of the Lord Jesus. Then they laid hands on them,
> and they received the Holy Spirit. Now when Simon saw that
> through the laying on of the apostles' hands the Holy Spirit
> was given, he offered them money, saying, "Give me this
> power also, that anyone on whom I lay hands may receive the
> Holy Spirit." But Peter said to him, "Your money perish with
> you, because you thought that the gift of God could be
> purchased with money!" (Acts 8:14-20).

From this account we understand that the people in Samaria had only
been converted for a few days, or at the most a few weeks. Yet they
received the Holy Spirit through the laying on of the apostles' hands as
a single, complete experience.

There was no question of waiting to see whether in the ensuing weeks
and months sufficient spiritual fruit would be manifested in the lives of
these new converts to prove that they really had received the Holy Spirit.
No, their receiving the Holy Spirit was a single, complete experience,
after which no further evidence or tests were needed.

The objection is sometimes raised that the Scripture does not
explicitly state that these people in Samaria spoke with tongues when
they received the Holy Spirit. This is quite true. However, the Scripture
does make it plain that, through the laying on of the apostles' hands,
there was an open demonstration of supernatural power such that Simon,
who had been a professional sorcerer, was willing to pay money to
receive the power to produce a similar supernatural demonstration in
anyone upon whom he might thereafter lay his hands.

If we accept that these people in Samaria, as a result of the laying on
of the apostles' hands, spoke with other tongues, this will fit in with
every detail of the story as it is recorded in Acts, and it will also bring
their experience into line with the cases of all the other people in the
book of Acts who received the baptism in the Holy Spirit.

On the other hand, if people prefer to assume that in this particular
incident in Samaria there was some supernatural manifestation other
than speaking with tongues, they must at least acknowledge that we have
no way of finding out what this other kind of manifestation was.

Upon this assumption, therefore, it is not possible to build any kind of positive doctrinal conclusion concerning the baptism in the Holy Spirit. For example, a person cannot say: "I have not spoken with tongues; nevertheless I know I have received the baptism in the Holy Spirit because I have received the same evidence or experience as the people of Samaria." If the people of Samaria did not speak with tongues, there is no way of knowing what else they may have done instead.

Thus this assumption leads only to negative and sterile conclusions. It cannot in any way affect the positive conclusions we have formed from the other cases where we know that people, on receiving the baptism in the Spirit, did speak with tongues.

Another case which is sometimes brought forward is that of Saul of Tarsus – later the apostle Paul.

> And Ananias went his way and entered the house; and laying his hands on him he said, "Brother Saul, the Lord Jesus, who appeared to you on the road as you came, has sent me that you may receive your sight and be filled with the Holy Spirit." Immediately there fell from his eyes something like scales, and he received his sight at once; and he arose and was baptised (Acts 9:17-18).

Surely if there was ever a case where the early church might justifiably have applied the test of fruit, it was in the case of Saul of Tarsus. Up to that time he had been, on his own admission, the bitterest opponent of the gospel and persecutor of the church. Yet here we find him receiving the Holy Spirit in a single experience, through the laying on of the hands of Ananias, and thereafter there is not the faintest suggestion that any further test of fruit in his life might have to be applied.

Once again, there are those who object that the Scripture does not state that Saul (later Paul) spoke with tongues when Ananias laid hands on him. It is true the Scripture gives no details of what happened to Paul. However, side by side with this account in Acts 9, we must set Paul's own testimony, as recorded in 1 Corinthians.

> I thank my God I speak with tongues more than you all (1 Cor. 14:18).

When we combine this testimony of Paul's with the other examples given in the book of Acts, it is reasonable to conclude that Paul first began to speak with tongues when Ananias laid his hands upon him for the infilling of the Spirit. This conclusion is strengthened by what happened when Paul in turn laid hands on new believers at Ephesus.

> And when Paul had laid hands on them, the Holy Spirit came upon them, and they spoke with tongues and prophesied (Acts 19:6).

It would be unnatural to suppose that Paul laid his hands upon these converts to transmit to them an experience he himself had never received.

One further and decisive case is that of Cornelius and his household, as related in Acts 10. Peter and the other believing Jews went to the house of Cornelius with reluctance, against their own inclinations, only because God had explicitly directed them to go. After Peter had preached a short while, the Holy Spirit fell upon all who heard his word. Peter and the other Jews were amazed because they heard these Gentiles speaking with tongues.

Up to this very moment Peter, like other Jewish believers, had not conceived that it was possible for Gentiles such as Cornelius to be saved and become Christians. Yet this one manifestation of speaking with tongues immediately convinced Peter and the other Jews that these Gentiles were now just as much Christians as the Jews themselves. Peter never suggested that it would be necessary to subject these Gentiles to any further tests or to wait for spiritual fruit or to look for any other kind of evidence. On the contrary, he immediately commanded that they be baptised, by which act they were openly accepted and attested as full Christians. Peter later gave an account of this incident to the other leaders of the apostolic church in Jerusalem.

> And as I began to speak, the Holy Spirit fell upon them, as upon us at the beginning . . . If therefore God gave them the same gift as He gave us when we believed on the Lord Jesus Christ, who was I that I could withstand God? (11:15,17).

We know from the previous chapter that Cornelius and his household all spoke with tongues. Yet in this account Peter does not find it necessary to mention this decisive manifestation. He merely says: "The Holy Spirit fell upon them, as upon us at the beginning . . . God gave them the same gift as He gave us." In other words, the manifestation of speaking with tongues was at this time so universally accepted as the evidence of receiving the Holy Spirit that Peter did not even need to mention it. Both he and the other church leaders took it for granted. The other church leaders concluded:

> When they heard these things they became silent; and they glorified God, saying, "Then God has also granted to the Gentiles repentance to life" (Acts 11:18).

What convinced Peter and the other apostles that Gentiles could experience salvation through faith in Christ just as fully as Jews? One thing, and one thing only: The fact that they heard these Gentiles speak with tongues. In the whole of this account there is never any suggestion that Peter or any other of the apostles ever looked for any other kind of evidence in the lives of these Gentiles, apart from the fact that they spoke with tongues. There was no question of waiting for spiritual fruit to be manifested.

In this the apostles were perfectly logical – not because fruit is unimportant, but because fruit is, by its very nature, totally different from a gift. A gift is received by a single act of faith; fruit is produced by a slow, gradual process, which includes planting, tending and cultivating.

The baptism in the Holy Spirit is a gift – a single experience – received by faith. The evidence that a person has received this gift is that he speaks with other tongues.

Thereafter, one main purpose for which the gift is given is to enable the person to produce more and better spiritual fruit than he could ever have produced otherwise. It is no error to emphasise the importance of fruit. The error consists in confusing a gift with a fruit, in confusing the evidence that a gift has been received with the purpose for which the gift has been given.

In the next chapter we will consider a number of other common misunderstandings connected with tongues as the evidence of having received the baptism in the Holy Spirit.

24
EMOTIONAL AND PHYSICAL REACTIONS

One common view today is that the baptism in the Holy Spirit is an intense emotional experience. One word often used in this connection is "ecstasy." This view of the baptism in the Holy Spirit draws its support mainly from two sources.

First, there are theologians who do not actually have the experience themselves but who theorise about it on the basis of passages in the New Testament or the writings of the early church fathers. For some reason, these theologians have chosen the word *ecstasy* or *ecstatic* to sum up the essential nature of this supernatural experience.

Second, many believers who have actually received the experience, when testifying of it to others, lay the main emphasis on their own subjective, emotional reactions. The result is that they convey, often without meaning to do so, the impression that the essential nature of the experience is emotional. Probably the emotion most commonly mentioned is joy.

The Place of Emotion

Now, in considering the relationship between the emotions and the baptism in the Holy Spirit, we do well to begin by acknowledging two important facts.

First, man is an emotional creature. His emotions constitute an integral and important part of his total makeup. Therefore, man's emotions have an important part to play in his total worship and service of God. True conversion neither suppresses nor obliterates the emotions. True conversion, on the contrary, first liberates and then redirects the emotions. If a man's emotions have not been brought under the control and power of the Holy Spirit, then the purpose of that man's conversion is not yet fulfilled.

Second, in Scripture the word *joy* is often closely associated with the Holy Spirit. For instance, the fruit of the Spirit, as listed in Galatians 5:22, is first love, then joy, and so on. In this list, joy comes immediately after love itself, which is the primary fruit of the Spirit. Again, we read concerning the early Christians in Antioch:

> And the disciples were filled with joy and with the Holy Spirit (Acts 13:52).

We see, then, that in the New Testament joy is often closely associated with the Holy Spirit.

Nevertheless, the teaching that intense joy or any other strong emotion by itself constitutes evidence of the baptism in the Holy Spirit cannot be reconciled with the New Testament. There are two main reasons for this.

First, in the actual passages where the baptism in the Holy Spirit is described, there is no direct mention of emotion. Never once is any form of emotion depicted either as the evidence, or as the direct consequence, of having received the Holy Spirit.

Any person who equates receiving the Holy Spirit with an emotional experience has no scriptural basis for his doctrine. This usually surprises the average religious person who does not base his opinions directly on the New Testament.

In fact, sometimes believers seeking the Holy Spirit receive a clear, scriptural experience of speaking with other tongues and yet afterward are unconvinced and dissatisfied with their experience simply because there was no intense emotion, as they had wrongly been led to expect.

We may illustrate this by the example of a little boy who asks his parents for a spaniel puppy as a birthday present. When the present arrives, it is a beautiful golden cocker spaniel puppy, exhibiting all the marks of a pedigree spaniel of its class.

Nevertheless, to the parents' dismay, the little boy is obviously far from satisfied with the gift. When his parents ask why, they discover that all the little fellow's friends have been telling him for weeks that all spaniels are black, and therefore he has formed in advance a strong expectation that his puppy will be black.

No matter how beautiful the golden puppy may be, it now cannot satisfy him, simply because it fails to live up to his expectation of being black. Yet his opinion that all spaniels are black has no basis in fact but has been formed merely by listening to the opinions of friends his own age who know no more about spaniels than he does.

So it is sometimes with Christians who ask their heavenly Father for the gift of the Holy Spirit. In answer to their prayer they receive an experience of speaking with other tongues, which is in perfect accord with the examples and teaching of the New Testament.

Yet they are not satisfied with this scriptural answer to their prayers simply because it was not marked by any intense emotional experience. They fail to realise that their anticipation of some intense emotion was based on the ill-considered opinions of misguided fellow Christians, not on the clear teaching of the New Testament.

The second reason why we cannot accept any strong emotion, like joy, as evidence of receiving the Holy Spirit is that there are instances in the New Testament of believers who experienced a wonderful sense of joy but who nevertheless had not yet received the Holy Spirit. An example is the first disciples' reactions after the ascension of Jesus (but before the day of Pentecost).

> And they worshipped Him, and returned to Jerusalem with great joy, and were continually in the temple praising and blessing God (Luke 24:52-53).

Here we find that the disciples, even before the day of Pentecost, experienced great joy in their worship of God. Nevertheless, we know it was not until the day of Pentecost that they were actually baptised in the Holy Spirit.

Again, after the people of Samaria had heard and believed the gospel of Christ preached to them by Philip, "there was great joy in that city" (Acts 8:8).

We see that the wholehearted acceptance of the gospel immediately brought great joy to these Samaritans. Nevertheless, as we read on in the same chapter we discover that it was only later, through the ministry of Peter and John, that these people received the Holy Spirit.

These two examples prove, therefore, that an intense emotional experience, such as great joy, is not an essential part of the baptism in the Holy Spirit and cannot be accepted as evidence of having received this baptism.

Physical Reactions

Another type of experience often associated with the baptism in the Holy Spirit is some kind of powerful physical sensation. Over the course of years I have asked many people on what grounds they based their claim to have received the baptism in the Holy Spirit. Their answer is often: some strong physical sensation or reaction.

The following are some of the experiences which have been mentioned to me: a sensation of a powerful electric current; a sensation of a fire or of intense heat in some other form; being prostrated forcefully on the floor; a powerful shaking of the whole body; seeing a very bright light; hearing the actual voice of God speaking; having a vision of heavenly glories; and so on.

Once again, in considering theories of this kind, we must acknowledge that they contain an important element of truth. Throughout the course of the Bible we find many instances where the immediate presence and power of almighty God produced strong physical reactions in those of His people who were counted worthy to come close to Him.

When the Lord appeared to Abraham and began to speak to him, Abraham fell upon his face (see Gen. 17:1-3). Several times in the books of Leviticus and Numbers, when God's presence and glory were visibly manifested among His people, both Moses and Aaron and others also of the children of Israel fell upon their faces. When the fire fell upon Elijah's sacrifice and all the people saw it, they fell upon their faces (see 1 Kin. 18:39). At the dedication of Solomon's temple:

> . . . the house of the Lord, was filled with a cloud, so that the priests could not continue ministering [more literally, could not stand to minister] because of the cloud; for the glory of the Lord filled the house of God (2 Chron. 5:13-14).

There are two passages in which the prophet Jeremiah gives his own

personal testimony of the strong physical effects produced within him by
the power of God's Word and God's presence.

> Then I said, "I will not make mention of Him [the Lord],
> Nor speak anymore in His name."
> But His word was in my heart like a burning fire
> Shut up in my bones;
> I was weary of holding it back,
> And I could not (Jer. 20:9).

Here Jeremiah testifies that the prophetic message of the Lord within
his heart produced the impression of a burning fire in his bones. Later he
says again:

> My heart within me is broken
> Because of the prophets;
> All my bones shake.
> I am like a drunken man,
> And like a man whom wine has overcome,
> Because of the Lord [more literally, from the face or presence
>   of the Lord],
> And because of His holy words (Jer. 23:9).

Here also Jeremiah's words indicate a powerful physical reaction to
God's presence.

Again, powerful physical effects came upon Daniel and his
companions because of a direct vision of the Lord.

> And I, Daniel, alone saw the vision, for the men who were
> with me did not see the vision; but a great terror [or
> trembling] fell upon them, so that they fled to hide
> themselves. Therefore I was left alone when I saw this great
> vision, and no strength remained in me; for my vigour was
> turned to frailty in me, and I retained no strength (Dan. 10:
> 7-8).

At the immediate presence of the Lord, Daniel and his companions –
just like Jeremiah – experienced strong and unusual physical reactions.

Reactions of this kind are not confined to the Old Testament. One
example is the vision of the Lord granted to Saul of Tarsus on his way
to Damascus. Saul saw a very bright light; he heard a voice speaking to

him from heaven; he fell to the earth; and his body trembled (see Acts 9:3-6).

When John describes a vision of the Lord that he received on the island of Patmos, he concludes:

And when I saw Him, I fell at His feet as dead (Rev. 1:17).

Here, too, there was obviously a very powerful and dramatic physical reaction to the immediate presence of the Lord.

In some of the older denominations of the Christian church there is a tendency to dismiss all such physical reactions or manifestations as "emotionalism" or "fanaticism." However, this attitude plainly goes far beyond what Scripture warrants. Doubtless, there can be occasions when manifestations of this kind are the product of "emotionalism" or "fanaticism" or possibly of a carnal desire for self-display. But who would dare to bring charges such as these against men like the prophets Moses, Jeremiah and Daniel or the apostles John and Paul? Too often the tendency to reject all forms of physical reaction to the presence and power of God is based on false, man-made traditions of what constitutes true holiness or of the kind of behaviour that is acceptable to God in the worship of His people.

We see, then, that the Scripture gives room for unusual reactions in the bodies of God's people, caused by His immediate presence or power. However, nowhere is it ever suggested that any of these physical reactions or manifestations constitutes evidence that a person has received the baptism in the Holy Spirit.

In the cases of the Old Testament prophets, we know that none of these received the baptism in the Holy Spirit because this experience was never granted to anyone before the day of Pentecost. In the cases of John and Paul in the New Testament, it is equally clear that their strong physical reactions to the presence of the Lord were not evidence of their receiving the baptism in the Spirit.

At the time when John received his vision on Patmos, he had already been baptised in the Spirit for more than fifty years. On the other hand, Saul's physical reactions on the Damascus road happened before he was filled with the Holy Spirit. He received this infilling as a separate, subsequent experience three days later when Ananias laid hands on him in Damascus.

No matter from what angle we approach this subject, we are always brought to the same conclusion: There is one, and only one, physical manifestation which constitutes evidence that a person has received the

Holy Spirit. That manifestation is speaking with other tongues, as the Spirit gives utterance.

Three Scriptural Principles

In closing this study, let us consider briefly three different, but basic, principles of Scripture, all of which confirm that speaking with other tongues is the appropriate evidence that a person has received the Holy Spirit.

First, Jesus says:

> For out of the abundance of the heart the mouth speaks (Matt. 12:34).

In other words, the heart of man, when it is filled to overflowing, overflows in speech through the mouth. This applies to the baptism in the Holy Spirit. When a person's heart has been filled to overflowing with the Holy Spirit, the overflow of the heart then takes place in speech through the mouth. Because the infilling is supernatural, the overflow is supernatural also. The person speaks a language which he has never learned and does not understand, using this to glorify God.

Second, Paul exhorts us as Christians:

> Present yourselves to God as being alive from the dead, and your members as instruments of righteousness to God (Rom. 6:13).

God's requirements go beyond the mere surrender of ourselves – that is, our wills – to Him. He demands that we actually present to Him our physical members, that He may control them according to His own will as instruments of righteousness.

However, there is one member of the body which none of us can control.

> But no man can tame [or control] the tongue. It is an unruly evil, full of deadly poison (James 3:8).

As the final evidence or seal that the presenting of our physical members to God has been made complete, the Spirit takes control of the very member which none of us can control – that is, the tongue – and then uses it in a supernatural way for God's glory.

The third principle of Scripture that establishes the relationship between tongues and the baptism in the Spirit is derived from the very nature of the Holy Spirit Himself.

In various passages Jesus emphasises that the Spirit is a real Person – just as real as God the Father and God the Son.

> However, when He, the Spirit of truth, has come, He will guide you into all truth; for He will not speak on His own authority, but whatever He hears He will speak (John 16:13).

Here Jesus emphasises the personality of the Holy Spirit in two ways: 1) by using the pronoun "He" rather than "it," 2) by attributing to the Holy Spirit the ability to speak. Reflection will show that the ability to communicate with words is one of the decisive, distinguishing features of personality. To anything capable of communicating with words for itself we naturally attribute the concept of a person; but if anything lacks this ability, we would not consider it a mature person. The fact that the Holy Spirit speaks directly for Himself is one of the great marks of His true personality.

Side by side with this we may set the words of Paul.

> Or do you not know that your body is the temple of the Holy Spirit who is in you? (1 Cor. 6:19).

Here Paul teaches that the physical body of the redeemed believer is the appointed temple in which the Holy Spirit desires to dwell. Appropriately, therefore, the evidence that the Holy Spirit as a Person has taken up His dwelling in this physical temple is that He speaks from within the temple, using the tongue and the lips of the believer to make this speech audible.

So it was also in the tabernacle of Moses. When Moses went into the tabernacle to commune with God:

> He heard the voice of One speaking to him from above the mercy seat (Num. 7:89).

Because Moses heard this voice – the mark of personality – he knew that the Person of the Lord was present in the tabernacle. In like manner today, when we hear the voice of the Holy Spirit speaking audibly from within the temple of a believer's body, we know by this evidence of personality that the Holy Spirit Himself – the third Person of the

Godhead – has taken up residence within the believer.

We find, then, that speaking with other tongues as the evidence of the baptism in the Holy Spirit accords with three great principles of Scripture.

1. The heart of the believer, supernaturally filled with the Holy Spirit, overflows supernaturally in speech through his mouth.
2. The evidence that the believer has yielded his physical members to God is that God's Spirit controls that member – the tongue – which the believer cannot control for himself.
3. By speaking from within the temple of the believer's body, the Holy Spirit demonstrates that He now dwells there as a Person.

25
THE PROMISE OF THE SPIRIT

In the preceding four chapters we have carefully analysed the teaching of the New Testament concerning the baptism in the Holy Spirit. Our analysis has included the following topics: the nature of the experience; the outward evidence by which it is attested; how it differs from the gift of "kinds of tongues"; the place of emotional and physical reactions.

This leads to a practical question: What conditions must be met before a person can be baptised in the Holy Spirit? There are two possible ways to approach this question. The first is from the viewpoint of God, the giver of the gift; the second is from the viewpoint of man, the receiver. In this chapter we shall approach the question from the first viewpoint – that of God Himself. In the next chapter we shall approach it from the human viewpoint.

The question which now confronts us is awesome in its implications. On what basis can a holy and omnipotent God offer to members of a fallen, sin-cursed race the gift of His own Spirit to indwell their physical bodies? What provision could God make to bridge the measureless gulf separating man from Himself?

The answer is supplied by a plan of redemption which was conceived in the Godhead before time began. Central to the outworking of this whole plan was the sacrificial death of Christ on the cross, which was followed first by His victorious resurrection and then by His triumphant ascension. Ten days later He poured out the Holy Spirit on His waiting disciples. Viewed in this light, the cross is the gate that opened the way to Pentecost.

A Personal, Permanent Indwelling

The direct connection between the ascension of Jesus and the outpouring of the Holy Spirit at Pentecost is unfolded in John 7:37-39.

> On the last day, that great day of the feast, Jesus stood and cried out, saying, "If anyone thirsts, let him come to Me and drink. He who believes in Me, as the Scripture has said, out of his heart will flow rivers of living water." But this He spoke concerning the Spirit, whom those believing in Him would receive; for the Holy Spirit was not yet given, because Jesus was not yet glorified.

The first two verses in this passage contain the promise of Jesus Himself, that every thirsty soul who comes to Him in faith will be filled and become a channel for rivers of living water. The last verse of the passage is an explanation of the two previous verses, added by the writer of the Gospel.

In this explanation the writer points out two things: 1) the promise of the rivers of living water refers to the gift of the Holy Spirit, 2) this gift could not be given while Jesus was still on earth in bodily form. It could only be made available to believers after Jesus had been received up to heaven again and entered into His glory at the Father's right hand.

What precisely is meant by saying that the Holy Spirit could not be given at that time? Obviously this does not mean that the Holy Spirit could not in any way be present, or move and work in the earth, until after the ascension of Christ into heaven. On the contrary, as early as the second verse of the Bible we already read of the Holy Spirit at work in the world.

> And the Spirit of God was hovering over the face of the waters (Gen. 1:2).

From this time onward, throughout the whole of the Old Testament and on into the days of Christ's earthly ministry, we read continually of the Holy Spirit moving and working in the world at large and more particularly among God's believing people. What, then, was the difference between the way in which the Holy Spirit worked up to the time of Christ's ascension and the gift of the Holy Spirit, which was reserved for Christian believers after Christ's ascension and was first received by the disciples in Jerusalem on the day of Pentecost?

Three descriptive words sum up the distinctive features of this gift of the Holy Spirit and distinguish it from all previous operations of the Holy Spirit in the world. These three words are personal, indwelling and permanent. Let us briefly consider, in turn, the significance of each of these three features.

First, the gift of the Holy Spirit is personal.

In His farewell discourse to His disciples, Jesus indicated that there was to be an exchange of divine Persons.

> Nevertheless I tell you the truth. It is to your advantage that I go away: for if I do not go away, the Helper will not come to you; but if I depart, I will send Him to you (John 16:7).

In effect, Jesus was saying: "In personal presence I am about to leave you and return to heaven. In My place, however, I will send you another Person – the Holy Spirit. This will be to your advantage."

The promise of the coming of the Holy Spirit as a Person was fulfilled at Pentecost. Since then, the Holy Spirit seeks to come to each believer individually, as a Person. We can no longer speak merely of an influence or an operation or a manifestation or of some impersonal power. The Holy Spirit is just as much a Person as God the Father or God the Son; and it is in this individual and personal way that He now seeks, in this dispensation, to come to the believer.

In the experience of salvation, or the new birth, the sinner receives Christ, the Son of God, the second Person of the Godhead. In the baptism in the Holy Spirit, the believer receives the third Person of the Godhead, the Holy Spirit. In each experience alike there is a real and direct transaction with a Person.

Second, the Holy Spirit in this dispensation comes to indwell the believer.

In the Old Testament the moving of the Holy Spirit among God's people is described by phrases such as these: "the Spirit of God came upon them"; "the Spirit of God moved them"; "the Spirit of God spoke through them." All these phrases indicate that some part of the believer's being or personality came under the Holy Spirit's control. But nowhere do we read in the Old Testament that the Holy Spirit ever came to take up His dwelling within the temple of a believer's physical body, thus taking control of his whole personality from within.

Third, the indwelling of the Christian by the Holy Spirit is permanent.

Under the old covenant, believers experienced the visitation of the Holy Spirit in many different ways and at many different times. But in all these cases the Holy Spirit was always a visitor, never a permanent resident. However, Jesus promised His disciples that when the Holy Spirit came to them, He would abide with them forever.

> And I will pray the Father, and He will give you another Helper [the Holy Spirit], that He may abide with you forever (John 14:16).

Thus we may characterise the gift of the Holy Spirit, as promised in the New Testament, by these three distinctive features: It is personal. It is an indwelling. It is permanent. Or, in one short phrase, it is a personal, permanent indwelling.

These distinctive features of the gift provide two reasons why it could not be given so long as Christ remained in bodily presence on earth.

First, while Christ was present on earth, He was the personal, authoritative representative of the Godhead. There was no need, and no place, for the Holy Spirit also to be personally present on earth at the same time. But after Christ's ascension into heaven, the way was then open for the Holy Spirit, in His turn, to come to earth as a Person. It is now He, the Holy Spirit, who in this present dispensation is the personal representative of the Godhead here on earth.

Second, the gift of the Holy Spirit could not be given until after Christ's ascension because the claim of every believer to receive it is in no way based upon his own merits, but simply and solely upon the merits of Christ's sacrificial death and resurrection. No one could receive the gift, therefore, until Christ's atoning work was complete.

The Father's Promise

Paul links the promise of the Spirit directly to Christ's atonement.

> Christ has redeemed us from the curse of the law, having become a curse for us (for it is written, "Cursed is everyone who hangs on a tree"), that the blessing of Abraham might

come upon the Gentiles in Christ Jesus, that we might receive
the promise of the Spirit through faith (Gal. 3:13-14).

Paul here establishes two facts of great importance concerning the gift
of the Holy Spirit to the Christian believer.

First of all, it is only through the redemptive work of Christ upon the
cross that the believer may now receive the promise of the Spirit. In fact,
this was one main purpose for which Christ suffered on the cross. He
died and shed His blood that He might purchase thereby a twofold legal
right: His own right to bestow, and the believer's right to receive, this
precious gift of the Holy Spirit.

Thus, the receiving of the gift does not depend in any way upon the
believer's own merits, but solely upon the all-sufficiency of Christ's
atonement. It is through faith, not by works.

Second, we notice that Paul uses the phrase "the promise of the
Spirit," for he says, "that we might receive the promise of the Spirit
through faith." This agrees with Jesus' final charge to His disciples just
before His ascension into heaven.

Behold, I send the Promise of My Father upon you; but tarry
in the city of Jerusalem until you are endued with power from
on high (Luke 24:49).

Jesus is here speaking to His disciples of the baptism in the Holy
Spirit which they were to receive in Jerusalem on the day of Pentecost.
He uses two phrases to describe this experience. He calls it an
enduement "with power from on high" and also "the Promise of My
Father."

This second phrase, "the Promise of My Father," gives us a wonderful
insight into the mind and purpose of God the Father concerning the gift
of the Holy Spirit. Someone has conservatively estimated that the Bible
contains seven thousand distinct promises given by God to His believing
people. But among all these seven thousand promises, Jesus singles out
one from all the rest as being in a unique sense the Father's special
promise for each of His believing children. What is this unique and
special promise? It is what Paul calls the "promise of the Spirit."

At Pentecost – on the very day the promise was fulfilled – Peter used
a similar form of speech.

Repent, and let every one of you be baptised in the name of
Jesus Christ for the remission of sins; and you shall receive

the gift of the Holy Spirit. For the promise is to you and to your children, and to all who are afar off, as many as the Lord our God will call (Acts 2:38-39).

Peter here joins together the words *gift* and *promise*. To what special, promised gift does he refer? To the same as that spoken of by Jesus and by Paul – the promise of the Spirit. This is indeed the promise of the Father which He had planned and prepared through many long ages, that He might bestow it upon His believing children through Jesus Christ in this present dispensation.

Paul also calls this promise "the blessing of Abraham" (Gal. 3:14). Thus he links it with the supreme purpose of God in choosing Abraham for Himself. When God first called Abraham out of Ur, He said:

I will bless you . . .
And you shall be a blessing . . .
And in you all the families of the earth shall be blessed
(Gen. 12:2-3).

In His subsequent dealings with Abraham, God reaffirmed His purpose of blessing many times.

In blessing I will bless you . . . In your seed all the nations of the earth shall be blessed (Gen. 22:17-18).

To what specific blessing did all these promises of God look forward? The words of Paul supply the answer: "the promise of the Spirit" (Gal. 3:14). It was to purchase this blessing, promised to the seed of Abraham, that Jesus shed His blood on the cross.

Heaven's Seal on Christ's Atonement

However, the final consummation of Christ's atoning work did not come on earth, but in heaven.

But Christ came as High Priest of the good things to come, with the greater and more perfect tabernacle not made with hands, that is, not of this creation. Not with the blood of goats and calves, but with His own blood He entered the Most Holy Place once for all, having obtained eternal redemption (Heb. 9:11-12).

As believers in the new covenant, we have come to:

> Jesus the Mediator of the new covenant, and to the blood of
> sprinkling that speaks better things than that of Abel (Heb.
> 12:24).

These passages in Hebrews reveal that the atoning work of Christ was
not finally consummated by the shedding of His blood upon the cross on
earth, but by His later entering with His blood into the presence of the
Father. There He presented that blood as the one final and sufficient
satisfaction and expiation for all sin. It is this blood of Christ, now
sprinkled in heaven, that speaks better things than that of Abel.

The blood of Christ is contrasted with that of Abel in two main
respects. First, Abel's blood was left sprinkled upon earth, while Christ's
blood was presented and sprinkled in heaven. Second, Abel's blood
called out to God for vengeance upon his murderer, while Christ's blood
speaks to God in heaven for mercy and pardon.

This revelation, given in Hebrews, of Christ completing the
atonement by presenting His own blood before the Father in heaven
enables us to understand why the gift of the Holy Spirit could not be
given until Christ had been glorified. The Holy Spirit is given not upon
the basis of the believer's own merits but upon the basis of Christ's
atonement.

This atonement was not consummated until the blood of Christ had
been presented in heaven and God the Father had declared His absolute
satisfaction with this atoning sacrifice. Thereafter the giving of the Holy
Spirit to those who believed in Christ was the public testimony of the
supreme court of heaven that the blood of Christ was forever accepted as
an all-sufficient propitiation for all sin.

> This is He who came by water and blood – Jesus Christ; not
> only by water, but by water and blood. And it is the Spirit
> who bears witness, because the Spirit is truth (1 John 5:6).

We see that the Holy Spirit bears witness to the blood of Jesus. In
other words, the giving of the Holy Spirit to those who believe in Jesus
constitutes the united testimony of the Father and the Spirit together to
the all-sufficiency of the blood of Jesus to cleanse the believer from all
sin.

This harmonises with Peter's teaching on the day of Pentecost
concerning the outpouring of the Holy Spirit. Having first spoken of

Christ's death and resurrection, Peter continues:

> Therefore being exalted to the right hand of God, and having
> received from the Father the promise of the Holy Spirit, He
> poured out this which you now see and hear (Acts 2:33).

Christ first purchased man's redemption by His atoning death and
resurrection. Then He ascended to His Father in heaven and there
presented the blood which was the evidence and seal of redemption.
Upon the Father's acceptance of the blood, Christ received from the
Father the gift of the Holy Spirit to pour out upon those who believed in
Him.

We may now sum up the revelation of Scripture concerning the plan
of God to bestow upon all believers the gift of the Holy Spirit.

Implicit in God's choice of Abraham was the promise of the blessing
of the Holy Spirit to all nations through Christ. By His blood shed upon
the cross, Christ purchased for all believers the legal right to this
blessing. After presenting His blood in heaven, Christ received from the
Father the gift of the Holy Spirit. On the day of Pentecost, the Spirit
Himself, who is the gift, was poured out from heaven upon the waiting
believers on earth.

Thus, Father, Son and Holy Spirit were all three concerned in
planning, purchasing and providing this, the supreme promise and the
greatest of all gifts, for all God's believing people.

In the next chapter we will view this same gift of the Holy Spirit from
the human standpoint and consider the conditions which must be met in
the life of each believer who desires to receive the gift.

26
HOW TO RECEIVE THE HOLY SPIRIT

W hat are the conditions which must be fulfilled in the life of a person who desires to receive the gift of the Holy Spirit?

By Grace Through Faith

As we consider the teaching of Scripture on this subject, we shall find that there is one basic principle which applies to every provision made for man by the grace of God.

> And if by grace, then it is no longer of works; otherwise grace is no longer grace (Rom. 11:6).

In this passage, as elsewhere in his epistles, Paul contrasts the expressions "grace" and "works." By grace Paul means the free, unmerited favour and blessing of God bestowed upon the undeserving, and even upon the ill-deserving. By works Paul means anything that a man may do of his own ability to earn for himself the blessing and favour of God.

Paul states that these two ways of receiving from God are mutually exclusive; they can never be combined. Whatever a man receives from God by grace is not of works; whatever a man receives from God by works is not of grace. Wherever grace operates, works are of no avail; wherever works operate, grace is of no avail.

This leads to the further contrast between grace and law: "For the law was given through Moses, but grace and truth came through Jesus Christ" (John 1:17).

Under the law of Moses men sought to earn the blessing of God by what they did for themselves. Through Jesus Christ the free, unmerited blessing and favour of God are now offered to all men on the basis of what Christ has done on man's behalf. This is grace.

All we receive in this way from God through Jesus Christ is by grace; the means by which we receive this grace is not by works but by faith.

> For by grace you have been saved through faith, and that not
> of yourselves: it is the gift of God, not of works, lest anyone
> should boast (Eph. 2:8-9).

The basic principle laid down by Paul in this passage can be summed up in three successive phrases: by *grace – through faith – not of works.* It applies in the receiving of every provision made for man by the grace of God. Specifically, Paul applies the principle to the receiving of the gift of the Holy Spirit.

> Christ has redeemed us from the curse of the law . . . that we
> might receive the promise of the Spirit through faith (Gal.
> 3:13-14).

Paul brings out two important and interrelated facts: 1) The gift of the Holy Spirit is made available to man through the redemptive work of Christ upon the cross; it is part of the total provision made for man by the grace of God through Jesus Christ. 2) This gift, like every other provision of God's grace, is received through faith, not by works.

This question of how the gift of the Holy Spirit is received had apparently been raised among the Christian churches in Galatia, and Paul makes several references to it.

> This only I want to learn from you: Did you receive the Spirit
> by the works of the law, or by the hearing of faith? (Gal. 3:2).

> Therefore He who supplies the Spirit to you . . . does He do

it by the works of the law, or by the hearing of faith? (Gal. 3:5).

. . . that we might receive the promise of the Spirit through faith (Gal. 3:14).

Three times, therefore, in these few verses Paul emphasises that the receiving of the Spirit is by faith.

In other words, the essential preparation for believers to receive the Holy Spirit is that they be instructed out of the Scriptures on the nature of God's provision for them and how they may claim this provision through faith in the redemptive work of Christ on the cross. If this kind of scriptural instruction is first given and received with faith by those seeking the Holy Spirit, there should be no need for great effort or delay in their receiving the gift.

Paul's epistle to the Galatians implies that the Christians there had originally received from him with faith the message of the gospel and the gift of the Holy Spirit, and had thus entered into the fullness of God's provision for them. Later, however, through other teachers, they had become involved in a legalistic system superimposed upon this gospel foundation and had begun to lose their first vision of the receiving of God's gift by grace through faith.

One main purpose of Paul's epistle is to warn them of the dangers of this and to call them back to the original simplicity of their faith.

Groups of Christians in various places today are being threatened by the same kind of error against which Paul warned the Galatians. There is in many places today a tendency to impose some kind of system or technique upon those seeking the gift of the Holy Spirit.

The precise form of technique varies from group to group. In some places the emphasis is upon some particular posture or attitude. In other places the emphasis is rather upon some special form of words or the repetition of certain phrases.

Instruction along these lines to those seeking the Holy Spirit is not necessarily unscriptural, but the great danger is that the particular posture or form of words, instead of being merely a help to faith, may become a substitute for it. In this case the technique defeats its own ends. Instead of helping seekers to receive the Holy Spirit, it actually prevents them from doing so.

As a result of this kind of technique we often meet the chronic seekers who say, "I've tried everything! I've tried praise . . . I've said, 'Hallelujah' . . . I've lifted my hands in the air . . . I've shouted . . . I've done everything, but it just doesn't work." Without realising it, they are making the same error that the Galatians were slipping into: They are substituting works for faith, a technique for the simple hearing of God's Word.

What is the remedy? Just what Paul proposes to the Galatians: to return to the hearing of faith. Chronic seekers like these do not need more praise, more shouting or more lifting up of their hands. They need fresh instruction from God's Word on the free provisions of God's grace.

As a general principle, wherever people are seeking the gift of the Holy Spirit, a period of instruction from God's Word should always precede any period of prayer. For my own part, if I were allotted thirty minutes to help believers seeking the gift of the Holy Spirit, I would spend at least half that time – the first fifteen minutes – giving scriptural instruction. The next fifteen minutes, devoted to prayer, would produce far more positive results than a full thirty minutes given to prayer without any instruction beforehand.

We see, then, that the basic requirement for receiving the gift of the Holy Spirit is defined by Paul as the *hearing of faith.*

We must be careful, however, to guard against a false interpretation of what is meant by faith. Faith is not a substitute for obedience. On the contrary, true faith is always manifested in obedience. Thus obedience becomes both the test and the evidence of faith. This applies as much to the receiving of the Holy Spirit as in any other area of God's grace.

In his defence to the Jewish council, Peter focuses upon obedience as the proper expression of faith.

> And we are His witnesses to these things, and so also is the Holy Spirit whom God has given to those who obey Him (Acts 5:32).

In speaking of the gift of the Holy Spirit, Paul stresses faith, while Peter stresses obedience. There is, however, no conflict between the two. True faith is always linked with obedience. Complete faith results in complete obedience. Peter says here that when our obedience is complete, the gift of the Holy Spirit is ours.

Six Steps of Faith

In seeking the gift of the Holy Spirit, how should complete obedience be expressed? We find six steps set forth in Scripture which mark the pathway of obedience leading to the gift of the Holy Spirit.

Repentance and Baptism

The first two steps are stated by Peter.

> Repent, and let every one of you be baptised in the name of
> Jesus Christ for the remission of sins; and you shall receive
> the gift of the Holy Spirit (Acts 2:38).

The two steps here stated by Peter are repent and be baptised.

Repentance is an inward change of heart and attitude toward God that opens the way for the sinner to be reconciled with God. Thereafter, baptism is an outward act by which the believer testifies to the inward change wrought by God's grace in his heart.

Thirsting

The third step to the fullness of the Holy Spirit is stated by Jesus.

> If anyone thirsts, let him come to Me and drink. He who
> believes in Me, as the Scripture has said, out of his heart will
> flow rivers of living water (John 7:37-38).

In the next verse John explains that this promise of Jesus refers to the gift of the Holy Spirit. This agrees with what Jesus says also:

> Blessed are those who hunger and thirst for righteousness, for
> they shall be filled (Matt. 5:6).

One essential condition for receiving the fullness of the Holy Spirit is to be hungry and thirsty. God does not squander His blessings on those who feel no need for them. Many professing Christians who lead good, respectable lives never receive the fullness of the Holy Spirit simply because they feel no need for it. They are satisfied without this blessing, and God leaves them that way.

From the human point of view, it sometimes happens that those who seem least deserving receive the gift of the Holy Spirit, and those who seem most deserving do not. This is explained by the Scripture.

> He [God] has filled the hungry with good things,
> And the rich He has sent away empty (Luke 1:53).

God responds to our sincere inner longings, but He is not impressed by our religious profession.

Asking

Jesus also presents the fourth step to receiving the Holy Spirit.

> If you then, being evil, know how to give good gifts to your
> children, how much more will your heavenly Father give the
> Holy Spirit to those who ask Him! (Luke 11:13).

Here Jesus places upon God's children an obligation to ask their heavenly Father for the gift of the Holy Spirit. We sometimes hear Christians make some such remark as this: "If God wants me to have the Holy Spirit, He will give it to me. I don't need to ask Him for it." This attitude is not scriptural. Jesus plainly teaches that God's children should ask their heavenly Father for this special gift of the Holy Spirit.

Drinking

After asking, the next step is receiving. Jesus calls this drinking, for He says, "If anyone thirsts, let him come to Me and drink" (John 7:37).

"Drinking" represents an active process of receiving. The infilling of the Holy Spirit cannot be received by a negative or passive attitude. No one can drink except of his own active volition, and no one can drink with a closed mouth. As it is in the natural, so it is in the spiritual. The Lord says, "Open your mouth wide, and I will fill it" (Ps. 81:10).

God cannot fill a closed mouth. Simple though it may seem, there are those who fail to receive the fullness of the Spirit simply because they fail to open their mouths.

Yielding

After drinking, the sixth and last step to receiving the Holy Spirit is yielding. Paul speaks to Christians of a twofold surrender to God.

> But present yourselves to God as being alive from the dead,
> and your members as instruments of righteousness to God
> (Rom. 6:13).

Two successive stages are here set before us as Christians. The first surrender is of *yourselves* – the surrender of the will and the personality. However, this is not all. There is a further degree of surrender of our physical *members*.

To surrender our physical members requires a much greater measure of confidence in God. In yielding ourselves – our wills – we yield obedience to the revealed will of God, but we still retain the exercise of our own understanding. We are willing to do what God asks of us, provided that we first understand what is asked.

However, in yielding our physical members we go beyond this. We no longer seek even to understand intellectually what God asks of us. We merely hand over unreserved control of our physical members and allow God to use them according to His own will and purpose without demanding to understand what God is doing or why He is doing it.

It is only as we make this second surrender that we come to the place of total, unconditional yieldedness. And it is just at this very point that the Holy Spirit comes in His fullness and takes control of our members.

The particular member He takes full control of is that unruly member which no man can tame – the tongue. Thus the yielding of our tongue to the Spirit marks the climax of yieldedness, of surrender, of complete obedience. It is by this that we receive the gift of the Holy Spirit.

We have outlined the six successive steps to receiving the fullness of the Holy Spirit: 1) repentance; 2) being baptised; 3) being thirsty; 4) asking; 5) drinking – that is, actively receiving; 6) yielding – that is, surrendering control of our physical members apart from the exercise of our intellectual understanding.

The question will naturally arise: Is it necessarily true that every person who receives the gift of the Holy Spirit has completely followed through all six steps?

The answer to this question is *no*. God's grace is sovereign. Wherever God sees fit, He is free to reach out in grace to needy souls beyond the conditions set forth in His Word. God's grace is not limited by the conditions He imposes. But, on the other hand, wherever those conditions are fully met, God's faithfulness will never withhold the blessing He has promised.

Of the steps just outlined, some are omitted by people who nevertheless do receive the gift of the Holy Spirit. In particular, the gift of the Holy Spirit is at times granted to people who have not been baptised and who have never specifically asked God for this gift.

This happened in my own experience. I received the gift of the Holy Spirit before I was baptised and without ever specifically asking for it. In these two points, God reached out to me in His free and sovereign grace beyond the conditions actually imposed in His Word. I realise, however, that this now makes me just so much the more a debtor to God's grace. It certainly opens no door to me for pride, carelessness or disobedience.

It would seem, however, that God never bestows the gift of the Holy Spirit where the other four conditions are not fulfilled. That is, God never bestows the Holy Spirit where there is not first of all repentance and then a spiritual thirst and willingness both to receive and to yield.

In concluding these studies on the baptism in the Holy Spirit, it is appropriate to emphasise once again the close connection between the fullness of the Holy Spirit and obedience. As Peter says, the gift of the Holy Spirit is for those who obey God. Even where God in His grace bestows this gift upon those who have not yet fully met the conditions of His Word, this still leaves no room for carelessness or disobedience.

As Peter preached in the house of Cornelius, the Holy Spirit fell upon all those who heard his word (see Acts 10). However, it is clear that this demonstration of God's grace was in no sense to be interpreted as a substitute for obedience to God's Word, for we read:

> He [Peter] commanded them to be baptised (Acts 10:48).

Even for those who have received the gift of the Holy Spirit, the ordinance of baptism in water still remains a commandment of God's Word that may not be set aside.

Above all, in this realm of spiritual gifts we need to be continually on our guard against spiritual pride. The more richly we receive of the gifts of God's grace, the greater is our obligation to be obedient and faithful in the exercise and stewardship of those gifts.

This principle of responsibility for grace received is summed up by Jesus' teaching on stewardship.

> For everyone to whom much is given, from him much will be required; and to whom much has been committed, of him they will ask the more (Luke 12:48).

The more abundantly we receive of God's gifts and graces through Jesus Christ, the greater becomes our obligation to humility, to consecration and to unfailing obedience.

27
OLD TESTAMENT PATTERNS FOR NEW TESTAMENT SALVATION

Throughout this section we have been considering that part of Christian doctrine which is called "the doctrine of baptisms" (Heb. 6:2).

The New Testament actually refers to four distinct types of baptism: 1) the baptism of John the Baptist, 2) Christian baptism in water, 3) the baptism of suffering and 4) the baptism in the Holy Spirit.

Of these four types of baptism, the two which are most directly related to the experience of all Christian believers in this dispensation are the second and the fourth – that is, Christian baptism in water and the baptism in the Holy Spirit. For this reason we have concentrated our attention mainly on these two forms of baptism.

The time has now come to see how they are related to each other and to the other parts of God's plan and provision for Christians. We may put the question in this form: What part do baptism in water and baptism in the Holy Spirit play in the total plan of God for all New Testament believers?

We shall follow an approach to this question frequently employed by the writers of the New Testament. We shall view God's deliverance of

Israel out of Egypt as a type or pattern of the greater deliverance from the slavery of sin and Satan offered to the whole human race through Jesus Christ. We will focus on three specific features of Israel's deliverance out of Egypt and use these to illustrate three main elements in the salvation provided for all men through Christ.

Salvation Through Blood

First of all, God sent His appointed deliverer, Moses, to Israel right where they were, in the midst of Egypt in their misery and slavery. There He saved them from wrath and from judgement through their faith in the blood of the sacrifice which He had appointed – the Passover lamb.

In the New Testament John the Baptist – the forerunner sent to prepare the way before Christ – introduced Him with the words: "Behold! The Lamb of God who takes away the sin of the world!" (John 1:29). Thus he proclaimed Jesus as the appointed Saviour whose sacrificial death and shed blood would accomplish all that had been foreshadowed by the Passover lamb.

Looking back on Christ's death and resurrection, Paul says: "Christ, our Passover, was sacrificed for us" (1 Cor. 5:7).

The Passover lamb provided temporary deliverance for Israel from physical slavery. The sacrifice of Jesus Christ provided eternal salvation for all who put their faith in His shed blood as the propitiation for their sins.

It was not God's purpose, however, for Israel to remain any longer in Egypt. The very same night that the Passover was sacrificed, Israel began their exodus, no longer a rabble of slaves but now an army in ordered ranks. There was urgency in all that they did. They took their bread before it was leavened. They marched in haste, with their loins girded and their staves in their hands.

In like manner, God meets the sinner right where he is in the world and saves him in the depths of his need and bondage. But God does not leave the sinner there. Immediately He calls him out into a totally new way of life – a life of separation and sanctification.

A Double Baptism

Paul describes the next two stages in Israel's deliverance out of Egypt.

Moreover, brethren, I do not want you to be unaware that all our fathers were under the cloud, all passed through the sea,

all were baptised into Moses in the cloud and in the sea, all
ate the same spiritual food, and all drank the same spiritual
drink. For they drank of that spiritual Rock that followed
them, and that Rock was Christ (1 Cor. 10:1-4).

Just a little further on in the same chapter Paul relates these experiences of Israel in the Old Testament to corresponding experiences of
Christians in the New Testament.

Now these things became our examples (1 Cor. 10:6).

Now all these things happened to them as examples [as types
or patterns of behaviour], and they were written for our
admonition [that is, to instruct and warn us], on whom the
ends of the ages have come [that is, for us who now live in the
closing dispensation of the present age] (1 Cor. 10:11).

In other words, Paul says these experiences of Israel in the Old
Testament are not merely interesting historical events in the past, but
they also contain an urgent and important message for us as Christians
in this age. They are specially recorded, by divine direction, as patterns
of behaviour which God intends to be carefully followed by all Christian
believers in this dispensation.

With this in mind, let us consider carefully just what examples or
lessons Paul sets before us in the first four verses of the chapter.

First of all we notice the very short but important word *all* occurs no
less than five times. Paul says:

All our fathers were under the cloud, *all* passed through the
sea, *all* were baptised into Moses in the cloud and in the sea,
all ate the same spiritual food, and *all* drank the same
spiritual drink (1 Cor. 10:1-4, italics added).

Clearly, Paul is emphasising that all these examples or patterns are to
be followed by all God's believing people. God does not leave room for
any exceptions. These things are for all His people.

What are the particular patterns to which Paul refers? There are four
successive experiences: 1) all were under the cloud; 2) all passed
through the sea; 3) all ate the same spiritual food; 4) all drank the same
spiritual drink.

These four experiences are also to be followed by God's people today:

1) passing under the cloud; 2) passing through the sea; 3) eating the same spiritual food; 4) drinking the same spiritual drink.

Just how do these four patterns relate to the experience of believers in this dispensation? What is their lesson for us as Christians today?

We notice, first of all, that these four experiences naturally fall into two distinct pairs. The first two – passing under the cloud and through the sea – were single experiences that occurred only once. The second two – eating and drinking spiritual food and drink – were continuing experiences that were regularly repeated over a long period of time.

Let us begin with the first pair of experiences – those that took place only once: passing under the cloud and through the sea. The key to understanding these is provided by a distinctive phrase which Paul uses in connection with them. He says: "All were baptised into Moses in the cloud and in the sea" (v. 2). Plainly, therefore, these two experiences correspond to two forms of baptism, both of which God has ordained for all Christians in this dispensation.

What are the two forms of baptism represented by these two experiences? In the light of our previous studies, it is now easy for us to supply the answer. The baptism in the cloud for Israel corresponds to the baptism in the Holy Spirit for the Christian. The baptism in the sea for Israel corresponds to baptism in water for the Christian.

If we now examine the details of these two experiences of Israel, we shall see just how appropriate each of them is as a pattern of the corresponding experience for Christians today.

The historical account of Israel passing under the cloud and through the sea is described in Exodus. After the sacrifice of the Passover lamb in Egypt, the Israelites began their exodus from Egypt the same night. When they came to the Red Sea, they miraculously passed through it, as on dry land.

Baptism in the Cloud

The first mention of their passing under the cloud is found in Exodus 13:20-21.

> So they took their journey from Succoth and camped in Etham at the edge of the wilderness. And the Lord went before them by day in a pillar of cloud to lead the way, and by night in a pillar of fire to give them light, so as to go by day and night.

Paul says, "All our fathers were under the cloud" (1 Cor. 10). This leads us to understand that at a certain point on Israel's journey out of Egypt, this unique, supernatural cloud came down over them from above and continued to rest over them.

Clearly this cloud was sensibly perceptible to Israel, and it took two different forms. By day it was a cloud, giving shadow from the heat of the sun. By night it was a pillar of fire, giving both light and warmth in the darkness and coldness of the night. By day and by night, it provided Israel with divine direction and guidance.

There are two further facts revealed about this wonderful cloud. First, God Himself – Jehovah – was personally present within the cloud. Second, this cloud served both to separate and to protect Israel from the Egyptians.

> And the Angel of God, who went before the camp of Israel, moved and went behind them; and the pillar of cloud went from before them and stood behind them. So it came between the camp of the Egyptians and the camp of Israel. Thus it was a cloud and darkness to the one [that is, to the Egyptians], and it gave light by night to the other [that is, to Israel], so that the one did not come near the other all that night (Ex. 14:19-20).

> Now it came to pass, in the morning watch, that the Lord looked down upon the army of the Egyptians through the pillar of fire and cloud, and He troubled the army of the Egyptians (Ex. 14:24).

From this account we see that the Lord Himself – Jehovah – the great Angel of God – was in the cloud and moved in the cloud. It was in the cloud that He moved over Israel from their front to their rear and in the cloud that He interposed His own presence between Israel and the Egyptians, to separate and protect His own people from their enemies.

The cloud had a very different meaning and effect for the Egyptians. For the Egyptians, "it was a cloud and darkness," but to Israel it "gave light at night" (Ex. 19:20). This cloud was darkness to Egypt, the people of this world; but it was light to Israel, the people of God.

Furthermore, when daylight came, the cloud was even more fearful for the Egyptians. As we read earlier:

> The Lord looked down upon the army of the Egyptians through the pillar of fire and cloud, and He troubled the army

of the Egyptians (v. 24).

We have said that this cloud is a type or picture of the baptism in the Holy Spirit. Let us now set out briefly, in order, the facts which we know about this cloud and see how perfectly each one of them applies to the baptism in the Holy Spirit.

1. This cloud came down over God's people from above, out of heaven.
2. It was not merely an invisible influence, but it was sensibly perceptible.
3. It provided shadow from the heat by day and light and warmth by night.
4. It gave God's people divine direction and guidance throughout their journeyings.
5. Within the cloud was the presence of the Lord Jehovah Himself, and it was in the cloud that the Lord came personally to the rescue of His people from their enemies.
6. The cloud gave light to the people of God, but to their enemies the same cloud was something dark and fearful.
7. The cloud came between God's people and their enemies, thus separating and protecting them.

Let us now see how perfectly each of these facts relates to the baptism in the Holy Spirit and what this experience means for God's people in this dispensation.

1. The baptism in the Holy Spirit is the presence of God Himself coming down over His people from heaven, enveloping and immersing them.
2. The baptism in the Holy Spirit is sensibly perceptible, and the effects it produces can be both seen and heard.
3. The Holy Spirit, coming in this way, is the appointed Comforter of God's people: He provides shade from heat, light and warmth in the midst of darkness and cold.
4. The Holy Spirit provides God's people with divine direction and guidance throughout their earthly pilgrimage.
5. Within this experience is contained the actual presence of the Lord Himself, for Jesus says:

> I will not leave you orphans; I [Myself personally] will come to you (John 14:18).

6. The baptism in the Holy Spirit brings a heavenly light to the people of God, but to the people of this world this supernatural experience remains something dark, incomprehensible, even fearful. As Paul says:

> The natural man does not receive the things of the Spirit of God, for they are foolishness to him; nor can he know them, because they are spiritually discerned (1 Cor. 2:14).

7. The baptism in the Holy Spirit, as a spiritual experience, marks a decisive separation between the people of God and the people of this world. It both separates and protects God's people from the sinful, corrupting influences of this world.

Baptism in the Sea

Let us now turn to the baptism in the sea.

> Then Moses stretched out his hand over the sea; and the Lord caused the sea to go back by a strong east wind all that night, and made the sea into dry land, and the waters were divided. So the children of Israel went into the midst of the sea on the dry ground, and the waters were a wall to them on their right hand and on their left (Ex. 14:21-22).

After this we read how the Egyptians attempted to follow Israel through the Red Sea.

> And Moses stretched out his hand over the sea; and when the morning appeared, the sea returned to its full depth, while the Egyptians were fleeing into it. So the Lord overthrew the Egyptians in the midst of the sea (Ex. 14:27).

Side by side with this account in Exodus, we should also read a New Testament comment on the event.

By faith they [that is, Israel] passed through the Red Sea as by
dry land, whereas the Egyptians, attempting to do so, were
drowned (Heb. 11:29, italics added).

In the light of these passages we can now list the main facts revealed
about the passing of Israel through the Red Sea and see how perfectly
each of them applies to Christian baptism in water.

1. The passing of Israel through the Red Sea was made
    possible only through a supernatural provision of God's
    power.
2. The Israelites could avail themselves of this provision
    only by their faith. The waters were first opened and then
    closed by an act of faith on the part of Moses, and Israel
    as a whole was able to pass through only by faith.
3. The Egyptians, attempting to do the same thing, but
    without faith, were not saved but destroyed.
4. Israel went down into the waters, passed through the
    waters and came up again out of the waters.
5. By passing through the waters, Israel was finally
    separated from Egypt and from the last threat of Egypt's
    dominion over them.
6. Israel came up out of the waters to follow a new leader,
    to live by new laws and to march to a new destination.

Let us now see how perfectly each of these facts corresponds to
Christian baptism in water and what this experience means for God's
people in this dispensation.

1. Christian baptism in water has been made possible for the
    believer only through the death and supernatural resur-
    rection of Jesus Christ.
2. Christian baptism is effectual only through personal faith
    on the part of the believer: "*he who believes* and is
    baptised will be saved."
3. Those who observe this ordinance without personal faith
    are like the Egyptians entering the Red Sea: Their act
    does not save them; it destroys them.
4. In every case where baptism in water is described in the
    New Testament, the person being baptised went down
    into the water, passed through the water and came up out

of the water again.

5. Baptism in water is intended by God to separate the believer from the world and from the continuing dominion of the world over him.

6. After baptism, the believer is directed by God into a new kind of life with a new leader, new laws and a new destination.

> Therefore we were buried with Him through baptism into death, that just as Christ was raised from the dead by the glory of the Father, even so we also should walk in newness of life (Rom. 6:4).

The Pattern of Salvation

We have seen that in their deliverance from Egypt, God's people under the Old Testament shared in two experiences common to them all: They all passed under the cloud and through the sea, and they were all baptised in the cloud and in the sea. Let us now consider briefly the place that these two experiences occupied in God's total plan of salvation for His people.

God delivered His people where they were, in Egypt, through their faith in the blood of the Passover sacrifice. However, once God had saved His people in Egypt, He no longer allowed them to remain there. On the contrary, He called them to march out the very same night of their deliverance, in haste, with their loins girded, no longer a mere rabble of slaves but now an army of men prepared for war.

When the Egyptians marched after the Israelites, intent upon bringing them back into bondage again, God's next two stages of deliverance for His people consisted in making them pass under the cloud and through the sea. By these two experiences God achieved two main purposes for His people: 1) He completed their deliverance out of Egypt's bondage; 2) He made the necessary provision for the new life into which He was leading them.

All these things are patterns of God's plan of deliverance or salvation for His people in this present dispensation. Immediately after the initial experience of salvation, God still today calls the sinner out from his old life, his old habits and his old associations. This call to come out and be separate is just as clear as God's call to Israel to come out of Egypt, for Paul says to Christians:

Come out from among them
And be separate, says the Lord.
Do not touch what is unclean,
And I will receive you.
I will be a Father to you,
And you shall be My sons and daughters,
Says the Lord Almighty (2 Cor. 6:17-18).

Still today also, Satan, the god of this world, seeks to do as Pharaoh did – pursue God's people as they move out from his dominion and bring them back under his bondage.

Because of this God has made for His believing people today a double provision corresponding to the double baptism of Israel in the cloud and in the sea. God has ordained that, after salvation, all His believing people should be baptised both in water and in the Holy Spirit.

By this double baptism it is God's intention that His people should finally be delivered from the association and dominion of this world and that the way back into the old life should forever be closed behind them. At the same time, God also makes the provision necessary for the new life into which He intends to lead His people.

Spiritual Food and Drink

Let us now consider briefly the other two experiences which God ordained for all His people under the Old Testament – eating the same spiritual food and drinking the same spiritual drink. Unlike the double baptism, which was never repeated, the food and drink represented God's ongoing provision, of which His people had to partake regularly every day until they had completed their pilgrimage.

Manna

The spiritual food which God ordained for Israel was the manna which came down to them every morning. Israel lived on this supernatural food throughout the forty years of their pilgrimage through the wilderness.

Speaking of this in the New Testament, Paul describes it as spiritual food. In other words, Paul indicates that for us as Christians this manna corresponds not to the natural food with which we must feed our bodies, but to the spiritual, supernatural food with which we must feed our souls.

What, then, is this spiritual, supernatural food of the Christian? Christ gives us the answer: "It is written, 'Man shall not live by bread alone, but by every word that proceeds from the mouth of God' " (Matt. 4:4). The spiritual food appointed by God for all believers in this dispensation is God's Word.

As we feed by faith upon the written Word of God, we receive within ourselves the divine life of the personal Word, that is, Jesus Christ Himself. For Jesus said of Himself:

> I am the living bread which came down from heaven (John 6:51).

Thus, it is through the written Word that the personal Word, the living bread from heaven, comes down to nourish the soul of the believer.

The ordinances for the gathering of manna by Israel are stated in Exodus 16. There are three main points: 1) it was gathered regularly; 2) it was gathered individually; 3) it was gathered early in the day.

The same three principles apply to the believer in this dispensation. Each Christian needs to feed upon God's Word regularly, individually and early in the day.

River From the Rock

Finally, there is the appointed spiritual drink of God's people. For Israel in the Old Testament this drink was a river that flowed out of a rock, and Paul tells us "that Rock was Christ" (1 Cor. 10:4).

For the Christian, the divinely appointed drink is the river of the Holy Spirit, flowing forth from within his own inner being. For Christ says of the Holy Spirit:

> If anyone thirsts, let him come to Me and drink. He who believes in Me, as the Scripture has said, out of his heart will flow rivers of living water (John 7:37-38).

For Israel this river flowed out of a smitten rock; for the Christian today this river flows out of the smitten side of the Saviour, for it was His atoning death upon the cross that purchased for all believers the indwelling fullness of the Holy Spirit.

The initial baptism in the Holy Spirit is a once-for-all experience that never needs to be repeated. But drinking from the river of the Spirit that now flows from within is something that each believer needs to do just as regularly as Israel drank from the rock in the desert.

For this reason Paul uses a continuing tense when he says: "Be [continually] filled [and refilled] with the Spirit" (Eph. 5:18). Continual drinking of the Spirit leads to the outward expressions Paul describes in the next two verses.

> Speaking to one another in psalms and hymns and spiritual songs, singing and making melody in your heart to the Lord, giving thanks always for all things to God the Father in the name of our Lord Jesus Christ (Eph. 5:19-20).

Continual feeding on God's Word and drinking of God's Spirit are essential for a life of victory and fruitfulness. Israel would have perished in the wilderness without their daily portion of manna from heaven and living water from the rock. The believer today is no less dependent upon the daily manna of God's Word and the daily filling, and refilling, of God's Spirit.

Let us now apply the complete pattern to the experience of the Christian in this dispensation.

God has ordained for each believer today five experiences, each typified by an experience of Israel in the Old Testament: 1) salvation through faith in the blood of Jesus Christ; 2) baptism in the Holy Spirit; 3) baptism in water; 4) daily feeding upon God's Word; 5) daily drinking of God's Spirit from within.

Of these five experiences, the first three – salvation, baptism in water and baptism in the Spirit – occur only once and need not be repeated. The last two – feeding upon God's Word and drinking of God's Spirit – are experiences which the believer must continue to practice regularly each day throughout his earthly pilgrimage.

PART IV

PURPOSES OF PENTECOST

BUT THE MANIFESTATION
OF THE SPIRIT IS
GIVEN TO EACH ONE
FOR THE PROFIT OF ALL.

1 CORINTHIANS 12:7

28
INTRODUCTION AND WARNING

In chapter 26 we considered the practical steps of faith and obedience by which a person may receive the baptism in the Holy Spirit. Leading on from that is a further practical question: Why is the baptism in the Holy Spirit given? Or, to put it another way, what results does God desire to produce in the life of the believer through baptising him in the Holy Spirit?

Before giving a scriptural answer to this question, however, it is first necessary to clear up common misunderstandings which often trouble people who have newly received the baptism in the Spirit and which thus prevent them from receiving the full benefits and blessings God intended for them through this experience.

The Holy Spirit Is Not a Dictator

The first point which needs to be emphasised is that, in the life of the believer, the Holy Spirit never plays the role of a dictator.

When Jesus promised the gift of the Holy Spirit to His disciples, He spoke of Him in terms such as Helper, Comforter, Guide or Teacher. The

Holy Spirit always keeps Himself within these limits. He never usurps the will or the personality of the believer. He never compels the believer to do anything against the believer's own will or choice.

The Holy Spirit is also called "the Spirit of grace" (Heb. 10:29). He is far too gracious to impose Himself upon the believer or to force His way into any area of the believer's personality where He is not received as a welcome guest.

Paul emphasises the freedom that proceeds from the Holy Spirit.

> Now the Lord is the Spirit; and where the Spirit of the Lord is, there is liberty [freedom] (2 Cor. 3:17).

Paul contrasts this freedom of the Spirit-baptised Christian believer with the bondage of Israel to the law of Moses, and he reminds Christians:

> For you did not receive the spirit of bondage [slavery] again to fear (Rom. 8:15).

It follows, therefore, that the extent to which the Holy Spirit will control and direct the believer is the extent to which the believer will voluntarily yield to the Holy Spirit and accept His control and direction. John the Baptist says:

> For God does not give the Spirit by measure (John 3:34).

The measure is not in God's giving; the measure is in our receiving. We may have as much of the Holy Spirit as we are willing to receive. But in order to receive Him, we must voluntarily yield to Him and accept His control. He will never force us to do anything against our own will.

Some believers make just this mistake when seeking the baptism in the Holy Spirit. They imagine that the Holy Spirit will move them so forcefully that they will be literally compelled to speak with other tongues, without any act of their own will. However, this will never happen. Consider the experience of the first disciples on the day of Pentecost, as recorded in Acts 2:4.

> And they were all filled with the Holy Spirit and [they] began to speak with other tongues, as the Spirit gave them utterance.

The disciples first began to speak themselves, and then the Holy Spirit gave them utterance. If the disciples had never voluntarily begun to speak, the Holy Spirit would never have given them utterance. He would never have forced utterance upon them without their own voluntary co-operation. In this matter of speaking with other tongues, there must be co-operation on the part of the believer with the Holy Spirit.

Someone has summed up this two-way relationship between the Holy Spirit and the believer as follows: The believer cannot do it without the Holy Spirit; the Holy Spirit will not do it without the believer.

This co-operation with the Holy Spirit continues to be just as necessary even after receiving the baptism in the Holy Spirit. Here again some believers make a great mistake in supposing that, after they have received the initial infilling of the Holy Spirit, with the evidence of speaking with tongues, thereafter the Holy Spirit will automatically exercise full control of their whole being without any further response or co-operation on their part. But this is far from being true.

We have already quoted Paul as saying, "The Lord is the Spirit" (2 Cor. 3:17). The Holy Spirit is indeed Lord – just as fully as God the Father and God the Son. But He, like the Father and the Son, waits for the believer to acknowledge His lordship.

In order to make the lordship of the Spirit an effective reality in his daily life, the believer must continually yield to the Spirit's control every area of his personality and every department of his life. Someone has very truly said that it requires at least as much faith, consecration and prayer to keep filled with the Spirit as it required to receive the initial infilling.

The baptism in the Holy Spirit is not the final goal of the Christian experience; it is an initial gateway leading into a new realm of Christian living. After entering in through this gateway, each believer has a personal responsibility to press on with faith and determination and to explore for himself all the wonderful potentialities of this new realm into which he has entered.

The believer who fails to realise and apply this truth will experience few, if any, of the benefits or blessings which God intended for him through the baptism in the Holy Spirit. In all probability, such a believer will become a disappointment and a stumbling block, both to himself and to other Christians.

Utilising God's Total Provision

This leads us to another area of misunderstanding which must be cleared up. A careful study of the New Testament makes it plain that God has made full provision to meet every need of every believer, in every area of his being and in every aspect of his experience. As clear proof of this, we may cite two very powerful verses from the New Testament.

> And God is able to make all grace abound toward you, that you, always having all sufficiency in all things, have an abundance for every good work (2 Cor. 9:8).

> His [God's] divine power has given to us all things that pertain to life and godliness, through the knowledge of Him who called us by glory and virtue (2 Pet. 1:3).

These verses reveal that God's grace and power combined, through the knowledge of Jesus Christ, have already made complete provision for every need of the believer. No need can ever arise for which God has not already made a perfect provision through Jesus Christ.

If we now go on to consider the various parts of God's total provision for the believer, we find that they are manifold and that one part of God's provision is not a substitute for any other part. It is here that so many believers make a serious mistake: They try to make one part of God's provision serve as a substitute for some other part. But God never intended it to be that way, and therefore it does not work.

As a practical example of God's provision for the believer, we may consider Paul's list of spiritual armour. Paul says: "Put on the whole armour of God" (Eph. 6:11). And again: "Therefore take up the whole armour of God" (Eph 6:13).

In both these verses Paul emphasises that, for full protection, the Christian must put on the complete armour, not just a few parts of it. In the next four verses Paul enumerates the following six items of armour: the girdle of truth; the breastplate of righteousness; the shoes of the preparation of the gospel; the shield of faith; the helmet of salvation; the sword of the Spirit.

The Christian who puts on all six items of armour is fully protected from the crown of his head to the soles of his feet. But if he omits only one part of the armour, his protection ceases to be complete.

For example, if a Christian puts on all the other five items but leaves off the helmet, he is likely to be wounded in the head. Once wounded there, his ability to make use of the rest of the armour will be impaired. Conversely, a Christian might put on the helmet and all the rest of the armour for the body, but omit the shoes. In this case his ability to march over rough ground would be affected, and thus his total usefulness as a soldier would be impaired. Or again, a Christian might put on all five items of defensive armour but fail to carry the sword. In this case he would have no means of keeping his enemy at a distance or wielding an active attack against him.

We see, therefore, that for full protection a Christian must put on all six items of armour which God has provided. He cannot omit any one piece and expect that another piece will serve as a substitute. God does not intend it that way. He has provided a complete set of armour, and He expects the Christian to put it all on.

The same principle applies to the whole of God's provision for the Christian. Epaphras prayed that the Christians at Colosse "may stand perfect and complete in all the will of God" (Col. 4:12). In order to stand thus perfect and complete in the fullness of God's will, a Christian must avail himself of all that God has provided for him through Christ. He cannot omit any part of God's total provision and then expect that some other part will serve as a substitute for that which has been omitted.

Yet it is just at this point that so many Christians go astray in their thinking. Consciously or unconsciously they reason that because they know they have availed themselves of some parts of God's provision for them, they do not need to concern themselves about other parts which they have omitted.

For instance, some Christians lay great emphasis upon witnessing by word of mouth but are neglectful about the practical aspects of daily Christian living. Conversely, other Christians are careful about their conduct but fail to witness openly to their friends and neighbours. Each of these types of Christians tends to criticise or despise the other. Yet both alike are at fault. Good Christian living is no substitute for witnessing by word of mouth. On the other hand, witnessing by word of mouth is no substitute for good Christian living. God requires both. The believer who omits either one or the other does not stand perfect and complete in all the will of God.

Many other similar instances could be quoted. For example, some believers lay great stress on spiritual gifts but neglect spiritual fruit. Others lay all their emphasis on spiritual fruit but display no zeal in seeking spiritual gifts. Paul says:

> Pursue love [that is, spiritual fruit], and desire spiritual gifts
> (1 Cor. 14:1).

In other words, God requires both spiritual gifts and spiritual fruit. Gifts are no substitute for fruit, and fruit is no substitute for gifts.

Again, in presenting the gospel, there are those who stress only the facts of God's foreknowledge and predestination; others present only those texts which deal with the free response of man's will. Often these two different lines of approach lead to some kind of doctrinal conflict. Yet each by itself is incomplete and even misleading. The total plan of salvation contains room both for God's predestination and for man's free choice. It is wrong to emphasise either to the exclusion of the other.

This same general principle applies also to the baptism in the Holy Spirit. For those believers who sincerely desire to enter into all the fullness of victorious and fruitful Christian living, the baptism in the Holy Spirit is the greatest single help that God has provided. But even so, it is no substitute for any of the other main parts of Christian experience or duty.

For example, the baptism in the Spirit is no substitute for regular personal Bible study or for a daily life of consecration and self-denial or for faithful participation in a spiritually minded local church.

A believer who is faithful in all these other aspects of the Christian life but who has not received the baptism in the Holy Spirit will probably prove a more effective Christian than one who has received the baptism in the Spirit but who neglects these other aspects of the Christian life. On the other hand, if the believer who is already faithful in these other duties receives the baptism in the Holy Spirit, he will immediately find that the benefits and the effectiveness of all his other activities will be wonderfully enriched and increased by this new experience.

We may illustrate this point by the example of two men, Mr. A and Mr. B, each of whom has the task of watering a garden. Mr. A has the advantage of using a hose attached directly to a tap. Mr. B has only a watering can which he must fill from the tap and then carry back and forth to each place in the garden where water is needed. Obviously Mr. A starts with a great advantage. He needs only to carry the nozzle of the hose in his hand and then direct the water wherever he wishes. Mr. B has the labour of carrying the can to and fro the whole time.

Let us suppose, however, that Mr. B has a great superiority of character over Mr. A. Mr. A is by nature lazy, erratic, unreliable. Sometimes he forgets to water the garden altogether. At other times he waters some areas but omits those which need watering most urgently. At other times he takes no care to direct the hose correctly, wasting large quantities of water in places where it is not needed and can do no good.

On the other hand, Mr. B is active, diligent and reliable. He never forgets to water the garden at any time. He never overlooks any areas that urgently need water. He never wastes any of the water from his can but carefully directs each drop where it will do the utmost good.

What will be the result? Obviously Mr. B will have a much more fruitful and attractive garden than Mr. A. However, it would be quite wrong to deduce from this that, as a means of watering a garden, a watering can is superior to a hose.

The superiority is not that of the watering can over the hose, but that of Mr. B's whole character over Mr. A's. This is proved by the fact that if Mr. B now changes over from the watering can to the hose and continues as faithful with the hose as he was previously with the can, the results he will be able to achieve with the hose will far excel those which he previously achieved with the can. Furthermore, he will save himself a great deal of time and effort, which he will be free to devote to other useful purposes.

Let us now apply this little parable to the experience of the baptism in the Spirit. Mr. A, with the hose, represents the believer who has received the baptism in the Spirit but who is lazy, erratic and unreliable in other main aspects of Christian duty. Mr. B, with the watering can, represents the believer who has not received the baptism in the Spirit but who is active, diligent and reliable in other areas of Christian duty.

In all probability Mr. B will prove to be a more fruitful and effective Christian than Mr. A. However, it would be quite illogical to conclude from this that there is anything amiss with the baptism in the Spirit as Mr. A received it. The fault lies not in the experience itself but in the failure of Mr. A to make the right use of it in his daily life.

Furthermore, although Mr. B's general faithfulness of character already makes him an effective and fruitful Christian, the same faithfulness, when enriched and empowered by the baptism in the Spirit, would enable him to become even more fruitful and effective than he was previously.

However much we may admire Mr. B's faithfulness, we still cannot deny that he is foolish not to seek and receive the baptism in the Spirit. He is foolish not to exchange the watering can for the hose.

We see, then, that the baptism in the Holy Spirit is not just an unusual and isolated phenomenon which can be detached from the whole context of Christian experience and duty as revealed in the New Testament. On the contrary, the baptism in the Spirit will only produce the benefits and blessings which God intends when it is joined together in active Christian service with all the other main parts of God's total provision for the believer. Isolated from the rest of Christian life and service, it loses its true significance and fails to achieve its true purpose.

In fact, to seek the baptism in the Spirit without sincerely purposing to use the power thus received in scriptural service for Christ can be extremely dangerous.

A New Realm of Spiritual Conflict

One reason for this is that the baptism in the Spirit does not merely lead into a realm of new spiritual blessing; it leads also into a realm of new spiritual conflict. As a logical consequence, increased power from God will always bring with it increased opposition from Satan.

The Christian who makes sensible, scriptural use of the power received through the baptism in the Spirit will be in a position to meet and overcome the increased opposition of Satan. On the other hand, the Christian who receives the baptism in the Spirit but neglects the other aspects of Christian duty will find himself in an exceedingly dangerous position. He will discover that the baptism in the Spirit has opened up his spiritual nature to entirely new forms of satanic attack or oppression, but he will be without the God-appointed means to discern the true nature of Satan's attack or to defend himself against it.

Quite often such a Christian will find his mind invaded by strange moods of doubt or fear or depression, or he will be exposed to moral or spiritual temptation which he never experienced before receiving the baptism in the Spirit. Unless he is forewarned and forearmed to meet these new forms of satanic attack, he may easily succumb to the wiles and onslaughts of the enemy and fall back to a lower spiritual level than he was on before he entered this new realm of conflict.

The life of Jesus provides a graphic example of this truth. At His baptism in the Jordan the Holy Spirit descended on Him in the form of a dove and remained on Him. Immediately after this the Holy Spirit led Him to a direct personal encounter with Satan.

> Then Jesus, being filled with the Holy Spirit, returned from the Jordan and was led by the Spirit into the wilderness, being tempted for forty days by the devil (Luke 4:1-2).

Luke emphasises at this point that Jesus was now "filled with the Holy Spirit." This was the very cause of His being thrust into direct conflict with the devil at this stage in His ministry.

In the next eleven verses Luke records how Jesus met and overcame the three successive temptations of Satan. He concludes:

Then Jesus returned in the power of the Spirit to Galilee
(Luke 4:14).

Notice the new phrase Luke uses here: "in the power of the Spirit."
When Jesus went into the wilderness, He was already "filled with the
Spirit." But when He came out of the wilderness, He came "in the power
of the Spirit." This represents a higher level of spiritual experience. The
full power of the Holy Spirit was now freely at His disposal for use in
His God-appointed ministry. How had He entered into this higher level
of experience? By meeting and overcoming Satan face-to-face.

Furthermore, in overcoming Satan, Jesus used one weapon, and only
one – "the sword of the Spirit, which is the word of God" (Eph. 6:17).
Each time Satan tempted Him, Jesus began His answer with the phrase
"It is written." That is, He encountered Satan with the direct quotation of
God's written Word. Against this weapon Satan has no defence.

This part of the experience of Jesus is a pattern for all those who will
follow Him into the Spirit-filled life and ministry. In the life of every
believer it is God's unchanging purpose that the fullness of the Holy
Spirit should be joined together with the regular, effective use of God's
Word. Only by this means can the believer expect to come victorious
through the new spiritual conflicts which the baptism in the Holy Spirit
will inevitably bring upon him.

Since the Word of God is called "the sword of the Spirit," it follows
that the believer who does not use God's Word automatically deprives
the Holy Spirit of the main weapon which He desires to use on the
believer's behalf. As a result, the believer's whole spiritual protection
becomes inadequate. On the other hand, the believer who at this stage
faithfully studies and applies God's Word will find that this weapon is
now being wielded on his behalf by a power and a wisdom far greater
than his own – the power and wisdom of the Holy Spirit Himself.

SECTION A

THE SPIRIT-FILLED
BELIEVER

29
POWER AND GLORY

We have seen that the Holy Spirit is not a dictator. He will not do for us – or through us – more than we allow Him to. There are three main areas to which we may apply this principle: 1) the life of the individual believer; 2) the worship and service of a congregation as a whole; 3) the ministry of a preacher of the gospel.

In this section we shall consider the first of these areas. What main results is the baptism in the Holy Spirit intended to produce in the life of each individual Christian? We shall look at eight specific results.

Power to Witness

Christ Himself points to the first of these results in two passages where He gives final words of direction to His disciples before His ascension into heaven.

> Behold, I send the Promise of My Father upon you; but tarry in the city of Jerusalem until you are endued with power from on high (Luke 24:49).

> But you shall receive power when the Holy Spirit has come
> upon you; and you shall be witnesses to Me in Jerusalem, and
> in all Judea and Samaria, and to the end of the earth (Acts
> 1:8).

In these passages Jesus gives His outline plan for the spread of the
gospel in the present age. It is extremely simple. It contains three
successive stages.

1. Each believer is to be personally empowered by the Holy
   Spirit.
2. Each believer, thus empowered by the Spirit, is by his
   personal testimony to win others to Christ.
3. These others (that are won) are in their turn to be
   empowered by the Spirit to win yet others.

In this way the testimony of Christ is to be extended outward from
Jerusalem in ever-widening circles of power until it has reached the end
of the earth; that is, until it has reached all nations and every creature.

This plan is both simple and practical. Whenever it is applied, it will
always work. It would make possible the evangelisation of the entire
world in any century in which the church would put the plan to work.
There is no other alternative plan which can accomplish the same result.

In these passages the key word is *power.* The Greek word is *dunamis,*
from which we get such English words as "dynamo," "dynamic,"
"dynamite." The impression produced by these English derivative words
is essentially that of a forceful, explosive impact.

In this respect, the New Testament observes a logical distinction
between the primary results of the new birth and the primary results of
the baptism in the Holy Spirit.

The primary concept associated with the new birth is authority.

> But as many as received Him [Christ], to them He gave the
> right to become children of God (John 1:12).

This passage describes the new birth, for in the next verse we are told
that these people who received Christ "were born of God." The Greek
word here translated "the right" is *exousia. Exousia* denotes a being or a
nature which is derived from some external source. In other words, the
person who receives Christ as Saviour receives, in Christ, the being or
nature of God Himself. The receiving of this new life or nature from God

produces within the believer the new birth.

The English word most commonly used to translate this Greek word *exousia* is "authority." This is the distinctive mark of the born-again child of God. He is no longer a slave of sin and Satan. He is a son of God. As such, he possesses a new authority. He no longer succumbs to temptation or opposition. He meets and overcomes these things by virtue of the new life within him. He is an overcomer. He has authority.

However, authority is not at all the same as power. The first disciples already had this authority from the time of Christ's resurrection onward. They were already "sons of God." They were able to lead godly, overcoming lives. They were no longer the slaves of sin. However, during the period from the resurrection to the day of Pentecost, these first disciples made very little positive impact upon the great majority of the inhabitants of Jerusalem. As a whole, during this period Jerusalem was very little changed or affected by the fact of Christ's resurrection.

All this was abruptly and dramatically changed, however, by the descent of the Holy Spirit on the day of Pentecost. As soon as the 120 believers in the upper room were baptised in the Holy Spirit, the whole of Jerusalem immediately felt the impact. Within an hour or two a crowd of many thousands had gathered, and before the day closed three thousand Christ-rejecting unbelievers had been gloriously converted, baptised and added to the church.

What produced these dramatic results? The adding of power to authority. Before the day of Pentecost the disciples already had authority. After Pentecost they had authority plus power – they had the power that was needed to make their authority fully effective.

The evidence and outworking of this new, supernatural power are conspicuous in the ensuing chapters of the book of Acts.

> And they were all filled with the Holy Spirit, and they spoke the word of God with boldness (4:31).

> And with great power the apostles gave witness to the resurrection of the Lord Jesus (4:33).

The high priest complained to the apostles:

> And look, you have filled Jerusalem with your doctrine (5:28).

The same city-shaking impact continued to make itself felt thereafter in every place where the early Christians presented the testimony of the risen Christ in the power of the Holy Spirit.

For instance, we read concerning Samaria:

And there was great joy in that city (8:8).

Concerning the city of Antioch in Pisidia, it says:

And the next Sabbath almost the whole city came together to hear the Word of God (13:44).

In the city of Philippi the opponents of the gospel complained concerning Paul and Silas:

These men, being Jews, exceedingly trouble our city (16:20).

In Thessalonica the opponents of the gospel said of Paul and Silas:

These who have turned the world upside down have come here too (17:6).

As a result of the opposition to Paul's preaching in Ephesus:

The whole city was filled with confusion (19:29).

One common feature marked the advent of these early Christian witnesses in every place: a mighty spiritual impact upon the whole community. In some places there was a revival, in some there was a riot; quite often there were both together. But there were two things that could not survive this impact: ignorance and indifference.

Today, in many places, the conduct and experience of professing Christians are very different. This applies even to many groups of Christians who have a genuine experience of the new birth. They meet regularly in a church building for worship; they lead decent, respectable lives; they cause no trouble; they provoke no riots; they arouse no opposition. But, alas! They make no impact. In the community all around them, ignorance and indifference concerning spiritual things prevail, unchanged and unchallenged.

The vast majority of their neighbours neither know nor care what these Christians believe or why they attend church.

What is lacking? The answer lies in one word: power. The explosive dynamite of the Holy Spirit has been left out of these Christians' lives. And nothing else can take its place.

The Christian church as a whole needs to face up to the challenge of Paul in 1 Corinthians 4:20.

> For the kingdom of God is not in word but in power.

Once again, the Greek word which Paul here uses is *dunamis* – explosive power. It is not a question merely of the words we speak but of the power which makes our words effective. The key to this spiritual power is the baptism in the Holy Spirit. For this there is no substitute.

We see, then, that according to the New Testament the primary result of the baptism in the Holy Spirit is a supernatural enduement with power from on high to become an effective witness for Christ.

Glorification of Christ

The second main result of the baptism in the Holy Spirit is indicated by Peter's speech on the day of Pentecost.

> Therefore being exalted to the right hand of God, and having received from the Father the promise of the Holy Spirit, He [Christ] poured out this which you now see and hear (Acts 2:33).

The baptism in the Holy Spirit, which Peter and the other disciples had just received, constituted for each of them direct, personal evidence and assurance that their risen Lord was now both exalted and glorified at the Father's right hand.

Ten days earlier a little group of them had stood on the Mount of Olives and watched Jesus be taken up from them out of their sight.

> And a cloud received Him out of their sight (Acts 1:9).

That was the last physical contact the disciples had with Jesus. Then, ten days later on the day of Pentecost, the Holy Spirit's coming gave to each disciple a new, direct and personal contact with Christ. Each one now knew with a fresh assurance that their Saviour, whom the world had despised, rejected and crucified, was henceforth and forever exalted and glorified at the right hand of the Father in heaven.

Only from the Father's presence could Jesus have received this wonderful gift of the Holy Spirit which He, in turn, imparted to His waiting disciples. Receiving this gift gave them total assurance that Jesus was actually in the glory of the Father's presence, invested with authority and power over the entire universe.

There are many Scripture passages which emphasise the supreme exaltation of Jesus Christ.

> He [God] raised Him [Jesus] from the dead and seated Him at His right hand in the heavenly places, far above all principality and power and might and dominion, and every name that is named, not only in this age but also in that which is to come. And He put all things under His feet, and gave Him to be head over all things to the church, which is His body, the fullness of Him who fills all in all (Eph. 1:20-23).

> Therefore God also has highly exalted Him and given Him the name which is above every name (Phil. 2:9).

> When He had by Himself purged our sins, [He] sat down at the right hand of the Majesty on high, having become so much better than the angels, as He has by inheritance obtained a more excellent name than they (Heb. 1:3-4).

Peter says of Christ after His resurrection:

> . . . who has gone into heaven and is at the right hand of God, angels and authorities and powers having been made subject to Him (1 Pet. 3:22).

Through these and other scriptures every believer understands by faith that Jesus Christ is not merely risen from the dead; He is also ascended and glorified at the Father's right hand. However, the believer who receives the baptism in the Holy Spirit receives with it a new kind of direct, personal evidence and assurance of Christ's exaltation in power and glory at the Father's throne.

Often when a loved one leaves us on a journey to some new destination, we urge him, "Be sure to send us a letter to let us know you have arrived safely." When the letter arrives in the loved one's own handwriting, postmarked with the name of the city of destination, we know with full assurance that he is in the very place he told us he would be.

So it is with the baptism in the Holy Spirit. For the disciples on the day of Pentecost – and for every individual believer who receives the same experience – it is like a personal letter from Christ. The postmark on the letter is "Glory," and the message reads: "I am here, just as I said, at the seat of all authority and power."

I am reminded of a conversation I once had, while serving as principal of a college in East Africa, with a minister of one of the older denominations. This minister was questioning me about my personal experience of receiving the baptism in the Holy Spirit. He designated the experience by the title "Pentecostalism," and he obviously regarded the whole thing with some suspicion, as the product of some new and eccentric religious sect.

"Now let me see," he said. "That started in America, I believe. It comes from the United States, doesn't it?"

"Oh, no!" I replied. "You're quite wrong about that! This thing started in Jerusalem, and it comes from heaven!"

So it is with every believer who has received the baptism in the Holy Spirit as the first disciples received it on the day of Pentecost. This experience gives him a new, direct contact in two directions: 1) with the glorified Christ at the Father's right hand in heaven; 2) with the New Testament church as it came into being in Jerusalem and as it is thereafter pictured in the book of Acts.

The baptism in the Holy Spirit gives a new meaning, a new reality, a new assurance, both concerning the exaltation of Christ and the life and activity of the New Testament church. Things that before were historical or doctrinal facts accepted by bare faith become, for each Spirit-filled believer, thrilling realities in his own experience.

This is in line with the statement that in the days of Christ's earthly ministry "the Holy Spirit was not yet given, because Jesus was not yet glorified" (John 7:39).

We have already seen earlier that the Holy Spirit could not be given to the church before Christ was glorified with the Father in heaven. Only the glorified Christ was worthy to exercise the privilege, bestowed by the Father, of giving this wonderful gift. Therefore, the fact that this gift was bestowed upon the disciples on the day of Pentecost was in itself evidence that Christ had been glorified.

Invariably, throughout the New Testament, we find perfect harmony and co-operation between the three Persons of the triune Godhead. When Jesus Christ, the second Person of the Godhead, came to earth, He came as the personal, authoritative representative of God the Father. He never sought any kind of honour or glory for Himself. His words and His works, His wisdom and His miracles, He invariably ascribed not to Himself but to His Father, dwelling and working in Him.

Likewise, when Jesus finished His earthly ministry and returned to the Father in heaven, He sent the Holy Spirit as His personal gift and representative to His church. The Holy Spirit, coming as the representative of the second Person, the Son of God, never seeks His own glory. His whole ministry on earth and in the church is always directed to uplifting, magnifying and glorifying the One He represents – Christ.

Jesus Himself spoke of this aspect of the Spirit's ministry.

> He will glorify Me, for He will take of what is Mine and declare it to you. All things that the Father has are Mine. Therefore I said that He will take of Mine and declare it to you (John 16:14-15).

Here we see the relationship between the three Persons of the Godhead very clearly unfolded. The Father bestows all His authority, power and glory upon the Son. The Son in turn appoints the Holy Spirit as His representative to reveal and interpret to the church all that He has received from the Father.

The Holy Spirit is just as much a Person as the Father and the Son. Therefore Christ, during the present dispensation, has one, and only one, personal and authoritative representative in the church and on earth. That representative is none other than the Holy Spirit.

This revelation of the Holy Spirit's ministry provides a simple way to test anything that claims to be inspired by the Spirit. Does it glorify Christ? If the answer is not a clear yes, we have every right to question whether we are dealing with a genuine operation or manifestation of the Holy Spirit.

We find, then, a kind of divine jealousy between Christ and the Holy Spirit. On the one hand, the Holy Spirit is jealous of any trend or teaching that detracts from the honour of Christ as head over the church. On the other hand, Christ refuses to lend His authority to any ministry or movement that does not recognise the unique position of the Holy Spirit as His representative within the church.

The glory of Christ and the ministry of the Holy Spirit are inseparably linked together.

30
ON THE SUPERNATURAL PLANE

In this chapter we shall continue to study the results which the baptism in the Holy Spirit is intended by God to produce in the life of each individual believer.

A Gateway to the Supernatural

For a third main result of this experience we may turn to the words of Hebrews 6:4-5, which speak of believers who:

> . . . have become partakers of the Holy Spirit, and have tasted the good word of God and the powers of the age to come.

These words indicate that those who have been made partakers of the Holy Spirit have tasted the powers of the age to come. The baptism in the Holy Spirit gives the believer a foretaste of an altogether new kind of power – a supernatural power that belongs, in its fullness, to the next age.

For this reason Paul describes the seal of the Holy Spirit as the guarantee of our inheritance.

> In Him you also trusted, after you heard the word of truth, the gospel of your salvation; in whom also, having believed, you were sealed with the Holy Spirit of promise, who is the guarantee of our inheritance until the redemption of the purchased possession, to the praise of His glory (Eph. 1:13-14).

An alternative translation for guarantee is "down payment." The Greek word, which is borrowed from Hebrew, is *arrabon*. This is a very interesting word which I have encountered – with slight variations – in four different languages: Hebrew, Greek, Arabic and Swahili.

Its meaning was brought home to me in a vivid way many years ago in Jerusalem. My first wife, Lydia, and I had moved with our children to a new home for which we needed to purchase about twenty yards of curtain material. We went to the Old City and found some suitable material for which, after some bargaining, we agreed to pay the equivalent of four dollars per yard, making a total of eighty dollars. I gave the storekeeper a down payment of twenty dollars (called in Arabic an *arbon*) and promised to come back within a week with the balance of sixty dollars.

I reminded the storekeeper that I now regarded the material as already my property. As such, he must set it aside until I returned, and he had no right to offer it to any other purchaser.

In the same way, the Lord gives us – through His Holy Spirit – a "down payment" of heavenly power and glory – a foretaste of the next age. This down payment sets us aside as His purchased property, not to be offered to any other purchaser. It is His guarantee, too, that at the appointed time He will return with the balance of payment and take us to His home, to be with Him forever. That is why Paul calls it "the guarantee of our inheritance until the redemption of the purchased possession."

Another beautiful illustration of what we receive through the baptism in the Holy Spirit is contained in the story of the healing of Naaman, the Syrian leper, recorded in 2 Kings 5. As a result of his miraculous healing Naaman came to acknowledge that the Lord Jehovah, the God of Israel, was the only true God. He knew, however, that he would shortly have to return to an unclean, heathen land and be associated with the idolatrous ceremonies of a heathen temple. With this in mind, Naaman had one special request to make before leaving the land of Israel.

> So Naaman said, "Then, if not, please let your servant be
> given two mule-loads of earth; for your servant will no longer
> offer either burnt offering or sacrifice to other gods, but to the
> Lord" (2 Kin. 5:17).

Why did Naaman desire to carry home soil from the land of Israel? He had realised the holiness of the Lord, and, in contrast, the uncleanness of his own land and people. He was determined, therefore, never again to offer worship from unclean earth.

The holiness of the Lord demanded that Naaman should stand and worship Him only on earth from the Lord's own land. Since Naaman could not remain permanently in Israel, he determined to carry a portion of Israel's earth home with him and to make there from that earth his own special place of worship.

So it is with the Spirit-baptised believer. He gains a new understanding of these words of Jesus:

> God is Spirit, and those who worship Him must worship in
> spirit and truth (John 4:24).

Such a believer can no longer be satisfied with the mere forms and ceremonies of man-made worship. He has been in the heavenly land; he has had a glimpse of its glories and the holiness of God. He has brought back a portion of that sacred soil with him. No matter where circumstances may take him, he worships now not on an unclean land, but on holy ground. He worships in Spirit – the Holy Spirit – and in truth.

What is true in the worship of the Spirit-filled believer is equally true in every other aspect of his experience. Through the baptism in the Spirit he has entered into a new kind of supernatural life. The supernatural has become natural.

If we study the New Testament with an open mind, we are compelled to acknowledge that the whole life and experience of the early Christians was permeated by the supernatural. Supernatural experiences were not something incidental or additional; they were an integral part of their lives as Christians. Their praying was supernatural; their preaching was supernatural; they were supernaturally guided, supernaturally empowered, supernaturally transported, supernaturally protected.

Remove the supernatural from the book of Acts, and you are left with something that has no meaning or coherence. From the descent of the Holy Spirit in Acts 2, it is impossible to find a single chapter in which the supernatural does not play an essential part.

In the account of Paul's ministry in Ephesus we find a most arresting and thought-provoking expression.

> Now God worked unusual miracles by the hands of Paul (Acts 19:11).

Consider the implications of that phrase "unusual miracles." The Greek could be translated, somewhat freely, "miracles of a kind that do not happen every day." Miracles were an everyday occurrence in the early church. Normally they would have caused no special surprise or comment. But the miracles granted here in Ephesus through the ministry of Paul were such that even the early church found them worthy of special record.

In how many churches today would we find occasion to use the phrase "miracles of a kind that do not happen every day"? In how many churches today do miracles ever happen – let alone happen every day?

The truth is, where we do not see and experience the supernatural, we have no right to speak of New Testament Christianity. These two things – the supernatural and New Testament Christianity – are inseparably interwoven.

Without the supernatural we may have New Testament doctrine, but it is bare doctrine, not experience. Such doctrine, divorced from supernatural experience, is of the kind described by Paul.

> For the letter kills, but the Spirit gives life (2 Cor. 3:6).

Only the Holy Spirit can give life to the letter of New Testament doctrine and make that doctrine a living, personal, supernatural way of life for each believer. One main purpose of the baptism in the Holy Spirit is to do just this.

Spirit-empowered Prayer

A fourth main purpose of the baptism in the Holy Spirit concerns the prayer life of the believer.

> Likewise the Spirit also helps in our weaknesses. For we do not know what we should pray for as we ought, but the Spirit Himself makes intercession for us with groanings which cannot be uttered. Now He who searches the hearts knows what the mind of the Spirit is, because He makes intercession

for the saints according to the will of God (Rom. 8:26-27).

Paul mentions one form of weakness which is common to all believers in their own natural condition and apart from the Holy Spirit. It is defined by Paul in the words "for we do not know what we should pray for as we ought." This weakness is not knowing how to pray in accordance with God's will.

The only One to whom we can turn for help in this weakness is the Holy Spirit, for Paul says:

> The Spirit also helps in our weaknesses . . . the Spirit Himself makes intercession for us . . . because He makes intercession for the saints according to the will of God (Rom. 8:26-27).

Paul here speaks of the Spirit as a Person who indwells the believer and who makes the believer a vessel, or a channel, through which He offers prayer and intercession.

This is prayer of a kind which is far above the level of the believer's own natural understanding or ability. In this kind of prayer the believer does not rely on his feelings or his understanding. He yields his body to the Holy Spirit as a temple in which the Spirit Himself conducts prayer, and he yields his members as instruments which the Spirit controls for purposes of supernatural intercession.

Concerning prayer, the New Testament sets a standard to which the believer can never attain in his own natural strength or understanding. In this way God deliberately shuts the believer up in a place where he is obliged either to fall below the divine standard or else to depend upon the supernatural assistance of the indwelling Spirit.

For example, Paul says:

> . . . praying always with all prayer and supplication in the Spirit (Eph. 6:18).

And again:

> Pray without ceasing . . . Do not quench the Spirit (1 Thess. 5:17,19).

No person in his own unaided strength or understanding can fulfil these commandments. No person can "pray always" or "pray without ceasing." But that which is impossible in the natural is made possible by the indwelling, supernatural presence of the Holy Spirit. For this reason, Paul is careful to emphasise the believer's dependence upon the Holy Spirit. He says, "Praying always . . . in the Spirit," and again, "Pray without ceasing . . . Do not quench the Spirit."

The Holy Spirit indwelling the believer in the New Testament corresponds to the fire supernaturally kindled upon the altar of the tabernacle in the Old Testament. Concerning this fire, the Lord ordained:

> A perpetual fire shall burn on the altar; it shall never go out (Lev. 6:13).

The corresponding New Testament ordinance is contained in the words of Paul: "Pray without ceasing . . . Do not quench the Spirit." Where the Spirit-baptised believer yields full control to the Spirit within and does not by carelessness or carnality quench the Spirit's fire, there burns within the temple of that believer's body a fire of supernatural prayer and worship which never goes out, day or night. Few people realise the limitless potentialities of Holy Spirit prayer within the temple of a believer's yielded body.

Some years ago when I conducted regular street meetings in London, England, a young woman of Catholic background from Ireland was saved and baptised in the Holy Spirit. She was working as a maid in a London hotel, and she shared a bedroom there with another young woman of her own age and background. One day this other woman came to her and said, "Tell me, what is that strange language you speak to yourself every night in bed after you seem to have gone to sleep?"

"I can't tell you that," the first young woman answered, "because I never even knew that I was speaking any language."

In this way she learned to her surprise that every night after she had gone to sleep, without the conscious exercise of her own faculties, she was speaking with other tongues as the Holy Spirit gave her utterance.

So it is to be filled with and yielded to the Holy Spirit. When we come to the end of our own natural strength and understanding, the Holy Spirit can take over our faculties and conduct His own worship and prayer through us.

This is the picture given of the bride of Christ in the Song of Solomon.

> I sleep, but my heart is awake (5:2).

The bride may sleep; she may be physically and mentally exhausted. But in the innermost depths of her being there dwells One who never slumbers or sleeps – the Holy Spirit Himself. Even through the hours of darkness there burns upon the altar of her heart a fire that never goes out – a fire of worship and prayer that is the life of the Holy Spirit within.

This is the Bible pattern for the prayer life of the church in this present age. But such a life of prayer is possible only through the supernatural, indwelling presence of the Holy Spirit.

Revelation of the Scriptures

A fifth great purpose of the baptism in the Holy Spirit is that the Spirit may become our guide and teacher in relation to the Scriptures. Christ promises this to His disciples in two passages in John's Gospel.

> But the Helper, the Holy Spirit, whom the Father will send in My name, He will teach you all things, and bring to your remembrance all things that I said to you (John 14:26).

During His earthly ministry Jesus taught His disciples much, especially concerning His death and resurrection, which they were unable either to understand or remember.

However, Jesus assured them that after the Holy Spirit came to dwell in them, He would become their personal teacher and enable them to remember and understand correctly all that Jesus had taught them during His earthly ministry. Nor would the Holy Spirit confine Himself only to interpreting the teachings of Jesus while on earth; He would also lead the disciples into a full understanding of God's whole revelation to man.

> However, when He, the Spirit of truth, has come, He will guide you into all truth [more literally, into all the truth]; for He will not speak on His own authority, but whatever He hears He will speak (John 16:13).

Here the phrase "all the truth" may be interpreted by reference to the words of Jesus: "Your word is truth" (John 17:17).

Jesus promises His disciples that the Holy Spirit will lead them into a correct understanding of the entire revelation of God to man through the Scriptures. This includes the Old Testament Scriptures, the teaching of Jesus during His earthly ministry and also the further revelation of truth given to the church after Pentecost through Paul and others of the apostles.

The Holy Spirit is given to the church to become the revelator, interpreter and teacher of the whole compass of divine revelation in the Scriptures.

The fulfilment of Christ's promise that the Holy Spirit would interpret the Scriptures for the disciples is dramatically illustrated in the events of the day of Pentecost. As soon as the Holy Spirit was poured out upon the disciples and they began to speak with other tongues, the question was raised: Whatever could this mean? Peter answered:

But this is what was spoken by the prophet Joel:

"And it shall come to pass in the last days, says
   God,
That I will pour out of My Spirit on all flesh"
(Acts 2:16-17).

Without a moment's hesitation, Peter quotes and interprets a prophecy concerning the last days given in the second chapter of Joel. In the sermon which follows, almost half of what Peter says is direct quotation from the Old Testament Scriptures. The teaching of these Scriptures is applied in a clear and forceful way to the events of Christ's death and resurrection and of the Holy Spirit's outpouring.

It is difficult to imagine any greater contrast between the exposition of the Old Testament Scriptures here given by Peter and the lack of understanding concerning the same Scriptures displayed by Peter and all the other disciples during the earthly ministry of Jesus and up to the day of Pentecost.

It would appear that this total change in the disciples' understanding of the Scriptures was not a gradual process but was produced instantaneously by the coming of the Holy Spirit. As soon as the Holy Spirit came to indwell them, their understanding of the Scriptures was supernaturally illuminated. Their previous doubts and confusion were immediately replaced by clear understanding and forceful application.

This same dramatic transformation continues to be a distinctive mark of Spirit-filled believers from the day of Pentecost onward.

For example, Saul of Tarsus had been trained in the knowledge of the Old Testament Scriptures by Gamaliel, the most famous teacher of his day. Yet in his early years he had no light or understanding on their correct application. It was only after Ananias in Damascus laid hands on Saul and prayed that he might be filled with the Holy Spirit that the scales fell from his eyes and he was able to understand and apply those Scriptures.

> Immediately he preached the Christ in the synagogues, that
> He is the Son of God (Acts 9:20).

Notice that word "immediately." There was not a slow, gradual struggle for understanding but rather an instant illumination. The moment the Holy Spirit came in, He cast an altogether new light upon Scriptures which Saul had known for many years but had never known how to apply or interpret.

What the Holy Spirit did for Peter and Saul, and for the New Testament Christians as a whole, He is still willing and able to do for all Christians today. But first each believer must, through the baptism in the Holy Spirit, personally receive this wonderful, indwelling guide, teacher and expositor.

31
CONTINUAL GUIDANCE
AND OVERFLOWING LIFE

L et us consider two further ministries of the Holy Spirit in the life of the believer: daily guidance in the path of God's will, and the impartation of life and health to the believer's physical body.

Daily Guidance

The first of these ministries, daily guidance, is described by Paul.

> For as many as are led by the Spirit of God, these are sons of God (Rom. 8:14).

It is important to see that Paul here uses a continuing present tense: "as many as are [being regularly] led by the Spirit of God." He is not talking about a few isolated experiences but about an ongoing way of life.

Many professing Christians, even among those who have been truly born again, do not attach sufficient importance to these words of Paul. They tend to place their whole emphasis on certain one-time experiences, such as the new birth or the baptism in the Holy Spirit, on which they base their claim to be considered Christians. It is certainly important to emphasise these decisive experiences, but not to the point where no mention is made of the need to walk daily in the grace of God.

In order to become a true Christian, a person must be born again of the Spirit of God. In order to become an effective witness for Christ, a person must be baptised in the Holy Spirit. But the work of the Holy Spirit should never end there. In order to live daily as a Christian, a person must be led by the Spirit.

The new birth transforms sinners into children of God. But it requires the continual leading of the Holy Spirit to make children into mature sons.

In Romans 8:14 Paul takes for granted the two preliminary experiences of being born of the Holy Spirit and baptised in the Holy Spirit. He points out, however, that the only way to achieve spiritual maturity and success in daily Christian living is to depend upon the Spirit for moment-by-moment direction in every aspect of life. Only this will make it possible for the Holy Spirit to accomplish all the purposes for which He actually came to indwell the believer. This is in harmony with Paul's comments.

> For we are His workmanship, created in Christ Jesus for good works, which God prepared beforehand that we should walk in them (Eph. 2:10).

As believers, Paul teaches, we are created anew by God through our faith in Christ. Thereafter, to continue in the Christian life, we do not have to plan our own ways and activities. On the contrary, the same God who first foreknew us and then created us anew in Christ also prepared from before the foundation of the world the good works which it was His will for each one of us to accomplish as Christians.

Therefore, we do not plan our own good works, but we seek to discover and then enter into the good works God has already planned for us. Here the guidance of the Holy Spirit becomes essential for each Christian. For it is the Holy Spirit who first reveals and then leads us into God's plan for our lives.

Unfortunately, many Christians today have reversed this process. They first plan their own ways and their own activities, and then they say some kind of perfunctory prayer asking God to bless those activities. In reality, almighty God will never allow His approval or blessing to become a mere rubber stamp superimposed upon plans and activities concerning which His counsel has never been sincerely sought.

This error is common not only in the lives of individual Christians, but also in the activities of churches and other Christian organisations. Countless hours of labour and vast sums of money are squandered and lost, without any enduring fruit, simply because the counsel of God was never sincerely sought before these various activities were initiated.

In fact, in many Christian circles today, the greatest enemy of true spirituality and fruitfulness is time-consuming, sweat-producing activity labelled "Christian" in name but lacking the divine inbreathing and directing of the Holy Spirit.

The end products of all such activity are "wood, hay, straw" – all of which will be consumed, without residue or remainder, in the fire of God's final judgement upon His people's works (see 1 Cor. 3:12).

In contrast, one of the distinguishing marks of the New Testament church is the direct, continued, supernatural guidance of the Holy Spirit in all its activities. Out of many possible examples of this in the book of Acts, let us consider one very characteristic incident from Paul's second missionary journey, on which he was accompanied by Silas.

> Now when they had gone through Phrygia and the region of Galatia, they were forbidden by the Holy Spirit to preach the word in Asia. After they had come to Mysia, they tried to go into Bithynia, but the Spirit did not permit them. So passing by Mysia, they came down to Troas. And a vision appeared to Paul in the night. A man of Macedonia stood and pleaded with him, saying, "Come over to Macedonia and help us." Now after he had seen the vision, immediately we sought to go to Macedonia, concluding that the Lord had called us to preach the gospel to them (Acts 16:6-10).

In considering this passage, we must bear in mind that Paul and Silas in their missionary undertaking were fulfilling the direct commission of Jesus to His disciples.

> Go therefore and make disciples of all the nations (Matt. 28:19).

> Go into all the world and preach the gospel to every creature (Mark 16:15).

Notice how all-inclusive this commission is: "all the nations . . . every creature."

In fulfilment of this commission, Paul and Silas had been preaching in Phrygia and Galatia – in the central part of what we today call Asia Minor. Their next obvious move would have been into the province of Asia, on the western edge of Asia Minor. However, the record of Acts says, "They were forbidden by the Holy Spirit to preach the word in Asia." As a result, they moved to the north of Asia, into Mysia.

From here, their next obvious move would have been northeast into Bithynia. However, at this point Acts records: "They tried to go into Bithynia, but the Spirit did not permit them" (Acts 16:7).

Both of the obvious doors of evangelisation – into Asia on the one side and into Bithynia on the other side – were closed to them by the direct, explicit decree of the Holy Spirit.

Doubtless, Paul and Silas began to wonder what God's plan for them could be or what course they should follow next. But at this point Paul had a vision in the night of a man of Macedonia saying, "Come over to Macedonia and help us" (v. 9). Without further question, they immediately realised that God was directing them to Macedonia – in the northern part of Greece and the southeastern corner of Europe. In this way the gospel was first brought out of Asia into Europe.

As we now look back over nineteen subsequent centuries of church history, we realise the decisive part played by the church in Europe, first in preserving the truth of the gospel and then in actively disseminating that truth throughout the rest of the world. We can understand, therefore, why, in the wisdom and foreknowledge of God, it was of the utmost urgency and importance that the gospel should, thus early, be planted in Europe by Paul himself, the chief apostle to the Gentiles.

However, Paul and Silas knew nothing of the course that history would take in the next nineteen centuries. Therefore, their taking of this epoch-making step into Europe was made possible solely through the supernatural revelation and direction of the Holy Spirit. If they had not been open to the Spirit's guidance, they would have missed God's plan, both for their own lives and also for the whole work of the gospel.

God's supernatural direction of Paul through the Holy Spirit at this point is made all the more remarkable when we consider certain subsequent phases of Paul's missionary activity.

Here in Acts 16 we read that Paul was forbidden by the Holy Spirit to preach the Word in the province of Asia, and therefore he journeyed past Asia and on into Europe. Yet in Acts 19 we read how Paul returned some time later to Ephesus, which was the main city of the province of Asia, and how there developed out of his preaching one of the greatest and most extensive revivals ever recorded in his whole ministry.

> And this continued for two years, so that all who dwelt in
> Asia heard the word of the Lord Jesus, both Jews and Greeks
> (Acts 19:10).

Surely this is worthy of our careful consideration. Earlier Paul had not been allowed by the Holy Spirit even to enter Asia or to speak to a single soul there. Now, returning there at God's appointed time and under the Holy Spirit's guidance, Paul witnessed such an impact through the preaching of the gospel that every single human dwelling in the entire province came to hear the testimony of Christ.

On the basis of these facts, we may form two conclusions: 1) If Paul had entered Asia on his first visit, contrary to the Spirit's direction, he would have encountered nothing but frustration and failure. 2) By visiting Asia prematurely, before the Spirit led him there, Paul could easily have hindered, or even totally prevented, the subsequent mighty move of God's Spirit which he was privileged to witness on his later visit.

What a lesson there is here for all who seek to preach the gospel or to witness for Christ in any way! In every course of proposed activity, there are two factors of related importance which we must take into account: 1) the place, 2) the time.

In this, the revelation of Scripture anticipates the basic inclusion of the modern scientific theory of relativity: that we can never accurately specify place unless we also specify time. These two are interrelated and can never be separated.

This same truth was stated many centuries ago by Solomon.

> To everything there is a season,
> A time for every purpose under heaven (Eccl. 3:1).

It is not enough merely to do the right thing or to have the right purpose. In order to enjoy success and the blessing of God, we must do the right thing at the right time, and we must carry out the right purpose at the right season. When God says, "Now," it is vain for man to say, "Later." And when God says, "Later," it is vain for man to say, "Now."

It is the God-appointed ministry of the Holy Spirit to reveal to the church not merely the right thing or the right purpose, but also the right time and the right season. Many sincere and well-meaning Christians who have not learned to make room for the guidance of the Holy Spirit encounter continual frustration in their lives simply through seeking to do the right thing at the wrong time and to carry out the right purpose at the wrong season. In this connection, the prophet Isaiah poses a very searching question.

> Who has directed the Spirit of the Lord,
> Or as His counsellor has taught Him? (Is. 40:13).

Yet this is just what many Christians are doing today: They are seeking to direct the Spirit of the Lord and to act as counsellor to the Holy Spirit. They plan their own activities, conduct their own services and then tell the Holy Spirit just what, when and how they expect Him to bless. In how many congregations today is there any real room left for the Holy Spirit either to direct or to intervene?

The result of this wrong attitude toward the Holy Spirit can be summed up in one word: frustration.

Such believers may have a genuine experience of the new birth and even of the baptism in the Holy Spirit. They may be perfectly sincere in their profession of faith in Christ. Nevertheless, in their daily lives they lack either victory or fruitfulness because they have overlooked this one cardinal rule of Christian living: "For as many as are led by the Spirit of God, these are sons of God" (Rom. 8:14).

Life for the Whole Person

The continual guidance of God in the life of the believer opens the way for yet another provision of His Spirit: overflowing life for his whole personality. The relationship between God's guidance and this all-sufficient life is described beautifully in Isaiah.

> The Lord will guide you continually,
> And satisfy your soul in drought,
> And strengthen your bones;
> You shall be like a watered garden,
> And like a spring of water, whose waters do not fail (Is. 58:11).

Isaiah depicts a person so continually guided by God that he has within him a spring of life which overflows throughout his whole personality, refreshing and renewing both his soul and his body.

In the New Testament Paul traces this overflowing life to its source:

the Holy Spirit indwelling the believer.

> [Jesus Christ was] declared to be the Son of God with power,
> according to the Spirit of holiness, by the resurrection from
> the dead (Rom. 1:4).

It was the "Spirit of holiness" – a Hebraic expression for "the Holy Spirit" – who raised up the dead body of Jesus from the grave, thus vindicating His claim to be the Son of God. The Holy Spirit will perform the same ministry for every believer whom He indwells.

> But if the Spirit of Him who raised Jesus from the dead
> dwells in you, He who raised Christ from the dead will also
> give life to your mortal bodies through His Spirit who dwells
> in you (Rom. 8:11).

This ministry of the Holy Spirit will receive its full and final outworking at the first resurrection, when He will raise up the righteous dead with the same kind of immortal body that Jesus already has.

> He [God] who raised up the Lord Jesus will also raise us up
> with Jesus, and will present us with you (2 Cor. 4:14).

However, this ministry of the Holy Spirit to the believer's body also has an intermediate application in the present age. Even now the Spirit of God, indwelling the believer, imparts to his physical body a measure of divine life and health sufficient to arrest and exclude the satanic inroads of disease and infirmity. This is the supreme purpose for which Christ came.

> I have come that they may have life, and that they may have
> it more abundantly (John 10:10).

It has been said that the first portion of divine life comes through the new birth, but the overflowing of life more abundant comes through the baptism in the Holy Spirit. It is God's purpose, even in the present age, that this divine, overflowing, abundant life shall suffice not merely for the spiritual needs of the inward man – man's spiritual nature – but also for the physical needs of the outer man – man's physical body.

In this present age the believer has not yet received his resurrection body, but he already enjoys resurrection life in a mortal body.

Paul depicts this miracle of resurrection life in a mortal body against a background of tremendous pressures, both physical and spiritual.

> We are hard pressed on every side, yet not crushed; we are perplexed, but not in despair; persecuted, but not forsaken; struck down, but not destroyed – always carrying about in the body the dying of the Lord Jesus, that the life of Jesus also may be manifested in our body. For we who live are always delivered to death for Jesus' sake, that the life of Jesus also may be manifested in our mortal flesh (2 Cor. 4:8-11).

What wonderful words! The very life of Jesus is to be manifested – its presence is to be demonstrated by the visible effects which it produces "in our body." For the sake of emphasis Paul says this twice, but the second time he speaks of "our mortal flesh." By this phrase he eliminates any interpretation which might seek to apply his words to a future state of the body after resurrection. He is talking about our present physical body. In the midst of all the pressures that come against it – both natural and satanic – it is sustained by an inner life which cannot be defeated.

This manifestation of the mighty, victorious, supernatural life of the risen Christ in the believer's body is not reserved merely for the resurrection, but it is to be effective even now while we still continue "in our mortal flesh." The open manifestation of Christ's life in our body here and now is the basic, scriptural principle of divine healing and divine health.

Central to this ongoing miracle is a paradox that runs through the whole Bible: Death is the gateway to life. In each place where Paul testifies to the manifestation of Christ's life, he first speaks of identification with His death: "always carrying about in the body the dying of the Lord Jesus."

Jesus did not die a natural death; He died by crucifixion. To be identified with Him is to be crucified with Him. But out of crucifixion comes resurrection to an inner life that owes no further debt to sin or to Satan, to the flesh or to the world.

Paul presents both the negative and the positive side of this exchange.

> I have been crucified with Christ; it is no longer I who live, but Christ lives in me; and the life which I now live in the flesh I live by faith in the Son of God, who loved me and gave Himself for me (Gal. 2:20).

The same process of crucifixion that ends our frail, transient life in this world opens the way for a new life that is the life of God Himself, taking up residence in a vessel of clay. The vessel is still as frail as ever, but the new life in it is undefeatable and inexhaustible.

As long as this present world order continues, however, there will always be an ongoing tension between the frailty of the flesh and the new life in the Spirit.

> Even though our outward man is perishing, yet the inward man is being renewed day by day (2 Cor. 4:16).

The physical body is still subject to sickness and decay from without, but the resurrection life from within has power to hold them at bay until the believer's life task is complete. After that, as Paul says, "to depart and be with Christ . . . is far better" (Phil. 1:23).

32
DIVINE LOVE OUTPOURED

We shall devote this chapter to one final, supremely important result produced in the believer by the baptism in the Holy Spirit. It is described by Paul in the latter part of Romans.

> The love of God has been poured out in our hearts by the Holy Spirit who was given to us (5:5).

We need to grasp the significance of that phrase, "the love of God." Paul is not speaking here about human love or even about love for God. He is speaking about the love of God – God's own love – which the Holy Spirit pours out in the believer's heart. This love of God, imparted by the Holy Spirit, is as high above any form of mere human love as heaven is above earth.

In the normal course of our lives we experience many different types of love. For instance, there is a form of love, so-called, which is mere sexual passion. Then there is the married love of husband and wife for each other. Again, within the human family, there is the love of parents for children and of children for parents. Outside the bonds of the family, there is the love of one friend for another, such as the love of David and Jonathan for each other.

The Nature of God's Love

All these and other forms of love, in varying degree, are found in all sections of the human race, even where the gospel of Christ has never been preached. The Greek language, which has a rich vocabulary, has various words to describe these different forms of love. There is one word, however, which is used primarily for love which is divine in its origin and nature. As a noun, this word is *agape*; as a verb, *agapao*.

Agape denotes the perfect love between the Persons of the Godhead – the Father, the Son and the Spirit. It denotes the love of God toward man – that is, the love which caused God the Father to give His Son, and Christ the Son to give His life, that man might be redeemed from sin and its consequences. It denotes also the love God through His Holy Spirit imparts to the hearts of those who believe in Christ.

This enables us to understand the words of the apostle in 1 John.

> Beloved, let us love one another, for love is of God; and everyone who loves is born of God and knows God. He who does not love does not know God, for God is love (4:7-8).

The Greek words which John uses are *agape* and *agapao*. John teaches that there is a kind of love, *agape*, which no one can experience unless he has been born of God. Love of this kind comes only from God.

Anyone who in any measure manifests this kind of love has, in that measure, come to know God through the new birth. Conversely, a person who has never known or manifested this love in any measure has never known God; for in the measure that a person comes to know God, he is in that measure changed and transformed by the divine love, so that he himself begins to manifest it to others.

As John here indicates, this manifestation of *agape* – of divine love – commences in human experience with the new birth. This is in harmony with the words of Peter.

> Since you have purified your souls in obeying the truth through the Spirit in sincere love of the brethren, love one another fervently with a pure heart, having been born again, not of corruptible seed but incorruptible, through the word of God which lives and abides forever (1 Pet. 1:22-23).

Where Peter says, "Love one another fervently with a pure heart," the verb for "love" which he uses is once again that for divine love – *agapao*. He directly connects this possibility of Christians' manifesting the divine love with the fact that they have been born again of the incorruptible seed of God's Word. That is to say, the potentiality of divine love is contained within the divine seed of God's Word implanted in their hearts at the new birth.

However, God intends for this initial experience of divine love, received at the new birth, to be immeasurably increased and expanded through the baptism in the Holy Spirit. For this reason, Paul says:

> The love of God has been poured out in our hearts by the
> Holy Spirit who was given to us (Rom. 5:5).

Once again, it is the word for divine love – *agape* – which Paul uses. The verb which he joins with it – "has been poured out" – is in the perfect tense. The use of the perfect tense indicates, as usual in Greek, finality and completeness. The meaning is that in this one act of baptising the believer in the Holy Spirit, God has emptied out into the believer's heart all the fullness of the divine love. Nothing has been reserved or held back; all has been poured out. Thereafter the believer does not need to seek more of God's love; he needs only to accept, to enjoy and to manifest that which he has already received within.

For the Spirit-baptised believer to ask God for more of His love is like a man who lives on the bank of the Mississippi River to seek for some other supply of water. Such a person already has at his disposal infinitely more than he can ever need to use. All that he needs is to utilise the supply already made available to him.

In like manner, Jesus says the Spirit-baptised believer already has within himself not merely one river, but "rivers of living water" – rivers of divine grace and love – infinitely in excess of any need that can ever arise in that believer's life (see John 7:38-39).

In his letter to the Romans, Paul defines the precise nature of this divine love, poured out within the believer by the Holy Spirit.

> For when we were still without strength, in due time Christ
> died for the ungodly. For scarcely for a righteous man will
> one die; yet perhaps for a good man someone would even
> dare to die. But God demonstrates His own love toward us, in
> that while we were still sinners, Christ died for us (5:6-8).

Paul points out that even natural love, apart from the grace of God, might impel a man to die for his friend, if that friend were a good and righteous man – just as natural love, in another form, might cause a mother to give her life for her child. Paul then shows that the super-natural, divine love of God is seen in the fact that Christ died for sinners who could have had no claim upon any kind of natural love whatever.

To describe the condition of those for whom Christ died, Paul uses three successive phrases: "without strength . . . ungodly . . . sinners." This means that those for whom Christ died were, at that time, utterly unable to help themselves, totally alienated from God and in open rebellion against Him. It was in dying for people such as this that Christ manifested *agape* – the divine love – in its perfect fullness.

John defines the divine love in a similar way.

> In this the love [*agape*] of God was manifested toward us, that God has sent His only begotten Son into the world, that we might live through Him (1 John 4:9).

The divine love does not depend upon anything worthy of love in those to whom it is directed, nor does it wait to be reciprocated before it gives all. On the contrary, it gives first and freely to those who are unlovable, unworthy and even in open rebellion. Jesus expressed this divine love in His prayer for those who were crucifying Him.

> Father, forgive them, for they do not know what they do (Luke 23:34).

The same divine love is expressed in the dying prayer of the martyr Stephen for those who were stoning him.

> Lord, do not charge them with this sin (Acts 7:60).

The same love is expressed again in the words of one who was an eager witness of Stephen's stoning – Saul of Tarsus, later the apostle Paul. Concerning his own Jewish brethren, who had consistently rejected and persecuted him, Paul says:

> I tell the truth in Christ, I am not lying, my conscience also bearing me witness in the Holy Spirit, that I have great sorrow and continual grief in my heart. For I could wish that I myself were accursed from Christ for my brethren, my kinsmen

according to the flesh (Rom. 9:1-3).

So greatly did Paul yearn for the salvation of his persecuting Jewish brethren that he would have been willing to forego all the blessings of salvation for himself and return under the curse of unforgiven sin with all its consequences, if this could bring his brethren to Christ. Paul acknowledges that the experience and realisation of this love was made possible only through the presence of the Holy Spirit within, for he says, ". . . my conscience also bearing me witness in the Holy Spirit."

Love Is the Greatest

We have said that among the various purposes for which God gives the gift of the Holy Spirit, this pouring out of divine love within the believer's heart occupies a place of unique importance. The reason for this is that, without the all-pervading influence of divine love in the believer's heart, all the other results which may be produced by the baptism in the Holy Spirit lose their true significance and fail to accomplish their true purpose.

Paul uses a vivid series of examples to emphasise the unique importance of this *agape* love.

> Though I speak with the tongues of men and of angels, but have not love, I have become as sounding brass or a clanging cymbal. And though I have the gift of prophecy, and understand all mysteries and all knowledge, and though I have all faith, so that I could remove mountains, but have not love, I am nothing (1 Cor. 13:1-2).

With characteristic humility, Paul puts himself in the place of a believer who exercises spiritual gifts but lacks divine love. In the previous chapter of 1 Corinthians he enumerated nine gifts of the Holy Spirit. He now imagines himself to be one who exercises various of these gifts, but who lacks love.

First he considers the possibility of exercising the gift of tongues on such a high supernatural plane that he speaks not only unknown human languages but even the language of angels. He says that if he were to do this without divine love, he would be no better than a gong or a cymbal that produces a loud noise when it is struck but is quite empty inside.

Then he considers the possibility of exercising other outstanding spiritual gifts – such as prophecy, or the word of wisdom, or the word of knowledge or faith. But he says that if he should exercise any or all of these gifts without divine love, he would be absolutely nothing.

These words of Paul provide the answer to a question which is being asked in many circles today: Is it possible to misuse the gift of tongues? The answer to this is clear: Yes, it is perfectly possible to misuse the gift of tongues. Any use of tongues apart from divine love is a misuse, because it renders the believer who exercises it no better than an empty, clanging gong or cymbal, and this was certainly never the purpose for which God bestowed the gift.

This applies equally to the other gifts which Paul mentions in the next verse – prophecy, the word of wisdom, the word of knowledge and faith. To use any of these gifts apart from divine love is to miss the whole purpose of God.

However, experience proves again and again that there is a special danger in misusing the three spiritual gifts which operate through the organs of speech – that is, tongues, interpretation and prophecy. This is confirmed by the fact that Paul devotes the greater part of the next chapter – 1 Corinthians 14 – to giving rules to control and regulate the use of these three particular gifts. If there were no possibility of believers misusing these gifts, there would be no need to give rules for their control. The fact that rules are given proves that rules are needed.

However, in interpreting the teaching of Paul in 1 Corinthians 13:1, it is necessary to pay close attention to the exact words he uses. He says:

> Though I speak with the tongues of men and of angels, but have not love, I have become as sounding brass or a clanging cymbal.

Note the phrase "I have become." These words indicate a change. The believer here pictured is not now in the same spiritual condition as he was when he was originally baptised in the Holy Spirit.

At that time, he had the assurance that his sins were forgiven and that his heart was cleansed through faith in Christ. He was willing to yield himself, as fully as possible, to the control of the Holy Spirit. In this condition, the initial manifestation of speaking with another tongue indicated that the Holy Spirit had come to indwell the believer and take control of his life.

However, in the period that has since elapsed, the believer here pictured by Paul has retained the outward manifestation but – through carelessness or disobedience – has not retained the same inward condition of cleansing and yieldedness to the Holy Spirit. Thus the process of speaking with tongues has degenerated into a mere outward physical manifestation without any corresponding inward spiritual reality.

To see this experience in its proper perspective, we must set side by side two facts which are confirmed both by Scripture and by experience.

First, at the time of being baptised in the Holy Spirit, a believer must fulfil two conditions: His heart must be purified by faith in Christ, and he must be willing to yield control of his physical members – in particular, his tongue – to the Holy Spirit.

Second, the fact that the believer was cleansed and yielded at the time of his baptism in the Spirit is not an automatic guarantee that he will always remain in that condition, even though he may still continue to speak in tongues.

At this point many people are likely to exclaim: "But surely if the person began to misuse God's gift, God would withdraw the gift from him altogether!"

However, this supposition is not supported either by logic or by Scripture.

From the viewpoint of logic, if a gift, once given, could thereafter be withdrawn at the will of the giver, then it was never a genuine gift in the first place. It was a loan or a conditional deposit, but not a free gift. A free gift, once given, passes out of the control of the giver and is thereafter under the sole control of the one who received it – whether to use, to abuse or not to use at all. Scripture confirms this point of logic: "For the gifts and the calling of God are irrevocable" (Rom. 11:29).

This word *irrevocable* used here of God, and not of man, indicates that once God has given a gift, He never withdraws the gift again. Thereafter the responsibility to make the proper use of the gift rests not with God, the giver, but with man, the receiver. This important principle applies in all areas of God's dealing with man, including that of the gifts of the Spirit.

This conclusion should be weighed with sober care by all those who are seeking or who have received the baptism in the Holy Spirit with the manifestation of speaking with other tongues. According to Scripture, it is not possible to receive this initial baptism without this outward manifestation. But it is possible, thereafter, to have the outward manifestation without retaining the inward fullness of the Spirit.

There is only one sure, scriptural test of continuing fullness of the Holy Spirit, and that is the love test. In the measure that we are filled with the Holy Spirit, in the same measure we shall be filled with divine love. We are not more filled with the Holy Spirit than we are filled with divine love. John applies this test in clear, simple terms.

> No one has seen God at any time. If we love one another, God abides in us, and His love has been perfected in us. By this we know that we abide in Him, and He in us . . . God is love, and he who abides in love abides in God, and God in him (1 John 4:12-13,16).

Likewise, Paul assigns to love a place of unique honour among all God's gifts and graces.

> And now abide faith, hope, love, these three; but the greatest of these is love (1 Cor. 13:13).

Of all the operations of the indwelling Spirit, the greatest and most enduring is the pouring out of divine love in the believer's heart.

In these last four chapters we have considered eight important results which God desires to produce in the life of each individual believer through baptising him in the Holy Spirit.

1. Power to witness.
2. The exalting and glorifying of Christ.
3. A foretaste of heaven's power and an entrance thereby into a supernatural life.
4. Help in prayer, lifting the believer far above his own natural strength or understanding.
5. A new understanding of the Scriptures.
6. Daily guidance in the path of God's will.
7. Life and health for the physical body.
8. The pouring out of God's love in the believer's heart.

In our next section we will consider results produced by this same experience in the life and worship of a Christian congregation.

THE SPIRIT-FILLED CONGREGATION

33
LIBERTY UNDER CONTROL

We shall now go beyond the life of the individual believer to consider the general life and worship of a Christian congregation as a whole. The questions we shall seek to answer are these:

1. What difference does the baptism in the Holy Spirit make in the life and experience of the congregation as a whole?
2. What are the main features which distinguish a congregation in which all or most of the members have received the baptism in the Holy Spirit and are free to exercise the power thus received?
3. How would such a congregation differ from one in which none of the members has received this experience?

To answer these questions, we shall examine two main ways in which a free congregation of Spirit-baptised believers differs from one in which the members have not received the baptism in the Holy Spirit.

Under the Spirit's Lordship

Now the Lord is the Spirit; and where the Spirit of the Lord
is, there is liberty (2 Cor. 3:17).

Paul points out two major facts about the presence and influence of
the Holy Spirit in a congregation. The first is that the Holy Spirit is Lord.
In the New Testament the word *Lord* corresponds in use and meaning to
the name *Jehovah* in the Old Testament. In this usage it is a title reserved
for the one true God, never given to any lesser being or creature.

This title belongs by right to each of the three Persons of the
Godhead. God the Father is Lord, God the Son is Lord, and God the
Holy Spirit is Lord. When Paul says, "The Lord is the Spirit," he is
emphasising the supreme sovereignty of the Holy Spirit in the church.

The second great fact pointed out by Paul is that where the lordship
of the Holy Spirit in the church is acknowledged, the result in a congregation is "liberty" or "freedom." Someone has sought to bring out the
true significance of the second part of this verse by a slight change in the
rendering. Instead of saying, "Where the Spirit of the Lord is, there is
liberty," we may say alternatively, "Where the Spirit is Lord, there is
liberty." True liberty comes to a congregation in measure as its members
acknowledge and yield to the lordship of the Holy Spirit.

Thus we may sum up this first main distinguishing feature of a Spirit-
baptised congregation by putting two words side by side. These two
words are *liberty* and *government*.

At first sight it might appear inconsistent to put these two words
together. Someone might feel inclined to object, "But if we have liberty,
then we are not under government. And if we are under government,
then we do not have liberty." People do, in fact, often feel that liberty and
government are opposite to each other. This applies not only to spiritual
things but also in the political realm.

I am reminded of the political situation in Kenya, in East Africa,
while I was serving there as a college principal from 1957 to 1961.
During that period the African people of Kenya were looking forward
with great eagerness to the time when their country would attain to
complete independence or self-government. The Swahili word used for
independence was *uhuru* – which means literally "liberty" or "freedom"
– and this word was upon everybody's lips. Many of the less-educated
Africans formed wonderful pictures of what this *uhuru* or liberty would
bring to them.

"When *uhuru* comes," they would say, "we shall be able to ride our bicycles on whichever side of the road we please. We shall be able to travel as far as we like in the buses without paying. We shall never have to pay any more taxes to the government."

To more sophisticated people in other lands, statements such as these might appear childish or ridiculous. Such people would argue that conditions such as these would not constitute true liberty but rather anarchy and disorder in their worst degree. Nevertheless, these simple African people were perfectly sincere in the picture of liberty which they had formed for themselves. Their own African political leaders often had difficulty in getting them to understand what liberty or independence would really entail.

The strange thing is that people who are perfectly sophisticated in their understanding of what political liberty means are sometimes quite childish in the picture they form of spiritual liberty.

Such people would smile at Africans who imagine that political liberty means they can ride their bicycles on either side of the road or travel in the buses without paying their fares. Yet the same people would behave in ways no less foolish or disorderly in the house of God, and then they justify their behaviour by the title of "spiritual liberty."

For example, in some congregations, when one member is asked to lead in prayer and to present certain prayer requests to God, there are others who speak so loud in other tongues that it becomes impossible for the rest of the congregation to hear what the appointed prayer leader is saying. This means it is impossible for the congregation to say "Amen" with understanding or faith to a prayer which they could not even hear. In this way, through this foolish misuse of tongues, the whole congregation loses the blessing and the effectiveness of united, wholehearted petition and intercession.

Or again, the preacher may be presenting a logical, scriptural message designed to show to the unsaved the need and the way of salvation. As the preacher approaches the climax of his message, someone in the congregation suddenly bursts out with a loud, ill-timed utterance in tongues. As a result, the whole congregation's attention is distracted from the salvation message. The unbelievers present are either irritated or frightened by what seems to be a senseless and emotional outburst. The force of the carefully prepared message on salvation is lost.

If the person responsible for this kind of foolishness should afterward be reproved, it quite often happens that he makes some such answer as this: "I couldn't help myself! The Holy Spirit made me do it. I had to obey the Holy Spirit." However, such an answer as this cannot be accepted because it is contrary to the clear teaching of the Scriptures.

> But the manifestation of the Spirit is given to each one for the
> profit of all (1 Cor. 12:7).

We may render this more freely: "The manifestation of the Spirit is always given for a useful, practical, sensible purpose."

Thus, if the manifestation is directed to fulfilling the purpose for which it is given, it will always be in harmony with the plan and purpose of the service as a whole and will make a positive contribution to accomplishing that purpose. It will never be meaningless or distracting or out of place.

God Makes Sons, Not Slaves

> And the spirits of the prophets are subject to the prophets. For God is not the author of confusion but of peace, as in all the churches of the saints (1 Cor. 14:32-33).

In other words, any spiritual evidence that is directed and controlled by God will produce peace and harmony, not confusion and disorder.

Any person responsible for an evidence that leads to confusion or disorder cannot excuse himself by saying, "I couldn't help myself! The Holy Spirit made me do it." Paul rules out this line of defence by saying, "The spirits of the prophets are subject to the prophets." In other words, the Holy Spirit never overrides the will of the individual believer and compels him to do something against his own will.

Even when a believer is exercising a spiritual gift, his spirit and his will still remain under his control. He is free to exercise that gift or not to exercise it. The responsibility for exercising it remains with him. As we have said earlier in this study, the Holy Spirit never plays the part of a dictator in the life of a believer.

This is one of the main features which distinguish genuine manifestations of the Holy Spirit from the phenomena of spiritism or demon possession. In many phases of spiritism or demon possession the person who plays the part of the medium (or other vessel of satanic power) is obliged to yield complete control of his whole will and personality to the spirit which seeks to possess him or to operate through him. Very often such a person is then obliged to say or to do things which of his own free will he would never have agreed to say or do.

In some phases of spiritism the person who comes under the control of the spirit loses all understanding or consciousness of what he is saying or doing. At the end of such an experience, the possessed person may come to himself again in entirely strange surroundings after a lapse of many hours, without any knowledge or recollection of what has happened in the intervening period. In this way, both the will and the understanding of the demon-possessed person are entirely set aside.

God the Holy Spirit never acts in this way with the true believer in Christ. Among the most precious of all the endowments which God has bestowed upon man are will and personality. Consequently, God never usurps the will or the personality of the believer. He will operate through them if He is permitted to do so, but He will never set them aside. Satan makes slaves; God makes sons.

We see, then, how wrong and unscriptural it is for Spirit-baptised believers to say concerning any spiritual manifestation: "I couldn't help it! The Holy Spirit made me do it." To speak like this is to represent the indwelling Spirit of God as some kind of despot and the believer as a slave in bondage. Believers who speak like this have not yet come to understand their privileges and responsibilities as sons of God.

> For you did not receive the spirit of bondage [slavery] again to fear, but you received the Spirit of adoption by whom we cry out, "Abba, Father." The Spirit Himself bears witness with our spirit that we are children of God (Rom. 8:15-16).

We are thus brought face-to-face with an important principle which holds good in all human affairs whether political or spiritual: True liberty is impossible without good government. The kind of liberty which seeks to set aside all government or control of any kind ends only in anarchy and confusion. The final result is a new form of slavery, far more severe than the previous form of government which was set aside.

We have seen this happen time after time in the political history of the human race, and the same principle applies equally in the spiritual life of the Christian church. True spiritual liberty is possible only where there is spiritual government. The government which God has appointed for the church is that of the Holy Spirit.

We come back then to the statement of Paul in 2 Corinthians 3:17:

> Now the Lord is the Spirit; and where the Spirit of the Lord is, there is liberty.

If we desire to enjoy the Spirit's liberty, we must first voluntarily acknowledge the Spirit's lordship. These two operations of the Holy Spirit can never be separated from each other.

We must also bear in mind another important fact about the Holy Spirit which we established earlier in this study. The Holy Spirit is both the author and the interpreter of the Scriptures. This means that the Holy Spirit will never direct a believer to say or do anything contrary to the Scriptures. If the Holy Spirit were ever to do this, He would be illogical and inconsistent with Himself, and this we know is impossible.

> But as God is faithful, our word to you was not Yes and No. For the Son of God, Jesus Christ, who was preached among you by us – by me, Silvanus, and Timothy – was not Yes and No, but in Him was Yes (2 Cor. 1:18-19).

Paul is saying that God is never inconsistent with Himself. Concerning any particular matter of doctrine or practice, God never says yes at one time and no at another. If God has ever said yes, then His answer always remains yes. He never changes to no later on. He is never changeable or inconsistent with Himself.

This applies to the relationship between the teaching of Scripture on the one hand and utterances and manifestations of the Holy Spirit on the other. The Holy Spirit, being Himself the author of Scripture, always agrees with Scripture. There is never a possibility of yes and no. Wherever the Bible says no, the Holy Spirit says no. No utterance or manifestation that is inspired and controlled by the Holy Spirit will ever be contrary to the teachings and examples of Scripture.

However, as we have already emphasised, the Holy Spirit in the life of the believer is not a dictator. He does not compel the believer always to act in a scriptural way. The Holy Spirit serves as interpreter and counsellor. He interprets the Scripture; He offers direction and counsel. But the believer still remains free to accept or to reject the Holy Spirit's counsel – to obey or to disobey.

This imposes a tremendous responsibility upon every Spirit-baptised believer. Every such believer is responsible to acquaint himself personally with the mind of the Holy Spirit as revealed in the Scriptures and then to direct his own conduct and behaviour in regard to the exercise of spiritual gifts or manifestations – as in all other matters – so that these harmonise with the principles and examples of Scripture.

If through laziness, indifference or disobedience a Spirit-baptised believer fails to do this and, as a result, exercises spiritual gifts or manifestations in a foolish, unscriptural way, the responsibility for this rests solely upon the believer himself, not upon the Holy Spirit.

In this connection, a special responsibility rests upon every minister called by God to lead the worship and service of a Spirit-baptised congregation. Not only must such a man direct his own spiritual ministry in line with the teaching of Scripture, but he must also allow himself to be, in God's hand, an instrument to direct the worship and ministry of the whole congregation in accordance with the same scriptural principles.

To do this successfully requires, in a high degree, special qualifications: first of all, a thorough, practical knowledge of the Scriptures, and then wisdom, authority and courage. Where these qualities are lacking in the leadership, a congregation that seeks to exercise spiritual gifts and manifestations will be like a ship at sea in the midst of powerful winds and treacherous shoals with an ill-trained and inexperienced captain in charge. Small wonder if the end is a wreck!

I have now been associated with full-gospel ministry for more than fifty years. During those years I have observed two things which have done more than anything else to hinder the acceptance of the testimony of the full gospel. The first is the failure to exercise proper control over the public manifestation of spiritual gifts, particularly the gift of tongues; the second is strife and division among Spirit-baptised believers, both among members of the same congregation and between one congregation and another. Each of these has its origin in one and the same error: the failure to acknowledge the effective lordship of the Holy Spirit.

We are now in a position to offer a definition of true spiritual liberty: Spiritual liberty consists in acknowledging the effective lordship of the Holy Spirit in the church. Where the Spirit is Lord, there is liberty.

Times and Seasons

So many Spirit-baptised believers have their own particular concept of liberty. Some imagine that liberty consists in shouting. If only we can shout loud enough and long enough, they seem to think, we shall work ourselves up into liberty. But the Holy Spirit is never worked up; He either comes down or He flows forth from within. In either case His manifestation is free and spontaneous, never laborious or wearisome.

Other Spirit-baptised believers lay all their emphasis on some other type of expression or manifestation, such as singing or clapping hands or dancing. In many cases the reason for this is that God once blessed them along those lines and they have come to believe that God's blessing will always continue to come along this same line and never along any other. God blessed them once when they were shouting, so they always want to shout. Or God blessed them once when they were dancing, so they always want to dance.

They have become so limited in their outlook and concept of the Holy Spirit that they can never conceive of God's blessing them in any other way. Quite often they even despise other believers who will not join them in their shouting or their dancing or their hand-clapping. They may suggest that these other believers are not really "free in the Spirit."

Let us be careful to add that there is not necessarily anything unscriptural in shouting or dancing or clapping hands. The Bible provides clear examples of all these things in the worship of God's people. But it certainly is unscriptural and also foolish to suggest that any of these forms of expression necessarily constitutes true spiritual liberty.

A person who believes he must always worship God by shouting or dancing or hand-clapping no longer enjoys true spiritual liberty; on the contrary, he has returned under a special kind of religious bondage of his own making. Such a person is as much under bondage as the Christian at the opposite end of the religious scale who knows of no other way to worship God than with the words and forms of a printed liturgy.

A wonderful key to true spiritual liberty is found in the words of Solomon.

> To everything there is a season,
> A time for every purpose under heaven:
> A time to be born,
> And a time to die;
> A time to plant,
> And a time to pluck what is planted;
> A time to kill,
> And a time to heal;
> A time to break down,
> And a time to build up;
> A time to weep,
> And a time to laugh;
> A time to mourn,
> And a time to dance;
> A time to cast away stones,
> And a time to gather stones;
> A time to embrace,
> And a time to refrain from embracing;
> A time to gain,
> And a time to lose;

A time to keep,
And a time to throw away;
A time to tear,
And a time to sew;
A time to keep silence,
And a time to speak;
A time to love,
And a time to hate;
A time of war,
And a time of peace (Eccl. 3:1-8).

Solomon here mentions twenty-eight forms of activity, set out in fourteen pairs of opposites. In each pair of opposites it is right at one time to do the one and at another time to do the other. We can never say without qualification, it is always right to do the one or always wrong to do the other. Whether each is right or wrong is decided by the time or the season.

Many of these pairs of opposites relate to the life and worship of a congregation, such as planting or plucking up; killing or healing; breaking down or building up; weeping or laughing; mourning or dancing; gathering or casting away; keeping silence or speaking.

None of these is either absolutely right or absolutely wrong. Each is right if done at the right time and wrong if done at the wrong time.

How, then, shall we know which to do, or when? The answer is, this is the sovereign office of the Holy Spirit as Lord in the church. He reveals and directs what to do, and when. A congregation that is directed by the Holy Spirit will do the right thing at the right time. This is the source of all true liberty, harmony and unity. Apart from this, there are only varying degrees of bondage, discord and disunity.

In the next chapter we shall go on to consider one further distinctive feature that marks the life and worship of a congregation where the members have been baptised in the Holy Spirit and have liberty to exercise this power.

34
TOTAL PARTICIPATION OF
THE MEMBERS

We shall now go on to examine a second distinctive feature of a Spirit-filled congregation.

In the regular services of most Christian churches today, almost all the real initiative and activity are confined to just a few individuals. The congregation may take part in certain pre-arranged activities, such as the singing of hymns from a book or the repetition of fixed prayers or responses. There may also be, within the main congregation, one or two smaller, specially trained groups – such as the choir or an orchestra. But apart from this all real initiative and activity are left in the hands of one or two individuals while most of the rest of the congregation remains passive.

One person leads the singing; one person prays; one person preaches. Sometimes two or more, even of these activities, may be combined in one person. From the rest of the congregation little more is expected or required than an occasional "Amen."

However, if we examine the life and worship of the early church as portrayed in the New Testament, we find there was active participation by all the believers present in any service. This was brought about by the supernatural presence and power of the Holy Spirit operating in and through the individual believers.

The Lamp on the Lampstand

Further study of this New Testament pattern reveals that the supernatural gifts or manifestations of the Holy Spirit are not given primarily to the individual believer. Rather they are given, through the vessel of the individual believer, to the church or congregation as a whole. Therefore they cannot achieve their proper purpose unless they are freely manifested and exercised in the life of the congregation.

In 1 Corinthians 12 Paul indicates how the gifts of the individual believers are intended to function within the corporate life of the congregation.

First he lists nine specific supernatural gifts or manifestations of the Holy Spirit, ending with the words:

> But one and the same Spirit works all these things, distributing to each one individually as He wills (1 Cor. 12:11).

This last phrase indicates that these gifts or manifestations are given in the first instance to individual believers. However, Paul does not end there.

In the next sixteen verses of the same chapter – verses 12-27 – Paul goes on to say that the Christian church is like one body with many members, and he likens each individual believer to a single member of the one body, ending with the words: "Now you are the body of Christ, and members individually."

The lesson therefore is that, though the spiritual gifts are given to individual believers, they are given to enable those believers to play their proper part in the church – the body of Christ – as a whole. Thus spiritual gifts are not intended primarily for the benefit of the individual but for the life and worship of the whole congregation.

Paul makes the same point again in the very next verse.

> And God has appointed these in the church: first apostles, second prophets, third teachers, after that miracles, then gifts of healings, helps, administrations, varieties of tongues (1 Cor. 12:28).

Paul says that all of these various ministries and giftings have been set by God in the church. That is, they are intended not merely for private use by individual believers but for public manifestation in the church, the congregation of God's people as a whole.

This same truth is vividly illustrated by a brief parable of Jesus.

> Nor do they light a lamp and put it under a basket, but on a lampstand, and it gives light to all who are in the house (Matt. 5:15).

The two main symbols used in this parable are the lamp and the lampstand. The symbol of the lampstand may be interpreted by reference to Revelation 1:20.

> The seven lampstands which you saw are the seven churches.

Throughout the whole of Scripture, a lampstand is used as a symbol of a church or a congregation.

The symbol of the lighted lamp may be interpreted by reference to Proverbs 20:27.

> The spirit of a man is the lamp of the Lord.

Thus the lighted lamp is a symbol of the spirit of the Spirit-baptised believer, made to burn and to shine by the fire of the indwelling Spirit.

Just as the lamp is appointed to take its place on the lampstand, so the Spirit-baptised believer is appointed to take his place in the public congregation of the church. A believer who has been baptised in the Holy Spirit but never exercises any spiritual gift in the service of the congregation is like a lamp under a basket. He fails to fulfil the purpose for which God gave him the gift.

When the presence and power of the Holy Spirit are publicly manifested through the various believers, the whole life and worship of the congregation are completely transformed. The main responsibility for the ministry and the conduct of the service is no longer borne by one or two individuals while the rest remain passive.

On the contrary, every member of the congregation participates actively in the service, and the various members minister to each other, rather than one or two ministering all the time to all the rest.

This is the pattern indicated by Paul's example of the body and its members, and it is confirmed by the words of Peter.

> As each one has received a gift, minister it to one another, as good stewards of the manifold grace of God. If anyone speaks, let him speak as the oracles of God. If anyone ministers, let him do it as with the ability which God supplies, that in all things God may be glorified through Jesus Christ (1 Pet. 4:10-11).

Peter here speaks of God's grace being manifold. That is, God's grace is so rich, so many-sided, that a different aspect of that grace can be manifested through each individual member in the total worship and service of God's people. In this way every member of the church may receive his own special manifestation and may thus have something to minister in turn to all the other members.

Peter emphasises that every member of the church is included; no one need be left without a gift or a ministry. He says: "As each one has received a gift, minister it to one another" (1 Pet. 4:10). And again, in the next verse: "If anyone speaks . . . If anyone ministers" (1 Pet. 4:11). There is no question here of a church with one or two "professional," full-time ministers, while all the remaining members are largely passive or inactive. Every member is included in God's programme of supernatural ministry in the church; each one may have a gift; anyone may speak; anyone may minister.

This picture of the church with every member active is confirmed by the words of Paul.

> For I say, through the grace given to me, to everyone who is among you, not to think of himself more highly than he ought to think, but to think soberly, as God has dealt to each one a measure of faith. For as we have many members in one body, but all the members do not have the same function, so we, being many, are one body in Christ, and individually members of one another. Having then gifts differing according to the grace that is given to us, let us use them: if prophecy, let us prophesy in proportion to our faith; or ministry, let us use it in our ministering; he who teaches, in teaching; he who exhorts, in exhortation; he who gives, with liberality; he who leads, with diligence; he who shows mercy, with cheerfulness (Rom. 12:3-8).

In these verses Paul once again likens the Christian church to a body, of which each individual believer is a member, and he lays great stress on the activity of each member. Notice the repetition of phrases such as "each one," "the members," "everyone."

Paul teaches that God has allotted to each member a special function, a special ministry. In conjunction with this, God has also made a double provision for the effective exercise of that ministry: 1) the measure of faith and 2) the special gifts which the ministry requires. In this way each member is fully equipped for his task.

Thus the New Testament picture of the church is that of a vigorous, active body in which each individual member properly fulfils his special function. A church in which only one or two members had any active ministry would be, by New Testament standards, like a body in which, let us say, the head, one hand and one foot were strong and active, and all the rest of the body was paralysed and useless. Obviously such a body, considered as a whole, could never fulfil its proper function.

Paul lays particular emphasis upon the supernatural ministry imparted by the Holy Spirit to every member of a New Testament church.

> But the manifestation of the Spirit is given to each one for the profit of all (1 Cor. 12:7).

And again, concerning the nine supernatural gifts of the Holy Spirit:

> But one and the same Spirit works all these things, distributing to each one individually as He wills (1 Cor. 12:11).

Notice carefully what Paul says here: "the manifestation of the Spirit [the manifest, public demonstration of the indwelling Spirit] is given to each one [to every member of the church]" (1 Cor. 12:7). And again: All these nine supernatural gifts the Holy Spirit distributes "to each one individually [to every member]" (1 Cor. 12:11).

The Exercise of Spiritual Gifts

These words make it plain that it is the express will of God for every member of the church to exercise spiritual gifts – that is, the open, public, supernatural manifestation of the indwelling Spirit. If all believers do not in fact have these gifts in operation, it is not because God withholds them but simply because such believers through ignorance or carelessness or unbelief fail to press on into the fullness of God's revealed will for His people.

Such believers have failed to obey Paul's exhortation to "earnestly desire the best gifts" (1 Cor. 12:31). He further urges believers to "pursue love, and desire spiritual gifts, but especially that you may prophesy" (1 Cor. 14:1).

There are three spiritual gifts about which Paul is particularly specific: tongues, interpretation and prophecy.

> I wish you all spoke with tongues, but even more that you prophesied (1 Cor. 14:5).

Since Paul is here writing under the inspiration of the Holy Spirit, his words impart to the church the revealed will of God for all His believing people both to speak with tongues and to prophesy. If there are believers who do not enjoy the exercise of these gifts, it is not because God has withheld them but simply because those believers have not entered into the fullness of their inheritance in Christ.

The Lord said to Joshua and to His people under the old covenant:

> There remains very much land yet to be possessed (Josh. 13:1).

So it is also with God's people under the new covenant today. Paul says also:

> Therefore let him who speaks in a tongue pray that he may interpret (1 Cor. 14:13).

God's Word never tells us to pray for something out of God's will. Therefore, we know it is God's will for anyone who speaks in tongues also to interpret that utterance. Since Paul has already said it is God's will for all to speak in tongues, it is therefore also God's will for all to interpret.

> For you can all prophesy one by one, that all may learn and all may be encouraged (1 Cor. 14:31).

Nothing could be plainer than this. It is within the revealed will of God for all the members of the church to exercise the spiritual gift of prophecy. Paul imposes only two limitations. Here in the verse just quoted he says, "One by one." That is, believers are to exercise this gift by turns, not more than one believer prophesying at any one time. The purpose of this is obvious and is stated a few verses further on. It is to avoid confusion.

> Let two or three prophets speak, and let the others [the other
> members] judge (1 Cor. 14:29).

Paul here limits the number who may prophesy in any service to "two
or three." The purpose of this is that the whole service should not be
monopolised by one particular form of spiritual manifestation. The
exercise of prophecy has its place in the service, but it does not make up
the whole service. The ministry of the Holy Spirit through God's people
is much more varied than that. Many other different forms of ministry
are required to make up a complete service.

In this verse Paul also says clearly that the exercise of the gift of
prophecy must be judged or tested. He says, "Let the others judge." The
"others" would include the rest of the Spirit-baptised believers present
who are capable of recognising the genuine manifestation of the gift of
prophecy. Even in this we see that Paul brings in all the members. He
does not specify merely one professional minister who is to judge, but
he makes the believers as a whole responsible to do this.

> Do not quench the Spirit.
> Do not despise prophecies.
> Test all things; hold fast what is good (1 Thess. 5:19-21).

These three verses are addressed to Christian believers generally, and
they must be taken closely together. It is wrong for believers to quench
the Spirit – to reject the moving and manifestation of the Holy Spirit in
their midst. It is also wrong for believers to despise prophesyings – to
adopt an attitude of criticism, contempt or unbelief toward the manifestation of the gift of prophecy.

On the other hand, when this gift is manifested, believers are responsible to test it by the standards of Scripture – and then to hold fast, to
accept, to retain only that which is good, only that which accords with
the standards of Scripture.

We see, then, that Paul is careful to guard against anything that might
be spurious or disorderly in the exercise or manifestation of spiritual
gifts. However, with this one qualification, he repeatedly and emphatically states that all believers in the church can and should exercise the
open manifestation of spiritual gifts. He particularly specifies the three
gifts of tongues, interpretation and prophecy.

What is the result in a church when all its members freely and publicly exercise supernatural spiritual gifts in this way?

Paul describes the kind of services which result from this.

> How is it then, brethren? Whenever you come together, each of you has a psalm, has a teaching, has a tongue, has a revelation, has an interpretation. Let all things be done for edification (1 Cor. 14:26).

That phrase "each of you has" sets a pattern. It implies active participation by all the members.

Generally speaking, when Christians come together today, they do so with the primary purpose of receiving, not of contributing. They come to get a blessing, to receive healing, to hear a preacher.

But this was not the way of the New Testament church. There the members came not primarily to receive but to contribute. Every one of them had something committed to him individually by the Holy Spirit which he was in turn able to contribute to the total worship and service of the church.

Paul mentions various possible forms of contribution. A *psalm* would denote some form of musical contribution. This might be the product either of natural talent or of the supernatural enabling of the Holy Spirit. A *teaching* would denote the ability to impart some truth from the teaching of God's Word. A *tongue* and an *interpretation* might be taken to cover generally the three gifts of supernatural utterance – tongues, interpretation and prophecy. A *revelation* would cover any one of the three main revelatory gifts – the word of wisdom, the word of knowledge and discernment of spirits.

In this way – mainly through the operation of the supernatural spiritual gifts – all the members had something of their own to contribute toward the total worship and service of the church. They were thus able to fulfil the injunction given by Peter.

> As each one has received a gift, minister it to one another (1 Pet. 4:10).

Peter brings out the same point as Paul. The ability of the members to minister effectively to one another was due mainly to the fact that they had received these supernatural spiritual gifts. They were thus lifted out of the limitations of their own education or natural talent into a much higher realm of spiritual freedom.

Had their ability to minister to each other depended on education or natural talent, many of them would have been left with very little to contribute. The result would have been just what we see in most churches today. The main burden of ministry would have fallen upon just a few of the members, while the rest would have remained largely passive or inactive, without any real opportunities for spiritual expression or development.

Why is it that so many professional ministers in our modern churches suffer mental or nervous breakdowns?

The answer is that, in many cases, one member is struggling to carry a burden of ministry which God never laid upon him. One member is seeking to fulfil a ministry which God intended to be divided up among all the members in the church. The almost inevitable result is some kind of breakdown.

The only escape from the limitations and frustrations of this situation is through the supernatural ministry of the Holy Spirit in the church, dividing spiritual gifts to all the members individually, according to His own will. This delivers believers from their own natural limitations and lifts them into a spiritual realm where they can share together the burden of the total ministry of the church.

When all the members are thus equipped to function in their individual ministries, the church as a whole can fulfil its corporate role as the body of Christ.

THE SPIRIT-FILLED
PREACHER

35
CONVICTION OF ETERNAL ISSUES

In the last two chapters we considered the effects of the baptism in the Holy Spirit upon the general life and worship of a Christian congregation.

We shall now focus our attention upon the special ministry of the preacher – that is, the believer called by God to the vital ministry of preaching God's Word. The questions we shall seek to answer are these:

1. What special results are produced in the ministry of the preacher by the baptism in the Holy Spirit?
2. In what main ways does the ministry of a preacher who is empowered by the Holy Spirit differ from that of one who is not?

In considering the relationship between the Holy Spirit and the ministry of the preacher, it is appropriate to begin with the words of Peter. He reminds the early church of the example and the standard set before them by the preachers who had brought the gospel message to them. He speaks of those "who have preached the gospel to you by the

Holy Spirit sent from heaven" (1 Pet. 1:12).

These words bring out the main distinctive nature of the New Testament preachers. They did not depend primarily upon education or eloquence or natural talents; they preached by the Holy Spirit sent from heaven. They reckoned and depended upon the real, personal presence and power of the Holy Spirit working in them, through them and with them. Every other means and talent they employed was kept subservient to this one controlling influence: the presence and power of the Holy Spirit.

What results follow when the pre-eminence of the Holy Spirit is thus acknowledged in the ministry of the preacher?

Sin, Righteousness and Judgement

> And when He [the Holy Spirit] has come, He will convict the world of sin, and of righteousness, and of judgement (John 16:8).

An alternative translation for "convict" is "convince." He "will convince the world of sin, and of righteousness, and of judgement."

We might paraphrase this: "The Holy Spirit will press home upon the attention of the unbelieving world the issues of sin, righteousness and judgement in such a way that it will no longer be possible for the world to ignore or deny these issues."

These three things – sin, righteousness and judgement – are the abiding eternal realities upon which all true religion is based.

Paul reminded the proud, intellectual, self-sufficient Athenian people of this basic issue of God's judgement.

> [God] has appointed a day on which He will judge the world in righteousness (Acts 17:31).

Judgement is a divine appointment. No one is excused; no one is exempted; no one can escape. God's appointment is with the world, the entire human race. In this judgement God is concerned with only one issue: righteousness. God will not judge men in respect of their wealth or their cleverness or their religious profession. He is concerned only about righteousness.

The nature of this issue is simply defined: "All unrighteousness is sin" (1 John 5:17). In respect of moral conduct, there is only one alternative to righteousness, and that is sin. Sin must be defined in terms of righteousness. The negative must be defined in terms of the positive.

If we were asked to explain the word *crooked,* the simplest way to begin would be by demonstrating the meaning of *straight.* We could draw a straight line and say, "This is straight." Then we could go on to say, "Any other line extending between the same two points that does not follow the course of this line is crooked."

The exact extent to which the crooked line deviates from the straight is a matter of secondary importance. It may deviate by one degree, or it may deviate by many degrees. This makes no difference. Whether it deviates by little or by much, it is still crooked.

So it is with sin and righteousness. All unrighteousness is sin. Every form of moral conduct that is not righteous is sinful. God has established His divine standard of righteousness. Anything which departs from that in any degree, small or great, is sinful.

What is God's standard of righteousness? The answer is given in the second part of the verse we have already quoted from Paul's speech at Athens.

> . . . because He has appointed a day on which He will judge the world in righteousness by the Man whom He has ordained. He has given assurance of this to all by raising Him from the dead (Acts 17:31).

What is God's standard of righteousness, here stated? It is not a moral code or a golden rule; it is not even the Ten Commandments. It is the one kind of standard perfectly suited to the human race. It is a man – that man whom God has ordained.

Who is this man? It is the man to whom God has given testimony or assurance by raising him from the dead. It is the Man Jesus Christ. He alone is God's standard of righteousness for the human race. To understand this standard we must study the life and character of Jesus as portrayed in the New Testament. Every aspect of human character or conduct that falls below the standard of Jesus falls below God's standard of righteousness.

Paul presents the same truth concerning the nature of righteousness and sin, as found in Romans 3:23.

> For all have sinned and fall short of the glory of God.

Paul does not specify any one particular type of sin. He does not specify pride or lust or murder or lies. There is only one point in which he asserts that all are alike guilty: All have come short of the glory of God; all have failed to live for God's glory; all have failed to live up to the divine standard; all have come short; all have missed the mark.

This standard of God's glory points us again to Jesus, both "the brightness of His [the Father's] glory and the express image of His person" (Heb. 1:3).

Jesus Christ alone of all men who have ever lived, lived out His entire life by this one standard and for this one purpose – the glory of God, His Father.

Here then, defined and demonstrated for all to see, are the three basic issues upon which the eternal destiny of every human soul depends – sin, righteousness and judgement.

Yet the human race, in its own natural, unregenerate condition, is totally unconcerned about these issues. This is because fallen man is the slave of his own carnal mind. His one normal means of contact with reality is through his fleshly nature – through his five senses. He is moved and impressed only by the aspects of reality which are revealed by his senses. He is therefore shut up in the realm of the carnal and the material. It is the things in this realm which impress him and influence him, which occupy his time, his thoughts, his energy.

Listen to people of the world talking casually together in any public place – a bus, a train or a restaurant. What is the most common topic of conversation? Without a doubt, it is money. I have proved this by personal observation, listening to people talk in many different languages and in many different lands.

After money there come a variety of other topics, all connected in some way with man's physical and material well-being, his pleasures, his comforts, his luxuries. Among the most common of these topics we might mention sports, entertainment, politics, food, business, farming, family affairs, cars, clothing and household equipment.

These are the things which normally monopolise the thought and speech of the people of this world. Among them no place is found for the three issues of sin, righteousness and judgement.

Why is this? The answer is simple. These three things cannot be apprehended through man's carnal senses. For the man who is shut up within the prison of his own senses and his own carnal understanding, sin, righteousness and judgement have no reality or importance whatever.

There is only one means by which these things can be made real for men and women, and that is through the working of God's Holy Spirit. He alone can convince the world of these unseen, eternal realities. In proportion as the Holy Spirit gains access to men's hearts and minds, they become concerned about sin, righteousness and judgement.

In Psalm 14:2-3 we are given a divinely inspired picture of the whole human race as God sees them, in their own natural, fallen condition, apart from the influence of God's grace and the working of God's Spirit. The psalmist here says:

> The Lord looks down from heaven upon the children of men,
> To see if there are any who understand, who seek God.
> They have all turned aside,
> They have together become corrupt;
> There is none who does good,
> No, not one.

Notice what the psalmist here says about man's natural condition. It is not merely that there is none who does good. Man's spiritual depravity goes much deeper than that. There is none who understands, none who seeks God. Even the understanding of spiritual things and the desire to know God are totally absent. Until God through His Holy Spirit reaches down to man, man, left to himself, never reaches out to God or seeks after God.

> And you He made alive, who were dead in trespasses and sins (Eph. 2:1).

Apart from the quickening influence of the Holy Spirit, man's spiritual condition is one of death. He is dead to God and to spiritual realities. Sin, righteousness and judgement have no meaning or reality for him.

This does not mean that man in this condition is necessarily without religion. On the contrary, religion may play a great part in his life. But religion apart from the moving of the Holy Spirit can be the most deadening of all influences, lulling man into a false sense of security and into callousness and indifference concerning those vital spiritual issues upon which the destiny of his soul depends.

Paul gives a prophetic picture of the main moral features which will characterise the human race at the close of the present age.

> But know this, that in the last days perilous times will come:
> For men will be lovers of themselves, lovers of money,
> boasters, proud, blasphemers, disobedient to parents,

> unthankful, unholy, unloving, unforgiving, slanderers, without self-control, brutal, despisers of good, traitors, headstrong, haughty, lovers of pleasure rather than lovers of God, having a form of godliness but denying its power. And from such people turn away! (2 Tim. 3:1-5).

Paul here lists eighteen major moral blemishes that will mar human life and conduct as this age draws to its close. The first two such moral blemishes in his list are "lovers of themselves" and "lovers of money." The last in the list is "lovers of pleasure rather than lovers of God." By the unerring insight of the Holy Spirit, Paul has pointed out three major marks of our contemporary civilisation: "love of self," "love of money," "love of pleasure."

In between these are fifteen other features of moral decline, all of which have been manifested in the twentieth century more openly and on a larger scale than at any previous period of world history.

Yet the most challenging aspect of this whole situation is that, in the midst of this universal moral decline, there is no absence of religion. After listing these eighteen moral blemishes, Paul adds, ". . . having a form of godliness, but denying its power."

In other words, the people guilty of these moral sins are not people without religion. They have a form of godliness – a form of religion – but it is a religion in which there is no room for the presence and power of the Holy Spirit. As a result, there is no sensitivity to spiritual things; no awareness of basic spiritual realities; no conviction of sin, righteousness or judgement.

It follows from this that to preach the gospel without the accompanying influence of the Holy Spirit is a totally useless endeavour. It is presenting a remedy to people who have no consciousness of a need; a cure to people who have no consciousness of being sick. The only reaction this can produce is indifference or scorn.

The greatest enemy of evangelistic activity is not communism or false cults. It is materialism and indifference. The only power that can break down this barrier of materialism is the power of the Holy Spirit. "When He [the Holy Spirit] has come, He will convict the world of sin, and of righteousness, and of judgement" (John 16:8).

It is not mere preaching that the world needs; it is preaching like that of the early church – preaching by the Holy Spirit sent from heaven.

Wielding the Spirit's Sword

Let us look briefly at the examples of this type of preaching recorded in the book of Acts and at the results it produced.

On the day of Pentecost, before the coming of the Holy Spirit, the 120 believers in the upper room in Jerusalem were an unimpressive, uninfluential minority. But after they had been filled with the Holy Spirit, Peter stood up and preached a sermon to a crowd of several thousand Jewish people who had gathered. What were the results of this one sermon?

> Now when they heard this, they were cut to the heart, and said to Peter and the rest of the apostles, "Men and brethren, what shall we do?" (Acts 2:37).

Notice the phrase "they were cut to the heart." This cutting to the heart is the operation of the Holy Spirit which Jesus foretold:

> When He [the Holy Spirit] has come, He will convict the world of sin, and of righteousness, and of judgement (John 16:8).

As a result of this conviction, before the day closed three thousand unbelieving Jews had repented, acknowledged Jesus as Lord and Saviour and been baptised.

However, it is important to emphasise that these results were not achieved by the supernatural manifestation of the Holy Spirit alone, but by this manifestation followed by the preaching of God's Word.

> It pleased God through the foolishness of the message preached to save those who believe (1 Cor. 1:21).

God has never ordained that men should be saved through witnessing miracles or through hearing prophetic utterances. These supernatural manifestations serve to arrest men's attention and to open their hearts to the truth. But it is only through the preaching of God's Word that men are actually saved.

This confirms Paul's statement that "the sword of the Spirit . . . is the word of God" (Eph. 6:17).

If Peter had not stood up on the day of Pentecost and preached a message from God's Word, the Holy Spirit would still have been mightily present with the disciples. But He would have been left without any sword to wield. There would still have been awe and amazement on the part of the unbelievers, but there would have been no conversions. It was the sharp, two-edged sword of God's Word, wielded by the Holy Spirit through the lips of Peter, that cut these unbelievers right to their hearts and brought them under such deep conviction.

Almost half of Peter's sermon consists of quotations from the Old Testament. So great is the impact of God's written Word when it is pressed home to the human heart by the power of the Holy Spirit.

In Acts chapters 6 and 7 we read how Stephen was accused of blasphemy and arraigned before the Jewish council in Jerusalem. At the opening of the trial scene Stephen is accused, and the members of the council are the accusers. But before the trial closes these roles have been reversed.

As Stephen, under the anointing of the Holy Spirit, expounds to the council the Old Testament Scriptures relating to Israel and the Messiah, it is Stephen who becomes the accuser and the members of the council who are accused.

> When they heard these things they [the council] were cut to the heart, and they gnashed at him with their teeth (Acts 7:54).

Notice the same phrase again: "cut to the heart." Once more we see that the sword of God's Word, wielded by the Holy Spirit, reached into the hearts of those unbelievers and wounded them there most deeply.

One of the witnesses of Stephen's trial and martyrdom was a young man named Saul of Tarsus. This incident evidently had an effect on Saul, for when Jesus appeared to him later on the Damascus road, He said:

> It is hard for you to kick against the goads (Acts 9:5).

What were these goads from which Saul was seeking vainly to escape? They were the sharp goads of God's Word, which had been pressed home to his heart by the Holy Spirit through the lips of Stephen.

Acts 24 describes another trial in which Paul was now the accused, arraigned concerning his faith in Christ, and the Roman governor Felix was the judge. In this trial, once again, the Holy Spirit reversed the roles of accuser and accused, for as Paul "reasoned about righteousness, self-control, and the judgement to come, Felix was afraid" (Acts 24:25). The Holy Spirit, through Paul, pressed home to the heart of Felix these truths of righteousness and judgement. The proud Roman governor, accustomed to having prisoners tremble before him, found himself trembling in the presence of an unseen judge and hastily dismissed the court without any judgement being pronounced.

These examples from the book of Acts illustrate the supernatural power of the Holy Spirit to convict men of sin, righteousness and judgement. But they also show that conviction is not the same as conversion, nor does it necessarily lead to conversion. There is one thing, however, that the Holy Spirit, by His convicting power, most surely does: He leaves no further room for neutrality. Jesus says:

> He who is not with Me is against Me, and he who does not gather with Me scatters abroad (Matt. 12:30).

Where the convicting power of the Holy Spirit is manifested, every person who comes under the influence of that power is compelled to take a definite stand – either with Christ or against Him; either gathering or scattering. Compromise or neutrality are no longer possible.

> Do not think that I came to bring peace on earth. I did not come to bring peace but a sword. For I have come to "set a man against his father, a daughter against her mother, and a daughter-in-law against her mother-in-law" (Matt. 10:34-35).

The sword of which Jesus here speaks is the sword of God's Word. As this Word is ministered in the power of the Holy Spirit, it is so sharp and so penetrating that it leaves no place anymore for neutrality or compromise. It divides even among members of the same family, compelling each one individually to take a stand, either with Christ or against Him.

We live in a civilisation marked by materialism, indifference, compromise and moral and spiritual decline. Is there anything that can arrest the course of this decline and turn our generation back to God?

Yes, there is one thing that can do this, and only one: the power of the Holy Spirit working through the Word of God, convincing the world of sin, of righteousness and of judgement.

36
SUPERNATURAL ATTESTATION

We shall now examine one further important result produced by the baptism in the Holy Spirit in the ministry of the preacher.

> How shall we escape if we neglect so great a salvation, which at the first began to be spoken by the Lord, and was confirmed to us by those who heard Him, God also bearing witness both with signs and wonders, with various miracles, and gifts of the Holy Spirit, according to His own will? (Heb. 2:3-4).

The writer here states three reasons why the gospel message should command the most careful attention of all who hear it: 1) because it was preached initially by the Lord Jesus Christ Himself; 2) because the message was then transmitted and recorded by men who themselves heard and saw all that took place; 3) because this message, so transmitted, was further supernaturally attested by the signs and wonders, miracles and gifts of the Holy Spirit which accompanied the message.

From this we see that one main ministry of the Holy Spirit, in relation to the preaching of the gospel, is to bear supernatural testimony, through signs, wonders, miracles and gifts, to the divine authority and truth of the message preached.

With Accompanying Signs

This is in line with the commission Jesus gave to His disciples at the close of His earthly ministry.

> Go into all the world and preach the gospel to every creature (Mark 16:15).

> And these signs will follow [or accompany] those who believe: In My name they will cast out demons; they will speak with new tongues; they will take up serpents; and if they drink anything deadly, it will by no means hurt them; they will lay hands on the sick, and they will recover (Mark 16:17-18).

In these verses Jesus specifies five supernatural signs ordained by God to accompany the preaching of the gospel message and to bear divine testimony to its truth.

1. The ability to cast out demons.
2. The manifestation of speaking with new tongues (elsewhere called "other tongues").
3. Immunity to harm from snakes.
4. Immunity to harm from poison in drink or food.
5. The ability to minister healing to the sick by laying hands on them in the name of Jesus.

The introductory phrase used by Jesus, "in My name," applies to each of the five signs that are specified. Each of them is effective only through faith in the name of Jesus.

It should also be pointed out that these five supernatural signs are not limited to any special class or category of people. Jesus does not say, "These signs will follow apostles," "These signs will follow preachers," or "These signs will follow the early church." He says, "These signs will follow those who believe." All true believers have a right to expect that these supernatural signs will accompany and confirm their testimony as, in obedience to Christ's command, they seek to proclaim the good news of the gospel to all men.

This was precisely how the first disciples interpreted and applied the commission of Jesus.

> So then, after the Lord had spoken to them, He was received up into heaven, and sat down at the right hand of God. And they went out and preached everywhere, the Lord working with them and confirming the word through the accompanying signs (Mark 16:19-20).

This supernatural testimony to the disciples' preaching only came into full effect after the Lord Jesus had been received up into heaven and had taken His place at the Father's right hand. Thereafter the Lord Jesus worked with His disciples and confirmed their testimony not by His own bodily presence on earth, but through the presence and power of the Holy Spirit poured out upon them on the day of Pentecost. Thus it was the Holy Spirit who was actually responsible for the supernatural confirmation of the disciples' testimony. It is His special office to bear supernatural testimony to the truth of God's message.

We find this illustrated in the ministry both of Jesus and of the disciples. Up to the time of His baptism by John in the river Jordan, there is no record that Jesus ever preached or performed a miracle. At the time of His baptism, the Holy Spirit descended upon Him from heaven in the form of a dove, and He was then led into the wilderness to be tempted for forty days by the devil. At the close of this period of temptation, Jesus immediately entered into His public preaching ministry. For the next three and a half years His message and ministry were continuously attested to by a great variety of miracles, signs and supernatural gifts.

By quoting a prophecy of Isaiah, Jesus publicly declared that this supernatural testimony to His ministry was the work of the Holy Spirit.

> The Spirit of the Lord is upon Me,
> Because He has anointed Me to preach the gospel to the poor.
> He has sent Me to heal the broken-hearted,
> To preach deliverance to the captives
> And recovery of sight to the blind,
> To set at liberty those who are oppressed,
> To preach the acceptable year of the Lord (Luke 4:18-19).

Here Jesus very clearly ascribes to the anointing of the Holy Spirit upon Him, both in His preaching and the miracles of mercy and deliverance that accompanied it.

> But if I cast out demons by the Spirit of God, surely the
> kingdom of God has come upon you (Matt. 12:28).

Here Jesus directly attributes to the Holy Spirit the power that He
possessed to cast out demons.

That the anointing of the Holy Spirit was responsible for the supernatural confirmation of Christ's ministry is stated also by Peter in the
book of Acts. He spoke to the Jews concerning Jesus in the following
terms:

> Jesus of Nazareth, a Man attested by God to you by miracles,
> wonders, and signs which God did through Him in your
> midst, as you yourselves also know (Acts 2:22).

Peter indicates that one purpose of the miracles, wonders and signs in
the ministry of Jesus was to approve or to attest the divine origin and
authority of His ministry, and that it was God Himself who gave this
testimony to the ministry of Jesus. Speaking to Gentiles in the household
of Cornelius, Peter describes the ministry of Jesus in the following
terms:

> God anointed Jesus of Nazareth with the Holy Spirit and with
> power, who went about doing good and healing all who were
> oppressed by the devil, for God was with Him (Acts 10:38).

Here Peter specifically attributes the supernatural ministry and
healing power of Jesus to the anointing of the Holy Spirit upon Him.

As it was in the ministry of Jesus, so it was also in the ministry of His
disciples. Before the day of Pentecost there was a measure of the supernatural in their ministry. The first twelve disciples whom Jesus sent out
are described this way:

> So they went out and preached that people should repent. And
> they cast out many demons, and anointed with oil many who
> were sick, and healed them (Mark 6:12-13).

The ministry of the seventy disciples whom Jesus sent out later was
described similarly.

> Then the seventy returned with joy, saying, "Lord, even the
> demons are subject to us in Your name" (Luke 10:17).

We see therefore that even during the earthly ministry of Jesus, His disciples shared in some measure in the supernatural aspect of that ministry toward the sick and the demon-possessed. But this would appear to be on a strictly limited scale and merely an extension of the earthly ministry of Jesus through His close presence with them.

However, after the day of Pentecost the disciples immediately entered into a full supernatural ministry of their own, in which they were no longer dependent upon the bodily presence of Jesus with them on earth.

As a result of the descent of the Holy Spirit, one of the five supernatural signs promised by Jesus in Mark 16 was immediately manifested: "They . . . all . . . began to speak with other [or with new] tongues" (Acts 2:4). The next chapter of Acts records the miraculous healing of the lame man at the beautiful gate.

The remainder of the book of Acts is an unbroken record of supernatural testimony by God, through the Holy Spirit, to the message and ministry of the disciples. This supernatural testimony to their ministry is summed up in the verse which we have already examined in Hebrews 2:4.

> God also bearing witness both with signs and wonders, and with various miracles, and gifts of the Holy Spirit, according to His own will.

Of the five supernatural signs which Jesus promised in Mark 16, four are actually recorded as taking place in the book of Acts. The speaking with other (or new) tongues was manifested on the day of Pentecost and on various subsequent occasions. The healing of the sick and the casting out of demons were manifested in the ministries of Philip, of Paul and of all the other apostles. Immunity to the bite of a poisonous snake was manifested in the experience of Paul on the island of Malta (see Acts 28:3-6). A modern record of these signs is contained in a small book titled *Signs Following*, published in the first half of the twentieth century. The author, William Burton, served for more than forty years as a missionary in the Belgian Congo.

In his book he considers each of the five signs in turn and records several detailed instances, attested to by his own observation and experience, in which each of these signs was manifested. In particular he records instances of immunity, on the part of missionaries and evangelists, both to the poison of snakes and also to other forms of poison placed in their food or drink by witch doctors opposed to the propagation of the gospel. Jesus promised that these signs would follow those who believe without any further limitations as to time or place or person.

> Most assuredly, I say to you, he who believes in Me, the
> works that I do he will do also; and greater works than these
> he will do, because I go to My Father (John 14:12).

Notice the central part of this promise: "He who believes in Me, the works that I do he will do also." The phrase "he who believes in Me" occurs frequently in the New Testament. It is absolutely general in its application. It means any true believer, anywhere. It is not limited to any special age or place or group or class of persons.

How can it be possible that every believer can do the works that Jesus Himself did? The answer is given in the last part of John 14:12, where Jesus says, "Because I go to My Father." A little further on Jesus says again:

> And I will pray the Father, and He will give you another
> Helper, that He may abide with you forever, even the Spirit of
> truth [that is, the Holy Spirit] (John 14:16-17).

This statement supplies the answer to the promise of verse 12. It is the abiding presence of the Holy Spirit, sent down upon the believer from the presence of the Father, that enables him to do the work that Jesus did.

The same anointing of the Holy Spirit, resting upon the believer as it rested first upon Jesus, leads the believer into the same type of super-natural ministry that Jesus entered into after the Holy Spirit came upon Him. This supernatural ministry is not due to any natural power or ability in the believer, but to the anointing of the Holy Spirit upon him.

Supernatural Revelation Demands
Supernatural Confirmation

If we study the whole record of Scripture carefully, we find that this supernatural testimony to the truth of the gospel is in line with God's dealings with His believing people through all ages. Whenever God has committed truth to man by divine revelation and man has been willing to obey that truth, God has always been willing to bear supernatural testimony to the truth which He reveals.

We find this at the very outset of human history in the account of the offerings brought to God by Cain and Abel (see Gen. 4:3-8). These two different types of offerings are typical of two main patterns of religion through the subsequent history of man.

Cain brought the fruit of the ground – but it was ground that had already come under God's curse (see Gen. 3:17). Cain's offering was the product of his own reason and his own works. There was no revelation of God; no acknowledgement of sin, with its ensuing curse; no acknowledgement of the need for a sacrifice to make propitiation for sin.

Abel brought of the firstlings of his flock, which he offered in sacrifice. By this act he acknowledged the fact of sin and the need for a propitiatory sacrifice with the shedding of blood. This came to him not through his own reason but by divine revelation. His religion was based not on his own works but on faith in God.

> By faith Abel offered to God a more excellent sacrifice than Cain, through which he obtained witness that he was righteous, God testifying of his gifts (Heb. 11:4).

As already explained in Section II of this book, "faith comes by hearing, and hearing by the word of God" (Rom. 10:17). That is, it is based on the revelation of God through His Word.

Because Abel received and obeyed such a revelation, God was pleased to bear supernatural testimony to his offering. Most commentators believe that the supernatural fire of God from heaven fell upon Abel's sacrifice and consumed it.

On the other hand, God refused to give His approval to Cain's offering.

> And the Lord respected Abel and his offering, but He did not respect Cain and his offering (Gen. 4:4-5).

In a similar way, ever since, God has always been pleased to give open, supernatural testimony to the truth which He reveals to man. In Exodus 4 we read that when God commissioned Moses to take His message of deliverance to the children of Israel in Egypt, God gave him three definite, supernatural signs which were to accompany and to attest his message.

Later, when Moses and Aaron had completed their sacrifices to God in the tabernacle:

> Fire came out from before the Lord and consumed the burnt offering and the fat on the altar. When all the people saw it, they shouted and fell on their faces (Lev. 9:24).

When Solomon had concluded his prayer at the dedication of the temple:

> Fire came down from heaven and consumed the burnt offering and the sacrifices; and the glory of the Lord filled the temple (2 Chron. 7:1).

The Lord similarly confirmed the message and the testimony of Elijah in his contest with the prophets of Baal.

> Then the fire of the Lord fell and consumed the burnt sacrifice [that is, Elijah's sacrifice], and the wood and the stones and the dust, and it licked up the water that was in the trench. Now when all the people saw it, they fell on their faces; and they said, "The Lord, He is God! The Lord, He is God!" (1 Kin. 18:38-39).

The supernatural testimony of God to the message of the prophets did not end with Elijah but continued on through the ministries of Elisha, Isaiah, Ezekiel, Daniel and many others.

In the New Testament, with the advent of the gospel, God's supernatural testimony to the truth of His Word was not decreased or withdrawn. On the contrary, it was greatly increased and extended, both in the ministry of Jesus Himself and in the subsequent ministry of the whole early church.

Throughout all ages it has been the special office of the Holy Spirit to bear supernatural testimony to God's revealed truth and to confirm the words of God's messengers. The more abundantly the Holy Spirit is poured out upon God's people, the more this supernatural testimony is strengthened and increased.

It has sometimes been suggested that a high degree of learning and education in God's ministers may render superfluous the special, supernatural testimony of the Holy Spirit. However, the outstanding example of the apostle Paul demonstrates that this is not correct. Intellectual learning, though useful on its own level, can never be a substitute for the supernatural power and ministry of the Holy Spirit.

Paul was a man of high intellectual gifts and wide learning, both in the field of religion and philosophy. Yet, in his presentation of the gospel, he deliberately renounced the appeal to his own learning or the use of purely human forms of reason and argument.

> And I, brethren, when I came to you, did not come with excellence of speech or of wisdom declaring to you the testimony of God. For I determined not to know anything among you except Jesus Christ and Him crucified. I was with you in weakness, in fear, and in much trembling. And my speech and my preaching were not with persuasive words of human wisdom, but in demonstration of the Spirit and of power, that your faith should not be in the wisdom of men but in the power of God (1 Cor. 2:1-5).

In presenting the gospel message, Paul deliberately renounced what he calls "excellence of speech or of wisdom," and again, "persuasive words of human wisdom."

He implies that, had he chosen to use such forms of appeal as these, it was in his power to do so. But he renounced them in favour of an altogether different type of proof of the truth of his message. This other proof Paul describes as "the demonstration of the Spirit [that is, the Holy Spirit] and of power."

Notice that word *demonstration.* This implies something open, public and perceptible to the senses. The Holy Spirit did not work with the apostle Paul merely as an invisible, imperceptible influence. The presence and power of the Holy Spirit were openly demonstrated in his ministry.

Why did God appoint, and Paul approve, this supernatural form of testimony to the truth of the gospel message? Paul tells us the answer: "that your faith should not be in the wisdom of men but in the power of God" (1 Cor. 2:5).

It is not God's purpose that the faith of His people should be based upon argument and proof on the level of human understanding. The only satisfactory foundation for the faith of each believer is in a direct personal experience of the power of the Holy Spirit in his own heart and life.

> For I will not dare to speak of any of those things which Christ has not accomplished through me, in word and deed, to make the Gentiles obedient – in mighty signs and wonders, by the power of the Spirit of God (Rom. 15:18-19).

Here Paul refuses to base the authority of the gospel message, committed to him by God, upon any personal qualities of his own – such as his own natural talents or learning. He states clearly that obedience to the gospel is not to be produced by any such qualities as these, but only by "mighty signs and wonders." And these, he says, are the work of the Spirit of God – the Holy Spirit.

Here, then, is one sovereign, unchanging office of the Holy Spirit: to bear testimony to the revealed truth of God by the open demonstration of supernatural power.

This supernatural testimony of the Holy Spirit commenced with Abel, the first believer and also the first martyr recorded in man's history after the fall. Nor will the Holy Spirit ever withdraw His supernatural testimony so long as God has on earth a people who believe and obey the revealed truth of His Word.

PART V

LAYING ON
OF HANDS

STIR UP THE GIFT OF GOD WHICH IS IN YOU
THROUGH THE LAYING ON OF MY HANDS.

2 TIMOTHY 1:6

37
IMPARTING BLESSING, AUTHORITY AND HEALING

Throughout this series of studies we are examining the six foundation doctrines of Christ which are listed in Hebrews 6:1-2:

1. Repentance from dead works
2. Faith toward God
3. The doctrine of baptisms
4. Laying on of hands
5. Resurrection of the dead
6. Eternal judgement

In the preceding sections we have systematically examined the first three doctrines in this list. Now we will move on to the fourth of these doctrines – that which is called "laying on of hands."

Had it been left to human understanding to determine the six basic doctrines of the Christian faith, it is quite probable that the laying on of hands would never have been included. However, in the last resort, the best commentary on Scripture is provided by Scripture itself. In this particular case we have the authority of Scripture itself for placing this doctrine among the great foundation doctrines of Christianity.

What are we to understand by this phrase, "laying on of hands"? "Laying on of hands" is an act in which one person places his hands upon another person with some definite spiritual purpose. Normally this act is accompanied by prayer or by prophetic utterance, or by both.

Outside the sphere of religion, this act of laying on of hands is not something strange or foreign to normal human behaviour. For example, in some parts of the world, when two men meet who are friends, it is normal for them to lay their hands upon each other's shoulders. This act constitutes an acknowledgement of their friendship and pleasure at meeting each other. Or again, when a child complains of headache or fever, it is quite natural – in fact, almost instinctive – for the mother to place her hand upon her child's brow to soothe or caress the child.

Within the sphere of religion, the practice of laying on of hands may thus be considered as an extension or an adaptation of what is basically a natural human action. As a religious act, the laying on of hands normally signifies one of three possible things.

1. The person laying on hands may thereby transmit spiritual blessing or authority to the one upon whom hands are laid.
2. The person laying on hands may thereby acknowledge publicly some spiritual blessing or authority already received from God by the one upon whom hands are laid.
3. The person laying on hands may thereby publicly commit to God for some special task or ministry the one upon whom hands are laid.

At times, all these three purposes may be combined in one and the same act of laying on hands.

Three Old Testament Precedents

The laying on of hands was an accepted practice in the earliest records of God's people. For instance, consider how Joseph brought his two sons Ephraim and Manasseh to his father, Jacob, and how Jacob blessed them.

> Then Israel [Jacob] stretched out his right hand and laid it on Ephraim's head, who was the younger, and his left hand on Manasseh's head, guiding his hands knowingly, for Manasseh

was the firstborn (Gen. 48:14).

At first Joseph thought his father had made a mistake, and he tried to make his father change his hands over, placing the right hand upon the head of Manasseh, the firstborn, and the left hand upon the head of Ephraim, the younger. However, Jacob indicated that he had been conscious of divine guidance in placing his right hand upon Ephraim and his left hand upon Manasseh. With his hands still kept crossed in this position, he proceeded to bless the two boys, giving the first and greater blessing to Ephraim and the lesser blessing to Manasseh.

This passage shows it was an accepted practice that the blessing of Jacob should be transmitted to his two grandsons by laying his hands upon their heads; and, furthermore, that the greater blessing was transmitted through Jacob's right hand and the lesser through his left hand.

As Moses came near to the end of his earthly ministry, he asked the Lord to appoint a new leader over Israel who should be ready to take his place.

> And the Lord said to Moses: "Take Joshua the son of Nun with you, a man in whom is the Spirit, and lay your hand on him; set him before Eleazar the priest and before all the congregation, and inaugurate him in their sight. And you shall give some of your authority to him, that all the congregation of the children of Israel may be obedient" (Num. 27:18-20).

Moses carried out this commandment of the Lord:

> So Moses did as the Lord commanded him. He took Joshua and set him before Eleazar the priest and before all the congregation. And he laid his hands on him and inaugurated him, just as the Lord commanded by the hand of Moses (Num. 27:22-23).

Moses' action produced a tremendous result in Joshua.

> Now Joshua the son of Nun was full of the spirit of wisdom, for Moses had laid his hands on him; so the children of Israel heeded him, and did as the Lord had commanded Moses (Deut. 34:9).

From these passages we see that this act of Moses laying his hands upon Joshua was one of great significance both for Joshua individually and for the whole congregation of Israel collectively. By this divinely ordained act, Moses accomplished two main purposes: 1) He transmitted to Joshua a measure of the spiritual wisdom and honour which he had himself received from God; 2) he publicly acknowledged before the whole congregation of Israel God's appointment of Joshua as the leader who was to succeed him.

Another significant act of laying on of hands took place when Joash, king of Israel, went down to pay his last respects to the prophet Elisha, who lay upon his deathbed. The following conversation occurred between Joash and Elisha.

> And Elisha said to him, "Take a bow and some arrows." So he [Joash] took himself a bow and some arrows. Then he said to the king of Israel, "Put your hand on the bow." So he put his hand on it, and Elisha put his hands on the king's hands. And he said, "Open the east window"; and he opened it. Then Elisha said, "Shoot"; and he shot. And he said, "The arrow of the Lord's deliverance and the arrow of deliverance from Syria; for you must strike the Syrians at Aphek till you have destroyed them" (2 Kin. 13:15-17).

Shooting the arrow eastward through the window symbolised the victory which Joash was to gain in battle over the Syrians. By this act, therefore, Elisha acknowledged God's appointment of Joash as the leader who would bring deliverance to Israel.

This divine appointment of Joash was made effective through Elisha's laying his hands upon the hands of Joash as the latter held the bow and shot the arrow, which was symbolic of victory and deliverance. Through the laying on of Elisha's hands, there were transmitted to Joash the divine wisdom and authority needed to equip him as the deliverer of God's people.

This incident is therefore closely parallel to the one in which Moses laid his hands upon Joshua. In each case the laying on of hands acknowledged a leader whom God had appointed for a special purpose. In each case this act also transmitted to that leader the divine wisdom and authority needed to carry out his God-appointed task. It is interesting also to notice that, in both cases, Joshua and Joash were appointed primarily as military commanders.

Two New Testament Ordinances for Healing

Let us now turn to the New Testament to see what part this ordinance of laying on of hands plays there. We shall find five distinct purposes for which laying on of hands may be used, according to the precepts and examples of the New Testament.

The first of these purposes is directly associated with the ministry of physical healing. Jesus authorised it in His final commission to His disciples (see Mark 16:17-18). In these verses Jesus appoints five super-natural signs which are to accompany the preaching of the gospel and which may be claimed by all believers through faith in the name of Jesus. The fifth of these supernatural signs appointed by Jesus is:

> In My name . . . they will lay hands on the sick, and they will recover (Mark 16:17-18).

Here the laying on of hands in the name of Jesus is appointed as a means for physical healing to be ministered to those who are sick.

Later on in the New Testament another slightly different ordinance is appointed.

> Is anyone among you sick? Let him call for the elders of the church, and let them pray over him, anointing him with oil in the name of the Lord. And the prayer of faith will save the sick, and God will raise him up. And if he has committed sins, he will be forgiven (James 5:14-15).

The ordinance here appointed is that of anointing the sick with oil in the name of the Lord.

Both these ordinances alike are effective only through the exercise of faith in the name of the Lord; that is, the name of Jesus. In the case of anointing with oil, it is specifically stated that prayer must accompany this act. In the passage about laying hands on the sick in Mark's Gospel, no specific mention is made of prayer. However, in most cases it would be natural to pray for the sick person, as well as laying hands on him.

Again, when anointing the sick with oil, it often seems natural – indeed, almost instinctive – to lay hands upon them at the same time. In this way the two ordinances become combined in one. However, this need not necessarily be so. It is perfectly scriptural to lay hands on the sick without anointing them with oil. Likewise, it is perfectly scriptural to anoint the sick with oil without laying hands on them.

The question naturally arises: Is there any difference in use or purpose between these two ordinances – that is, laying hands on the sick and anointing the sick with oil? Are there times or situations when it is more appropriate to use one ordinance rather than the other? And if so, what are the scriptural principles guiding their use?

The passage in the epistle of James about anointing with oil begins:

> Is anyone among you sick? Let him call for the elders of the church (James 5:14).

Since the epistle of James is addressed primarily to professing Christians (albeit among the Jewish people), the phrase "among you" would seem to refer mainly to believers. This fits in also with the commandment which follows: "Let him call for the elders of the church."

A person who made no profession of faith and was not associated with any Christian church would not be included in the phrase "among you"; nor would such a person know who were the church elders for whom to send. It would seem, therefore, that this ordinance of anointing with oil is intended primarily for those who already profess faith in Christ and are associated with some Christian church.

Interpreted in this way, this ordinance contains two lessons of great practical importance for every professing Christian. First, God expects every sick Christian to seek Him first, for healing through faith and by spiritual means. This does not mean it is necessarily unscriptural for a Christian who is sick to seek the advice or help of a medical doctor. But it is absolutely contrary to Scripture for any professing Christian who is sick to seek for human medical aid without first seeking for divine help from God Himself, through the appointed leaders of the church.

Today the great majority of professing Christians who fall sick automatically call for their doctor without giving any thought to seeking help from God or from the leaders of the church. All Christians who do this are guilty of direct disobedience against the ordinances of God as set forth in the New Testament. For the Scripture says plainly, without any qualification: "Is anyone among you sick? Let him call for the elders of the church . . ." In the face of this, any Christian who falls sick and calls for the doctor, without calling for the elders of the church, is guilty of open disobedience.

The implications of this act are plain enough if we pause to consider them. It amounts to saying to God: "God, I do not need You. I do not really believe You can help me or heal me. I am content to accept the

best that man can do for me without seeking You for guidance or help."
This prevailing attitude among professing Christians is one main reason
why so much sickness also prevails among them.

For the most part, Christians today have simply set aside the claims of
God to heal the body and have closed the doors of their homes and
churches against Christ the healer.

The second important lesson contained in this passage from the
epistle of James is that God expects all Christians to associate
themselves with a church and that the leaders of this church shall be
ready to minister in faith, according to the Scripture, to the physical
needs of their church members.

The phrase "let him call for the elders of the church, and let them pray
over him, anointing him with oil in the name of the Lord" (James 5:14)
carries both these implications: 1) that every Christian shall be
associated with a church in such a way that its leaders both know him
and are known to him; 2) that these leaders shall be ready to minister
physical healing to their members in faith, according to the ordinances
appointed by God for the church.

In connection with this ordinance of anointing the sick with oil, there
are two further points which need to be made plain. First of all, there is
no suggestion that oil is to be used because of any natural healing
properties it may possess. Here, as in many other passages of Scripture,
the oil is simply a type or picture of the Holy Spirit.

Thus, placing the oil upon the sick person represents the claim of faith
on behalf of that person that the Spirit of God shall minister divine life
and healing to his sick body. This claim is based upon a clear promise
from God.

> But if the Spirit of Him who raised Jesus from the dead
> dwells in you, He who raised Christ from the dead will also
> give life to your mortal bodies through His Spirit who dwells
> in you (Rom. 8:11).

Here the phrase "to give life to your mortal bodies" means to impart
divine life and power to the mortal, physical body of the believer in
whom the Spirit of God dwells. The great agent of the Godhead who
imparts this divine life is the third Person, the Holy Spirit.

The second point which must be established is that anointing the
believer with oil, according to the New Testament, is never intended as
a preparation for death but, on the contrary, as a way of imparting to the
believer the exact opposite of death – that is, divine life and health and

strength.

Thus, to make anointing with oil a preparation for death is to reverse the true meaning of the ordinance. It is ignoring God's warning not to "put darkness for light and bitter for sweet" – to put the darkness and bitterness of death and sickness in place of the light and sweetness of life and health (see Is. 5:20).

We may sum up this ordinance of anointing with oil by saying that it is an appointed act of faith by which the impartation of divine life and health through the Holy Spirit is claimed for the body of a sick Christian.

If we now turn back to the ordinance of laying hands on the sick, as set forth in Mark 16, we shall see that the context suggests that this ordinance is intended to go together with the preaching of the gospel to the unconverted and that its primary use is for those who are not yet converted or who have newly come to the faith.

We form this conclusion from the fact that this, like the other supernatural signs ordained by Jesus, follows immediately upon His commandment to evangelise the whole world.

> And He said to them, "Go into all the world and preach the gospel to every creature. He who believes and is baptised will be saved; but he who does not believe will be condemned. And these signs will follow those who believe" (Mark 16:15-17).

Jesus immediately enumerates the five supernatural signs, ending with the healing of the sick through the laying on of hands. This indicates that each one of these supernatural signs, including the healing of the sick, is intended by God to bear testimony to the divine truth and authority of the gospel message in places where this message has not previously been heard or believed.

This is in line with the closing account of the disciples' evangelistic activity in Mark's Gospel.

> And they went out and preached everywhere, the Lord working with them and confirming the word through the accompanying signs. Amen (Mark 16:20).

This indicates that the primary purpose of these supernatural signs – including the healing of the sick through the laying on of hands – is to confirm the truth of the gospel message among people who have not previously accepted it. It seems clear, therefore, that ministering to the sick through laying on of hands in the name of Jesus is primarily intended not for established Christians who are members of churches but for the unconverted, or for those who have newly come to the faith.

How Healing Comes

In what way will healing come as a result of the laying on of hands?

The Scripture does not give any precise or detailed answer to this question. Jesus says merely, "They will lay hands on the sick, and they will recover." In place of the phrase "they will recover," we might translate alternatively, "they will become well," or more simply still, "they will be well."

By these words of Jesus two things are still left within the sovereignty of God: 1) the precise way in which healing will be manifested and 2) the precise length of time that the process of healing will take. Side by side with this we may set the words of Paul.

> And there are diversities of activities [or operations], but it is the same God who works all in all (1 Cor. 12:6).

In the laying on of hands there are what Paul calls "diversities of operations"; that is, the process of healing does not always operate in the same way each time.

In one case the laying on of hands may be a channel through which the supernatural gift of healing operates. In such a case the person who lays on hands by this act transmits the supernatural healing virtue or power of God to the body of the one on whom hands are laid. Very often this latter person actually feels within his body the supernatural power of God.

At other times, however, there is no sensation of power at all, but the laying on of hands is simply an act of naked faith and obedience to God's Word. However, if there is genuine faith, healing will follow, even though there may be no dramatic or supernatural experience.

Again, Christ does not specify the length of time that the healing process will take.

Sometimes complete healing is received instantly, as soon as hands are laid upon the sick person. At other times, however, healing comes only as a gradual process. In this latter case it is most important that the person seeking healing continue to exercise active faith until the process of healing is complete.

It quite often happens that a sick person who is ministered to by the laying on of hands receives a measure of deliverance but not complete healing. The reason for this usually is that the sick person did not exercise active faith for a long enough period of time to allow the process of healing to be completed. When the person's faith ceases to be active, the process of healing is then arrested.

For this reason it is important to give scriptural instruction to those seeking healing through laying on of hands and to warn them in advance of the necessity of holding out in active faith until the process of healing is complete.

Experience has convinced me that in every case where genuine faith is exercised by laying hands on the sick in the name of Jesus, the process of healing begins to operate. However, if the sick person then loses faith, the healing may be either completely lost or at best never fully consummated.

There are two main ways in which a sick person may exercise active faith after hands have been laid upon him for healing. The first is by thanking God continually for the measure of healing already received. The other is by maintaining a consistent testimony of faith in the truth of God's Word – even in the face of negative symptoms.

At this point, there is a delicate balance between faith and realism. If a person continues to experience obvious symptoms of sickness even after the laying on of hands, it is unrealistic to pretend that the symptoms are no longer there or to claim that complete healing has taken place. It is better to acknowledge the symptoms but to focus on the Word of God.

Such a person may say, "I recognise that I still have symptoms of sickness, but I believe that God's healing has been released within my body through my obedience to His Word, and I trust Him to complete what He has begun."

It is also perfectly reasonable for such a person to ask for continuing prayer.

There are thousands of people, alive and well today, who have received healing through these scriptural means.

38
IMPARTING THE HOLY
SPIRIT AND SPIRITUAL
GIFTS

The next main purpose of laying on of hands, as practised in the New Testament, is to help those seeking the baptism in the Holy Spirit.

To form a proper estimate of the part played in this by the laying on of hands, it is necessary to consider briefly all the accounts in the book of Acts of how people received the baptism in the Holy Spirit. There are altogether five such accounts.

1. The first disciples in the upper room in Jerusalem on the day of Pentecost (see Acts 2:1-4).
2. The new converts in Samaria (see Acts 8:14-20).
3. Saul of Tarsus, later the apostle Paul, in the city of Damascus (see Acts 9:17).
4. Cornelius and his household (see Acts 10:44-46).
5. The disciples at Ephesus, to whom Paul preached and ministered (see Acts 19:1-6).

In three of these cases those seeking the baptism in the Holy Spirit were ministered to by other believers through the laying on of hands.

Ministering the Holy Spirit

In Samaria the apostles Peter and John laid hands on the new converts and prayed for them.

> Through the laying on of the apostles' hands the Holy Spirit was given (Acts 8:18).

In Damascus the disciple Ananias laid his hands upon Saul of Tarsus that he might receive his sight and also be filled with the Holy Spirit. In this case both physical healing and the baptism in the Holy Spirit were ministered to Saul by Ananias through the one ordinance of laying on of hands.

In Ephesus the disciples to whom Paul ministered received the Holy Spirit only after Paul had laid his hands upon them.

If we now summarise these facts as percentages, we may say that in more than 50 percent of the cases in Acts where people received the baptism in the Holy Spirit, it was through other believers' laying hands upon them.

Certainly this is not the only way in which people may receive the baptism in the Holy Spirit. In the upper room in Jerusalem and in the house of Cornelius those present received the experience directly, without anyone's laying hands upon them.

However, on the basis of all the cases considered, we may say that it is both normal and scriptural for those seeking the baptism in the Holy Spirit to be ministered to by other believers through laying on of hands.

It is sometimes suggested that it was only the apostles or special officers of the church who were able to exercise this ministry of laying hands upon other believers that they might be filled with the Holy Spirit. However, this is not supported by Scripture. Ananias, who laid hands for this purpose upon Saul of Tarsus in Damascus, is described merely as "a certain disciple" (Acts 9:10). There is no suggestion that he held any special ministry or office in the church. Yet he was directed by God Himself to lay hands upon the one who was destined to become the great apostle to the Gentiles. This is in line with what Jesus says.

> And these signs will follow those who believe: In My name . . . they will speak with new tongues . . . they will lay hands on the sick, and they will recover (Mark 16:17-18).

Here Jesus joins closely together the two supernatural signs of

speaking with new (or other) tongues and of laying hands upon the sick
for healing, and He says that both these signs shall follow (or
accompany) the testimony of those who believe. That is to say, the
exercise of these supernatural signs is not confined to any special class
of believers, such as apostles or bishops or evangelists or pastors, but is
open to all believers. Just as the Scripture leaves open to all believers the
ministry of laying hands upon the sick for healing, so the Scripture
leaves open also to all believers the ministry of laying hands upon other
believers that they may receive the Holy Spirit.

However, the Scripture also warns us that this ordinance of laying
hands upon believers is not to be practised lightly or carelessly. For Paul
tells Timothy:

> Do not lay hands on anyone hastily, nor share in other
> people's sins; keep yourself pure (1 Tim. 5:22).

In this one verse Paul gives three distinct warnings to Timothy: 1) do
not lay hands on anyone hastily, 2) nor share in other people's sins, and
3) keep yourself pure.

It is no accident that the two latter warnings follow immediately upon
the first warning not to lay hands on anyone hastily. For if this act of
laying hands upon another believer – particularly for the baptism in the
Holy Spirit – is to be more than a mere religious ceremony, if it is to
produce a real spiritual effect, then there must of necessity be a direct
spiritual contact between the two believers.

In this contact between two spirits there is always the possibility of
spiritual harm resulting to one or both of the believers. If the spirit of one
believer is not altogether pure – if it is defiled in any way by unconfessed
sin or by evil associations – then there is the possibility that the spirit of
the other believer may be harmfully affected by this defiling contact.
That this danger is real is made plain by the two warnings which Paul
gives in this particular context: "nor share in other people's sins" and
"keep yourself pure."

This naturally leads to the question: Since the ministry of laying on of
hands is endorsed by Scripture, how can we guard against the spiritual
dangers connected with it?

The answer is that there are four main safeguards for the believer who
desires to exercise this ministry.

1. This ministry should never be exercised lightly or
   carelessly but always in a spirit of prayer and humility.

2. The guidance and direction of the Holy Spirit should be sought at every stage: with whom to pray, when to pray, how to pray.
3. The believer who lays on hands must know how to claim on behalf of his own spirit the continual purifying and protecting power of the blood of Christ.
4. The believer who lays on hands must himself be so empowered by the Holy Spirit that he is able to overcome any kind of evil spiritual influence seeking to work in or through the one upon whom hands are laid.

Where these four safeguards are not carefully observed, there is a real danger that harmful spiritual results may follow the practice of laying on of hands – either in the one who lays on hands or in the one on whom hands are laid, or in both.

This danger exists in all cases of laying on of hands, but it is greatest where the purpose of laying on of hands is for the baptism in the Holy Spirit. In a figurative way, we may say that the Holy Spirit is heaven's electricity, and the same principle applies in the heavenly as in the earthly realm: The greater the power involved, the greater the need for adequate protection and safeguards.

Imparting Spiritual Gifts

The next purpose for the laying on of hands is the imparting of spiritual gifts. From the passages in the New Testament where this is referred to, it would appear that it is commonly associated with the exercise of the gift of prophecy.

First of all it is necessary to establish that there is scriptural authority for a believer imparting spiritual gifts to others.

> For I long to see you, that I may impart to you some spiritual gift, so that you may be established – that is, that I may be encouraged together with you by the mutual faith both of you and me (Rom. 1:11-12).

Here Paul says that one reason why he desires to visit the Christians at Rome is that he may be able to impart to them "some spiritual gift." He explains also the effect which he intends this to produce upon the Christians there, for he adds, "so that you may be established." In other words, the imparting of spiritual gifts to Christians is one scriptural way of establishing or strengthening them in their faith and spiritual experience.

In the next verse Paul explains more fully the results that would follow from the manifestation of new spiritual gifts among the Christians at Rome.

> That is, that I may be encouraged together with you by the mutual faith both of you and me (Rom 1:12).

The free operation of spiritual gifts within a congregation enables the various members to comfort, to encourage and to strengthen one another. In this way, not only would Paul, as a preacher, be ministering to the Christian congregation at Rome, but, through the operation of the spiritual gifts, the members of the congregation would also be able to minister to Paul. The result would thus be the mutual ministry of the various members to each other.

The operation and the effect of spiritual gifts within a congregation are described by Paul in somewhat similar terms in 1 Corinthians.

> I thank my God always concerning you for the grace of God which was given to you by Christ Jesus, that you were enriched in everything by Him in all utterance and all knowledge, even as the testimony of Christ was confirmed in you, so that you come short in no gift, eagerly waiting for the revelation of our Lord Jesus Christ, who will also confirm you to the end, that you may be blameless in the day of our Lord Jesus Christ (1 Cor. 1:4-8).

Paul here thanks God on behalf of the Christians at Corinth because they are enriched by God in all spiritual gifts. In particular Paul specifies the gifts of utterance and of knowledge. Paul also mentions two results which follow from the operation of the spiritual gifts in the Corinthian church. First, the testimony of Christ is confirmed in them. Second, they are themselves confirmed or strengthened by God through these gifts.

Furthermore, Paul indicates that it is the revealed purpose of God that these spiritual gifts continue to operate in the Christian church right up to the return of Christ. In this connection he uses two phrases, each of which carries the same implication.

> So that you come short in no gift, eagerly waiting for the revelation of our Lord Jesus Christ (1 Cor. 1:7).

That you may be blameless in the day of our Lord Jesus
Christ (1 Cor. 1:8).

Both these phrases indicate plainly that the church of Christ at the end
of this age will not be considered by God to be complete or blameless
unless she is fully equipped with all the supernatural spiritual gifts.

In many sections of the Christian church today there is an unhealthy
tendency to treat these supernatural spiritual gifts like extra chrome
fittings or fancy gadgets on a car. The suggestion is that the person who
wishes to pay a little extra may have the chrome or the gadgets on his
car, but that these are not of any real consequence, and the car would
really function just as well without them. In the same way, Christians
often seem to think that the supernatural gifts are optional – a kind of
unnecessary spiritual luxury which people may seek after if they wish,
but which are not in any way essential to the proper functioning of the
church. However, this attitude is not at all in line with Scripture.

According to the New Testament, the supernatural spiritual gifts are
an integral, built-in part of God's total plan for the church. Without these
gifts in operation the church can never function on the level of power and
efficiency God intended.

Example of Timothy

Having thus established the importance of spiritual gifts in the church
today, let us now consider what Paul teaches about the way in which they
may be imparted. The person Paul refers to in this connection is his own
co-worker, Timothy.

Do not neglect the gift that is in you, which was given to you
by prophecy with the laying on of the hands of the presbytery
(1 Tim. 4:14).

In another epistle Paul refers to the same incident in Timothy's
spiritual experience.

Therefore I remind you to stir up the gift of God which is in
you through the laying on of my hands (2 Tim. 1:6).

In order to complete the picture of this particular incident in
Timothy's life, we should look at one more reference.

> This charge I commit to you, son Timothy, according to the
> prophecies previously made concerning you, that by them
> you may wage the good warfare (1 Tim. 1:18).

By putting these three passages of Scripture together, we are able to
establish certain definite facts about the incident here described by Paul.

First of all, Timothy received some definite spiritual gift. The precise
nature of this gift is never specified by Paul, and for the purposes of our
present study it is not of any special importance.

Second, we learn that this spiritual gift was imparted to Timothy
through the laying on of hands. In one passage Paul says, "with the
laying on of the hands of the presbytery" (1 Tim. 4:14). In another
passage he says, "through the laying on of my hands" (2 Tim. 1:6).

The word *presbytery* in the New Testament is simply a collective
noun denoting the elders of a local church. The elders referred to by Paul
may have been those in the church at Lystra, where Timothy began his
Christian life.

> [Timothy] was well spoken of by the brethren who were at
> Lystra and Iconium (Acts 16:2).

Or Paul may be referring to the elders of the church at Ephesus, where
Timothy was when Paul wrote his first epistle to him. In this case, the
same group of elders would be referred to in Acts 20:17, where we read:

> From Miletus he [Paul] sent to Ephesus and called for the
> elders of the church.

Turning back again to Paul's epistles to Timothy, we see that in one
place Paul says it was he himself who laid hands upon Timothy, and in
another place he says it was the elders of the church who did this. Most
likely, therefore, Paul acted in conjunction with the church elders. He
and they together laid hands upon Timothy.

The third important fact revealed by these passages from the epistles
to Timothy is that the imparting of a spiritual gift to Timothy by the
laying on of hands was also associated with prophetic utterance.

In one passage Paul says this gift was given "by prophecy" (1 Tim.
4:14). This indicates that the will of God for Timothy to receive this gift
was supernaturally revealed through the gift of prophecy; thereafter the
impartation of this gift to Timothy was made effective through the laying
on of the hands of Paul and the church elders. In other words, the laying

on of hands was the means by which the revealed will of God for Timothy was actually made effective in his experience.

In another passage Paul explains a further spiritual purpose for which the prophetic revelation of God's will was given to Timothy, for he says:

> This charge I commit to you, son Timothy, according to the prophecies previously made concerning you, that by them you may wage the good warfare (1 Tim. 1:18).

This indicates that God had a special charge committed to Timothy, a special ministry for him to exercise, a special purpose in life for him to fulfil. The nature of this ministry was revealed to him in advance – on more than one occasion, it would appear – by prophetic utterances. On one of these occasions it was also revealed that Timothy would need a certain spiritual gift to fulfil the ministry committed to him, and on that occasion the particular gift that he needed was imparted to him through the laying on of hands.

Once again, it must be emphasised that this was not a question of the unnecessary or ostentatious use of spiritual gifts. On the contrary, this was something that was vitally necessary to the success of Timothy's ministry. Paul states the purpose for which these prophecies were given to Timothy: "that by them you may wage the good warfare" (1 Tim. 1:18).

The Christian life – and especially the life of a minister – is a warfare, a continual contest against unseen forces of darkness and wickedness.

> For we do not wrestle against flesh and blood, but against principalities, against powers, against the rulers of the darkness of this age, against spiritual hosts of wickedness in the heavenly places (Eph. 6:12).

Two main weapons used by these unseen forces of darkness are doubt and fear. Many times in his ministry Timothy most likely passed through periods of great difficulty and opposition and of apparent failure and frustration. At such periods he could easily be tempted to doubt the reality of his God-given calling. For this reason Paul reminds him of the prophecies which had outlined beforehand God's plan for his life, and he urges him to be encouraged and strengthened by these so that he may go on to the fulfilment of his God-given task.

In particular Paul warns Timothy against yielding to fear. Immediately after he urged him to stir up the gift that is in him by the laying on of hands, Paul says:

> For God has not given us a spirit of fear, but of power and of
> love and of a sound mind (2 Tim. 1:7).

What is the remedy that Paul recommends against the insidious attacks of this spirit of fear? The remedy is twofold: 1) that Timothy should stir up – rekindle into flame – the spiritual gift that he had received through the laying on of hands; 2) that Timothy should recall and be encouraged by the prophecies which outlined in advance the course that God had planned for his life.

We see, therefore, that the ordinance of laying on of hands was combined in Timothy's experience with the gift of prophecy as a means whereby he might be directed, encouraged and strengthened in the fulfilment of his God-given ministry.

According to God's Word, the same means to direct, to encourage and to strengthen are still available today to God's people, and especially to God's appointed ministers. Furthermore, God's people and ministers still stand in need of these things as much today as in the days of Paul and Timothy.

39
COMMISSIONING MINISTERS

The next purpose of the laying on of hands is connected with the sending out of apostles from a local church.

The Local Church at Antioch

The local church at Antioch in Syria provides the clearest example of this.

> Now in the church that was at Antioch there were certain prophets and teachers: Barnabas, Simeon who was called Niger, Lucius of Cyrene, Manaen who had been brought up with Herod the tetrarch, and Saul. As they ministered to the Lord and fasted, the Holy Spirit said, "Now separate to Me Barnabas and Saul for the work to which I have called them." Then, having fasted and prayed, and laid hands on them, they sent them away. So, being sent out by the Holy Spirit, they went down to Seleucia, and from there they sailed to Cyprus (Acts 13:1-4).

This passage provides a great deal of information about the way in which, according to the New Testament, a local church conducted its affairs.

First of all we notice that in this church at Antioch two definite spiritual ministries were present and were recognised by the church: those of prophet and teacher. Within the congregation five men were recognised and mentioned by name as exercising these ministries.

Second, we notice that these leaders in the congregation not only prayed, but they also fasted. Furthermore, they did not merely fast privately as individuals, but they fasted together in a group.

This is in line with Joel's prophetic exhortations for the last days.

> Consecrate a fast,
> Call a sacred assembly;
> Gather the elders
> And all the inhabitants of the land
> Into the house of the Lord your God,
> And cry out to the Lord (Joel 1:14).

> Blow the trumpet in Zion,
> Consecrate a fast,
> Call a sacred assembly (Joel 2:15).

After these exhortations to united fasting by God's people, there follows the promise of the outpouring of the Holy Spirit.

> And it shall come to pass afterward
> That I will pour out My Spirit on all flesh (Joel 2:28).

This prophecy of the outpouring of the Holy Spirit upon all flesh received its initial fulfilment on the day of Pentecost and in the experience of the early church. Now in our day, once again, a similar outpouring of the Holy Spirit upon all flesh, but on an even greater scale, is being re-enacted around the world. The early church received "the former rain" of the Holy Spirit, as promised in Joel 2:23. Today we are experiencing "the latter rain," as promised in the same verse.

Since the promise of the outpouring of the Holy Spirit is for us in these days, it is only logical to acknowledge that the exhortations to united fasting in the same prophecy of Joel are also for us. It would be illogical to apply the exhortations to fasting to some past or future age, while reserving the actual outpouring of the Holy Spirit for the present.

In fact, the whole context of Joel's prophecy makes it plain that periods of united fasting and prayer are one main preparation which God's people should make if they wish to enter into the fullness of the outpouring of the Holy Spirit upon all flesh, as promised by God for these last days.

Joel's prophecy lays special emphasis on the leaders of God's people. Joel 1:14 specifies "the elders"; Joel 2:17 specifies "the priests, who minister to the Lord." Thus the spiritual leaders of God's people are called upon to set a public example in this matter of fasting. Clearly the leaders of the church at Antioch understood this, for "they ministered to the Lord and fasted" (Acts 13:2).

Paul and Barnabas Sent Out

The outcome of their waiting upon God with fasting was guidance from the Holy Spirit.

> The Holy Spirit said, "Now separate to Me Barnabas and Saul for the work to which I have called them" (Acts 13:2).

One reward which they received was that the Holy Spirit spoke directly to them and in this way revealed to them the mind and purpose of God for the extension of His work through them. The phrase "the Holy Spirit said" indicates that the words following, "separate to Me Barnabas and Saul . . . ," are the actual words spoken by the Holy Spirit.

In the light of other New Testament teaching on the operation of the gifts of the Holy Spirit, it is reasonable and scriptural to suppose that the Holy Spirit spoke on this occasion through a human instrument, either by the gift of prophecy or by the gifts of tongues and interpretation.

It is important to notice the exact words used by the Holy Spirit.

> Separate to Me Barnabas and Saul for the work to which I have called them (Acts 13:2).

The verb phrase "I have called" is in the perfect tense. This indicates that God had already spoken privately and individually to Paul and Barnabas about the work that He wanted them to do before He spoke publicly concerning them and their work to all the leaders of the church.

Thus the words spoken by the Holy Spirit publicly to the group of leaders were both a revelation and a confirmation of the call which Paul and Barnabas had already received privately from God. Since Paul and Barnabas were both mentioned by name in the public utterance of the Holy Spirit, it is plain that this utterance was not given through either of them, but through one of the other men present.

How did these men react to this supernatural revelation of God's will?

> Then, having fasted and prayed, and laid hands on them, they sent them away (Acts 13:3).

Notice that they did not immediately send Paul and Barnabas off on their God-appointed mission. First they set aside further time for fasting and prayer. This was the second time they had fasted and prayed together. Through their first period of prayer and fasting they received the supernatural revelation of God's plan. In their second period of prayer and fasting it is reasonable to suppose that they united together to claim on behalf of Paul and Barnabas the divine grace and power which they would need for the accomplishment of God's plan.

Thereafter, the sending forth of Paul and Barnabas from the church at Antioch was consummated by one further ordinance. The other leaders of the church laid their hands upon Paul and Barnabas and so sent them forth.

In contemporary Christianity the title usually given to Christian workers sent forth from a local church is "missionaries." However, the actual word used in the New Testament is "apostles."

This becomes apparent if we compare the phraseology used in Acts 13:1 with that used in Acts 14:4 and 14. In Acts 13 Paul and Barnabas are described as "prophets and teachers." In Acts 14 they are called "apostles." The word *apostle* means literally "one sent forth." Thus this title was applied to Paul and Barnabas after they had been sent forth from the church at Antioch.

By its origin the word *missionary* likewise means "one who is sent." Thus the words *apostle* and *missionary* have the same original meaning. However, in modern Christianity the word *missionary* is applied in many cases where it would not be scriptural to use the word *apostle*.

An apostle is, by definition, someone sent forth by divine authority to accomplish a special task. Many Christians have the impression that the apostles of the New Testament were limited to the twelve originally appointed by Jesus while on earth. However, a careful study of the New Testament does not support this view. In Acts 14, both Paul and Barnabas are called apostles, yet neither of them was appointed during the earthly ministry of Jesus.

A similar conclusion follows from a comparison of two verses in 1 Thessalonians. In 1 Thessalonians 1:1 three men are named as joint writers of the epistle: Paul, Silvanus (or Silas) and Timothy. In 1 Thessalonians 2:6 these three men say of themselves: "We might have made demands as apostles of Christ." That is, all three of them were recognised as apostles.

In fact, a thorough examination of the New Testament reveals more than twenty men who are called apostles. However, it is outside the scope of the present study to analyse the full extent of the apostolic ministry.

Returning to the original sending forth of Paul and Barnabas, we need to ask: What was the purpose for which the other leaders laid hands on them?

First, this act represented the open, public acknowledgement by the church leaders that God had chosen and called Paul and Barnabas to a special task and ministry. Second, by laying hands upon Paul and Barnabas, the other church leaders claimed for them the special spiritual wisdom, grace and power which they would need for the successful accomplishment of their God-given task.

In this respect, this use of laying on of hands in the New Testament is closely parallel to the incident already referred to in the Old Testament where Moses laid hands upon Joshua, publicly acknowledging God's choice of Joshua as the leader who was to succeed him and also imparting to Joshua the spiritual wisdom and authority needed for his God-appointed task.

God's own summary of the process by which Paul and Barnabas were appointed and sent forth from the church at Antioch is given in the next verse.

> So, being sent out by the Holy Spirit, they went down to Seleucia (Acts 13:4).

Notice that phrase "being sent out by the Holy Spirit . . ." The church at Antioch and its leaders were the human instruments by which God revealed and worked out His will for the sending forth of these two apostles. But behind and through these human instruments there operated the wisdom, foreknowledge and direction of the Holy Spirit.

In the final analysis it was He, the Holy Spirit, the executive agent of the Godhead now present on earth, who was responsible for the commissioning and sending forth of these two apostles.

In the whole procedure followed at Antioch we find a perfect example of divine and human co-operation – God and His church working as partners together.

Let us now consider briefly what was the outcome of this first missionary journey of Paul and Barnabas into which they had entered by the direction of the Holy Spirit, with prayer and fasting, and with the ordinance of laying on of hands.

> From there they sailed [back] to Antioch, where they had been commended to the grace of God for the work which they had completed. And when they had come and gathered the church together, they reported all that God had done with them, and that He had opened the door of faith to the Gentiles (Acts 14:26-27).

There are three points of interest to notice here.

1.   We are here given an authoritative, scriptural account of the purpose for which the church leaders had laid their hands upon Paul and Barnabas. We are told that, by this ordinance, Paul and Barnabas had been commended to the grace of God for the work. Thus, the laying on of hands constitutes a means by which God's servants may be commended to the grace of God for a special work to which God has called them.

2.   We must observe the outcome of the labour of Paul and Barnabas. The Scripture states that they completed their God-given work. This means that they successfully accomplished their work, without omissions or failures. Someone has said, "God's callings are God's enablings." In other words, when God calls a man to a special task, He also makes available to that man all the means and the spiritual grace required for the complete and successful accomplishment of that task.

3.   We should notice the impact of their ministry upon the Gentiles. The Scriptures state: "God . . . had opened the door of faith to the Gentiles" (Acts 14:27). Paul and Barnabas did not beat against a closed door. Wherever they went they found that God had gone before them to open the doors and prepare the hearts. Such is the power of united prayer and fasting: to open doors that

otherwise would remain closed. The power thus generated by prayer and fasting was made available to Paul and Barnabas according to the needs that lay before them, through the ordinance of laying on of hands.

In this connection I would add my own conclusion, based on varied experiences in many different lands: New Testament results can be achieved only by New Testament methods.

Appointing Deacons and Elders

It remains to consider one further use, recorded in the New Testament, of the ordinance of laying on of hands. This use is somewhat similar to that which we have just examined.

Now in those days, when the number of the disciples was multiplying, there arose a murmuring against the Hebrews by the Hellenists, because their widows were neglected in the daily distribution. Then the twelve summoned the multitude of the disciples and said, "It is not desirable that we should leave the word of God and serve tables. Therefore, brethren, seek out from among you seven men of good reputation, full of the Holy Spirit and wisdom, whom we may appoint over this business; but we will give ourselves continually to prayer and to the ministry of the word." And the saying pleased the whole multitude. And they chose Stephen, a man full of faith and the Holy Spirit, and Philip, Prochorus, Nicanor, Timon, Parmenas, and Nicolas, a proselyte from Antioch, whom they set before the apostles; and when they had prayed, they laid hands on them (Acts 6:1-6).

Here we have an account of the appointment of seven men to an administrative office in the church at Jerusalem. By the common consent of almost all interpreters, it is agreed that the office to which these men were appointed was that which came to be designated by the official title of "deacon." We find that the appointment of these men as deacons was made effective through the laying on of hands by the church leaders.

In order to understand this procedure more clearly, it is necessary to analyse briefly the structure of leadership in the local church of the New Testament. This basic structure was extremely simple. It consisted of two – and only two – classes of administrative officers. These two classes were elders and deacons.

To those who are familiar only with the 1611 King James Version of the New Testament, it might appear that there are, in addition to elders and deacons, two other classes of church officers – namely, bishops and overseers. However, a closer examination of the actual words used in the original Greek will reveal that this is not so. In fact, the three titles "bishop," "overseer" and "elder" are merely three different names for one and the same office. The English word *bishop* is derived, with a few small changes, from the Greek word *episkopos*. The plain, literal meaning of this Greek word *episkopos* is "overseer." Sometimes the 1611 King James Version rendered the word as "overseer," at other times as "bishop."

Some of this confusion still persists in the New King James Version. For example, in Acts 20:28 and in 1 Peter 5:2 this Greek root *episkopos* is translated by the English word *overseer*. On the other hand, in Philippians 1:1, in 1 Timothy 3:2 and in Titus 1:7 the same Greek word *episkopos* is translated by the English word *bishop*. No matter which word may be used in translation, each alike describes one and the same office. If we desire the plainest and most literal translation of the Greek word *episkopos*, undoubtedly this would be "overseer."

Again, the examination of these and other New Testament passages reveals clearly that the title "elder" denotes precisely the same office as that of "bishop" or "overseer."

For example, in Acts 20:17 we read that from Miletus Paul:

> . . . sent to Ephesus and called for the elders of the church.

In verse 28 of the same chapter Paul said to these men:

> Therefore take heed to yourselves and to all the flock, among which the Holy Spirit has made you overseers (Acts 20:28).

Thus, by putting these two verses together, we learn that the two titles "elder" and "overseer" denoted one and the same office.

Again, Paul writes to Titus:

> For this reason I left you in Crete, that you should set in

order the things that are lacking, and appoint elders in every
city as I commanded you (Titus 1:5).

In verse 7 of the same chapter Paul describes the qualifications which
an elder should possess, and he says:

For a bishop must be blameless, as a steward of God.

In other words, Paul uses the two words *elder* and *bishop* interchangeably to describe one and the same office. Peter's use of these
titles agrees with that of Paul. In 1 Peter 5:2 he writes to the elders and
says:

Shepherd the flock of God . . . serving as overseers.

The same persons are called both elders and overseers.

Thus we find that these three words, *bishop, overseer* and *elder,* are
merely three different titles used to designate one and the same office.
Probably the title most commonly used for this office is that of elder.

In addition to the elders, we find, as already stated, the deacons.
Apart from these two – elders and deacons – no other administrative
officers of the local church are recorded in the New Testament.

The main qualifications for these two offices are set forth in the
following passages of Scripture: Acts 6:3, 1 Timothy 3 and Titus 1:5-9.

Upon the basis of these passages, we may summarise the main
features of these two offices as follows. The primary task of the elders
is to give spiritual direction and instruction to the church.

Let the elders who rule well be counted worthy of
double honour, especially those who labour in the
word and doctrine (1 Tim. 5:17).

Here the two main duties of elders are described as "ruling" and as
"labouring in the word and doctrine."

On the other hand, the word *deacon,* in its original form, means a
"servant." In Acts 6:2 the primary task of the deacons is to serve tables
– that is, to minister to the material needs of the congregation. In doing
this, they were also serving the apostles.

The procedure for appointing deacons is outlined in Acts 6:3-6. The
apostles delegated to the congregation as a whole the responsibility for
choosing from among their own number men suited to fill the office of

deacon. After these men had been chosen by the congregation, they were brought before the apostles, who first prayed over them and then laid hands upon them.

This act of laying hands upon the deacons served three main purposes.

1. The apostles publicly acknowledged thereby that they accepted these men as fitted to hold the office of deacon.
2. They publicly committed these men to God for the task for which they had been chosen.
3. They transmitted to these men a measure of their own spiritual grace and wisdom needed for the task that they had to carry out. Two of these men appointed as deacons – Stephen and Philip – subsequently developed outstanding spiritual ministries of their own.

For an account of the appointment of elders we may turn to Acts.

> And when they [Paul and Barnabas] had preached the gospel to that city [Derbe] and made many disciples, they returned to Lystra, Iconium, and Antioch, strengthening the souls of the disciples, exhorting them to continue in the faith, and saying, "We must through many tribulations enter the kingdom of God." So when they had appointed elders in every church, and prayed with fasting, they commended them to the Lord in whom they had believed (Acts 14:21-23).

Various features of this account are significant. First, the appointment of elders, like the sending forth of apostles, was accompanied by corporate prayer and fasting. Clearly the New Testament church understood that this was the scriptural way to obtain the direction of God in making all important decisions.

Second, the people to whom Paul and Barnabas returned at this point are first called merely disciples. After the appointment of elders, however, they are described corporately as a church. It is the appointment of elders that marks the transition from a group of individual disciples to the corporate entity of a church.

Third, the appointment of elders was the responsibility of the apostles, as representatives of God's authority. In this, however, they did not rely on their own judgement but were the instruments of the Holy Spirit. Speaking to the elders of the church at Ephesus, Paul says:

> Therefore take heed . . . to all the flock, among which the Holy Spirit has made you overseers (Acts 20:28).

According to the divine pattern, all appointments in the church should proceed from the Holy Spirit.

In Acts 14:21-23 no specific mention is made of laying on of hands. However, Scripture provides two strong reasons for believing that Paul and Barnabas did, in fact, lay hands on those whom they appointed as elders.

First, this appointment exactly answered to the two main purposes for which laying on of hands is used throughout Scripture. By it, the apostles endorsed and set apart the chosen leaders of the local congregation. At the same time they imparted to them the wisdom and authority they would need for their task.

Second, in 1 Timothy 5:17-22 Paul is giving Timothy a series of instructions on how to relate to the local elders. He concludes by saying: "Do not lay hands on anyone hastily." Although this warning is appropriate for any of the various uses of laying on of hands, it seems probable that Paul is here referring to this ordinance primarily as a way of ordaining elders.

This would indicate that the accepted way to ordain elders was by laying hands on them.

In closing this study, let me enumerate the five main purposes indicated in the New Testament for the laying on of hands: 1) to minister healing to the sick, 2) to help those seeking the baptism in the Holy Spirit, 3) to impart spiritual gifts, 4) to send out apostles and 5) to ordain deacons and elders in a local church.

In order to understand these five uses of laying on of hands, we have examined the pattern of daily life and administration of a local church, as revealed in the New Testament.

If we now sum up the lessons learned in these three chapters that have been devoted to the laying on of hands, we see that this ordinance has a close and vital connection with many important aspects of the Christian life and ministry.

It is directly connected with the ministry of healing; with the equipping of believers for active witness through the baptism in the Holy Spirit; and with the commissioning of specially called Christian workers. It is often associated with the gift of prophecy. It also strengthens the life of the local church in two ways: spiritually, through the impartation of spiritual gifts; and practically, through the appointment of deacons and elders.

For all these reasons, the ordinance of laying on of hands logically takes its place in Hebrews 6:2 among the great foundation doctrines of the Christian faith.

PART VI

RESURRECTION OF THE DEAD

IF, BY ANY MEANS, I MAY ATTAIN TO
THE RESURRECTION OF THE DEAD.

PHILIPPIANS 3: 11

40
AT THE END OF TIME

In Part V we examined the fourth of the foundation doctrines listed in Hebrews 6:1-2, which is called "laying on of hands." It now remains for us to examine the last two doctrines in the list: resurrection of the dead and eternal judgement.

The examination of these last two doctrines leads us into an altogether new realm of study. The four doctrines we have already considered have all been directly related to this present world and to the realm of time. However, in the study of the two doctrines now remaining, we are taken, by the revelation of God's Word, out of this present world and beyond the realm of time into the realm of eternity. The stage where the resurrection of the dead and eternal judgement will be enacted belongs not to time but to eternity.

Eternity: The Realm of God's Being

Many people are confused by this word *eternity*. They think of eternity as being merely an immensely long period of time, beyond the power of the human mind to conceive. However, this is not correct.

Eternity is not merely the endless extension of time. Eternity differs in its nature from time. Eternity is an altogether different realm, a different mode of being. Eternity is God's own mode of being, the realm in which God Himself dwells.

In Genesis 21:33 and in Isaiah 40:28, God is called "the Everlasting God."

In Psalms 90:2 Moses addresses God and says:

> Before the mountains were brought forth,
> Or ever You had formed the earth and the world,
> Even from everlasting to everlasting, You are God.

God Himself also defines His own eternal nature and realm.

> For thus says the High and Lofty One
> Who inhabits eternity, whose name is Holy:
> "I dwell in the high and holy place" (Is. 57:15).

These scriptures reveal that eternity is an aspect of God's own nature, the realm in which God has His being. When Moses asked God by what name He wished to make Himself known to the children of Israel, God gave Moses the following reply.

> And God said to Moses, "I AM WHO I AM." And He said, "Thus you shall say to the children of Israel, 'I AM has sent me to you' " (Ex. 3:14).

Here God gives Moses two forms of His name: "I AM" and "I AM WHO I AM." This reveals the eternal and unchanging nature of God. God is always "I AM." He is not in any way changed or affected by the course of time, which is but a part of His own creation. For God, past, present and future are ever united in an eternal present – an eternal "I AM."

Out of this revelation granted to Moses came the sacred form of God's name, consisting of four Hebrew consonants, represented in English as *YHWH*. Traditionally this has been rendered as "Jehovah." Modern scholars suggest that it could more accurately be represented by the form *YAHWEH* – meaning "HE IS" or, alternatively, "HE WILL BE." Some translators have sought to express the meaning of this name by the title "the Eternal."

In the New Testament the same truths concerning the eternal, unchanging nature of God are brought out in the revelation granted to the apostle John on the isle of Patmos.

> "I am the Alpha and the Omega, the Beginning and the End," says the Lord, "who is and who was and who is to come, the Almighty" (Rev. 1:8).

Alpha is the first letter of the Greek alphabet, and Omega the last. Thus, the whole alphabet of time, from its beginning to its ending, is contained within the nature of God Himself. The phrase "who is and who was and who is to come" sums up present, past and future, and thus exactly corresponds to the revelation of God's nature given to Moses: "I AM WHO I AM."

The other title of God here used, "the Almighty," corresponds to the Hebrew form used from the book of Genesis onward – *El Shaddai.*

For instance, in Genesis 17:1 we read that the Lord – that is, *Yahweh* – revealed Himself to Abraham by this name *El Shaddai,* the almighty God, for it says:

> When Abram was ninety-nine years old, the Lord appeared to Abram and said to him, "I am Almighty God [*El Shaddai*]; walk before Me and be blameless."

The root meaning of the form *El Shaddai* would appear to be "God who is sufficient" – that is, "the all-sufficient God" – the One in whom all creation is summed up, from its beginning to its ending.

The same picture of the absolute all-sufficiency of God is contained in the New Testament as well.

> For of Him and through Him and to Him are all things (Rom. 11:36).

All things have their origin in God. All things are kept in being by God. And all things find their end and their completion in God.

Thus we find that the various biblical names and titles of God contain within them a revelation of God's own eternal nature. As we contemplate the eternal nature of God, we begin to form a true picture of eternity.

Eternity, correctly understood, is not time in endless duration; rather, eternity is the nature and mode of God's own being, the uncreated realm in which God Himself exists.

Out of eternity, by the act of creation, God brought into being the present world, and with it the order of time as we now know it – past, present and future. By another divine act God will one day bring this present world to an end, and with it time, as we now know it, will once again cease to be. Time is directly and inseparably related to our present world order. With this world order time came into being, and with this world order time will once again cease to be.

Within the limits of this present world order, all creatures are subject to the processes of time. Time is one factor in man's total experience which he has no power to change. All men in this world are creatures and slaves of time. No man has the power to arrest the course of time, nor to reverse it.

This inexorable dominion of time in the affairs of men has always occupied the thought and imaginations of thinking men and women throughout the recorded history of the human race. In different ways and at different periods men have sought to escape from time's dominion – but always in vain. The English poet Andrew Marvel gave utterance to the cry of the human race when he said:

> For ever at my back I hear
> Time's winged chariot drawing near.

In countless different forms and figures of speech, poets and philosophers from all ages and all backgrounds have given expression to the same thought – time's unalterable course and inexorable dominion over all men and all created things.

In recent years the science of physics, through the theory of relativity, has made a notable contribution to man's understanding of time. Briefly, this theory states that the two categories of time and space are inseparably related to each other, so that neither can be properly defined or explained except in relation to the other. We cannot accurately define space without relation to time, nor time without relation to space. Together these two constitute what science calls "the space-time continuum."

If we seek to relate this modern theory to the revelation of the Bible, we may say that this space-time continuum is the framework within which the whole of the present world order exists. By a sovereign act of God, this space-time continuum came into being together with the present world order; and by another sovereign act of God this present world order, together with the space-time continuum in which it exists, will once again cease to be. Before, behind and beyond the whole space-time continuum, the eternal nature and being of God continue unchanged.

The Bible reveals that, for the present world order as a whole, the end of time will come at a moment preordained by God. However, there is a sense in which every individual even now alive must bow before this divine edict that time shall end.

As individuals we do not need to wait for the end of the present world order. A moment lies ahead for each one of us when time shall be no longer – a moment when each one of us shall come to the end of time's course and step out into eternity.

In the home of the late Chaim Weizmann, the first president of Israel, the hands of the clock were stopped at the hour of the president's death. This is a picture of what awaits each man, no matter what his station in life may be. For each man individually there comes an hour when the hands of the clock stand still – a moment when time ceases and eternity begins.

Someone has expressed this same thought by saying, "The clock behind all other clocks is the human heart." When this clock ceases to beat, then all other clocks cease to tick. For each individual, the end of life is the end of time.

What awaits each departing soul as it steps from time into eternity? What is on the other side of time?

Two Universal Appointments

Doubtless there are many mysteries and things unknown that await each departing soul, concerning which the Bible does not lift the veil separating time from eternity. However, beyond the immediate threshold of eternity the Bible reveals two things which are the ultimate destiny of all souls: the resurrection of the dead and eternal judgement.

> For as in Adam all die, even so in Christ all shall be made
> alive (1 Cor. 15:22).

Just as death is the universal fate of all, through their descent from Adam, so resurrection from the dead is the universal appointment of God for all; and this is made possible through the death and resurrection of Christ.

To this universal appointment of resurrection from the dead, the Bible admits only one class of exceptions. The exception is a wholly logical one: Those who never die will never need to be resurrected from the dead.

> Behold, I tell you a mystery: We shall not all sleep, but we
> shall all be changed – in a moment, in the twinkling of an eye,
> at the last trumpet. For the trumpet will sound, and the dead
> will be raised incorruptible, and we shall be changed. For this
> corruptible must put on incorruption, and this mortal must put
> on immortality (1 Cor. 15:51-53).

When Paul says here "we shall not all sleep," he is referring only to Christians. He means that all true Christians who are alive at the time of Christ's return for His church will not sleep – that is, they will not die or will not sleep in death. Instead, their bodies will be instantaneously and miraculously changed, and they will find themselves arrayed in bodies of an entirely new and supernatural kind. Corruption will be replaced by incorruption, mortality by immortality. Thereafter there will remain no further possibility either of death or of resurrection from the dead.

Besides this class of true Christians who will be alive at the time of Christ's return, we may leave open the possibility of two other exceptions to the universal appointment of resurrection from the dead. These are provided by Enoch and Elijah, the two men recorded in the Old Testament who were translated from earth to heaven without seeing death.

The Bible nowhere gives clear details as to what will be the ultimate experience of these two men. But one thing remains certain: Those who never die will never need to be resurrected from the dead. On the other hand, the Bible does clearly reveal that all who do die will also be resurrected from the dead.

The other great appointment of God in eternity for all men is judgement. Paul warned the people of Athens that the whole world must one day face the judgement of God.

> Truly, these times of ignorance God overlooked, but now
> commands all men everywhere to repent, because He has
> appointed a day on which He will judge the world in right-
> eousness by the Man whom He has ordained. He has given
> assurance of this to all, by raising Him from the dead (Acts
> 17:30-31).

God's appointment of judgement is made with the world at large, with the whole human race. This is why all men are commanded to repent, because all men will one day be judged.

Paul warns Christians that they, too, must be prepared to stand before God's judgement.

> But why do you judge your brother? Or why do you show contempt for your brother? For we shall all stand before the judgement seat of Christ.
>> For it is written:
>>
>>> "As I live," says the Lord,
>>> "Every knee shall bow to Me,
>>> And every tongue shall confess to God"
>>> (Rom. 14:10-11).

Here Paul is writing to Christians. Therefore, the phrase "your brother" denotes a fellow Christian. Similarly, the phrase "we shall all" denotes all Christians. Furthermore, that there are no exceptions to judgement is indicated by the universal application of the two phrases "every knee shall bow" and "every tongue shall confess to God."

Later in this series of studies we shall examine in detail God's programme of judgement for all men, and we shall then see that there will be different scenes and purposes of judgement according to the various categories of men to be judged. Meanwhile, this basic principle has been established, that all who die will be both resurrected and judged.

> And as it is appointed for men to die once, but after this the judgement (Heb. 9:27).

Here the phrase "it is appointed for men" includes the whole human race.

We may say, therefore, that for every human soul who, through death, passes out of time into eternity, there remain two universal, irrevocable appointments of God: resurrection and judgement.

Even those Christians who will be caught up, still alive, to meet Christ at His return must still appear before the judgement appointed for all Christians.

> For we shall all stand before the judgement seat of Christ (Rom. 14:10).

Almost exactly the same words occur again in 2 Corinthians.

> For we must all appear before the judgement seat of Christ
> (5:10).

In each of these two passages the phrase "we . . . all" denotes all Christians, without any exceptions.

Resurrection and judgement are inseparably connected by the logic of Scripture.

Resurrection always precedes judgement. In no case will anyone appear before God for judgement as a disembodied soul; but in every case it will be the complete human personality, consisting of spirit, soul and body, that will appear before the judgement of God. For this reason, the resurrection of the body must necessarily precede the final judgement. It is in this order that these two things are always presented to us in Scripture: first resurrection, then eternal judgement.

Paul indicates the underlying principle which determines this order.

> For we must all appear before the judgement seat of Christ,
> that each one may receive the things done in the body,
> according to what he has done, whether good or bad (2 Cor.
> 5:10).

Judgement concerns the things done in the body while on earth. Since it is for the things done in the body that man must answer, God has ordained that man shall appear in his body before Him to answer for those things.

Therefore resurrection of the body must precede eternal judgement. In this, as in all points, the programme of God is logical and consistent.

41
DIVERGING DESTINIES AT DEATH

In this chapter we shall begin to examine in detail what the Bible teaches about the resurrection of the dead.

The first point which must be clearly established is that the part of man which is to be resurrected is his body – not his spirit or his soul. More precisely defined, the resurrection of which the Bible speaks is a resurrection of the body.

In order to understand what this entails, it is necessary to analyse briefly the total nature of man as revealed in the Bible.

Man's Triune Being

Paul offered the following prayer on behalf of the Christians in Thessalonica.

> Now may the God of peace Himself sanctify you completely; and may your whole spirit, soul, and body be preserved blameless at the coming of our Lord Jesus Christ (1 Thess. 5:23).

In the first part of this verse Paul uses the phrase "sanctify you completely." This indicates that he is concerned with the total nature or personality of each of the Christians for whom he prays. In the second part of the verse Paul enumerates the three elements which make up man's total nature or personality: spirit, soul and body.

Again, we read:

> For the word of God is living and powerful, and sharper than any two-edged sword, piercing even to the division of soul and spirit, and of joints and marrow (Heb. 4:12).

This verse gives the same threefold division of man's total personality into spirit, soul and body. In this instance the body is represented by the actual physical parts here mentioned – that is, the joints and marrow.

For further understanding concerning the constitution of man's total personality, we may turn to the original account of man's creation, as given at the beginning of the Bible.

> Then God said, "Let Us make man in Our image, according to Our likeness" (Gen. 1:26).

In this verse two words are used to express the relationship of man, the creature, to God, the Creator. The first of these words is *image*; the second is *likeness.*

The original Hebrew word, here translated "image," is in many other passages of the Old Testament translated by "shade" or "shadow." In modern Hebrew the same root occurs today in the verbal form which means "to have one's photo taken." These other associations of the word indicate that its primary reference here in the creation of man is to man's external form or appearance. Even in man's external form there is a correspondence between man and God which is not found in the lower animal creation.

However, the correspondence between man and God goes further than mere external form. The second Hebrew word used here, translated "likeness," is much more general in its application. It refers to the total personality of man. It indicates that there is a correspondence between this total personality of man and the being or nature of God Himself.

One important aspect of this correspondence between the nature of God and the nature of man is contained in the revelation of the three elements of man's total personality – spirit, soul and body. Thus we may say that man is revealed as a triune being – one total personality, yet composed of the three constituent elements: spirit, soul and body.

In a corresponding way, the Bible also reveals that the being of God is triune – that is, there is one true God, yet within this one Godhead we discern the three distinct Persons of the Father, the Son and the Spirit.

Thus the Bible presents us with a likeness, or a correspondence, between the total personality of man and the total nature of God. Briefly, we may sum up this correspondence of man to God as follows: The Bible reveals a triune man, created in the likeness of a triune God.

In Genesis we are given further details concerning the original creation of man.

> And the Lord God formed man of the dust of the ground, and
> breathed into his nostrils the breath of life; and man became
> a living being [soul] (2:7).

Here we see that the total personality of man has its origin in two absolutely distinct and separate sources. The physical, material part of man – his body – is formed out of the dust of the earth. The invisible, immaterial part of man has its origin in the breath of almighty God. This invisible, immaterial part of man is here called "the soul." However, as we have already said, in other passages of Scripture it is more fully defined as the combination of spirit and soul together.

The Bible indicates that spirit and soul are not identical but are two distinct elements together making up the immaterial part of man. It is outside the scope of our present study, however, to attempt to draw a precise line of demarcation between man's spirit and his soul.

For our present purposes it is sufficient to say that the total personality of man has two different original sources: 1) The physical, material part of man (his body) is from below – from the earth. 2) The invisible, immaterial part of man (his spirit and soul) is from above – from God Himself.

At death, the invisible, immaterial element of man (his spirit and soul) is released from its earthly vessel. Thereafter, by the process of burial, man's material part (his body) is restored again to the earth from which it came and through decomposition returns again to its original elements. Even where there is no actual burial, man's body, after death, is always subjected to some process of disintegration or decomposition, which ultimately restores it to its original material elements. Consequently, it will be man's body also which, by resurrection, will be raised up again from the same material elements.

Man's Spirit Separated From His Body

There is no suggestion anywhere in the Bible that, after death, man's immaterial part – his spirit and soul – will be subjected to the same processes of burial and decomposition that await his body. On the contrary, there is evidence in many passages of Scripture that the destiny of man's spiritual part, after death, is quite different from that of his body.

For the first such passage, we may turn to the book of Ecclesiastes. When considering the teaching of this book, it is necessary to bear in mind a definite limitation which the author, Solomon, sets to all the inquiries and conclusions contained in the book. This is clearly indicated by one particular phrase that is repeated again and again throughout the book.

For example, in Ecclesiastes 1:3 Solomon asks:

> What profit has a man from all his labour
> In which he toils under the sun?

This question, with slight variations in the wording, is repeated several times throughout the book. In all, the phrase "under the sun" occurs twenty-nine times.

This particular phrase, "under the sun," indicates a deliberate limitation which Solomon sets to all his inquiries and conclusions throughout the book. The entire book is concerned only with things under the sun – that is, with things which are temporal and material – things which belong to the realm of time and to this present world order.

We may better understand this particular limitation by reference to the words of Paul.

> For the things which are seen are temporary, but the things
> which are not seen are eternal (2 Cor. 4:18).

Here Paul draws a clear dividing line between two different classes of things: the things which are seen and which are temporal; and the things which are unseen and which are eternal.

If we now apply this twofold classification to the book of Ecclesiastes, we find that the whole material contained within the book falls within the first class of things – those things which are seen and which are temporal.

In this book Solomon never seeks to pursue his studies beyond the boundary of the temporal realm into the eternal realm. Whenever he reaches this boundary, he stops and turns back to some new aspect of the temporal realm. This is indicated by the repetition of the phrase "under the sun." Nothing in the book deals with the realm that is *not* subject to the sun's influence – the invisible and eternal realm. However, this invisible and eternal realm is referred to in various ways by nearly all the other books and authors of the Bible – and also by Solomon himself in his other writings.

The realisation of this particular limitation of Ecclesiastes helps us better to appreciate the teaching of the book as a whole and also clears up apparent conflicts between the conclusions of Ecclesiastes and the teaching of other books in the Bible.

With this in mind, we may turn to the particular passage in Ecclesiastes which indicates a difference between the destiny of man's body at death and that of his spirit.

> I said in my heart, "Concerning the estate of the sons of men, God tests them, that they may see that they themselves are like beasts." For what happens to the sons of men also happens to beasts; one thing befalls them: as one dies, so dies the other. Surely, they all have one breath; man has no advantage over beasts, for all is vanity. All go to one place: all are from the dust, and all return to dust. Who knows the spirit of the sons of men, which goes upward, and the spirit of the beast, which goes down to the earth? (Eccl. 3:18-21).

In accordance with the whole theme of this book, Solomon lays his main emphasis upon the physical, material part of man – his body. Quite correctly, therefore, he points out that in this respect there is no difference between the destiny at death of man and of the lower animals. At death, the body of man, just like that of any other animal, is returned to the earth from which it came and there decomposes once again into its component elements.

However, Solomon goes on to point out that this similarity between the destiny at death of man and of the lower animals ends with the physical body. It does not apply to man's spirit. Man's spirit – his immaterial part – has a different destiny from the spirit of the lower animals.

> . . . the spirit of the sons of men, which goes upward, and the spirit of the beast, which goes down to the earth? (Eccl. 3:21).

Solomon introduces this verse with a question: "Who knows . . . ?" This is as if he were to say: "We recognise that there is a difference between man and the beasts, but it is outside the scope of our present studies. Therefore, we can only mention it briefly; we cannot pursue it any further."

What are we to understand by the phrase which Solomon uses concerning the spirit of man at the death of the body? He says: "the spirit of the sons of men . . . goes upward."

First of all we note that this is in accord with the account of man's creation, which shows that man's body came from below, from the earth, but that his spirit came from above, from God (see Gen. 2:7). Because at death man's spirit is released from the body, the direction of his spirit is once again upward – toward God.

> Then the dust will return to the earth as it was,
> And the spirit will return to God who gave it (Eccl. 12:7).

Thus the teaching of Solomon in Ecclesiastes concerning the destiny of man's spirit at death is brief, but clear, and agrees with indications given in many other passages of Scripture. At death, man's body returns to the dust, but the destiny of his spirit is upward, toward God.

What takes place when the spirit of man, at death, is released from the body and is brought before God, the Creator?

There appears to be no definite revelation of Scripture concerning this point. However, Scripture does enable us to establish two definite principles in this connection. First, this appearance of the spirit of man before God is not the final judgement, which will take place only after the resurrection. Second, the spirits of the wicked and the ungodly can have no permanent access to the presence of God.

We may therefore conclude that this appearance of the spirit of man before God immediately after death is for one main purpose: to hear the divine sentence appointing to each spirit the state and the place it must occupy from the time of death up to the time of resurrection and final judgement. Thereafter, each spirit is consigned to its duly appointed state and place and continues there until called forth again at the resurrection of the body.

The Righteous Separated From the Wicked

What is the condition of departed spirits in this period that intervenes between death and resurrection?

Doubtless there is much concerning this that God has not seen fit to reveal in the Bible. However, two facts are made clear: 1) After death there is a complete and permanent separation between the departed spirits of the righteous and the wicked. 2) The condition of the departed spirits of the righteous was different in the period before the death and resurrection of Christ from their condition now, in this present dispensation.

Over and above these two clearly established facts, the Bible does from time to time lift a corner of the veil between this world and the next, giving us a momentary glimpse of that which lies beyond.

An example is the biblical account of God's judgement upon the oppressing king of Babylon.

> Hell [Sheol] from beneath is excited about you,
> To meet you at your coming;
> It stirs up the dead for you,
> All the chief ones of the earth;
> It has raised up from their thrones
> All the kings of the nations.
> They all shall speak and say to you:
> "Have you also become as weak as we?
> Have you become like us?" (Is. 14:9-10).

This account reveals certain definite facts about the condition of departed spirits. It does not indicate that they have any awareness of events currently transpiring on earth. It does, however, reveal that there is at least some recollection of events that have transpired during the earthly lifetimes of these departed spirits.

Beyond this, it is clear that personality remains intact after death; there is recognition of one person by another; there is communication between one person and another; and there is awareness of present conditions in this place of departed spirits. Furthermore, there is a correspondence in some measure between a man's state in this world and his state in the next. For those who were kings in this world are still recognised as kings in the next.

We are given a somewhat similar picture of the descent into Sheol of the departed spirit of the king of Egypt (see Ezek. 32:17-32).

> Son of man, wail over the multitude of Egypt,
> And cast them down to the depths of the earth,
> Her and the daughters of the famous nations,

With those who go down to the Pit:
"Whom do you surpass in beauty?
Go down, be placed with the uncircumcised" (Ezek. 32:18-
19).

The king of Egypt was received by the spirits of other great men who went down into the pit before him.

The strong among the mighty
Shall speak to him out of the midst of hell [Sheol]
With those who help him:
"They have gone down,
They lie with the uncircumcised, slain by the sword" (Ezek. 32:21).

A careful examination of this passage shows that it reproduces the same features already noted in the passage from Isaiah. There is persistence of personality; recognition of one person by another; communication between one person and another; and awareness of present conditions in this place of departed spirits.

Let us now turn to the New Testament and see what further light this sheds upon the destiny of man's spiritual part at death.

The first New Testament passage that we shall consider is the well-known story of the beggar Lazarus who was laid daily at the rich man's gate (see Luke 16:19-31). There is no suggestion that this story is a mere parable. It is related by Christ Himself as an actual historical incident that had taken place at some time prior to that point in Christ's earthly ministry – that is, in the dispensational period prior to Christ's death and resurrection. Following is Christ's description of the destinies of Lazarus and the rich man after their deaths.

So it was that the beggar died, and was carried by the angels to Abraham's bosom. The rich man also died and was buried. And being in torments in Hades, he lifted up his eyes and saw Abraham afar off, and Lazarus in his bosom. Then he cried and said, "Father Abraham, have mercy on me, and send Lazarus that he may dip the tip of his finger in water and cool my tongue; for I am tormented in this flame." But Abraham said, "Son, remember that in your lifetime you received your good things, and likewise Lazarus evil things; but now he is comforted and you are tormented. And besides all this,

between us and you there is a great gulf fixed, so that those
who want to pass from here to you cannot, nor can those from
there pass to us" (Luke 16:22-26).

There is much in this passage that confirms the conclusions we had
already formed from the Old Testament. At death the body by burial is
returned to the earth, but the spirit moves out into a new kind of
existence. In this existence after death there is persistence of personality;
there is recognition of one person by another; there is consciousness of
present conditions. There is also some recollection of the previous life
on earth. This is brought out by the words of Abraham to the rich man:
"Son, remember . . ."

All this agrees with the picture given in the Old Testament.

However, this account in Luke adds one further, very important fact.
After death the destiny of the spirits of the righteous is quite different
from that of the spirits of the wicked.

Both Lazarus and the rich man found themselves within the realm of
departed spirits called in Hebrew "Sheol" and in Greek "Hades," but
their destinies there were quite different. The rich man's spirit was in a
place of torment; the spirit of Lazarus was in a place of rest. Between
these two places was fixed an impassable gulf that could not be crossed
from either side.

The place of rest, set apart for the departed spirits of the righteous, is
here called "Abraham's bosom." This title would indicate that this place
is ordained for the spirits of all those who in their earthly pilgrimage
followed in the footsteps of faith and obedience marked out by
Abraham, who for this reason is called "the father of all those who
believe."

42
CHRIST THE PATTERN
AND THE PROOF

Hitherto, the facts which we have gleaned from Scripture concerning the destiny of departed spirits all deal with events that transpired prior to the death and resurrection of Christ. We shall now go on to see what the Bible reveals about the experience of Christ Himself during the period between His death and resurrection.

Between Death and Resurrection

The first passage we shall consider is a prophetic anticipation of the death, burial and resurrection of Christ.

> I have set the Lord always before me;
> Because He is at my right hand I shall not be moved.
> Therefore my heart is glad, and my glory rejoices;
> My flesh also will rest in hope.
> For You will not leave my soul in Sheol,
> Nor will You allow Your Holy One to see corruption.
> You will show me the path of life;

> In Your presence is fullness of joy;
> At Your right hand are pleasures forevermore (Ps. 16:8-11).

In Acts 2:25-28 Peter quotes these verses in full. In Acts 13:35 Paul quotes one of these verses. Both Peter and Paul alike interpret these words as a direct prophecy of the burial and resurrection of Christ. Peter points out that, though these words were spoken by David, they do not apply to David because David's soul was left for many centuries in Sheol and his body suffered the process of corruption. Therefore this is one of many messianic prophecies in the Old Testament, spoken by David, yet referring not to David himself but to David's promised seed, the Messiah, Jesus Christ.

Applied in this way to Christ, these words of David in Psalm 16 reveal two things that transpired at the death of Christ. First, His body was laid in the tomb but did not suffer any process of corruption. Second, His Spirit descended into Sheol (the place of departed spirits) but did not remain there for longer than the period between His death and His resurrection.

This Old Testament revelation is confirmed by the more detailed revelation of the New Testament. Jesus said to the penitent thief beside Him on the cross:

> Assuredly, I say to you, today you will be with Me in Paradise (Luke 23:43).

The word *paradise* means literally "a garden" and is one of the names given to that place in the next world which is reserved for the departed spirits of the righteous.

> And when Jesus had cried out with a loud voice, He said, "Father, 'into Your hands I commend My spirit.' " And having said this, He breathed His last (Luke 23:46).

By the words "Father, into Your hands I commend my spirit," we understand that Jesus here committed the destiny of His spirit at death into the hands of His heavenly Father. His body, He knew, was to be laid aside in the tomb; but the destiny of His spirit was to be decided by God, His Father.

In all this we see that Jesus, having taken upon Himself, in addition to His divine nature, the nature of humanity, passed through the same experiences that await each human soul at death. His body was committed to the tomb in burial, by the hands of men; but His spirit was committed into the hands of God, and its destiny was settled by the sentence of God.

What happened to the spirit of Christ after it was thus released at death from the earthen vessel of His body? Paul says, concerning Christ:

> (Now this, "He ascended" – what does it mean but that He also first descended into the lower parts of the earth? He who descended is also the One who ascended far above all the heavens, that He might fill all things.) (Eph. 4:9-10).

Again, in 1 Peter 3:18-20 we read:

> For Christ also suffered once for sins, the just for the unjust, that He might bring us to God, being put to death in the flesh but made alive by the Spirit, by whom also He went and preached to the spirits in prison, who formerly were disobedient, when once the long-suffering of God waited in the days of Noah.

If we combine the various revelations contained in these passages, we may form the following outline of the experiences through which the spirit of Christ passed.

His spirit descended into Sheol, the place of departed spirits. On the day of His death upon the cross, He went first to the place of the spirits of the righteous, called "Paradise" or "Abraham's bosom." Since the Gospel record indicates that the death of Christ on the cross preceded the death of the two thieves, it seems natural to suppose that Christ was in Paradise to welcome the departed spirit of the penitent thief who followed Him there.

From Paradise Christ then went further down into that area of Sheol reserved for the spirits of the wicked. It would appear that His descent into this place of torment was necessary for Him to complete the work of atonement for man's sin, since He had to endure in full not merely the physical but also the spiritual consequences of sin.

At some stage while in this lower realm of Sheol, Christ preached to the spirits of those who had lived wickedly in the days of Noah – that is, the antediluvian age – and who had consequently been consigned to a special place of imprisonment in Sheol. (The Greek verb here translated "preached" is directly connected with the Greek noun herald. It does not therefore necessarily indicate that Christ "preached the gospel" to the spirits in prison, but merely that He made to them some proclamation such as a herald would make.)

Then, at God's appointed moment, when all the divine purposes of the atonement had been accomplished, the spirit of Christ ascended up again from the realm of Sheol to this present temporal world. At the same time His body, which had been lying lifeless in the tomb, was raised up from death, and spirit and body were once again reunited to form a complete personality.

> But now Christ is risen from the dead, and has become the firstfruits of those who have fallen asleep . . . For as in Adam all die, even so in Christ all shall be made alive (1 Cor. 15:20,22).

Paul indicates that the resurrection of Christ from the dead set a pattern which is to be followed by all men. In this pattern we may distinguish two main threads: 1) Man's immaterial part – his spirit – is to come forth once again from the realm of departed spirits; 2) his material part – his body – is to be raised up again from death.

In this way spirit and body are once again to be reunited, thus reconstituting the complete personality of man, with its material and immaterial parts – its three elements of spirit, soul and body.

Destiny of the Christian at Death

In order to complete our brief outline of this subject, it is necessary to carry our study beyond the time of Christ's own death and resurrection and to consider what the New Testament reveals concerning the destiny at death of true Christians in this present dispensation. We shall see that the New Testament indicates one important difference between the period that preceded Christ's resurrection and that which followed it.

As we have already seen, prior to Christ's resurrection the departed spirits of the righteous were consigned to a certain area of Sheol, the netherworld, which was called "Paradise" or "Abraham's bosom." Once full atonement for sin had been accomplished, however, by the death and resurrection of Christ, thereafter the way was open for the spirits of the righteous to ascend immediately and directly into heaven and into the presence of God Himself.

This is made plain by a number of passages in the New Testament, including the account of the stoning of Stephen, the first Christian martyr (see Acts).

But he [Stephen], being full of the Holy Spirit, gazed into heaven and saw the glory of God, and Jesus standing at the right hand of God, and said, "Look! I see the heavens opened and the Son of Man standing at the right hand of God!" (Acts 7:55-56).

Then the account closes as follows.

And they stoned Stephen as he was calling on God and saying, "Lord Jesus, receive my spirit." Then he knelt down and cried out with a loud voice, "Lord, do not charge them with this sin." And when he had said this, he fell asleep (Acts 7:59-60).

In the moments just before death, Stephen was granted a vision of Christ in glory at the right hand of God. His prayer, "Lord Jesus, receive my spirit," expressed his assurance that immediately upon the death of his body, his spirit would ascend into heaven into the presence of God.

This is confirmed by the way in which Paul also speaks about death.

Therefore we are always confident, knowing that while we are at home in the body we are absent from the Lord . . . We are confident, yes, well pleased rather to be absent from the body and to be present with the Lord (2 Cor. 5:6,8).

These words of Paul imply two things: 1) While the spirit of the believer remains within his body, it cannot be in the immediate presence of God. 2) As soon as the spirit of the believer is released by death from the body, it has direct access to the presence of God.

Paul returns to the same thought again in Philippians, where he weighs the relative merits of being released by death from his physical body or of remaining longer in his body in order to complete his earthly ministry.

For to me, to live is Christ, and to die is gain. But if I live on in the flesh, this will mean fruit from my labour; yet what I shall choose I cannot tell. For I am hard pressed between the two, having a desire to depart and be with Christ, which is far better. Nevertheless to remain in the flesh is more needful for you (Phil. 1:21-24).

Here Paul considers two alternatives before him: 1) to remain in the flesh – that is, to continue longer in his present life here on earth in his physical body, or 2) to depart and be with Christ – that is, for his spirit to be released from his body by death and thus to enter directly into the presence of Christ in heaven.

These examples of Stephen and Paul make it plain that, when a true Christian in this present dispensation dies, his spirit is released from his body and goes immediately and directly into the presence of Christ in heaven. This direct access for the Christian believer into the presence of God in heaven has been made possible only through the death and resurrection of Christ, by which full and final atonement has been made for sin.

Prior to Christ's atonement, the departed spirits of the righteous were consigned to a special area in Sheol, the netherworld. This special area was a place of rest and comfort, not of torment or punishment. Nevertheless, it was far removed from the immediate presence of God.

We may now apply the conclusions we have reached to the doctrine of the resurrection. The pattern for the resurrection of all men is set by the resurrection of Christ Himself. That is to say, the departed spirit is called forth from the place to which it has been consigned by the sentence of God – whether in the realm of heaven or of the netherworld. At the same time, the body is raised up by resurrection from death. Spirit and body are thus reunited, and the complete personality of man is reconstituted.

Resurrection Reassembles the Original Body

At this point there is a difficulty that often troubles the carnal mind concerning the resurrection of man's physical body.

Suppose that a man has been dead two or three thousand years and that his body has been totally resolved into its original material elements. Or suppose that a man has been killed in war by the explosion of a bomb or a shell, and his body has been totally disintegrated by the force of the explosion so that no humanly recoverable traces of the body remain. Is it reasonable, in such circumstances, to expect that, at the moment of resurrection, the material elements of bodies such as these shall be regathered, reconstituted and resurrected complete once again?

The answer must be that, for those who acknowledge the unlimited wisdom, knowledge and power of God, there is nothing incredible or impossible in this doctrine. Furthermore, when we take time to consider what the Bible reveals concerning the wisdom and knowledge of God displayed in the original creation of man's body, the doctrine of the resurrection of the body appears both natural and logical.

In Psalm 139 David speaks of the original process by which God formed man's physical body. Nearly the whole of this psalm is devoted to extolling the fathomless wisdom, knowledge and power of God. In several verses David deals in particular with these attributes of God as displayed in the formation of his human, physical body.

> For You have formed my inward parts;
> You have covered me in my mother's womb.
> I will praise You, for I am fearfully and wonderfully made;
> Marvellous are Your works,
> And that my soul knows very well.
> My frame [that is, my physical body] was not hidden from You,
> When I was made in secret,
> And skilfully wrought in the lowest parts of the earth.
> Your eyes saw my substance [my physical body], being yet unformed.
> And in Your book they all were written,
> The days fashioned for me,
> When as yet there were none of them (Ps. 139:13-16).

Here David is speaking not about the immaterial part of his nature – his spirit and soul – but about the material part of his nature – his physical body – which he denotes by the phrases "my substance" and "my frame."

Concerning the process by which God brought his physical body into being, David reveals two facts of great interest and importance: 1) The material, earthly elements out of which David's body was to be formed were specially appointed and prepared a great while beforehand by God, while these material elements were still in the lowest part of the earth. 2) God had appointed the precise number, dimensions and material of all the constituent members of David's body long before his body ever actually came into being.

David's account of the process that produced the materials for his body is remarkably confirmed by the conclusions of Dr. Fujita, a prominent Japanese pharmacologist who spent many years seeking an answer to the question, What is life? His research was confined to the material realm. Within this realm he analysed many different forms of life, both animal and vegetable. Eventually he concluded that minerals are the basic, common constituent in all these forms.

However, the revelation of Scripture goes beyond these bare scientific facts. It discloses that God keeps a complete and detailed record of all the elements that make up our bodies. There is no part too small or too unimportant to be included in God's record. Jesus tells us:

> But the very hairs of your head are all numbered (Matt. 10:30).

In the light of this revelation, we find that there is a close and illuminating parallel between the original process by which God formed man's physical body and the process by which He will once again resurrect that body from death.

In the original process of forming man's body, God first appointed and prepared its various material elements while they were still in the earth. Then, as these appointed elements were assembled together to constitute man's body, God kept a precise and careful record of each part and each member.

After death the body decomposes once again into its material elements. But God, who foreordained the special elements of each individual body, still keeps a record of each element. At the moment of resurrection, by His same creative power, He will once again reassemble every one of the original elements and thus reconstitute the same body.

The only major difference is that the original process of forming the body was apparently gradual, while the process of reconstituting the body at the resurrection will be instantaneous. However, in relation to God's supreme and sovereign control of both time and space, the actual length of time required is of no significance whatever.

If we do not accept this biblical account of the destiny of man's body, then we have no right to speak of a resurrection – that is, of a process of raising again the second time. If the elements which make up man's body at resurrection are not the same as those which originally made up his body, then there is no logical or causal connection between the first and the second body. The two bodies are in no way related to each other, either in time or in space. In that case we should not be able to say that God resurrected (or raised up) man's body. We should have to say instead that God equipped man's spirit with a totally new body, unconnected in any way with the previous body.

This is not what the Bible teaches. The Bible teaches that there is direct continuity between man's original body and the body with which he will be provided at the resurrection. The continuity consists in this:

that the same material elements which formed the original body will once again be reassembled to form the resurrection body.

Confirmation of this wonderful truth is found first and foremost in the resurrection of Christ Himself. When Jesus first appeared to His disciples in a group after His resurrection, they were frightened, supposing that what they saw was a ghost, a disembodied spirit. However, Jesus immediately reassured them and gave them positive proof of His identity and of the reality of His body.

> "Behold My hands and My feet, that it is I Myself. Handle Me and see, for a spirit does not have flesh and bones as you see I have." When He had said this, He showed them His hands and His feet (Luke 24:39-40).

One of the disciples, Thomas, was not present on this occasion, and he would not accept the account of the incident which the other disciples gave him. However, a week later Jesus appeared to the disciples again when Thomas was also present, and this time He addressed Himself directly to Thomas.

> Then He said to Thomas, "Reach your finger here, and look at My hands; and reach your hand here, and put it into My side. Do not be unbelieving, but believing" (John 20:27).

From these passages we see that Jesus was careful to give His disciples the plainest evidence that after His resurrection He had a real body, and that His body was the same that had been crucified. The evidence was in His hands and feet and in His side, which still bore the marks of the nails and of the spear.

In other respects His body had undergone important changes. It was no longer subject to the limitations of a mortal body in this present world order. Jesus could now appear or disappear at will; He could enter a closed room; He could pass between earth and heaven. However, with due allowance made for these changes, it was still in other respects the same body that had been crucified.

Furthermore, Jesus also promised His disciples that their bodies would be resurrected no less complete than His own. In Luke 21 Jesus first warned His disciples of great opposition and persecution awaiting them. In particular He warned them that some of them would actually be put to death. Nevertheless, He went on to give them a clear promise of the resurrection of their bodies.

You will be betrayed even by parents and brothers, relatives
and friends; and they will send some of you to your death.
And you will be hated by all for My name's sake. But not a
hair of your head shall be lost (Luke 21:16-18).

Notice carefully what Jesus says here. The disciples will be hated,
persecuted, killed. Yet, at the end of it all, "not a hair of your head shall
be lost." This does not refer to the preservation of their physical bodies
intact in this life. We know that many of the early Christians – as also
those of later ages – suffered violent death, mutilation, burning and other
processes that marred and destroyed their physical bodies. Therefore the
promise of every hair being perfectly preserved does not refer to this
present life but to the resurrection of their bodies from the dead.

At the resurrection every element and member of their original
physical bodies, foreordained, numbered and recorded by God, will by
God's omnipotence once again be regathered and reconstituted – a
perfect body, a glorified body, but still the same body that had previously
suffered death and decomposition.

Such is the picture that the Bible gives of the resurrection of man's
body – wonderful in its revelation of God's unlimited wisdom,
knowledge and power, yet perfectly consistent with logic and with the
principles of Scripture.

43
RESURRECTION FORETOLD IN THE OLD TESTAMENT

We shall now go on to show that the divine promise of the resurrection runs as one continuous thread throughout the whole Bible, both Old and New Testament alike.

In 1 Corinthians 15:4 Paul makes the following statement concerning the burial and resurrection of Christ.

> That He was buried, and that He rose again the third day according to the Scriptures.

Bear in mind that during the period in which Paul wrote these words the only complete, acknowledged Scriptures were those of the Old Testament. Consequently, when Paul says here that Christ rose again the third day "according to the Scriptures," he means that the resurrection of Christ was a fulfilment of the Old Testament Scriptures.

Furthermore, Paul refers to the Old Testament Scriptures as being the first and basic authority for the doctrine of the resurrection. He goes on to cite the evidence of men still alive at that time who had been eyewitnesses of the risen Christ. However, in Paul's presentation of this doctrine, the evidence of contemporary eyewitnesses is secondary to that of the Old Testament Scriptures.

Let us therefore consider some of the main passages in the Old Testament which foretell the resurrection.

The Psalms

In the previous chapter we have already shown that there is a clear promise of the burial and resurrection of Christ in Psalm 16:8-11. We pointed out that, although these verses were spoken in the first person by David, they do not actually apply to David himself but rather to David's promised seed, the Messiah, Jesus Christ. They are also applied to Christ in the New Testament both by Peter and by Paul.

In Psalm 71:20-21 a similar passage foretells the resurrection of Christ. David is here speaking directly to God, and he says:

> You, who have shown me great and severe troubles,
> Shall revive me again,
> And bring me up again from the depths of the earth.
> You shall increase my greatness,
> And comfort me on every side.

This passage is another example of messianic prophecy. That is to say, the words are spoken in the first person by David; yet they do not apply primarily to David but to David's promised seed, the Messiah, Jesus.

Understood in this way, this passage prophetically sets forth five successive stages that Christ was to pass through in making atonement for man's sin. These may be summarised as follows.

1. Great and severe troubles – the rejection, suffering and crucifixion of Christ.
2. Christ was to descend into the depths of the earth – into Sheol or Hades, the place of departed spirits.
3. Christ was to be revived – made alive again.
4. Christ was to be brought up again from Sheol – that is, the resurrection of Christ.
5. After the resurrection of Christ, He was to be increased in greatness and comforted – that is, restored once again to His place of fellowship and supreme authority at the right hand of God His Father.

Time and space are not sufficient to quote the many passages in the New Testament which confirm that this prophecy was completely fulfilled in the experience of Christ.

However, the two Old Testament passages which we have so far examined, Psalm 16 and Psalm 71, refer primarily to the resurrection of Christ Himself as the Messiah. Let us now examine other passages of the Old Testament which foretell the resurrection of others besides Christ Himself.

Genesis

Let us begin by considering one of God's promises made to Abraham.

> Also I give to you and your descendants after you the land in which you are a stranger, all the land of Canaan, as an everlasting possession (Gen. 17:8).

There are two important points to notice in this promise. First of all, the order of possession is important. God says, ". . . to you and your descendants after you." That is to say, Abraham himself is to possess the land first, and then his descendants after him.

Second, the extent and duration of possession are important. God says, ". . . all the land of Canaan, as an everlasting possession." This promise cannot be fulfilled by any occupation of the land that is partial or temporary. Its fulfilment demands a complete and permanent possession of the whole land.

It is plain therefore that up to now this promise of God to Abraham has never been fulfilled. The only part of the land that Abraham himself has hitherto received for a permanent possession is just space enough in which to be buried – that is, the burial place in the cave of Machpelah in the field of Ephron the Hittite, near Hebron.

As for Abraham's seed, the nation of Israel, until now they have enjoyed temporary or partial occupation of the land, but they have never known the complete and permanent possession promised by God. At present the state of Israel clings tenaciously, in the face of every kind of opposition, to an area that is a small fraction of the total possession promised by God.

Even if in the years that lie ahead Israel should continue to extend its area of occupation until it gains control of the whole land promised by God, this still would not constitute a complete fulfilment of God's original promise to Abraham, which was "to you and your descendants after you." That is to say, Abraham himself must first enjoy possession of the whole land, and then his descendants after him.

Thus, this promise of God cannot be fulfilled apart from the resurrection. The cave of Machpelah must first give up its dead. Abraham himself must be resurrected. Only in this way can he ever enter into the full possession of the land in which he now lies buried. If there is no resurrection, then God's promise to Abraham can never be fulfilled. The promise of God here made to Abraham assumes, and depends upon, the resurrection.

We find therefore that this promise to Abraham concerning the everlasting possession of the land of Canaan includes within it the promise of Abraham's own resurrection from the dead. In this way the truth of the resurrection is already revealed in Genesis, the first book of the Old Testament.

Job

Let us now turn to another book of the Old Testament which is usually attributed to an early date – the book of Job. In the midst of overwhelming grief and affliction, when his earthly future appears to be without a single ray of hope, Job gives utterance to an amazing confession of faith concerning the eternal destiny of his soul and the resurrection of his body.

> For I know that my Redeemer lives,
> And He shall stand at last on the earth;
> And after my skin is destroyed, this I know,
> That in my flesh I shall see God,
> Whom I shall see for myself,
> And my eyes shall behold, and not another (Job 19:25-27).

The language of Job is so terse and so charged with meaning that it is difficult to find any one translation which adequately brings out the full force of the original. The following is an alternative translation of the central section of the passage just quoted.

> After I shall awake, though this body be destroyed, yet out of
> my flesh shall I see God . . .

Whichever translation we may prefer, certain facts stand out with absolute clarity from this passage. Job knows that his physical body will suffer the process of decomposition. Nevertheless, he looks forward to a period at the end of time when he will again be clothed with a body of flesh and appear in that body directly before God. This assurance of Job is based on the life of one whom he calls "my Redeemer."

Thus the whole passage is a clear anticipation of the final resurrection of Job's body, made possible through the resurrection of the Redeemer, Jesus Christ.

Isaiah

We may now turn to the prophet Isaiah, who lived about seven hundred years before Christ. Isaiah makes a confession of faith in the resurrection, somewhat similar to that of Job.

> Your dead shall live;
> Together with my dead body they shall arise.
> Awake and sing, you who dwell in dust;
> For your dew is like the dew of herbs,
> And the earth shall cast out the dead (Is. 26:19).

Isaiah speaks about his own dead body arising from the dust, and together with this he associates a group whom he calls, at the beginning of the verse, "Your dead," and again, more generally, at the end of the verse, "the dead." It is plain that Isaiah contemplates a general resurrection of many, if not all, of the dead.

The prospect is one that brings joy to those concerned, for Isaiah says, "Awake and sing, you who dwell in dust." It would seem therefore that Isaiah's message is addressed primarily to the righteous dead, who, through the resurrection, will be ushered into their final, eternal reward.

In agreement with conclusions reached in earlier studies, we see that Isaiah views the resurrection as affecting primarily the material part of man – his body. He speaks about those "who dwell in dust." The picture which he presents is that of men's dead bodies arising or awakening out of their sleep in the dust.

Isaiah also depicts the supernatural power which will affect the resurrection as "dew."

> For your dew is like the dew of herbs,
> And the earth shall cast out the dead (Is. 26:19).

The picture is one of dry seeds lying buried in the dust and requiring moisture to make them germinate and spring up.

This moisture is provided by the dew settling upon them. In many passages of Scripture, dew – like rain – is a figure of the operation of the Holy Spirit. Thus Isaiah foretells that the resurrection of the dead bodies of believers will be effected through the power of the Holy Spirit.

This is confirmed by Paul.

> But if the Spirit of Him who raised Jesus from the dead dwells in you, He who raised Christ from the dead will also give life to your mortal bodies through His Spirit who dwells in you (Rom. 8:11).

Paul states that the same power of the Holy Spirit that raised the dead body of Jesus out of the tomb will also raise up the dead bodies of those who believe in Jesus and who are indwelled by the Holy Spirit.

Daniel

The next main Old Testament prophecy of the resurrection which we shall consider is found in Daniel 12:1-3. These verses are part of a lengthy prophetic revelation concerning the last days, given to Daniel by the angel Gabriel, who was sent to him by God for that special purpose. This part of the revelation, which deals specifically with the resurrection, reads as follows.

> At that time Michael shall stand up,
> The great prince who stands watch over the sons of your people;
> And there shall be a time of trouble,
> Such as never was since there was a nation,
> Even to that time.
> And at that time your people shall be delivered,
> Every one who is found written in the book.
> And many of those who sleep in the dust of the earth shall awake,
> Some to everlasting life,
> Some to shame and everlasting contempt.
> Those who are wise shall shine
> Like the brightness of the firmament,
> And those who turn many to righteousness
> Like the stars forever and ever.

The first part of this revelation refers specifically to Daniel's own people, Israel, and speaks of a time of trouble even greater than any that Israel has hitherto passed through. This is undoubtedly the same time of trouble referred to in Jeremiah.

> Alas! For that day is great,
> So that none is like it;
> And it is the time of Jacob's trouble,
> But he shall be saved out of it (30:7).

Jeremiah indicates that though this time of trouble will be greater than any that Israel has previously passed through, yet Israel will be saved out of it and not destroyed. This agrees with the statement in Daniel 12:1.

> And at that time your people shall be delivered,
> Every one who is found written in the book.

At this time of greatest tribulation God Himself will ultimately intervene and save the chosen remnant of Israel whom in His grace He has foreknown and foreordained for salvation.

No doubt this time of Israel's trouble is one main phase of the total period of intense trouble destined to come upon the entire world, called in the New Testament "the great tribulation."

Directly associated with this final period of tribulation is a prophecy of the resurrection, for Gabriel says in Daniel 12:2:

> And many of those who sleep in the dust of the earth shall awake,
> Some to everlasting life,
> Some to shame and everlasting contempt.

The language used in Daniel is closely parallel to that of Isaiah. Both speak of those that "dwell in the dust"; both speak of the resurrection as an "awakening" out of the dust. However, the revelation of Daniel goes further than that of Isaiah, for it indicates that there will be two distinct phases of the resurrection – one for the righteous, who will be ushered into everlasting life, and one for the wicked, who will be doomed to shame and everlasting contempt.

The reward of the righteous at the resurrection will be based on their faithfulness in serving God and in making known His truth while on earth.

> Those who are wise shall shine
> Like the brightness of the firmament,
> And those who turn many to righteousness
> Like the stars forever and ever (Dan. 12:3).

Here there is a distinction between those who are wise to the salvation of their own souls and those who go further than this and turn many others also to righteousness. Both alike will enter into glory, but the glory of the latter will be greater than the glory of the former.

From the passages we have considered, we see that the theme of the resurrection runs like a thread all through the Old Testament. The details of this revelation become progressively clearer until in Daniel we are told that the resurrection will be closely associated with the period of the great tribulation and that it will occur in two distinct phases: one for the righteous and one for the wicked.

Before we close this study of Old Testament prophecies of the resurrection, there is one further point of great interest and importance which needs to be established.

Hosea

In the passage already quoted from 1 Corinthians 15:4, Paul says that Christ "rose again the third day according to the Scriptures." Not merely was the resurrection of Christ foretold in the Old Testament, but it was even foretold that Christ would rise from the dead *the third day*. We may ask: Where in the Old Testament can we find this specific prophecy that Christ would rise again on the third day? Hosea provides the answer.

> Come, and let us return to the Lord;
> For He has torn, but He will heal us;
> He has stricken, but He will bind us up.
> After two days He will revive us;
> On the third day He will raise us up,
> That we may live in His sight.
> Let us know,
> Let us pursue the knowledge of the Lord.
> His going forth is established as the morning;
> He will come to us like the rain,
> Like the latter and former rain to the earth (6:1-3).

This prophecy commences with a promise of forgiveness and healing to those who will return to the Lord in repentance and faith. Then, in the second verse, comes the clear prediction of the resurrection on the third day: "On the third day He will raise us up, that we may live in His sight" (Hos. 6:2). This promise is given in the plural, not the singular: "He will raise *us* up . . . *we* may live in His sight." That is to say, the promise refers not only to the resurrection of Christ but also includes all those who obey the exhortation to return to God in repentance and faith.

In order to understand the full implications of this prophecy, we must turn to the complete revelation of the gospel as given by God to the church through Paul in the New Testament.

All Believers Included in Christ's Resurrection

In Romans 6:6 Paul says:

> Our old man was crucified with Him [that is, with Christ].

Again, in Galatians 2:20 he says:

> I have been crucified with Christ.

These and other similar passages reveal that in making atonement for man's sin, Christ deliberately made Himself one with the sinner: He took the sinner's guilt. He made Himself one with the sinner's corrupt and fallen nature. He died the sinner's death. He paid the sinner's penalty.

Thereafter, it remains for us as sinners to accept by faith our identification with Christ. When we do this, we find that we are identified with Him not only in His death and burial, but also in His resurrection from the dead and in the new, immortal resurrection life which He now enjoys.

> God . . . made us alive together with Christ . . . and raised us
> up together [that is, from the dead], and made us sit together
> in the heavenly places in Christ Jesus (Eph. 2:4-6).

As soon as we are willing, by faith, to accept our identification with Christ in His death for our sins, we find that we are also identified with Christ in His resurrection and in His victorious life upon God's throne. Entering in through His death, we become partakers also of His resurrection.

In brief but powerful words, Jesus conveyed the same truth to His disciples.

> Because I live, you will live also (John 14:19).

This is why the prophetic revelation states in Hosea 6:2:

> On the third day He will raise us up,
> That we may live in His sight.

This prophecy reveals not only that Christ was to be raised on the third day, but also that, according to God's eternal purpose in the gospel, all those who believed in Christ were to be identified with Him in His resurrection. In this respect, Hosea's prophecy is characteristic of Old Testament prophecy as a whole in that it does not merely predict an event which is to take place, but at the same time it also reveals the true spiritual significance of that event and its connection with God's whole purpose in the gospel.

However, Hosea also warns that this secret of God's purpose in the resurrection of Christ will be revealed only to those who are willing to seek the truth with faith and diligence, for he says in the next verse:

> Let us know,
> Let us pursue the knowledge of the Lord (Hos. 6:3).

This revelation is only for those who "pursue the knowledge of the Lord."

For those who do, Hosea continues: "His going forth is established as the morning" (Hos. 6:3). That is, the resurrection of Christ from the dead is as sure and certain in God's purpose as the rising of the sun after the darkness of night. This is closely parallel to the prophecy of Christ's resurrection in Malachi.

> But to you who fear My name
> The Sun of Righteousness shall arise
> With healing in His wings (4:2).

Again we notice a limitation of those to whom this revelation of the risen Christ will be granted: It is not for all men but "to you who fear My name."

Finally, Hosea indicates that the resurrection of Christ will be closely followed by the outpouring of the Holy Spirit, for he continues:

He will come to us like the rain,
Like the latter and former rain to the earth (Hos. 6:3).

The rain is here a figure of the Holy Spirit's outpouring, divided into two main visitations – the former rain and the latter rain.

In accurate fulfilment of this prophecy, the New Testament records that on the day of Pentecost, fifty days after Christ's resurrection, the former rain of the Holy Spirit began to be poured out upon His waiting disciples – those who had pursued the knowledge of the Lord.

As we look back over the Old Testament prophecies of the resurrection of the righteous quoted in this chapter, one feature emerges which is common to them all: The saints of the Old Testament are to be included in it.

We saw, for instance, that God's promise of Canaan as an everlasting possession was made to Abraham first, then to his seed (descendants) after him. Paul says to Christians: "You are Abraham's seed [descendants]" (Gal. 3:29). The resurrection of these New Testament descendants of Abraham will not precede that of Abraham himself.

Job said, concerning himself: "I know that my Redeemer lives . . . in my flesh I shall see God" (Job 19:25-26). Through faith in his Redeemer he looked forward to sharing in the resurrection of the righteous.

Likewise, Isaiah spoke of a joyful resurrection of the righteous dead in which he was to be included.

Your dead shall live;
Together with my dead body they shall arise.
Awake and sing, you who dwell in dust (Is. 26:19).

Gabriel told Daniel that there was to be a resurrection of both the righteous and the wicked (see Dan. 12:2-3). Then the angel said to Daniel personally:

You shall rest [in the grave], and will arise [be resurrected] to your inheritance at the end of the days (Dan. 12:13).

Clearly, Daniel was to be included in the resurrection of the righteous. In Hosea's prediction of the resurrection he said:

On the third day He will raise *us* up,
That we may live in His sight (Hos. 6:2, italics added).

Hosea included himself in the predicted resurrection.

For confirmation from the New Testament, we may turn to the words of Jesus.

> And I say to you that many will come from east and west, and sit down with Abraham, Isaac, and Jacob in the kingdom of heaven (Matt. 8:11).

Jesus speaks of believers from many different nations and backgrounds coming together at the resurrection with the three Old Testament patriarchs: Abraham, Isaac and Jacob. This indicates that both Old Testament and New Testament believers will participate together in the resurrection of the righteous.

All who will participate in this resurrection have one qualification in common: faith in Christ's atoning sacrifice. There is, however, a difference between the saints of the old covenant and those of the new. Under the old covenant believers looked forward – through various prophetic revelations – to a sacrifice that had not yet been offered. Under the new covenant believers look back to the historical facts of Christ's death and resurrection.

Throughout the remainder of these studies we will assume, as an established fact, that the resurrection of the righteous will include the believers or saints of the old covenant as well as those of the new.

44
CHRIST THE FIRSTFRUITS

In the last chapter we examined some of the main passages of the Old Testament which foretell the resurrection. We saw that the Old Testament foretells the following three main events: 1) Christ Himself will be raised from the dead. 2) Those who believe in Christ will share His resurrection. 3) There will also be a resurrection of the wicked for purposes of judgement and punishment.

If we now turn to the New Testament, we find that the revelation it gives concerning the resurrection of the dead agrees exactly in these three main points with that of the Old Testament. However, a good deal more information is also given, to make the whole picture clearer and more detailed.

Three Successive Phases of Resurrection

The first New Testament passage we shall consider is found in John. Jesus says:

Most assuredly, I say to you, the hour is coming, and now is,

> when the dead will hear the voice of the Son of God; and
> those who hear will live (John 5:25).

> Do not marvel at this; for the hour is coming in which all who
> are in the graves will hear His voice and come forth – those
> who have done good, to the resurrection of life, and those
> who have done evil, to the resurrection of condemnation
> (John 5:28-29).

Jesus here uses two different phrases. In verse 25 He uses "the dead"; in verse 28 He uses "all who are in the graves." The context seems to indicate that these two phrases are not identical but are contrasted with each other.

If this is so, then the first phrase, "the dead," must be taken to describe not those who are physically dead but rather those who are spiritually dead in sin. This is in line with the language which Paul uses in Ephesians 2:1.

> And you He made alive, who were dead in trespasses and
> sins.

Here the context makes it plain that Paul is not speaking about people who were physically dead, but he is speaking about people who, as a result of sin, were spiritually dead and alienated from God.

Again, Paul uses language borrowed from Isaiah to exhort the sinner.

> Awake, you who sleep,
> Arise from the dead,
> And Christ will give you light (Eph. 5:14).

Here, too, the one whom Paul exhorts to awake and arise from the dead is not physically dead but spiritually dead in sin.

It would seem, therefore, that we should apply this interpretation to the words of Jesus.

> Most assuredly, I say to you, the hour is coming, and now is,
> when the dead will hear the voice of the Son of God; and
> those who hear will live (John 5:25).

Jesus is here speaking about the response of those who are dead in sin to the voice of Christ, brought to them through the preaching of the gospel: "those who hear will live." That is, those who receive the gospel message with faith will thereby receive forgiveness and eternal life.

This is confirmed by the fact that Jesus says, "The hour is coming, and now is." That is to say, the preaching of the gospel to men dead in sins had already commenced at the time that Jesus spoke these words.

We notice the contrast between this and the words of Jesus in John 5:28-29.

> The hour is coming in which all who are in the graves will hear His voice and come forth – those who have done good, to the resurrection of life, and those who have done evil, to the resurrection of condemnation.

This passage differs from the previous one in three main respects.

First, Jesus says, "The hour is coming," but He does not add, "and now is." That is to say, the events of which Jesus here speaks are still entirely in the future; they have not yet begun to be fulfilled.

Second, Jesus uses the phrase "all who are in the grave." This clearly refers to those who have actually died and been buried. Furthermore, He says that *all* these, without exception, will hear; whereas in the previous passage, concerning the dead, He indicated that only some would hear, not all.

Third, in this second passage Jesus actually uses the word *resurrection.* He says that all those in the graves will "come forth . . . to resurrection."

We conclude therefore that in the first passage Jesus is speaking about the response of those who are spiritually dead in sin; while in the second passage He is speaking about the literal resurrection of those who have actually died and been buried.

In this second passage Jesus speaks about two distinct aspects of resurrection: 1) the resurrection of life; 2) the resurrection of condemnation. This agrees with the revelation of the Old Testament in Daniel 12:1-3.

In each case the resurrection is spoken of in two distinct phases, that of the righteous and that of the wicked; and in each case the resurrection of the righteous precedes that of the wicked.

In addition, we learn from the words of Jesus one further point not revealed in Daniel: The voice that will call all the dead forth to resurrection will be that of Christ Himself, the Son of God.

If we now turn to 1 Corinthians 15, we find there a yet fuller and more detailed account of the resurrection.

> For as in Adam all die, even so in Christ all shall be made
> alive. But each one in his own order: Christ the firstfruits,
> afterward those who are Christ's at His coming. Then comes
> the end, when He [Christ] delivers the kingdom to God the
> Father, when He puts an end to all rule and all authority and
> power (1 Cor. 15:22-24).

Notice the phrase "each one in his own order." The word translated
"order" is used to describe a rank of soldiers. Thus Paul here pictures the
resurrection as occurring in three successive phases, like three ranks of
soldiers marching past, one behind the other.

The first phase consists of Christ Himself – "Christ the firstfruits."

The second phase consists of all true believers when Christ returns –
"those who are Christ's at His coming." This corresponds to the resurrection of the righteous foretold in Daniel and by Christ Himself.

The third phase is called "the end" – that is, the end of Christ's earthly
reign of one thousand years, at the close of which He will deliver up the
kingdom to God the Father. Of those resurrected at this stage, the
majority – but not all – will belong to the resurrection of the wicked as
foretold in Daniel and by Christ. Concerning this third phase, Paul says
nothing more here in 1 Corinthians. However, we shall see in due course
that further details concerning this are given in Revelation 20.

In the meanwhile, let us examine more closely what Paul says about
the first two phases.

Typology of the Firstfruits

The first phase, Paul says, is "Christ the firstfruits." By this phrase
Paul compares the resurrection of Christ to the ceremony of presenting
the firstfruits of the harvest to the Lord, as ordained for the children of
Israel under the law of Moses.

> Speak to the children of Israel, and say to them: "When you
> come into the land which I give to you, and reap its harvest,
> then you shall bring a sheaf of the firstfruits of your harvest
> to the priest. He shall wave the sheaf before the Lord, to be
> accepted on your behalf; on the day after the Sabbath the
> priest shall wave it" (Lev. 23:10-11).

This sheaf of the firstfruits waved before the Lord is a picture of
Christ coming forth from the dead as the sinner's representative and as

the beginning of a new creation.

Notice how accurate the picture is. The sheaf of the firstfruits was the first complete fruit to rise up out of the seed that had been buried earlier in the earth. Moses told the children of Israel that the priest was to wave this sheaf before the Lord "to be accepted on your behalf . . ."

In Romans 4:25 Paul tells us that Christ "was delivered up because of our offences, and was raised because of our justification."

The resurrection of Christ not only vindicated His own righteousness, but it also made it possible for the believer to be reckoned equally righteous with Christ before God.

Furthermore, this sheaf of the firstfruits was to be waved before the Lord "on the day after the Sabbath." Since the Sabbath was the seventh or last day of the week, the day after the Sabbath was the first day of the week – the day on which Christ did in fact rise from the dead.

Finally, the waving of the firstfruits was an act of worship and of triumph, for the appearing of the firstfruits at the appointed season gave assurance that the rest of the harvest would be gathered safely in. In like manner, the resurrection of Christ gives assurance that all the remaining dead will also in their due season be resurrected.

However, there is yet one further prophetic revelation concerning Christ's resurrection contained in this Old Testament ordinance of the firstfruits. Jesus spoke prophetically of His own impending death and burial, and He compared this to a grain of wheat being buried in the earth. He said:

> Most assuredly, I say to you, unless a grain of wheat falls into the ground and dies, it remains alone; but if it dies, it produces much grain (John 12:24).

By this Jesus taught that the fruit of His ministry of reconciliation between God and man could come only as a result of His own atoning death and resurrection. If He were to stop short of death on the cross, no fruit could come forth out of His ministry. Only through His death, burial and resurrection could there come forth the fruit of a great harvest of sinners justified and reconciled to God. This truth He presented to His disciples in the picture of a grain of wheat being buried in the earth, germinating and springing up again as a fruitful stalk out of the earth.

In nature, although a single grain of wheat is buried in the earth, the stalk which springs up out of it never bears merely one single grain but a whole head or cluster of grains upon the one stalk. As Jesus indicated in the parable of the sower, the ratio of increase out of the single grain may be thirtyfold or sixtyfold or a hundredfold.

This truth of natural law applies also in the spiritual counterpart of Christ's resurrection. Jesus was buried alone, but He did not rise alone. This fact, which has received surprisingly little attention from the majority of Bible commentators, is clearly stated in Matthew 27:50-53. These verses record the death of Jesus upon the cross and various events which followed His death and resurrection.

> Jesus, when He had cried out again with a loud voice, yielded up His spirit. And behold, the veil of the temple was torn in two from top to bottom; and the earth quaked, and the rocks were split, and the graves were opened; and many bodies of the saints who had fallen asleep were raised; and coming out of the graves after His resurrection, they went into the holy city and appeared to many.

Though these events are here presented in close succession one after the other, it is clear that the total period of time which they covered extended over three days. The death of Jesus on the cross took place on the eve of the Sabbath, but His resurrection took place early in the morning of the first day of the new week. In connection with this, Matthew states:

> The graves were opened; and many bodies of the saints who had fallen asleep were raised; and coming out of the graves after His resurrection . . . appeared to many (Matt. 27:52-53).

At what precise moment the graves were opened we do not know; but we do know that it was only after the resurrection of Christ Himself that these resurrected saints arose and came out of their graves.

In this way the Old Testament type of the firstfruits was perfectly fulfilled by the resurrection of Christ. Christ was buried alone – a single grain of wheat that fell into the ground. But when He arose again from the dead, He was no longer alone – no longer one single grain. Instead, there was a handful – a sheaf of the firstfruits – brought forth together with Him out of the dead and waved in triumph before God as a token of the defeat of death and hell and Satan, and as an assurance that all believers who had been buried would also in their due season be resurrected.

Concerning these Old Testament saints resurrected together with Jesus, two interesting questions naturally suggest themselves.

The first question is: Did these resurrected saints comprise all the righteous believers of the Old Testament? Were all the Old Testament saints resurrected together with Jesus?

To this question the answer would appear to be no. Matthew says: "Many bodies of the saints . . . were raised." This phrase, "many . . . of the saints," in normal usage would indicate that it was not *all* the saints that arose.

This conclusion is supported by the words of Peter on the day of Pentecost.

> Men and brethren, let me speak freely to you of the patriarch David, that he is both dead and buried, and his tomb is with us to this day (Acts 2:29).

Peter is here speaking fifty days after the resurrection of Christ. Yet his words suggest that the body of David was still in his tomb at that time. This would indicate that David, one of the greatest of the Old Testament saints, had not yet been resurrected at the time when Peter spoke on the day of Pentecost. Therefore this resurrection of Old Testament saints on the first Easter Sunday morning was a resurrection of some, but not of all.

The second interesting question concerning these resurrected Old Testament saints is: What became of them after their resurrection?

From the account given, it would appear that these Old Testament saints were, in the true sense, "resurrected" – that is, they were raised up once and for all out of the dominion of death and the grave, never to return again under that dominion. In this respect, there is a complete difference between these saints and the people whom Jesus raised from the dead during His earthly ministry.

Those whom Christ raised from the dead were called back out of death to the same kind of natural, earthly life which they had previously. They still remained subject to all the weaknesses of mortal flesh, and in due course they died again and were buried. These people had merely been restored to natural, earthly life; they had not been resurrected from the dead. On the other hand, the saints who rose with Jesus shared His resurrection with Him. They entered into a totally new kind of life; they received new, spiritual bodies, just like that which Jesus Himself received.

> Coming out of the graves after His resurrection, they [the resurrected saints] went into the holy city [that is, Jerusalem],

and appeared to many (Matt. 27:53).

These words indicate that these saints had bodies of the same kind that Jesus had after His resurrection. They could appear or disappear at will. They were no longer subject to the physical limitations of a normal, earthly body.

If this is so, then there can be no thought that they ever returned again into their graves and submitted themselves afresh to the process of decomposition. In putting on these resurrection bodies, they had passed once and for all out of the shadow and dominion of death and the grave, never to return thereunder again.

What became of these saints after this? The New Testament does not give any definite or final answer to this question. However, it seems natural to suppose that these saints, having shared with Jesus in His resurrection, shared with Him also in His ascension into heaven. Let us therefore glance briefly at the description of the ascension of Jesus into heaven.

> Now when He had spoken these things, while they watched,
> He was taken up, and a cloud received Him out of their sight
> (Acts 1:9).

We notice that Jesus passed out of His disciples' sight into a cloud and that within this cloud He then continued His ascent to heaven. Immediately after this, two angels appeared to the disciples and gave them the following assurance concerning the return of Christ.

> This same Jesus, who was taken up from you into heaven,
> will so come in like manner as you saw Him go into heaven
> (Acts 1:11).

This indicates that there is to be a close parallel between the ascent of Christ into heaven and His return again from heaven to earth. He will so come in like manner as He was seen to go.

What does this imply? In Mark 13:26 (and in other passages also) it is stated that Christ will come again in the clouds – more literally, in clouds. Again, Zechariah 14:5 and Jude verse 14 reveal that Christ will come with His saints.

Combining these two statements, we find that Christ will come "in clouds, with His saints." We know also that the ascension of Christ into heaven and His return from heaven are closely parallel. We know, further, that Christ ascended into heaven "in a cloud." We are therefore completing the parallel if we suggest that Christ ascended into heaven together with those of his saints who had at that time been resurrected.

There is one further point of interest to notice in this connection.

> Therefore we also, since we are surrounded by so great a cloud of witnesses, let us lay aside every weight, and the sin which so easily ensnares us, and let us run with endurance the race that is set before us (Heb. 12:1).

What is this "cloud of witnesses" to which the writer of Hebrews refers? The context makes it plain that he is referring to the Old Testament saints whose exploits of faith had been recorded in the previous chapter – Hebrews 11.

These Old Testament saints are pictured as a cloud of witnesses surrounding each Christian believer who undertakes to run the race of faith in this dispensation. In this way the figure of a cloud is once again linked to the saints of the Old Testament.

From all these considerations it seems both logical and scriptural to suggest that, on the day of His ascension, Jesus was taken up into heaven within a cloud that also contained the Old Testament saints who had been resurrected with Him. In this way the resurrection and ascension of Christ would exactly and completely fulfil all that is indicated in the typology of the Old Testament ordinance of the firstfruits. It would also be exactly parallel to the method of His promised return from heaven to earth.

However, this conclusion should be taken as no more than a logical inference from various indications of Scripture. It should not be put forward dogmatically as an established doctrine.

45

THOSE WHO ARE
CHRIST'S AT HIS COMING

In the last chapter we considered the first phase of the resurrection, called by Paul "Christ the firstfruits." We saw how exactly and completely the account of Christ's resurrection given in the New Testament fulfilled the prophetic typology of the ordinance of the first-fruits as ordained for Israel in the Old Testament.

We shall now go on to consider the second main phase of the resurrection – that which Paul refers to as "those who are Christ's at His coming" (1 Cor. 15:23).

Marks of True Believers

Notice carefully the exact phrases which Paul uses concerning this second phase of the resurrection. First, the Greek word here translated "coming" is *parousia*. This is the word mainly used throughout the New Testament to denote that aspect of Christ's second coming which primarily concerns the church – that is, Christ's coming as the Bridegroom to take His bride, the church, to Himself.

Second, we must notice how carefully Paul specifies those who will take part in this second phase of the resurrection. He says, "Those who are Christ's." This phrase indicates possession. It is equivalent to saying "those who belong to Christ." This certainly does not include all those who make a profession of faith in Christ. It covers only those who have so fully and unreservedly yielded themselves to Christ that they are entirely His. They are no longer their own; they belong to Christ.

Paul describes a double "seal" that marks those who fulfil this requirement.

> Nevertheless the solid foundation of God stands, having this seal: "The Lord knows those who are His," and, "Let everyone who names the name of Christ depart from iniquity" (2 Tim. 2:19).

In the last resort, only the Lord Himself knows exactly who are those that belong to Him. In outward conduct, however, all such believers have one feature in common: They "depart from iniquity." Any who lack this second, outward seal are not among those whom the Lord acknowledges as His.

In Galatians Paul gives a further mark by which such people are distinguished.

> And those who are Christ's have crucified the flesh with its passions and desires (5:24).

Professing Christians who lead careless, carnal, self-indulgent lives will not be numbered among those whom Christ will receive to Himself.

Christ is coming, it is true, "like a thief," but He certainly is not coming to steal. He will take to Himself only those who are already His own.

With this warning in mind, let us consider what will take place at this second main phase of the resurrection. Since Paul states that it will take place "at Christ's coming," it is clear that this second phase is directly associated with the return of Christ.

The return of Christ is one of the main themes of biblical prophecy. Someone has estimated that for every promise in the Bible concerning the first coming of Christ, there are at least five promises concerning His second coming. This shows how great a part the theme of the second coming of Christ plays in the total revelation of Scripture. For this reason it is outside the scope of our present studies to discuss in detail every question related to Christ's second coming.

It is, however, helpful to point out that, in the eternal counsel of God, the second coming of Christ is ordained to accomplish a number of different purposes. These purposes are in some sense distinct from each other, yet all are interrelated in God's overall plan. Each of these purposes constitutes one main aspect of Christ's second coming, one main part of the total event as foretold in Scripture.

Five Purposes of Christ's Second Coming

Briefly, we may mention the five main purposes for which Christ will come again.

1. Christ will come for the church. He will come again as the Bridegroom to receive to Himself all true believers as His bride. They will be united with Christ, either by resurrection or by instantaneous change in their bodies while still alive. Jesus promised His disciples:

> And if I go and prepare a place for you, I will come again and receive you to Myself; that where I am, there you may be also (John 14:3).

2. Christ will come for the national salvation of Israel. The national remnant of Israel that has survived the fires of the great tribulation will acknowledge Jesus as Messiah and thus be reconciled to God and restored to His favour and blessing. This is foretold in the promise of God through Isaiah, quoted by Paul.

> And so all Israel will be saved, as it is written:

> > "The Deliverer will come out of Zion,
> > And He will turn away ungodliness
> >   from Jacob;
> > For this is My covenant with them,
> > When I take away their sins"
> >   (Rom. 11:26-27).

3. Christ will come for the overthrow of Antichrist and of Satan himself.

> And then the lawless one [the Antichrist] will be revealed, whom the Lord will consume with the breath of His mouth and destroy with the brightness of His coming [*parousia*] (2 Thess. 2:8).

4. Christ will come for the judgement of the Gentile nations. He Himself gave this prediction:

> When the Son of Man comes in His glory, and all the holy angels with Him, then He will sit on the throne of His glory. All the nations will be gathered before Him, and He will separate them one from another, as a shepherd divides his sheep from the goats (Matt. 25:31-32).

In the verses that follow, Jesus describes in detail the procedure of judgement.

5. Christ will come for the establishment of His millennial kingdom on the earth. This is included in the passage in Matthew 25 and predicted in Isaiah.

> Then the moon will be disgraced
> And the sun ashamed;
> For the Lord of hosts will reign
> On Mount Zion and in Jerusalem
> And before His elders, gloriously (Is. 24:23).

It is also predicted in Zechariah.

> The Lord will be king over the whole earth. On that day there will be one Lord, and his name the only name (14:9, NIV).

The period of time for which Christ will thus reign is given in Revelation 20:4, where it speaks of the martyrs of the tribulation period:

And they lived and reigned with Christ for a thousand years.

(*Millennium* is a Latin word meaning "a period of a thousand years.")

Thus we may briefly summarise the five main purposes for which Christ will come.

1. Christ will come for the church, to receive all true believers to Himself.
2. Christ will come for the national salvation of Israel.
3. Christ will come for the overthrow of Antichrist and of Satan himself.
4. Christ will come for the judgement of the Gentile nations.
5. Christ will come to establish His millennial kingdom upon earth.

While there is general agreement among Bible believers concerning these main purposes of Christ's second coming, there has been much discussion and controversy concerning the details and the precise relationship of each to all the rest. Some of the main questions that have been asked are: Will all these purposes of Christ's return be accomplished together as one single event, or will there be definite intervals of time between some of them? If so, in what order will they take place? Is it possible that some will partly overlap others?

In our present study we shall avoid entering unnecessarily into these controversial questions, and we shall confine ourselves to that particular aspect of Christ's return which is directly associated with the resurrection of the righteous.

Resurrection and Rapture of True Believers

Paul describes how Christians will be resurrected to meet Christ at His coming.

> But I do not want you to be ignorant, brethren, concerning those who have fallen asleep, lest you sorrow as others who have no hope. For if we believe that Jesus died and rose again, even so God will bring with Him those who sleep in Jesus. For this we say to you by the word of the Lord, that we who are alive and remain until the coming of the Lord will by no means precede those who are asleep. For the Lord Himself will descend from heaven with a shout, with the voice of an archangel, and with the trumpet of God. And the dead in Christ will rise first. Then we who are alive and remain shall be caught up together with them in the clouds to meet the

Lord in the air. And thus we shall always be with the Lord. Therefore comfort one another with these words (1 Thess. 4:13-18).

The primary purpose of Paul's teaching here is to comfort Christian believers concerning other Christians – relatives or other loved ones – who have died. These Christians who have died are described as "those who have fallen asleep," or, more precisely, "those who sleep in Jesus." This means those who have died in the faith of the gospel. Paul's message of comfort is based on the assurance that these, and all other true believers, will be resurrected.

The actual picture which Paul gives of this phase of the resurrection is as follows.

First, there will be three dramatic sounds to herald it. The first sound will be the shout of the Lord Jesus Christ Himself, as He Himself had predicted.

All who are in the graves will hear His voice and come forth – those who have done good, to the resurrection of life, and those who have done evil, to the resurrection of condemnation (John 5:28-29).

It is the voice of Christ alone that has power to call the dead out of their graves. However, at this particular moment He will call forth only the righteous dead – only those who have died in the faith. The calling forth of the unrighteous dead will be reserved for a later phase of resurrection.

The other two sounds that will be heard at this point will be the voice of an archangel and the trumpet of God. The archangel here referred to is probably Gabriel, since it appears to be his special ministry to proclaim upon earth impending interventions of God in the affairs of men.

All through the Bible, one main use of the trumpet is to gather the Lord's people together in any special time of crisis. The sound of the trumpet at this point will be the signal for all the Lord's people to gather together with Him as He descends from heaven to meet them.

Upon earth two great events will occur in swift succession. First, all true believers who have died in the faith will be resurrected. Second, all true believers alive on earth at that moment will undergo an instantaneous, supernatural change in their bodies.

Then both these companies of believers – those who were resurrected and those whose bodies were changed without dying – will together be swiftly raised by God's supernatural power from the earth up into the air. There they will be received into clouds, and within these clouds they will be reunited with their Lord and with each other. Thereafter the Lord and His redeemed believers will forever be united in unbroken harmony and fellowship.

There is special significance in two of the Greek words that Paul uses in this passage. Where he says "we shall be caught up," the Greek verb translated "to catch up" is *harpazo*. This denotes a sudden, swift, violent grab. It is used four times in the New Testament to describe people being caught up to heaven.

In addition, it is used in Acts 8:39, where we read that "the Spirit of the Lord caught Philip away" from the Ethiopian eunuch. It is used by Jesus in John 10:12 to describe the wolf "catching" the sheep. It is used by Him also in Matthew 13:19 to describe the birds snatching away the seed sown by the wayside. It is used in Jude verse 23 to describe people being pulled out of the fire.

Traditionally, Bible commentators have rendered *harpazo* by the word *rapture* – either as a noun or as a verb. *Rapture* is derived from a Latin verb which means precisely the same as *harpazo* – "to seize, to snatch away." Throughout the rest of these studies, *rapture* will be used in this sense as the equivalent of *harpazo*.

Paul's use of *harpazo* is deliberately intended to give the impression of one single, swift, sudden, violent act. Indeed, it suggests particularly the act of a thief. In this respect it is in line with other scriptures which compare this aspect of Christ's coming to that of a thief.

> Behold, I am coming as a thief (Rev. 16:15).

> Watch therefore, for you do not know what hour your Lord is coming. But know this, that if the master of the house had known what hour the thief would come, he would have watched and not allowed his house to be broken into (Matt. 24:42-43).

Notice the suggestion of violence in the statement that the house is to be "broken into."

We may say, therefore, that the coming of Christ for His church at this point will be like that of a thief in the following respects. It will be sudden, unexpected, without warning; it will culminate in one single, violent act of snatching away. Furthermore, that which is to be snatched away will be earth's most valuable treasure – the true Christians. However, as we have already said, Christ's coming will differ from that of a thief in one extremely important respect: He will take away only that which is already His by right of redemption.

First Thessalonians 4:17 contains one other significant Greek word. Paul says that we shall meet the Lord "in the air." The Greek word used here is *aer*.

This is one of two Greek words normally translated "air." The other word is *aither*. The difference between these two words is that *aer* denotes the lower air in immediate contact with the earth's surface; *aither* denotes the higher, rarer air, some considerable distance above the earth's surface. Since Paul uses the word *aer* in relation to the Lord's return, he indicates that the Lord's gathering together with His raptured saints will take place in the lower air, quite close to the earth's surface.

Paul refers again to this same moment of resurrection and rapture in 1 Corinthians.

> Behold, I tell you a mystery: We shall not all sleep, but we shall all be changed – in a moment, in the twinkling of an eye, at the last trumpet. For the trumpet will sound, and the dead will be raised incorruptible, and we shall be changed (15:51-52).

Paul here unfolds "a mystery" – that is, a previously unrevealed secret of God's plan for the church. The secret thus revealed is this: All true believers will be raptured together at the Lord's coming, but not all those to be raptured will have died and been resurrected.

Those who are alive at the Lord's coming will not die at all but will simply undergo an instantaneous and miraculous change in their bodies. By this change their bodies will be rendered exactly like those of the other believers who have been resurrected from the dead.

In the next verse Paul briefly summarises the nature of the change that will take place.

> For this corruptible must put on incorruption, and this mortal must put on immortality (1 Cor. 15:53).

Instead of being mortal and corruptible, the new body of each believer will be immortal and incorruptible.

Does this account given by Paul constitute a complete picture of the resurrection of all believers before the establishment of Christ's kingdom in the millennium?

To this question the answer would appear to be no. For it would seem that at least two further stages in the resurrection of the righteous are recorded in the book of Revelation.

Witnesses and Martyrs

In Revelation 11 we read the account of God's two witnesses during the tribulation period and of their eventual martyrdom "by the beast that ascends out of the bottomless pit" – the Antichrist.

> Then those from the peoples, tribes, tongues, and nations will see their dead bodies three and a half days, and not allow their dead bodies to be put into graves . . . Now after the three and a half days the breath of life from God entered them, and they stood on their feet . . . And they heard a loud voice from heaven saying to them, "Come up here." And they ascended to heaven in a cloud, and their enemies saw them (Rev. 11:9,11-12).

The account makes it plain that this was in the fullest sense a resurrection. Although their bodies had not been buried, these two martyrs had been dead for three and a half days. Then, in the open sight of their enemies, their bodies were resurrected, and they ascended into heaven. It is interesting to notice that their ascension into heaven is similar to each of the other cases that we have already considered in that it takes place in a cloud.

It seems clear that this resurrection of the two witnesses is distinct from the resurrection of Christians described in 1 Thessalonians 4:16-17. It is not associated with the descent of Christ from heaven, nor is there any mention of other accompanying features, such as a trumpet or the voice of an archangel.

If we now turn to Revelation, we find the account of what appears to be a further stage in the resurrection of the righteous.

> And I saw thrones, and they sat on them, and judgement was committed to them. And I saw the souls of those who had been beheaded for their witness to Jesus and for the word of God, who had not worshipped the beast or his image, and had not received his mark on their foreheads or on their hands. And they lived and reigned with Christ for a thousand years.

> But the rest of the dead did not live again until the thousand
> years were finished. This is the first resurrection. Blessed and
> holy is he who has part in the first resurrection (20:4-6).

The people whose resurrection is described here are those who were
beheaded as martyrs of Jesus during the period of the Antichrist's rule.
These tribulation saints are shown as being resurrected at the close of the
great tribulation, just prior to the establishment of Christ's millennial
kingdom. They thus share with Christ Himself, and with all other resurrected saints, the privilege of ruling and judging the nations on earth
during the millennium.

Some commentators believe that these tribulation martyrs are
included in the resurrection of Christians described in 1 Thessalonians
4:16-17. Others view it as a distinct and subsequent stage in the resurrection of the righteous. There is little to be gained by making this a
subject of controversy.

John closes the account of the resurrection of these martyrs with the
words:

> This is the first resurrection. Blessed and holy is he who has
> part in the first resurrection (Rev. 20:5-6).

By these words John apparently indicates that "the first resurrection"
is now complete. All those who take part in this resurrection are called
"blessed and holy." That is to say, they are all righteous believers. (Up to
this point, none of the unrighteous has been resurrected. The second
resurrection, in which the unrighteous have their part, is described by
John in the latter part of Revelation 20.)

If we now combine the revelations given by Paul and John, we may
offer the following summary of the resurrection of the righteous.

The total resurrection of the righteous, from the moment of Christ's
own resurrection down to the resurrection of the tribulation martyrs just
prior to the millennium, is called by John "the first resurrection." All
those who take part in this resurrection are "blessed and holy"; that is,
they are all righteous believers.

However, within this total resurrection of the righteous we may
discern at least four distinct events.

1. "Christ the firstfruits" – that is, Christ Himself and those
   of the Old Testament saints who were resurrected at the
   time of Christ's resurrection.

2. "Those who are Christ's at His coming" – the true Christians who are ready to meet Christ at His return, together with those who died in the faith – all these together being caught up in clouds to meet Christ in the air.
3. The "two witnesses" of the tribulation period, who are left dead but unburied for three and a half days and are then resurrected and ascend to heaven in a cloud.
4. The remainder of the tribulation martyrs, who are resurrected at the close of the tribulation period in time to share with Christ and the other saints in the privilege of ruling and judging the nations on earth during the millennium.

Such, in brief outline, is the New Testament picture of the resurrection of the righteous.

In the next chapter we shall go on to consider the third and final phase of the resurrection.

46
THEN COMES THE END

W̲e shall now consider the final, closing phase of the resurrection. Paul indicates that this will be preceded by the resurrection of true believers – "those who are Christ's at His coming" – and will coincide with the consummation of Christ's millennial kingdom.

> But each one in his own order: Christ the firstfruits, afterward those who are Christ's at His coming. Then comes the end, when He [Christ] delivers the kingdom to God the Father, when He puts an end to all rule and all authority and power. For He must reign till He has put all enemies under His feet. The last enemy that will be destroyed is death (1 Cor. 15:23-26).

At the Close of the Millennium

In verse 24 Paul moves on to the final phase of the resurrection. This he refers to in the phrase "Then comes the end." He goes on to indicate the other main events that will be associated with this final phase of the resurrection.

At this time Christ will have completed His earthly reign of one
thousand years, by the end of which God the Father will have brought all
Christ's enemies into subjection to Him. The last of these enemies will
be death.

Thereafter, Christ the Son will in turn offer up His kingdom to God
the Father. In accordance with His position as the Son, He will voluntarily place Himself and His kingdom in subjection to His Father.

This closing event of Christ's earthly reign is described by Paul two
verses later.

> Now when all things are made subject to Him [Christ], then
> the Son Himself will also be subject to Him who put all things
> under Him, that God may be all in all (1 Cor. 15:28).

As we study this prophetic picture of the end, we notice the perfect
harmony that exists within the Godhead between the Father and the Son.
First God the Father will, during the millennium, establish Christ the
Son as His appointed representative and ruler over all things. By the
close of this period the Father will have brought all Christ's enemies into
subjection to Him – the last enemy being death. Thereafter Christ the
Son will in turn offer up in subjection to the authority of the Father both
Himself and all that the Father has made subject to Him. In this way,
Paul says, God the Father, through Christ, will be "all in all."

This offering up of the completed kingdom by Christ to the Father
represents the climax and culmination of God's plan for all the ages.
Paul also describes this glorious culmination of God's purpose.

> [God has] made known to us the mystery of His will,
> according to His good pleasure which He purposed in
> Himself, that in the dispensation [or administration] of the
> fullness of the times He might gather together in one all
> things in Christ, both which are in heaven and which are on
> earth (Eph. 1:9-10).

This gathering together of all things in Christ by God the Father, Paul
says, will usher in "the administration of the fullness of the times" – that
is, the period which will mark the culmination and consummation of
God's plan that has been gradually maturing throughout all preceding
ages.

If we now turn to Revelation 20 we shall see just how the final resurrection of all the remaining dead will be related to the other parts of God's plan for the consummation of Christ's millennial reign.

John describes Satan's last attempt to oppose the authority of God and of Christ and to stir up rebellion against it. This occurs at the end of the millennium.

> Now when the thousand years have expired, Satan will be released from his prison and will go out to deceive the nations which are in the four corners of the earth, Gog and Magog, to gather them together to battle, whose number is as the sand of the sea. They went up on the breadth of the earth and surrounded the camp of the saints and the beloved city. And fire came down from God out of heaven and devoured them. And the devil, who deceived them, was cast into the lake of fire and brimstone where the beast and the false prophet are. And they will be tormented day and night forever and ever (Rev. 20:7-10).

John uses the phrases "the camp of the saints" and "the beloved city" to describe the city of Jerusalem and the territory surrounding that. During the millennium Jerusalem will be the earthly centre of Christ's administration and rule over the nations of the earth.

During this period Satan will be kept confined as a prisoner in the bottomless pit, but at its close he will be allowed to go free just long enough to stir up this final rebellion among the Gentile nations, which will culminate in an attempt to attack Jerusalem.

God will intervene, however, with fire from heaven. The rebellion will be totally defeated. And Satan himself will be cast into the lake of eternal fire, there to be tormented forever together with the beast (the Antichrist) and the false prophet. Both of these will already have been cast into the lake of fire at the time of Christ's return to earth and of the commencement of the millennium.

The Final Resurrection

After this John describes the final resurrection of all the remaining dead.

> Then I saw a great white throne and Him who sat on it, from whose face the earth and the heaven fled away. And there was found no place for them. And I saw the dead, small and great,

standing before God, and books were opened. And another
book was opened, which is the Book of Life. And the dead
were judged according to their works, by the things which
were written in the books. The sea gave up the dead who were
in it, and Death and Hades delivered up the dead who were in
them. And they were judged, each one according to his
works. Then Death and Hades were cast into the lake of fire.
This is the second death. And anyone not found written in the
Book of Life was cast into the lake of fire (Rev. 20:11-15).

In this account we notice that resurrection comes first, then
judgement. This same principle is observed at every stage of resurrection. Since it is in their bodies that men have committed acts of good
or evil, it is in their bodies also that they must appear before God to hear
His judgement upon those acts.

We have already seen that all those who have trusted Christ for
salvation will have been resurrected prior to the millennium. This will
include both the saints of the old covenant and the saints of the new
covenant. It would seem, therefore, that the majority of those to be resurrected at the close of the millennium will be people who have died in sin
and unbelief.

In this connection it is significant that John refers to those resurrected
at the close of the millennium as "the dead." He says, "I saw the dead,
small and great, standing before God." This is different from the
language which he uses to describe the resurrection of the righteous dead
at the beginning of the millennium. Concerning these he says, "And they
lived and reigned with Christ for a thousand years" (Rev. 20:4).

Thus, concerning the resurrected righteous, John says not only that
they were resurrected, but also that "they lived" – they were in the fullest
and truest sense alive. On the other hand, those whom John saw resurrected at the close of the millennium are still "the dead." Although
resurrected from the grave in their bodies, they are still spiritually dead
– dead in trespasses and sins, alienated and cut off from the presence and
fellowship of God. They are brought before God for the last time, only
to hear His final sentence of condemnation upon them. Thereafter their
destiny is the lake of fire, "the second death," the place of final, eternal
banishment from God's presence, the place which offers henceforth no
hope either of change or of return.

Among all these, however, Scripture indicates that there will be at
least two categories of people who will come forth to the resurrection of
life and not of condemnation.

One such category includes people such as the queen of the South (Sheba) and the men of Nineveh referred to by Jesus.

> The queen of the South will rise up in the judgement with the men of this generation and condemn them, for she came from the ends of the earth to hear the wisdom of Solomon; and indeed a greater than Solomon is here. The men of Nineveh will rise up in the judgement with this generation and condemn it, for they repented at the preaching of Jonah; and indeed a greater than Jonah is here (Luke 11:31-32).

In each of these examples it is clear that the men of this generation (who rejected the mercy offered them through Jesus) will rise up (be resurrected) for the judgement of condemnation. Together with them, however, two groups will be resurrected who will receive mercy at the judgement: the queen of the South and the men of Nineveh.

Unlike the saints of the old covenant, these two groups were not granted a revelation of Christ's atoning sacrifice – foreshadowed in type and in prophecy – in which they could trust for salvation. Consequently they will not be included in the resurrection of those who are Christ's at His coming. They did, however, respond in faith to the limited measure of light that came to them. At the close of the millennium, therefore, they will be delivered from condemnation and enter into the resurrection of life.

Will there be others in the same category as the queen of the South and the men of Nineveh? If so, who? And how many? The answers to these questions can come only from the omniscience of God Himself. One thing, however, is certain: Those who have heard and rejected the gospel of Christ have forever shut themselves off from the mercy of God.

A second category of people who will be delivered from condemnation at the final resurrection will be the righteous who have died during Christ's millennial reign on earth.

Concerning this millennial period, we find the following prophetic account in Isaiah.

> No more shall an infant from there live but a few days,
> Nor an old man who has not fulfilled his days;
> For the child shall die one hundred years old,
> But the sinner being one hundred years old shall be accursed (65:20).

The picture here given by Isaiah of life on earth during the millennium indicates that though the span of human life will be greatly extended, nevertheless both the righteous and the sinner will still be subject to death. From this we may conclude that the righteous who die during the millennium will be resurrected at its close but will not be subject to God's judgement upon the unrighteous who are to be resurrected at the same time.

If we now turn again to Revelation 20 we notice the completeness and the finality of the resurrection depicted by John.

> The sea gave up the dead who were in it, and Death and Hades delivered up the dead who were in them. And they were judged, each one according to his works (Rev. 20:13).

To this final resurrection of the remaining dead there are no exceptions. It includes "each one." None is omitted. Every realm of God's created universe is called upon by divine authority to give up the dead which are in it. The three words which John uses in this connection are "the sea," "Death" and "Hades."

The Greek word *Hades* corresponds to the Hebrew word *Sheol* used in the Old Testament. Hades or Sheol is a place of temporary confinement for departed spirits, prior to their final resurrection and judgement. After final resurrection and judgement, all the unrighteous are consigned to the lake of fire. The usual Hebrew word used in the Old Testament for this lake of fire is not *Sheol* but *Gehenna.*

There is therefore a clear distinction between Sheol, or Hades, and Gehenna, or the lake of fire. Sheol is a place of temporary confinement to which are consigned the spirits, but not the bodies, of the departed. Gehenna is a place of final, unending punishment to which is consigned, after resurrection, the total personality of every unrighteous person – spirit, soul and body together.

This distinction between Sheol and Gehenna is further brought out by the statement of John in Revelation 20:14.

> Then Death and Hades were cast into the lake of fire.

Death and Hades Are Persons

Just what is the true nature of Death and Hades as revealed in the New Testament? John's famous vision of the four horsemen sheds light on this question. Concerning the fourth horseman, John says:

> And I looked, and behold, a pale horse. And the name of him
> who sat on it was Death, and Hades followed with him (Rev.
> 6:8).

It is obvious from this account that both Death and Hades were
revealed to John as being persons. Only a person could sit on a horse,
and only another person could follow along with this first one. This
passage therefore casts light on the nature of Death and Hades as
revealed in the Scriptures.

In one sense death is a state or condition. It is the cessation of life, the
experience which results in the separation of the spirit from the body.
However, Death is also a person. Death is the dark angel, the minister of
Satan who claims the spirit of every unrighteous person that is separated
from his body when he dies.

A similar truth applies also to Hades. In one sense Hades is a place of
confinement for departed spirits. In another sense, however, Hades is a
person. Hades, like Death, is a dark angel, a minister of Satan, following
close upon the heels of Death. Hades takes charge of the spirits of the
unrighteous which have been claimed by Death and conducts them to the
realm of departed spirits from which he receives his name – that is,
Hades.

Thus Death and Hades are both dark angels, ministers of Satan's
infernal kingdom. But the difference between them is this: Death first
claims the departing spirits of all who die in unrighteousness; Hades
receives them from Death and conducts them to their appointed place of
imprisonment. For this reason John saw them moving among men in that
order: first Death, claiming the departing spirits, then Hades, taking
them to their prison in the lower world.

This scene from Revelation casts light on the words of Jesus.

> Most assuredly, I say to you, if anyone keeps My word he
> shall never see death (John 8:51).

Jesus does not say here that the believer will not experience physical
death. He says that the believer will not "see death." He is not referring
to the physical condition of death which results from the separation of
the spirit from the body. When He speaks of "seeing death," He is
referring to the person of the dark angel whose name is Death, and to the
other dark angel, his companion, whose name is Hades.

Jesus means that the spirit of the true believer, on departing from the
body, will never come under the dominion of these two dark angels,

Death and Hades. Rather, like the poor beggar Lazarus, the departing spirit of the true believer will be met by God's angels – the angels of light – and by them be escorted to Paradise.

With this in mind, too, we can understand Paul's statement that "the last enemy that will be destroyed is death" (1 Cor. 15:26); and also John's statement that "then Death and Hades were cast into the lake of fire" (Rev. 20:14).

In each of these passages the primary reference is to Death and Hades as persons, as dark angels, ministers of Satan and enemies of God and the human race. The last of all God's enemies to receive the judgement due him will be Death. Together with Hades he will be cast into the lake of fire, there to join their master, Satan, and all the rest of Satan's servants and followers both angelic and human.

By this final act of judgement, the last of God's enemies will forever have been banished from His presence.

47
WITH WHAT BODY?

In the last three chapters we have considered in succession the three main phases of the resurrection as stated by the apostle Paul (see 1 Cor. 15:23-24).

1. "Christ the firstfruits" – the resurrection of Christ Himself, together with those of the Old Testament saints who were resurrected with Him.
2. "Those who are Christ's at His coming" – all believers who have died during the preceding ages and who will be resurrected at Christ's second coming, prior to the establishment of His millennial kingdom.
3. "The end" – the final resurrection of all the remaining dead at the close of the millennium.

We shall devote most of this final chapter to considering what the Scripture reveals about the nature of the body with which Christian believers will be resurrected.

In our earlier studies on this subject we have already pointed out that there is direct continuity between the body that dies and is buried and the body that is later resurrected. The basic material of the body that is to be resurrected is the same as that of the body that is buried. That is to say, resurrection is the raising up of the same body that was buried, and not the creation of a completely new body.

However, once this fact is established, we must also add that, in the case of the Christian believer, the body that is resurrected undergoes certain definite and tremendous changes.

Analogy of Grain

This whole question is raised and discussed by Paul.

> But someone will say, "How are the dead raised up? And with what body do they come?" Foolish one, what you sow is not made alive unless it dies. And what you sow, you do not sow that body that shall be, but mere grain – perhaps wheat or some other grain. But God gives it a body as He pleases, and to each seed its own body (1 Cor. 15:35-38).

Here Paul uses the analogy of a grain of wheat planted in the ground to illustrate the relationship between the body that is buried and the body that is raised up in resurrection. Out of this analogy there emerge three facts which may be applied to the resurrection of the body.

1. There is direct continuity between the seed that is planted in the ground and the plant that later grows up out of the ground from that seed. The basic material of the original seed is still contained in the plant that grows up out of it.
2. The plant that grows up out of the original seed undergoes, in that process, certain definite and obvious changes. The outward form and appearance of the new plant is different from that of the original seed.
3. The nature of the original seed determines the nature of the plant that grows up out of it. Each kind of seed can produce only the kind of plant that is appropriate to it. A wheat seed can produce only a stalk of wheat; a barley seed can produce only a stalk of barley.

Let us now apply these three facts taken from the analogy of a seed to the nature of the body that is to be resurrected.

1. There is direct continuity between the body that is buried and the body that is resurrected.
2. The body that is resurrected undergoes, in that process, certain definite and obvious changes. The outward form and appearance of the new, resurrected body are different from those of the original body that was buried.
3. The nature of the body that is buried determines the nature of the body that is resurrected. There will be a direct logical and causal connection between the condition of the believer in his present earthly existence and the nature of his resurrected body.

Paul gives further details about the nature of the changes that the believer's body will undergo at resurrection.

All flesh is not the same flesh, but there is one kind of flesh of men, another flesh of beasts, another of fish, and another of birds. There are also celestial bodies and terrestrial bodies; but the glory of the celestial is one, and the glory of the terrestrial is another. There is one glory of the sun, another glory of the moon, and another glory of the stars; for one star differs from another star in glory. So also is the resurrection of the dead. The body is sown in corruption, it is raised in incorruption. It is sown in dishonour, it is raised in glory. It is sown in weakness, it is raised in power. It is sown a natural body, it is raised a spiritual body. There is a natural body, and there is a spiritual body (1 Cor. 15:39-44).

To complete this picture, we should add Paul's statement in verse 53.

For this corruptible must put on incorruption, and this mortal must put on immortality.

This analysis given here by Paul of the nature of the changes that the believer's body will undergo at resurrection may be expressed in the form of a series of statements.

1. Paul points out that, even among the bodies of creatures with which we are familiar in the present natural order, there are differences of nature and constitution. He mentions the following main classes: men, animals,

fishes and birds. This is in line with the conclusions of modern science that there is no discernible difference in the chemical makeup of the blood of different racial groups within the human family, but that there is a difference between the chemical makeup of the blood of human beings and that of other orders of the animal kingdom.

2. Paul points out that, over and above all bodies of the order with which we are familiar here on earth, there is another and higher order of bodies, which he calls the "celestial" or "heavenly" order. Once again, this is in line with recent scientific discoveries. Science has now succeeded in putting men into space. But in order to keep them alive, it has to confine them in a capsule and surround them with the atmosphere and conditions of earth. To be truly at home any distance from the surface of the earth, man must be equipped with a body of an altogether different order from his present one. But for this he must depend upon God; he cannot do it for himself.

3. Paul points out that, among the various heavenly bodies which we can see – that is, the sun, the moon and the stars – there are differences of nature and of brightness. The sun produces its own light; the moon merely reflects the light of the sun. Among the stars there are many different orders of brightness. Paul states that the same will be true of the bodies of believers when they are resurrected from the dead. There will be many different orders of glory among them.

This is foretold in the prophecy of the resurrection given in Daniel 12:2-3.

> And many of those who sleep in the dust of the earth shall
>   awake,
> Some to everlasting life,
> Some to shame and everlasting contempt.
> Those who are wise shall shine
> Like the brightness of the firmament,
> And those who turn many to righteousness
> Like the stars forever and ever.

Here Daniel foretells the differences in rewards and in glory among the resurrected saints. Those who have been most faithful and diligent in making known God's truth to others will shine the most brightly.

This picture of the saints resurrected with glorious bodies like those of the stars is also the fulfilment of God's promise to Abraham.

> There He brought him outside and said, "Look now toward heaven, and count the stars if you are able to number them." And He said to him, "So shall your descendants be" (Gen. 15:5).

Included by God among Abraham's seed are all those who believe and obey the word of God's promise just as Abraham did – those who accept by faith in their hearts the divine seed of God's Word. In fact, it is this incorruptible seed of God's Word, received by faith in the heart of each believer, that makes possible his resurrection among the righteous.

In the day of the final fulfilment of God's promise, at the resurrection, all the believers then raised up on the basis of their faith in God's Word will be like the stars that God showed to Abraham – as numerous, as glorious and as diverse from each other in their glory.

Five Distinctive Changes

In his analysis of the nature of the believer's resurrection body, Paul closes by listing a series of specific changes that will take place.

1. The present body is corruptible, subject to corruption – to sickness, decay and old age. The new body will be incorruptible – free from all these evils.
2. The present body is mortal – subject to death. The new body will be immortal – incapable of death.
3. The present body is a body of dishonour. In Philippians 3:21 it is called "our lowly body." But a more literal translation of this would be "the body of our humiliation." Man's present body is the outcome of his sin and disobedience to God. It is a continual source of humiliation – a continual reminder of the fall and of the resultant physical frailty and insufficiency. No matter how great man's achievements may be in the realms of art or science, he is continually humbled and brought low by the physical needs and limitations of his body. However,

the new resurrection body will be a body of beauty and glory, free from all of man's present limitations.

4. The present body is committed to the grave in weakness. The act of burial is the final acknowledgement of man's debt to death; it is the supreme confession of man's weakness. But the new body will be raised up from the grave by the power of almighty God, and the resurrection will thus be a testimony of God's omnipotence, swallowing up the power of death and the grave.

5. The present body is a natural body – literally, a "soulish" body. (The Greek word translated natural is *psuchikos,* directly derived from *psuche*, the word for "soul." It is a pity that English does not use the corresponding adjective, *soulish.*)

According to God's original pattern in creation, man was to be a triune being consisting of spirit, soul and body. Of these three elements, man's spirit was capable of direct communication and fellowship with God and was intended to control the lower elements of man's nature – the soul and the body. However, as a result of man's yielding to temptation at the fall, these lower elements of his nature – the soul and the body – gained control. This produced far-reaching changes both in man's inner personality and in his physical body. His body became "soulish." Henceforth, its organs and functions were given over to the expression and satisfaction of the lower desires of his soul but were incapable of fully expressing the higher aspirations of his spirit.

In some sense this "soulish" body is a prison – a place of confinement and restriction for man's spirit. However, the new resurrection body will be "spiritual." It will be perfectly adapted to express and fulfil the highest aspirations of man's spirit. Clothed in this new body, the spirit will once again be the controlling element, and the whole personality of the resurrected believer will function in harmony and perfection under the spirit's control.

Paul sums up the differences between the old and the new body by contrasting the body of Adam with that of Christ and by saying that the resurrected body of the believer will be similar to the Lord's.

> The first man was of the earth, made of dust; the second Man is the Lord from heaven. As was the man of dust, so also are those who are made of dust; and as is the heavenly Man, so also are those who are heavenly. And as we have borne the

image of the man of dust, we shall also bear the image of the heavenly Man (1 Cor. 15:47-49).

That is to say, man's present body is similar, in its earthly nature, to the body of the first created man, Adam, from whom all other men are descended. But the resurrection body of the believer will be similar to that of Christ, who, through the new creation, has become the head of a new race in which are included all those redeemed through faith in Him from sin and its consequences.

Paul gives a similar picture of the believer's resurrection body.

> For our citizenship is in heaven, from which we also eagerly wait for the Saviour, the Lord Jesus Christ, who will transform our lowly body that it may be conformed to His glorious body, according to the working by which He is able even to subdue all things to Himself (Phil. 3:20-21).

Translated more literally, this last verse states that Christ is able to transform the body of our humiliation so that it becomes similar in form to the body of His glory.

In 1 John 3:2 we glimpse a similar picture of the transformation of the believer at the return of Christ.

> Beloved, now we are children of God; and it has not yet been revealed what we shall be, but we know that when He is revealed, we shall be like Him, for we shall see Him as He is.

Even those Christians who are alive at Christ's return and who therefore will not need to be resurrected will at that time undergo a similar instantaneous and miraculous change in their bodies.

> Behold, I tell you a mystery: We shall not all sleep, but we shall all be changed – in a moment, in the twinkling of an eye, at the last trumpet. For the trumpet will sound, and the dead will be raised incorruptible, and we shall be changed (1 Cor. 15:51-52).

Where Paul says, "We shall not all sleep," he means, "We shall not all die." Then he goes on to say, "But we shall all be changed." In other words, all true believers, whether resurrected or raptured alive, will undergo the same instantaneous and miraculous change in their bodies.

Concerning the nature of Christ's own body after His resurrection, the Gospels give us certain interesting indications. It would appear that He was no longer subject to those limitations of time and space with which we are familiar in our present earthly body. He could appear or disappear at will; He could pass through locked doors; He could appear in different forms in different places. He could also ascend to heaven and descend again to earth. In these and in other respects which are perhaps not yet revealed, the body of the redeemed believer after resurrection or rapture will be like that of his Lord.

So far we have spoken only about the resurrection body of the redeemed believer. What about the unrighteous? those who are not redeemed? those who die in their sins?

The Scripture reveals clearly that these, too, in their own order, will be resurrected for judgement and for punishment. With what kind of bodies will they be clothed at their resurrection?

To this question no clear answer or even indication is found in the Bible. We must therefore be content to leave it unanswered.

The Unique Importance of the Resurrection

There are three main reasons why the doctrine of the resurrection occupies a special, central place in the Christian faith.

The first reason is that the resurrection is God's own vindication of Jesus Christ.

[Christ was] declared to be the Son of God with power, according to the Spirit of holiness, by the resurrection from the dead (Rom. 1:4).

Previously, Christ had been brought before two human courts – first the religious court of the Jewish council, and then the secular court of the Roman governor Pontius Pilate. Both these courts had rejected Jesus' claim to be the Son of God and had condemned Him to death. Furthermore, both these courts had united in seeking to prevent any breaking open of the grave of Jesus. To this end, the Jewish council had provided their special seal, and the Roman governor had provided an armed guard of soldiers.

However, on the third day God intervened. The seal was broken, the armed guard was paralysed, and Jesus came forth from the tomb. By this act God reversed the decisions of the Jewish council and the Roman governor, and He publicly vindicated the claim of Christ to be the sinless

Son of God.

The second main reason for the importance of the resurrection is that it is the sure seal upon God's offer of forgiveness and salvation to every repentant sinner who will put his faith in Christ.

> [Christ was] delivered up because of our offences, and was raised because of our justification (Rom. 4:25).

This shows that the sinner's justification is dependent upon Christ being raised again from the dead. Had Christ remained on the cross or in the tomb, God's promise to the sinner of salvation and eternal life could never have been fulfilled. It is only the risen Christ, received and confessed by faith, who brings to the sinner pardon, peace, eternal life and victory over sin.

> If you confess with your mouth the Lord Jesus [or Jesus as Lord] and believe in your heart that God has raised Him from the dead, you will be saved (Rom. 10:9).

Salvation is dependent upon two things: 1) openly confessing Jesus as Lord; 2) believing in the heart that God raised Jesus from the dead. Thus, saving faith includes faith in the resurrection. There can be no salvation for those who do not believe in the resurrection of Christ.

Logic and intellectual honesty permit no other conclusion. If Christ is not risen from the dead, then He has no power to pardon or to save the sinner. But if He is risen, as the Scripture states, then this is logical proof of His power to pardon and to save.

> Therefore He is also able to save to the uttermost those who come to God through Him, since He ever lives to make intercession for them (Heb. 7:25).

Christ's resurrection is an absolute, logical necessity as a basis of God's offer of salvation.

> And if Christ is not risen, then our preaching is vain and your faith is also vain (1 Cor. 15:14).

> And if Christ is not risen, your faith is futile; you are still in your sins! (1 Cor. 15:17).

The condition of contemporary Christendom abundantly confirms these plain statements of Scripture. Those theologians who reject the personal, physical resurrection of Christ may moralise and theorise as much as they please, but one thing they never come to know in personal experience is the peace and joy of sins forgiven.

Finally, the third reason for the importance of the resurrection is that it constitutes the culmination of all our hopes as Christians and the supreme goal of our life of faith here on earth.

Paul says that the resurrection is the supreme goal and consummation of all his earthly endeavours. Speaking of the motivating purpose of his life as a Christian, he says:

> That I may know Him [Christ] and the power of His resurrection, and the fellowship of His sufferings, being conformed to His death, if, by any means, I may attain to the resurrection from the dead. Not that I have already attained, or am already perfected; but I press on, that I may lay hold of that for which Christ Jesus has also laid hold of me (Phil. 3:10-12).

Notice particularly the two phrases "that I may know . . . the power of His resurrection" and "if, by any means, I may attain to the resurrection from the dead." Paul did not intend to let anything in this world prevent him from attaining to the consummation of all his beliefs and labours – the resurrection of the dead. In this respect, the attitude of every Christian believer should be the same as that of Paul.

If there is no resurrection, then the Christian faith and the Christian life are a pathetic deception.

> If in this life only we have hope in Christ, we are of all men the most pitiable (1 Cor. 15:19).

On the other hand, if we really believe in the resurrection, our life's aim and purpose will be like Paul's: to attain it.

PART VII

ETERNAL JUDGEMENT

EVERY ONE OF YOUR RIGHTEOUS
JUDGEMENTS ENDURES FOREVER.

PSALM 119:160

48
GOD THE JUDGE OF ALL

Throughout this study we have been systematically examining the six foundation doctrines of Christ which are listed in Hebrews 6:1-2.

1. Repentance from dead works
2. Faith toward God
3. The doctrine of baptisms
4. Laying on of hands
5. Resurrection of the dead
6. Eternal judgement

We will now examine the sixth and last of these foundation doctrines: eternal judgement.

In this chapter we shall consider the following two aspects of divine judgement: 1) the general revelation of Scripture concerning God as the Judge of all; 2) the main principles according to which God's judgement is administered.

Judgement Tempered by Mercy

For an introduction to the teaching of the Bible concerning God as the Judge, we turn to Hebrews.

> But you have come to Mount Zion and to the city of the living God, the heavenly Jerusalem, to an innumerable company of angels, to the general assembly and church of the firstborn who are registered in heaven, to God the Judge of all, to the spirits of just men made perfect, to Jesus the Mediator of the new covenant, and to the blood of sprinkling that speaks better things than that of Abel (12:22-24).

These three verses present a picture of God in His heavenly dwelling and of the saints and the redeemed who dwell with Him there. The key to the proper analysis of these verses is the number three.

First of all, the verses fall naturally into three main parts: 1) a description of God's dwelling place, 2) an enumeration of those who dwell there with God and 3) a presentation of God Himself.

Then each of these three main parts falls naturally into a further threefold subdivision.

The description of God's dwelling is threefold: 1) "Mount Zion," 2) "the city of the living God" and 3) "the heavenly Jerusalem."

The enumeration of those who dwell there is likewise threefold: 1) "an innumerable company of angels," 2) "the general assembly and church of the firstborn who are registered in heaven" and 3) "the spirits of just men made perfect." Concerning these three groups, we may offer the following brief explanation.

The "angels" here referred to are those who kept their proper domain, joining neither in Satan's first rebellion nor in the universal wickedness of both men and angels in the period before the flood. The "church of the firstborn" represents the saints of the new covenant, who, through the experience of the new birth, have their names registered in heaven and thus have become a firstfruits of God's new creation in Christ. The "spirits of just men made perfect" represent the saints of previous ages, who, through a lifetime's walk of faith, were gradually made perfect.

Finally, the presentation of God Himself is likewise threefold: 1) "God the Judge of all," 2) "Jesus the Mediator of the new covenant" and 3) "the blood of sprinkling [that is, the sprinkled blood of Jesus], that speaks better things than that of Abel."

With the eye of faith and the light of Scripture, let us survey this heavenly scene. In the centre of it all we observe one solemn, majestic and awe-inspiring figure – "God the Judge of all." Here God is revealed to us in His sovereign, eternal authority as Judge – Judge of all, Judge of heaven and earth, Judge of angels and Judge of men.

However, if God were revealed only as Judge, there would be no place here for sinful men – neither for the perfected spirits of the Old Testament nor for the reborn saints of the New. In mercy, therefore, the revelation of God's Word leads us on from the figure of God the Judge to the figure of Jesus the Mediator – the only One who can come between a righteous, holy God and lost, sinful men and reconcile the one to the other. The picture is completed by the revelation of the blood of Jesus, being both the means and the price by which reconciliation has been achieved.

In this picture the blood of Jesus is contrasted with the blood of Abel. There are three main points of contrast.

1. The blood of Abel was shed without his own will or consent, spilled suddenly by a murderer's blow without warning; the blood of Jesus was freely given of His own consent as the price of man's redemption.
2. The blood of Abel was sprinkled upon the earth; the blood of Jesus was sprinkled before the mercy seat in heaven.
3. The blood of Abel cried out to God for vengeance upon his murderer; the blood of Jesus pleads for mercy and forgiveness for the sinner.

We see, therefore, that this revelation of God as Judge of all is tempered by the revelation of God's mercy and grace manifested in the mediatorial office and the shed blood of Christ. This revelation of God as a God of judgement tempered by grace and mercy is in harmony with the total revelation of Scripture upon this theme.

The entire Bible reveals that, by sovereign, eternal right, the office of judge belongs to God Himself. This theme runs through the whole of the Old Testament. For instance, Abraham said to the Lord:

Shall not the Judge of all the earth do right? (Gen. 18:25).

Other Old Testament sources say:

May the Lord, the Judge, render judgement this day (Judg. 11:27).

Surely He [God] is God who judges in the earth (Ps. 58:11).

The psalmist says to God:

Rise up, O Judge of the earth (Ps. 94:2).

(For the Lord is our Judge . . .) (Is. 33:22).

However, the truest and most perfect expression of God's eternal nature is not in judgement but in grace, not in wrath but in mercy. This truth is illustrated in the description of God's wrath and impending judgement given in Isaiah 28:21.

The Lord will rise up as he did at Mount Perazim, he will
   rouse himself as in the Valley of Gibeon –
to do his work, his strange work, and perform his task, his
   alien task (NIV, italics added).

Here the prophet Isaiah pictures the Lord rising up to administer wrath and judgement upon His adversaries. However, he describes this act as strange and alien.

The administration of wrath and judgement is alien to God's nature. It is not something He naturally desires to do. It is rather the inevitable response of God to the unthankful and unholy behaviour of man. It is the warped and twisted character and conduct of man, the creature, which calls forth this strange manifestation of wrath and judgement from God, the Creator.

As we move on from the Old Testament into the New, we enter into a fuller revelation of the motives and methods of God's judgement. Renewed emphasis is laid upon the fact that wrath and judgement are alien to the abiding nature and purpose of God.

For God did not send His Son into the world to condemn the world, but that the world through Him might be saved (John 3:17).

The Lord is not slack concerning His promise, as some count slackness, but is long-suffering toward us, not willing that any should perish but that all should come to repentance (2 Pet. 3:9).

These scriptures – and many others like them – reveal that God delights to offer mercy and salvation but that He is reluctant to administer wrath and judgement. However, the New Testament revelation takes us still further along this line of truth. The reluctance of God to administer judgement finds expression also in the way in which God's judgement will ultimately be carried out.

The Father – The Son – The Word

In the first instance and by sovereign eternal right, judgement belongs to God the Father. The apostle Peter speaks of "the Father, who without partiality judges according to each one's work" (1 Pet. 1:17).

Here judgement of all men is declared to be the office of God the Father. However, in John 5 Christ reveals that the Father has chosen in His sovereign wisdom to commit all judgement to the Son.

> For the Father judges no one, but has committed all judgement to the Son, that all should honour the Son just as they honour the Father. He who does not honour the Son does not honour the Father who sent Him (John 5:22-23).

> For as the Father has life in Himself, so He has granted the Son to have life in Himself, and has given Him authority to execute judgement also, because He is the Son of Man (John 5:26-27).

Here it is explicitly stated that the office of judgement has been transferred from the Father to the Son. Two reasons are given for this: 1) because with the office of judge goes also the honour due to the judge, and in this way all men will be obliged to show the same honour toward God the Son as they would toward God the Father; 2) because Christ is also the Son of man as well as the Son of God. That is, He partakes of the human as well as of the divine nature, and thus in His judgement He is able to make allowance, from His own experience, for all the infirmities and temptations of human flesh.

So gracious and merciful, however, is the divine nature in the Son, as in the Father, that Christ, too, is unwilling to administer judgement. For this reason He has, in His own turn, transferred the final authority of judgement from His own Person to the Word of God. Jesus says:

> And if anyone hears My words and does not believe, I do not
> judge him; for I did not come to judge the world but to save
> the world. He who rejects Me, and does not receive My
> words, has that which judges him – the word that I have
> spoken will judge him in the last day (John 12:47-48).

The final authority of all judgement is vested in the Word of God.
This is the impartial, unchanging standard to which all men must one
day answer.

The same revelation concerning God's Word is given in the Old
Testament, for David says to God:

> The entirety of Your word is truth,
> And every one of Your righteous judgements endures forever
>   (Ps. 119:160).

This is to say, all the standards and principles of God's judgement are
contained within His Word; like that very Word, of which they are part,
these standards and principles of judgement endure unchanged forever.

Four Principles of Judgement by the Word

What, then, are the principles of divine judgement revealed in God's
Word? Paul unfolds four main principles which may be summarised as
follows.

First, Paul declares that God's judgement is according to truth.

> Therefore you are inexcusable, O man, whoever you are who
> judge, for in whatever you judge another you condemn
> yourself; for you who judge practice the same things. But we
> know that the judgement of God is according to truth against
> those who practice such things (Rom. 2:1-2).

Paul is here speaking primarily to religious people who judge other
people by one standard and themselves by another standard. Paul says
that this is not the way of God's judgement. God's judgement is
according to truth. If we see and acknowledge the truth of God's
judgement as applied to others, we must apply precisely the same truth
to ourselves and our own lives. God's standard does not vary. It is always

the truth – the revealed truth of God's Word.

Jesus Himself says to the Father, "Your word is truth" (John 17:17). This revealed standard of God's truth applies just as much to the one who judges as to the one who is judged.

Second, God's judgement is according to "deeds": "[God] will render to each one according to his deeds" (Rom. 2:6).

This principle of divine judgement is repeated many times over in Scripture.

> The Father . . . judges *according to each one's work* (1 Pet. 1:17, italics added).

Again, in the account of the final judgement in Revelation 20:12, we read that:

> Books were opened . . . And the dead were judged according to their works, by the things which were written in the books.

The use of the word *books* in this connection is interesting and illuminating. In modern English the word *book* normally denotes a number of paper pages bound together at one edge. However, in New Testament times a book normally took the form of a long sheet of parchment, leather or other material which was kept rolled up and was unrolled in order to be read. A scroll of this kind, sealed with seven successive seals, actually plays a prominent part in the imagery of the book of Revelation.

Among the various means developed by modern technology for recording and transmitting information, there is one which resembles an ancient scroll far more closely than a modern book does, and that is electromagnetic recording tape. This is kept rolled up in precisely the same manner as an ancient scroll but must be unrolled in order to transmit the information recorded on it.

With this picture of an electromagnetic tape in mind, it becomes easy for us to realise that there is an individual record kept in heaven of the entire life of every human being. Just as a man's words may be recorded and preserved on earth by means of electromagnetic tape, so on a special "book" or scroll in heaven God preserves a complete and flawless record of the entire life of every person. According to this record of his deeds preserved upon this heavenly scroll, each person will one day be judged.

However, we must be careful not to limit the meaning of the word *deeds* merely to external actions such as can be observed by other human beings. The whole Bible makes it plain that God, in His judgement of man, takes into account not merely external actions but also the deepest and most secret thoughts, impulses and motives of the heart.

> . . . the day when God will judge the secrets of men by Jesus Christ, according to my gospel (Rom. 2:16).

> Therefore judge nothing before the time, until the Lord comes, who will both bring to light the hidden things of darkness and reveal *the counsels of the hearts*; and then each one's praise will come from God (1 Cor. 4:5, italics added).

This same truth is actually contained in the revelation that judgement will be by the Word of God.

> For the word of God is living . . . piercing even to the division of soul and spirit . . . and is *a discerner of the thoughts and intents of the heart.* And there is no creature hidden from His sight, but all things are naked and open to the eyes of Him to whom we must give account (Heb. 4:12-13, italics added).

We see, therefore, that God's record of men's deeds covers not merely their external, observable actions but also their thoughts and intents, the deepest motives and impulses of their minds and hearts. It is in this all-embracing sense that God's judgement of men will be according to their deeds.

The third principle of God's judgement is stated in Romans 2:11: "For there is no partiality with God."

In place of "partiality" the 1611 King James Version uses the phrase "respect of persons [literally, faces]." This expression implies that God is not influenced in His judgement by a person's external characteristics. These do not necessarily give a correct indication of that person's real character and conduct.

Men are often influenced in forming their judgements by such external things as race, religion, profession, social position, physical appearance, wealth, education and so on. However, God's judgement is not influenced or diverted by any of these things.

> For the Lord does not see as man sees; for man looks at the outward appearance, but the Lord looks at the heart (1 Sam. 16:7).

Not only is God Himself never moved by respect of persons; He also strictly charges all those who exercise judgement in human affairs never to yield to this influence. There can scarcely e any principle of Scripture which is stated more often than this. It is mentioned nine times in the Old Testament and seven times in the New Testament – a total of sixteen times in all.

The fourth principle of God's judgement is: "according to light." This is implied in Romans.

> For as many as have sinned without law will also perish without law, and as many as have sinned in the law will be judged by the law (2:12).

Applied generally, this means that each person will be judged according to the measure of moral light and understanding made available to him. Those who have had the full knowledge of God's moral standards revealed to them through the law of Moses will be judged by that law. But those who did not have the fuller revelation of the law of Moses will not be judged by that law, but only in accordance with the general revelation of God granted to the human race as a whole through the wonders of creation.

> For since the creation of the world His [God's] invisible attributes are clearly seen, being understood by the things that are made, even His eternal power and Godhead, so that they are without excuse (Rom. 1:20).

Paul here states that a general revelation of God's nature, that is, His eternal power and Godhead, is given through creation to all men everywhere – irrespective of race or religion – who attain to normal understanding.

This, therefore, is the basic standard by which all men will be judged. However, those who receive an additional and special revelation through God's Word will be judged by the higher standard of moral knowledge thus granted to them. Therefore, judgement is according to light – according to the measure of moral knowledge granted to each person.

This same principle of judgement according to light is contained in the words of Jesus to the people of His own day.

> Then He began to upbraid the cities in which most of His mighty works had been done, because they did not repent:

"Woe to you, Chorazin! Woe to you, Bethsaida! For if the mighty works which were done in you had been done in Tyre and Sidon, they would have repented long ago in sackcloth and ashes. But I say to you, it will be more tolerable for Tyre and Sidon in the day of judgement than for you. And you, Capernaum, who are exalted to heaven, will be brought down to Hades; for if the mighty works which were done in you had been done in Sodom, it would have remained until this day. But I say to you that it shall be more tolerable for the land of Sodom in the day of judgement than for you" (Matt. 11:20-24).

Jesus here shows that the sinful cities of the ancient world – Tyre, Sidon and Sodom – will be judged according to the measure of moral knowledge available to them in their day. On the other hand, the cities of His own day – Chorazin, Bethsaida and Capernaum – will be judged according to the much greater measure of knowledge granted to them through His personal presence and ministry. For this reason, the judgement of these latter cities will be much more severe than the judgement of the former.

Let us bring this principle down to our own day. We who are alive today will be judged by the measure of moral light and knowledge available to our generation. For those of us who live in countries with a long history of Christianity, such as America or Great Britain, there is probably a greater measure of moral knowledge more easily available than there has ever been to any previous generation in earth's history. For this reason, the standards by which we shall be judged will be the highest of all. The following words of Jesus apply to us in our generation.

For everyone to whom much is given, from him much will be required; and to whom much has been committed, of him they will ask the more (Luke 12:48).

Such, then, are the four main principles of judgement according to the Word of God.

1. According to truth.
2. According to deeds.
3. Without partiality (or respect of persons).
4. According to the light available to those being judged.

49
GOD'S JUDGEMENTS
IN HISTORY

Having established in chapter 48 the general principles of divine judgement, we shall now go on to point out two distinct and separate stages in which God's judgement is administered to the human race.

Historical vs. Eternal Judgements

The first of these two stages is God's judgement in time; that is, that part of God's judgement which is carried out upon the scene of human history. The second of these two stages is God's judgements in eternity. It is this second stage of judgement which is called "eternal judgement" (Heb. 6:2). Eternal judgement is not carried out upon the scene of time or of human history. Eternal judgement is the judgement which awaits every human soul in eternity, after time and history have closed.

The main purpose of our present studies is to examine the teaching of Scripture concerning God's judgement in eternity. However, it will be helpful to begin by a brief examination of the first stage, God's judgement in history. In this way, as we carefully observe this logical and scriptural distinction between God's judgement in history and God's judgement in eternity, we shall be able to reconcile certain statements of Scripture which seem inconsistent with each other. Take, for example, the following commandment and warning given to Israel by God.

> You shall not make for yourself any carved image, or any likeness of anything that is in heaven above, or that is in the earth beneath, or that is in the water under the earth; you shall not bow down to them nor serve them. For I, the Lord your God, am a jealous God, visiting the iniquity of the fathers on the children to the third and fourth generations of those who hate Me, but showing mercy to thousands, to those who love Me and keep My commandments (Ex. 20:4-6).

Jeremiah reminded the Lord of both the promise and the warning which He had given to Israel.

> You show lovingkindness to thousands, and repay the iniquity of the fathers into the bosom of their children after them (Jer. 32:18).

These passages of Scripture and others like them make it clear that – in certain cases, at least – the sins of one generation cause the judgement of God to come upon succeeding generations, as far as down to the third or fourth generation. Conversely, the righteousness of one generation can cause the blessing of God to come upon many thousands of their descendants. Such passages as these all deal with God's judgements in time; that is, in history.

In order to obtain a complete picture of God's total judgement, however, we must also consider the many passages of Scripture which deal with God's judgement in eternity. A very clear picture of this is given in the following message of the Lord to His people Israel through the prophet Ezekiel.

> The word of the Lord came to me again, saying,
> "What do you mean when you use this proverb concerning
>   the land of Israel, saying:
> 'The fathers have eaten sour grapes,
> And the children's teeth are set on edge'?
> "As I live," says the Lord God, "you shall no longer use
>   this proverb in Israel.

"Behold, all souls are Mine;
The soul of the father
As well as the soul of the son is Mine;
The soul who sins shall die" (Ezek. 18:1-4).

This passage indicates that, when God through His prophets rebuked Israel for their backsliding, the people tried to excuse themselves by placing the blame for their condition upon the sinfulness of preceding generations. They implied that the national decline of Israel in their day was due to the sins of their ancestors and so God could not justly hold them responsible for their present moral condition. However, God, through this message by Ezekiel, entirely rejects this form of excuse.

Although national decline may have been brought about by the failure of preceding generations, God warns them that He holds each one of them individually responsible for his own moral condition and that each one of them will be judged – in eternity – solely for his own character and conduct, and not at all for anything that his ancestors may or may not have done. This warning is repeated yet more emphatically a little further on.

The soul who sins shall die. The son shall not bear the guilt of the father, nor the father bear the guilt of the son. The righteousness of the righteous shall be upon himself, and the wickedness of the wicked shall be upon himself (Ezek. 18:20).

The whole application of this passage is individual and personal. "*The soul* who sins shall die." This is not the judgement of a nation or a family; this is the judgement of each individual soul – the judgement by which the destiny of each soul is settled for eternity.

This point is again brought out in verse 24 of the same chapter.

But when a righteous man turns away from his righteousness and commits iniquity, and does according to all the abominations that the wicked man does, shall he live? All the righteousness which he has done shall not be remembered; because of the unfaithfulness of which he is guilty and the sin which he has committed, because of them he shall die.

The final words of this verse, "because of them he shall die," indicate that God is speaking of the condition in which each individual soul passes from time into eternity. The condition of each soul at this moment will determine the destiny of that soul for eternity. The soul that dies in sin can never be admitted into the presence of God thereafter. In Ecclesiastes the same truth is presented under the picture of a tree falling.

> And if a tree falls to the south or to the north,
> In the place where the tree falls, there it shall lie
> (Eccl. 11:3).

The tree falling corresponds to a man dying. "In the place where the tree falls, there it shall lie." The position in which the tree falls decides the position in which it will lie. The condition in which a man dies – the condition of his soul at death – decides what will be his condition throughout eternity. In this respect, each soul is answerable for himself alone and responsible only for his own condition.

These passages in Ezekiel and Ecclesiastes deal with the eternal judgement of God upon each individual soul. The destiny of each soul is settled by the condition in which it dies.

On the other hand, the passages which we considered earlier in Exodus and Jeremiah dealt with the judgements of God in history, worked out from generation to generation in the experience of families, of nations and of whole races.

Viewed in this light, there is no conflict or inconsistency between these two presentations of God's judgement. In history, the behaviour of one generation has an important effect, for good or for evil, upon the course of succeeding generations. This is part of God's judgement in history. But in eternity, after time and history have closed, each soul will answer to God solely for his own character and conduct. No soul will be justified by the righteousness of another, and no soul will be condemned for the wickedness of another. This is God's judgement in eternity.

Examples of Historical Judgements

We shall now consider briefly some biblical examples of God's judgement in history.

There are a number of such judgements recorded in Scripture which set forth God's attitude toward certain sinful acts or conditions in such a clear and dramatic way that they constitute a warning to all those in succeeding generations who might be tempted to follow in sins of the same kind.

One clear example of this kind is provided by God's judgement upon the cities of Sodom and Gomorrah.

> Then the Lord rained brimstone and fire on Sodom and Gomorrah, from the Lord out of the heavens. So He overthrew those cities, all the plain, all the inhabitants of the cities, and what grew on the ground (Gen. 19:24-25).

New Testament writers refer to this event several times.

> [God] turning the cities of Sodom and Gomorrah into ashes, condemned them to destruction, making them an example [or a pattern] to those who afterward would live ungodly (2 Pet. 2:6).

Peter points out that the sudden, dramatic and complete overthrow of Sodom and Gomorrah was an example, a pattern, setting forth God's attitude toward the sins of which these cities were guilty.

Ezekiel gives a very interesting account of the basic moral and social conditions which produced the decline of Sodom, for God says to Jerusalem:

> Look, this was the iniquity of your sister Sodom: She and her daughter had pride, fullness of food, and abundance of idleness; neither did she strengthen the hand of the poor and needy (Ezek. 16:49).

God here specifies four basic causes of Sodom's moral decline: pride, fullness of food, abundance of idleness and a lack of concern for the poor and underprivileged in their midst. Out of these basic causes there grew up that particular form of sexual perversion which has ever since been called by the name "sodomy."

The amazing accuracy of the Bible is once again confirmed as we observe how, in many of the great population centres of our modern civilisation, the same moral and social causes are producing the same form of sexual perversion. The Bible does not suggest that this form of sin will in every subsequent case be visited with the same dramatic form of historical judgement, but it does teach that the unchanging attitude of God toward this form of sin has once and for all time been demonstrated by His judgement upon Sodom.

In the light of this revealed judgement of God, all who thereafter turn aside into this form of sexual perversion are left without any excuse. Even though no open judgement of God may fall upon them on the scene of time, their judgement in eternity will be nonetheless severe on that account.

Another dramatic instance of God's judgement is provided by the story of Ananias and Sapphira (see Acts 5:1-10).

Ananias and his wife, Sapphira, were what we would call religious hypocrites. They sold a possession and brought part of the price to the apostles as an offering to the work of God. This, by itself, was to be commended. However, their sin consisted in pretending that the money which they brought represented the full price of the possession which they had sold. They did this in order to gain the praise and favour of the apostles and their fellow Christians.

However, by the supernatural revelation of the Holy Spirit, Peter discerned their hypocrisy and charged first Ananias and later Sapphira with lying and seeking to deceive the Holy Spirit. Such intense conviction of sin came upon them that each, in turn, fell down at Peter's feet, dead. This judgement of God had a strong effect on the people who heard of it.

> So great fear came upon all the church and upon all who heard these things (Acts 5:11).

Of course, there is no suggestion that God will always judge this kind of behaviour by professing Christians in such a swift and dramatic way. But the unchanging attitude of God toward lying and hypocrisy on the part of professing Christians is demonstrated by this incident as a warning to all succeeding generations of the church.

On a larger scale, the record of God's people Israel from the time of Moses down to the present day abounds with examples of God's judgements in history. At the time when God first gave the law to Israel, before they ever entered into the promised land, God warned them through Moses of the judgements He would bring upon them if they should thereafter turn away from Him in disobedience and rebellion.

One such passage of prophetic warning to Israel is found in Leviticus 26:14-45. God first warns Israel of various judgements for disobedience that He will bring upon them while they are still in their own land. Then He warns them that continued disobedience will bring upon them judgements yet more severe, by which they will be scattered abroad as exiles from their land.

> And after all this, if you do not obey Me, but walk contrary to
> Me, then I also will walk contrary to you in fury; and I, even
> I, will chastise you seven times for your sins. You shall eat the
> flesh of your sons, and you shall eat the flesh of your
> daughters. I will destroy your high places, cut down your
> incense altars, and cast your carcasses on the lifeless forms of
> your idols; and My soul shall abhor you. I will lay your cities
> waste and bring your sanctuaries to desolation, and I will not
> smell the fragrance of your sweet aromas. I will bring the
> land to desolation, and your enemies who dwell in it shall be
> astonished at it. I will scatter you among the nations and draw
> out a sword after you; your land shall be desolate and your
> cities waste (Lev. 26:27-33).

Through the invasion of the land of Israel by the Roman armies under
Titus in 70 A.D., and through subsequent invasions, every detail of this
prophecy was exactly fulfilled in the experience of Israel.

In the siege of Jerusalem by Titus, the Jews there were reduced to
such straits of hunger that they literally ate the flesh of their sons and
daughters. Thereafter, all their sanctuaries and religious centres were
destroyed. Great numbers of the people were massacred; others were
sold into slavery and scattered abroad as exiles. Gentiles from the
surrounding countries moved in and took possession of the land thus left
desolate. God goes on to warn Israel of their pitiful condition during the
ensuing centuries of their dispersion among the Gentiles.

> And as for those of you who are left, I will send faintness into
> their hearts in the lands of their enemies; the sound of a
> shaken leaf shall cause them to flee; they shall flee as though
> fleeing from a sword, and they shall fall when no one pursues.
> They shall stumble over one another, as it were before a
> sword, when no one pursues; and you shall have no power to
> stand before your enemies (Lev. 26:36-37).

Once again, as we look back over the history of Israel, we see that
every one of these prophecies has been fulfilled over and over again in
the shame, the fear, the degradation and the persecutions that have
marked eighteen centuries of dispersal.

However, before the prophecy closes, God also gives a promise that
His mercy will never be fully or finally withdrawn from Israel.

> Yet for all that, when they are in the land of their enemies, I
> will not cast them away, nor shall I abhor them, to utterly
> destroy them and break My covenant with them; for I am the
> Lord their God (Lev. 26:44).

Just as surely as God's warnings of judgement have been fulfilled, so
has His promise of mercy been fulfilled, even in the midst of judgement.

Viewed thus in the light of prophetic Scripture, the whole history of
Israel becomes a demonstration on a world-wide scale of both the
judgement and the mercy of God; for even in the midst of judgement
God still delights to administer mercy.

Perhaps the most striking example of God's mercy in the midst of
judgement is contained in the story of Rahab, as recorded in Joshua
chapters 2 and 6.

From the standpoint of both background and environment, Rahab had
everything against her. She was a harlot, belonging to a race appointed
to judgement, living in a city appointed to destruction. Yet in humility
and faith she dared to cast herself upon the mercy of God, with the result
that she and her whole household were spared, and she herself, through
marriage to an Israelite, became a member of the direct line from which
the genealogy of Christ was derived.

Thus the case of Rahab proves that no soul is necessarily damned by
background or environment. No matter how dark the background or how
corrupt the environment, personal repentance and faith on the part of any
individual will cancel God's judgement and call forth His mercy instead.

We find, then, that history, illuminated by Scripture, unfolds the
outworking in human affairs of both the judgement and the mercy of
God. Even in the midst of the severest judgements, the underlying
purposes of God are still those of grace and mercy. For this reason, the
revelation of God at work in history is summed up in Psalm 107:43.

> Whoever is wise will observe these things,
> And they will understand the lovingkindness [more fully,
>   the covenant-keeping mercies] of the Lord.

For the believer, the supreme lesson of history is the revelation of
God's unchanging faithfulness in working out His covenants of grace
and mercy. However, we must not make the mistake of supposing that
full and final judgement upon all men's actions is administered upon the
scene of time. Paul warns:

Some men's sins are clearly evident, preceding them to judgement, but those of some men follow later. Likewise, the good works of some are clearly evident, and those that are otherwise cannot be hidden (1 Tim. 5:24-25).

A similar warning is contained in Ecclesiastes 8:11.

Because the sentence against an evil work is not executed speedily, therefore the heart of the sons of men is fully set in them to do evil.

Both these passages warn us that God's judgements are not fully revealed in time. This applies both to the punishment of the wicked and to the reward of the righteous. For the full revelation of God's final judgements, we must pass beyond the scene of time into eternity.

50
THE JUDGEMENT SEAT
OF CHRIST

The New Testament reveals three main, successive scenes upon which eternal judgement will be carried out. Each of these scenes is marked out from the others by one distinctive feature: the type of seat upon which the Judge will sit while carrying out the judgement.

In the first scene the seat upon which the Judge will sit is called "the judgement seat of Christ." Those to be judged here will be Christ's own followers and servants, the true Christians.

In the second scene the seat of judgement is called "the throne of [Christ's] glory." Those to be judged here will be the Gentile nations remaining upon earth at the close of the great tribulation, prior to the setting up of Christ's millennial kingdom upon earth.

In the third scene the seat of judgement is called "a great white throne." Those to be judged here will be all the remaining dead who will be resurrected at the close of the millennium.

Christians Will Be Judged First

We shall begin by considering the picture given in the New Testament of the first of these three judgement scenes – that which is to be carried out before the judgement seat of Christ. As we have said, those to be judged here will be the true Christians. To some it may perhaps appear surprising that Christians are to be judged at all – even more so that they will be the first to be judged. However, this principle is based on Scripture.

> For the time has come for judgement to begin at the house of God; and if it begins with us first, what will be the end of those who do not obey the gospel of God? Now
>
> > "If the righteous one is scarcely saved,
> > Where will the ungodly and the sinner appear?"
> > (1 Pet. 4:17-18).

Here Peter, writing as a Christian, says that judgement must begin with "us" – the house of God. It is obvious that by these two phrases he is referring to Christians. This is confirmed by the fact that those thus described are contrasted with "those who do not obey the gospel of God"; that is, with the unbelievers. Peter makes it clear, therefore, that the first judgement will be that of the true Christians.

The scene upon which this judgement of Christians will be carried out is referred to by Paul twice, in very similar language, in two different passages of his epistles.

> But why do you judge your brother? Or why do you show contempt for your brother? For we shall all stand before the judgement seat of Christ (Rom. 14:10).
>
> So then each of us shall give account of himself to God (Rom. 14:12).

In these two verses the phrase "your brother," which occurs twice, and the phrase "each of us" make it clear that Paul is speaking only about the judgement of Christians. Paul's thought is that as Christians we should not seek to pass final judgement upon one another because Christ Himself will do that upon each one, and each one of us will have to answer for himself to Christ.

As always, where we are considering eternal judgement, it will be an entirely individual matter. This is stressed by the emphatic phrase which Paul uses: "each of us." Paul uses very similar language to describe this judgement of Christians in other passages.

> For we must all appear before the judgement seat of Christ,
> that each one may receive the things done in the body,
> according to what he has done, whether good or bad (2 Cor.
> 5:10).

Once again, both the language and the context make it plain that Paul is speaking only of Christians. Again, too, there is the same emphasis upon the individual – "each one."

Paul also states that the things which will be brought up for judgement at this time will be "the things done in the body" – the acts and behaviour of each Christian during his life here on earth.

Paul indicates, too, that every act performed by a Christian while here on earth must fall into one of two categories – either "good" or "bad." There is no third category, no neutrality. Every act of a Christian has definite value of some kind – either positive or negative. Every act that is not performed in faith and obedience, for the glory of God, is unacceptable to God and therefore bad. It is upon this simple basis, clearly revealed, that each one of us as Christians must expect to be judged.

In both these passages, speaking of the place which Christ will occupy while judging Christians, Paul uses the phrase "the judgement seat of Christ." The Greek word here translated "judgement seat" is *bema.* This word suggests a raised platform used for public address. In other passages of the New Testament it denotes the place of judgement used by the Roman emperor or by one of his deputies to hear and pronounce judgement on cases brought before them.

For instance, when Paul exercised his right as a Roman citizen to be judged by the emperor, he said:

> I stand at Caesar's judgement seat, where I ought to be judged
> (Acts 25:10).

The word which Paul uses for Caesar's judgement seat is *bema* – the same which he uses elsewhere for the place from which Christ will judge all Christians.

Not for Condemnation But for Reward

What will be the nature of the judgement administered to Christians by Christ upon His judgement seat?

First of all we must state clearly and emphatically that this judgement of Christians will not be a judgement of condemnation. This vitally important fact, that the true believer in Christ is cleared from all fear of final condemnation, is affirmed in various passages of the New Testament. Jesus says:

> He who believes in Him [Christ] is not condemned; but he who does not believe is condemned already, because he has not believed in the name of the only begotten Son of God (John 3:18).

Here there is a clear and sharp distinction. The true believer in Christ is not condemned; the unbeliever is condemned already on the ground of his unbelief.

Further on in John's Gospel, Christ gives the same assurance to each sincere believer.

> Most assuredly, I say to you, he who hears My word and believes in Him who sent Me has everlasting life, and shall not come into judgement, but has passed from death into life (5:24).

Here Christ gives a definite, threefold assurance to every believer who accepts in faith His word through the gospel. Such a believer already has everlasting life; he has already passed from spiritual death into eternal life; he will never come into condemnation. Paul repeats the same assurance of freedom from condemnation.

> There is therefore now no condemnation to those who are in Christ Jesus, who do not walk according to the flesh, but according to the Spirit (Rom. 8:1).

All these passages make it plain that true believers in Christ will never have to face a judgement of which the outcome will be final condemnation. In fact, the true believer in Christ will never need to be judged at all for sins he has committed. When a person comes as a sinner in faith to Christ, receiving Him as Saviour and confessing Him as Lord, the whole record of that person's past sins is immediately and eternally blotted out by God, never to be remembered anymore. Twice, in two successive chapters of Isaiah, God gives this promise to those whom He has redeemed.

> I, even I, am He who blots out your transgressions for My
>   own sake;
> And I will not remember your sins (Is. 43:25).

> I have blotted out, like a thick cloud, your transgressions,
> And like a cloud, your sins (Is. 44:22).

In both these passages there is mention both of sins and of transgressions. "Sins" are wrong acts that are committed without any necessary reference to a known law; "transgressions" are wrong acts committed in open disobedience of a known law. Sins are therefore compared to "a cloud," but transgressions to "a thick cloud." That is to say, transgressions are the darker of the two. However, God's grace and power are more than sufficient to blot out both.

In the previous chapter we stated that there is a complete record preserved in heaven of the life that every human soul leads here on earth. We compared the type of "book" on which this record is made to electromagnetic tape. The parallel extends not only to the way in which the record is made but also to the way in which it may be erased.

If there is any error made on tape, it may be completely erased in a few moments by running the recording head past that particular stretch of tape a second time.

There is even an instrument called a bulk eraser which can completely erase in a few seconds the whole recorded contents of an entire tape. A completely clean tape is produced, on which a new message may be recorded without any trace remaining of the previous message.

So it is with the heavenly record of the sinner's life. When a sinner comes for the first time in repentance and faith to Christ, God applies His heavenly "bulk eraser." The whole record of the sinner's former sins is thereby instantly and completely erased, and a clean "tape" is made available, upon which a new life of faith and righteousness may be recorded. If at any time thereafter the believer should fall again into sin, he needs only to repent and confess his sin. God erases that particular section of the record, and once again the tape is clean.

If we confess our sins, He is faithful and just to forgive us our sins and to cleanse us from all unrighteousness (1 John 1:9).

> My little children, these things I write to you, that you may
> not sin. And if anyone sins, we have an Advocate with the

Father, Jesus Christ the righteous. And He Himself is the
propitiation for our sins, and not for ours only but also for the
whole world (1 John 2:1-2).

These passages teach that if a believer in Christ sins and thereafter
repents and confesses his sin, the record of his sin is erased, and he
himself is cleansed from all unrighteousness.

This is why the true believer in Christ need not fear final condemnation. God's provision both to cleanse the sinner himself and to erase
the record of his sins means that there will be no record of sin remaining
upon which any just judgement of condemnation could be based.

If, then, there is no possibility of final condemnation for the true
believer, for what purpose will Christians be judged?

The answer is that the judgement of Christians will be to assess their
rewards. The true believer will be judged not in respect of righteousness
but in respect of service rendered to Christ.

The reason why the believer will not be judged in respect of righteousness is simple and logical: The righteousness of the true believer is
no longer his own but the righteousness of Christ Himself, imputed to
him by God on the basis of his faith.

> [Christ] became for us wisdom from God – and righteousness
> and sanctification and redemption (1 Cor. 1:30).

None other than Christ Himself has become our righteousness from
God.

> For He [God] made Him [Jesus] who knew no sin to be sin
> for us, that we might become the righteousness of God in
> Him (2 Cor. 5:21).

Through this exchange we have become the righteousness of God in
Christ. Obviously, where the believer receives salvation on this basis, it
would be utterly illogical for God to judge, or even to call into question,
His own righteousness imparted to the believer.

We conclude, therefore, that the judgement of Christians will deal not
with their righteousness but with their service rendered to Christ. The
purpose of the judgement will not be to decide upon either acquittal or
condemnation but rather to assess the reward due to each believer for his
service to Christ while on earth.

The Test of Fire

This judgement of believers for rewards is described by Paul.

> For no other foundation can anyone lay than that which is laid, which is Jesus Christ. Now if anyone builds on this foundation with gold, silver, precious stones, wood, hay, straw, each one's work will become manifest; for the Day will declare it, because it will be revealed by fire; and the fire will test each one's work, of what sort it is. If anyone's work which he has built on it endures, he will receive a reward. If anyone's work is burned, he will suffer loss; but he himself will be saved, yet so as through fire (1 Cor. 3:11-15).

Paul makes it clear that this is a judgement not of every man's soul but of every man's work. Even if a man's works are totally burned up, yet his soul will be saved. In the first verse of this passage Paul explains why such a man's soul is secure.

> For no other foundation can anyone lay than that which is laid, which is Jesus Christ (v. 11).

This judgement concerns only those who have built their faith not upon their own works or their own righteousness but upon the foundation of Jesus Christ and His righteousness. So long as their faith remains unmoved upon this foundation, their souls are eternally safe.

When it comes to the assessment of believers' works, these are placed by Paul in one of two categories. On the one hand there are "gold, silver, precious stones." On the other hand there are "wood, hay, straw."

The basis on which these two categories are separated from each other is the ability to stand the test of fire. The items in the first category – gold, silver, precious stones – will be able to pass through the fire without being consumed. The items in the second category – wood, hay, straw – will be consumed in the fire.

One thought immediately emerges from contrasting these two categories: Quality is of infinitely greater importance to God than quantity. Gold, silver and precious stones are all things that are normally found in small quantities but are nevertheless of great value. Wood, hay and straw are all things that take up much space and are obtainable in large quantities but are of relatively little value.

Just what is this fire by which the works of Christians will be tried?

Let us remember that the glorified Christ will be sitting upon His judgement seat and that each one of us will stand directly before Him. We shall see Him then as John saw Him in his vision on the island of Patmos.

> His head and His hair were white like wool, as white as snow, and His eyes like a flame of fire; His feet were like fine brass, as if refined in a furnace, and His voice as the sound of many waters (Rev. 1:14-15).

In this vision Christ's feet "like fine brass" in a burning furnace typify the fires of tribulation in which He will judge the sinful acts of the ungodly while His eyes "like a flame of fire" typify the penetrating and consuming insight with which He will assess the works of His own believing people. In the fiery rays of those eyes, as each one stands before His judgement seat, all that is base, insincere and valueless in His people's works will be instantly and eternally consumed. Only that which is of true and enduring value will survive, purified and refined by fire.

As we consider this scene of judgement, each of us needs to ask himself: How may I serve Christ in this life so that my works will stand the test of fire in that day?

There are three points concerning which each one of us should examine ourselves: motive, obedience, power.

1. We should examine our motives. Is the aim of our service to please ourselves, for our own satisfaction and glory, or do we sincerely seek to glorify Christ and to do His will?
2. We should examine ourselves on the point of obedience. Are we seeking to serve Christ according to the principles and methods revealed in the Word of God? Or are we fashioning our own forms of worship and service and then attaching to them the name of Christ and the titles and phrases of New Testament religion?
3. We should examine ourselves in respect of power. Paul reminds us, "The kingdom of God is not in word but in power" (1 Cor. 4:20). Are we seeking to serve God in the inadequacy of our own carnal strength? Or have we been renewed and empowered by the Holy Spirit? If so, then we can say like Paul: "To this end I also labour, striving

according to His working which works in me *mightily*"
(Col. 1:29, italics added).

Upon the answers to these questions of motive, obedience and power will depend the issues of our judgement in that day when each one of us shall stand before the judgement seat of Christ.

51

THE JUDGEMENT OF CHRISTIAN SERVICE

We shall now consider in greater detail the principles by which believers will be rewarded for their service. These are set forth by Christ in the form of two parables: the parable of the talents (see Matt. 25:14-30) and the parable of the minas (see Luke 19:11-27).

Assessment of Christian Service

The central theme of both parables is the same. Each concerns a man of wealth and authority who commits a certain sum to each of his servants to administer on his behalf and then takes a journey to a distant country. After a considerable lapse of time, this wealthy man returns and holds an individual reckoning with his servants as to the way in which each has handled the money committed to him.

In both parables three servants are mentioned individually: the first two are faithful in administering their master's money; the third is unfaithful. This is how the money was distributed in the parable of the talents:

And to one he gave five talents, to another two, and to another
one, to each according to his own ability (Matt. 25:15).

(A talent was a considerable quantity of money, perhaps as much as
fifteen years' wages.)

Notice that this verse reveals the principle according to which the
talents are distributed: "to each according to his own ability." That is,
God distributes to each believer the maximum number of talents that his
own ability will permit him to use effectively. God does not give to any
believer either more or less than he is able to use effectively.

In this parable the first two servants each achieved an increase of 100
percent. The servant who had received five talents gained five more; the
servant who had received two talents gained two more. The lord assessed
the faithfulness of these servants not by their net gain but by their
percentage increase. The servant who gained five talents was not
considered more faithful than the servant who had gained two talents,
although his net gain in talents was greater. Rather, each of these
servants was considered equally faithful because each had achieved the
same proportionate increase: 100 percent.

This is indicated by the fact that the words of commendation spoken
to these two servants, recorded in Matthew 25:21 and 23, are exactly the
same in each verse.

His lord said to him, "Well done, good and faithful servant;
you were faithful over a few things, I will make you ruler over
many things. Enter into the joy of your lord."

Each of them had originally received the maximum number of talents
that his ability would allow him to use effectively; each of them had
achieved the maximum gain possible – 100 percent. It is on their faithfulness, as expressed in the percentage increase achieved, that their
judgement is based. The fact that one man originally received five talents
and the other two is not the basis on which their faithfulness is assessed.

In this parable of the talents the third servant merely hid the one talent
he had received and later brought it back to his lord in exactly the same
condition in which he had received it. For this he was not only deprived
of any reward, but he was also totally and finally rejected and cast out
from his lord's presence.

But his lord answered and said to him, "You wicked and lazy
servant, you knew that I reap where I have not sown, and

gather where I have not scattered seed. Therefore you ought
to have deposited my money with the bankers, and at my
coming I would have received back my own with interest.
Therefore take the talent from him, and give it to him who has
ten talents. For to everyone who has, more will be given, and
he will have abundance; but from him who does not have,
even what he has will be taken away. And cast the unprof-
itable servant into the outer darkness. There will be weeping
and gnashing of teeth" (Matt. 25:26-30).

There can be no doubt whatever about the meaning of these words.
This third servant not only received no reward; he was actually deprived
of the one talent which he had originally received, and he himself was
cast out from his lord's presence.

Let us now turn to the parable of the minas in Luke 19. (A mina was
a quantity of money equivalent to about three months' wages.)

In this parable ten servants are mentioned, although only the cases of
three of them are described in detail. Originally, all ten servants received
the same amount committed to them by their lord: one mina each.

Of the three servants whose cases are described, the first gained ten
minas, the second gained five minas, and the third merely hid his mina
away and eventually brought it back in the same condition in which he
had received it.

It would appear that each of these three servants possessed equal
ability, since each received the same amount committed to him.
However, they were not equally faithful. The first gained twice as much
with his mina as the second. For this reason his reward was twice as
great.

Then came the first, saying, "Master, your mina has earned
ten minas." And he said to him, "Well done, good servant;
because you were faithful in a very little, have authority over
ten cities." And the second came, saying, "Master, your mina
has earned five minas." Likewise he said to him, "You also be
over five cities" (Luke 19:16-19).

We notice that, in two respects, the reward of the first servant was
greater than that of the second. First, the first servant was specifically
commended by his lord as a good servant; the second servant received
no such special commendation. Second, the first servant was given
authority over ten cities; the second servant was given authority only

over five cities. That is to say, their rewards were in exact proportion to the increase which each had achieved.

One further conclusion we may draw from this parable is that rewards for serving Christ faithfully in this present age will consist in positions of authority and responsibility in the administration of Christ's kingdom in the following age. In other words, faithful service in the present age leads to continued and extended opportunities of service in the next age. For those who truly love Christ there can be no greater joy or privilege than that of continuing to serve their Lord. For those who are faithful, this privilege, begun here in time, will be extended throughout the ages of eternity.

In this parable of the minas, as in that of the talents, the third servant was condemned for being unfaithful and failing to make any use at all of the mina committed to him.

> And he said to him, "Out of your own mouth I will judge you, you wicked servant. You knew that I was an austere man, collecting what I did not deposit and reaping what I did not sow. Why then did you not put my money in the bank, that at my coming I might have collected it with interest?" And he said to those who stood by, "Take the mina from him, and give it to him who has ten minas" (Luke 19:22-24).

In this parable, as in that of the talents, the unfaithful servant not only received no reward, but even the one mina he had originally received was taken away from him. The final end of the servant with the one mina is not revealed in this parable. However, it seems reasonable to conclude that, like the unfaithful servant in the parable of the talents, he was rejected and cast out from his lord's presence.

In both these parables alike, failure to make active use of the talent or mina committed to each servant is described by the very strong word *wicked*. In each case the lord commences his judgement of the unfaithful servant by the phrase "you wicked servant."

From this we learn that, by God's standards, wickedness consists not only in actively doing that which is bad, but just as much in the failure to do good when it lies within our power to do it.

> Therefore, to him who knows to do good and does not do it,
> to him it is sin (James 4:17).

In other words, the sins of omission are no less serious than the sins of commission.

The same thought is contained in Malachi's prophetic revelation of God's judgement.

> Then you shall again discern
> Between the righteous and the wicked,
> Between one who serves God
> And one who does not serve Him (Mal. 3:18).

Here we find a clear and sharp distinction made by God between the righteous and the wicked. The righteous are defined as those who serve God; the wicked as those who do not serve God. Once again the lesson is plain: Not to serve God is in itself wickedness.

It was this wickedness that led to the condemnation and rejection of the unfaithful servant in each of the two parables we have studied. In neither of these parables did the rejected servant do anything evil; in each case the ground of his rejection was merely that he failed to do the good which it was in his power to do. In both these parables Christ indicates that this same principle of judgement will be applied to all those who claim to be His followers and servants.

In the previous chapter we examined the passage that speaks about the Christian whose works are rejected and burned up in the fire of judgement, yet he himself is saved (see 1 Cor. 3:11-15). On the other hand, in the parables which we have now considered, it appears that the unfaithful servant is not only deprived of any reward, but he himself is rejected and cast out forever from his lord's presence.

This naturally leads us to ask an important question: What is the difference, in God's estimation, of these two cases? Why should it be that, in the case described by Paul, the man's works are rejected but he himself is saved, whereas in the parable of Jesus the unfaithful servant not only loses his reward but is himself also rejected and cast out?

The difference appears to be this. In the case described by Paul, the man actually did try to do something active for his master; in fact, the examples of wood, hay and straw suggest that he did a great deal. However, his work was not of the kind or quality that would stand the test of fire. Yet this activity of his – though misguided and unrewarded – did at least serve to prove that his actual faith in Christ was genuine. For this reason the salvation of his soul was assured even though his works were burned up.

On the other hand, the unfaithful servant with the one talent did nothing at all for his master – either good or bad. This failure to act at all showed that his profession of faith and service was vain and insincere.

> Faith without works is dead also (James 2:26).

A faith that does not result in activity of any kind is a dead faith; it is empty, worthless, insincere. Not only does it fail to produce any works of service which can be rewarded; it even fails to secure for the one who professes it the salvation of his own soul. A person who professes faith in Christ without ever seeking to serve Christ actively is a hypocrite.

For this reason, the judgement of such a person is to be cast "into the outer darkness. There will be weeping and gnashing of teeth." A careful examination of passages concerning similar judgements (see Matt. 24:51 and Luke 12:46) shows that this place of outer darkness, with its weeping and gnashing of teeth, is the place reserved for the hypocrite and the unbeliever. The unfaithful servant who does nothing at all for his master must take his place in this same category; he is in reality a hypocrite and an unbeliever. The place appointed for him is outer darkness.

Angels Will Eliminate All Hypocrites

This judgement upon the hypocritical servant leads us to one further important conclusion in connection with the events that will lead up to the judgement seat of Christ.

Before the true Christians are admitted to the place of Christ's judgement seat, all hypocrites and false Christians will first be separated out from among God's believing people and will receive the judgement due to them for their hypocrisy and falsehood.

This judgement of hypocrites is described in two parables concerning the kingdom of heaven (see Matt. 13). These two parables are the parable of the wheat and the tares and the parable of the dragnet cast into the sea.

In studying these and other parables in this chapter it is important to determine what is meant by the phrase "the kingdom of heaven." In Matthew 12:25-28 and in Luke 11:17-20 Jesus speaks about two kingdoms which are in opposition to each other: the kingdom of God (or of heaven) and the kingdom of Satan. Until the present age closes, these two kingdoms will continue to coexist. The kingdom of God includes all created beings who are submitted to His righteous government; the kingdom of Satan includes all who are in rebellion against God's government.

In Ephesians Paul reveals two levels of Satan's kingdom. He describes a host of wicked angels who had followed Satan in his initial rebellion against God (see Eph. 6:12). Paul also speaks of human beings who are in rebellion against God. He calls these latter "the sons of disobedience" and indicates that they are controlled by Satan as "the prince of the power of the air" (Eph. 2:2).

The "gospel of the kingdom," proclaimed by Jesus and His apostles, is an invitation extended by God to rebellious men – but never to rebellious angels – to escape from Satan's kingdom and to enter into God's kingdom. All who desire to accept this invitation must fulfil two conditions: They must repent of their rebellion and submit themselves in faith to Christ as God's appointed ruler.

These two parables – the wheat and the tares, and the dragnet – both reveal that some of those who appear to belong to God's kingdom have not, in fact, fulfilled these two conditions. They have made an outward pretence of repentance and submission, but it did not come from a sincere heart. Consequently it did not produce the deep, inner reformation of character which alone is appropriate to the kingdom of God. One main purpose of both parables is to reveal the special judgement of God which will come upon these hypocrites at the close of the present age.

In the first of the two parables the servants ask the owner of the field if they should attempt to pull up the tares.

> But he said, "No, lest while you gather up the tares you also uproot the wheat with them" (Matt. 13:29).

This indicates that it would have been very hard for the servants to distinguish the tares from the wheat. Obviously this would not be true if the tares represented people who had not made any profession of faith in Christ. Jesus goes on to give a full interpretation of the whole parable.

> He answered and said to them: "He who sows the good seed is the Son of Man. The field is the world, the good seeds are the sons of the kingdom, but the tares are the sons of the wicked one. The enemy who sowed them is the devil, the harvest is the end of the age, and the reapers are the angels. Therefore as the tares are gathered and burned in the fire, so it will be at the end of this age. The Son of Man will send out His angels, and they will gather out of His kingdom all things

that offend, and those who practice lawlessness, and will cast them into the furnace of fire. There will be wailing and gnashing of teeth. Then the righteous will shine forth as the sun in the kingdom of their Father. He who has ears to hear, let him hear!" (Matt. 13:37-43).

Jesus identifies the tares as "the sons of the wicked one." Their presence in the field is no accident. They have been deliberately sown among the wheat by the devil. In other words, it is part of Satan's strategy to plant hypocrites among the true Christians. It is one way in which he seeks to discredit the testimony of the church.

Jesus goes on to say that, in the judgement at the end of this age, the angels will first gather out all false Christians from among the true and cast them into a place of fire, where there is wailing and gnashing of teeth. After this has been done, "*then* the righteous will shine forth as the sun in the kingdom of their Father." In other words, the false Christians will first be separated out and cast into a place of fiery judgement. After that, the true Christians will be manifested in their resurrection glory.

The parable of the dragnet contains the same revelation.

Again, the kingdom of heaven is like a dragnet that was cast into the sea and gathered some of every kind, which, when it was full, they drew to shore; and they sat down and gathered the good into vessels, but threw the bad away. So it will be at the end of the age. The angels will come forth, separate the wicked from among the just, and cast them into the furnace of fire. There will be wailing and gnashing of teeth (Matt. 13:47-50).

In this parable the dragnet cast into the sea represents the gospel of the kingdom proclaimed in all the world. The various creatures caught in the net represent all those who have made a positive response to the gospel invitation. These include people of every kind – both good and bad, both just and wicked.

At the close of the age, the angels will separate out the wicked from the just and cast them into a place of punishment. Only after that will the good and the righteous go on to receive the blessings and rewards of eternity with Christ.

In this revelation we see yet another reason why the judgement conducted before the judgement seat of Christ will not result in final condemnation for any who appear there. Before this judgement of the true believers takes place, the angels will already have separated out and cast into a place of punishment all hypocrites and false Christians. Thus those who appear before Christ's judgement seat to receive their rewards will be only the true and righteous believers, the salvation of whose souls is eternally assured through their sincere faith based on Christ's own righteousness.

The Psalms prophetically refer to this process of separating out the hypocrites and false believers prior to judgement of the true believers.

> The ungodly are not so,
> But are like the chaff which the wind drives away.
> Therefore the ungodly shall not stand in the judgement,
> Nor sinners in the congregation of the righteous (Ps. 1:4-5).

In this prophecy the ungodly are compared to the chaff, while – by implication – the righteous are compared to the wheat. Before the wheat is gathered into the barn, the chaff is first driven away. Before the righteous enter into their eternal reward, the wicked are first severed out from among them and cast out into a place of punishment.

For this reason the psalmist goes on to say that the ungodly and the sinners will never be allowed to take their place in the judgement of the righteous (before the judgement seat of Christ), nor will they ever be admitted to the congregation of true believers in eternity.

We may state this conclusion as follows: Only true, sincere believers will appear before the judgement seat of Christ. Prior to this, by the intervention of angels, all hypocrites and false Christians will have been purged out and cast into a place of fiery punishment.

52
THREE FINAL JUDGEMENTS

We pointed out in chapter 50 that the eternal judgements of God will be carried out in three successive scenes.

The first scene will be the judgement of Christian believers before the judgement seat of Christ.

The second scene will be the judgement of the Gentile nations at the close of the great tribulation, carried out before the throne of Christ's glory.

The third scene will be the judgement of all the remaining dead at the close of the millennium, carried out before a great white throne.

We have already examined the first of these three scenes, the judgement of Christians before the judgement seat of Christ. Now we shall move on to the next scene: the judgement of the Gentiles at the close of the great tribulation.

First, however, we need to consider the main events which will lead up to this judgement. This will help us to understand why God has ordained a special judgement reserved only for the Gentile nations.

Paul refers to three different categories into which God has divided the human race.

> Give no offence, either to the Jews or to the Greeks [Gentiles]
> or to the church of God (1 Cor. 10:32).

The Jews are a special nation, separated out by God for purposes of His own from all other nations. The Gentiles are all the remaining nations, except Israel. The church of God consists of all true believers who have been born again through faith in Jesus Christ. These are no longer reckoned by God according to their original nationality, whether Jew or Gentile, but as being "a new nation" in Christ.

Scripture makes it clear that the judgement we are now considering, before the throne of Christ's glory, will be for Gentiles only. No member of either of the other two groups will appear here for judgement. There will be no Jews and no Christians. This fact agrees with the general revelation of Scripture concerning the close of this present age.

There will be no Christians at this judgement because all these will already have undergone their own special judgement before the judgement seat of Christ.

There will be no Jews present at this judgement because by this time Israel, as a nation, will already have passed through her own special judgement. All Jews who survive this special judgement will have been reconciled to God through the acknowledgement of Jesus as Saviour and Messiah.

God's final dealings with Israel at this time will complete the historical process of judgement through which He has been bringing them for nearly four thousand years. The subsequent judgement of the Gentile nations will mark a transition from historical to eternal judgement.

Tribulation Judgement of Israel

In considering this special judgement of Israel, it is helpful to observe two general principles according to which God deals with the human race: in blessing and in judgement. These may be briefly stated as follows.

1. *A principle of blessing.* God normally blesses the Gentiles through the Jews, but He blesses the Jews directly.
2. *A principle of punishment.* God normally punishes the Jews through the Gentiles, but He punishes the Gentiles directly.

These two principles will direct God's dealings with the human race at the close of the present age.

First, in the closing stages of the great tribulation, God will judge and punish Israel for the last time as a nation, through the instrumentality of the Gentiles. When this final judgement of Israel is complete, God Himself will intervene directly in judgement upon the Gentiles. Jeremiah describes this final judgement upon Israel after they have returned as a nation to their own land.

> "For behold, the days are coming," says the Lord, "that I will bring back from captivity My people Israel and Judah," says the Lord. "And I will cause them to return to the land that I gave to their fathers, and they shall possess it." Now these are the words that the Lord spoke concerning Israel and Judah.
>
> > For thus says the Lord:
> > "We have heard a voice of trembling,
> > Of fear, and not of peace.
> > Ask now, and see,
> > Whether a man is ever in labour with child?
> > So why do I see every man with his hands on his
> >   loins
> > Like a woman in labour,
> > And all faces turned pale?
> > Alas! For that day is great,
> > So that none is like it;
> > And it is the time of Jacob's trouble,
> > But he shall be saved out of it.
> > For it shall come to pass in that day,"
> > Says the Lord of hosts,
> > "That I will break his yoke from your neck,
> > And will burst your bonds;
> > Foreigners shall no more enslave them.
> > But they shall serve the Lord their God,
> > And David their king,
> > Whom I will raise up for them" (Jer. 30:3-9).

Notice the order of events here foretold by Jeremiah.

1. God will bring Israel back to their own land.
2. There will be for Israel a time of national peril and

distress, more terrible than any that they have previously passed through.

3. The Lord Himself will eventually intervene against the foreigners – the Gentile enemies of Israel – and will save Israel from them.

4. The national kingdom of Israel will again be restored upon the throne of David, under the supreme government of the Lord Jesus Himself. This period of the restored kingdom will be the millennium.

This end-time gathering of the Gentile nations against Israel, and the direct intervention of the Lord on behalf of Israel, are further described in Zechariah.

> And it shall happen in that day that I will make Jerusalem a very heavy stone for all peoples; all who would heave it away will surely be cut in pieces, though all nations of the earth are gathered against it (Zech. 12:3).

> For I will gather all the nations to battle against Jerusalem . . .
> Then the Lord will go forth
> And fight against those nations,
> As He fights in the day of battle.
> And in that day His feet will stand on the Mount of Olives
>   (Zech. 14:2-4).

Here again we see that the present age will close with a concerted attack against Israel and Jerusalem by the Gentile nations but that the Lord Himself will intervene to save Israel. This intervention will culminate in His personal return to the Mount of Olives – the very point from which He ascended into heaven at the commencement of this present dispensation.

As a result of this final period of national peril and distress, all rebellious elements will finally be purged out from among Israel, and those who survive this final purging will then be ready to be reconciled in repentance and humility to their God.

This final purging of Israel is described in Ezekiel 20:37-38, where the Lord first predicts their regathering in their own land and then describes how He will deal with them there.

> I will make you pass under the rod, and I will bring you into

the bond of the covenant; I will purge the rebels from among
you, and those who transgress against Me.

The phrase used here, to "make you pass under the rod," refers to the
process by which a shepherd used to inspect each one of his sheep before
admitting them to the fold. As a result of this process, all rebels will be
purged out from Israel, and those who are left will be brought into a new
covenant relationship with the Lord – through the new covenant in Jesus
Christ.

The intervention of the Lord against the persecuting Gentile nations
and His final reconciliation with Israel are further described in
Zechariah.

> It shall be in that day that I will seek to destroy all the nations
> that come against Jerusalem. And I will pour on the house of
> David and on the inhabitants of Jerusalem the Spirit of grace
> and supplication; then they will look on Me whom they have
> pierced; they will mourn for Him as one mourns for his only
> son, and grieve for Him as one grieves for a firstborn (12:9-
> 10).

It is the Lord Himself here speaking in the first person concerning
Israel, and He says, "They will look on Me whom they have pierced . . ."
Here is one of the clearest predictions in all Scripture of the rejection and
crucifixion of Christ. However, at this point Israel will at last
acknowledge their terrible error, and in great mourning and repentance
they will be reconciled with their Messiah, whom they have so long
rejected.

In the New Testament Paul describes this final reconciliation of Israel
to God.

> And so all Israel will be saved, as it is written:
>
> > "The Deliverer will come out of Zion,
> > And He will turn away ungodliness from Jacob"
> > (Rom. 11:26).

After Israel has thus passed through the fires of the great tribulation
and been reconciled again to God through Jesus Christ, there will be no
further need for God to judge them. Thereafter, when Christ sets up His
earthly kingdom and takes His seat upon the throne of His glory, He will

need only to judge the Gentile nations remaining alive on earth at the close of the great tribulation.

Judgement of Gentile Nations

Jesus gives a vivid picture of the judgement of the Gentile nations (see Matt. 25:31-46). There is no suggestion that this is a parable. It is a direct, prophetic prediction, using the analogy of a shepherd dealing with his flock. Let us examine the opening scene.

> When the Son of Man comes in His glory, and all the holy angels with Him, then He will sit on the throne of His glory. All the nations will be gathered before Him, and He will separate them one from another, as a shepherd divides his sheep from the goats. And He will set the sheep on His right hand, but the goats on the left (Matt. 25:31-33).

The purpose of the judgement that follows is to separate the sheep (those whom God accepts) from the goats (those whom God rejects). The sheep will be received into the kingdom God has prepared for them – that is, Christ's millennial kingdom. The goats will have final, irrevocable judgement pronounced upon them, by which they will be banished into everlasting fire prepared for the devil and his angels.

These rejected Gentiles will be sent forth not to Sheol or Hades but directly to the place of final punishment of all rebels – the lake of fire. Into this lake the beast – the Antichrist – and his false prophet already will have been cast.

The separation between sheep and goats is based upon one decisive issue: the way in which those being judged have treated the brothers of Jesus; that is, the Jewish people.

Many passages of Scripture make it clear that at the close of this age there will be world-wide hostility toward the Jewish people and the state of Israel. Not only will there be a concentrated attack by the Gentile nations against Israel, but Jews in other countries will be subjected to various forms of persecution. In the midst of all this, however, there will be some Gentiles who take their stand – either as individuals or as nations – on the side of the Jewish people. These will do everything in their power to protect the Jews and to alleviate their suffering. At the ensuing judgement, this will mark them out as sheep, counted worthy to enter into Christ's kingdom established on earth.

Joel presents a similar picture of the end-time gathering of the nations for God's judgement.

> For behold, in those days and at that time,
> When I bring back the captives of Judah and Jerusalem,
> I will also gather all nations,
> And bring them down to the Valley of Jehoshaphat;
> And I will enter into judgement with them there
> On account of My people,
> My heritage Israel,
> Whom they have scattered among the nations;
> They have also divided up My land (Joel 3:1-2).

God declares that He will first bring back the captives of Judah and Jerusalem – that is, He will regather the scattered Jewish people in their own land. Then He will gather all the Gentile nations and bring judgement upon them.

The basis of the judgement is the same as that described by Jesus in Matthew 25. God says He will enter into judgement with the nations "on account of My people Israel." At this stage in history when anti-Semitism is becoming continually more widespread and more aggressive, it is tremendously important for all nations to be warned that they will be judged by God on the basis of their treatment of the Jewish people.

Once the sheep have been separated from the goats, the judgement of the Gentile nations will be complete. By this time all those who are accounted worthy to enter into the period of Christ's millennial kingdom will have passed through the refining judgements of God. First, Israel will be purged in the fires of the great tribulation. Then, at the close of the tribulation, the Gentiles will be purged by Christ's own direct intervention and judgement.

After these purging judgements upon both Jew and Gentile, there will ensue a thousand years of peace and prosperity, with Christ ruling as King over all the earth.

At the close of this period of one thousand years, Satan will make one final attempt to organise the Gentile nations in rebellion against Christ and His kingdom, but this rebellion will be brought to nought by the direct intervention of God.

At this time Satan himself will at last be banished forever from earth and will be cast into the lake of fire, to join the Antichrist and the false prophet who will already be there.

With this defeat of Satan's final uprising, all the rebellious among those living at that time upon the earth will be purged out, and it will then remain to judge the dead of all previous ages. For this purpose, all the dead who have not previously been resurrected will at this time be called forth for judgement. In this way the stage will be set for the third and final scene of God's eternal judgement.

The Great White Throne

> Then I saw a great white throne and Him who sat on it, from whose face the earth and the heaven fled away. And there was found no place for them. And I saw the dead, small and great, standing before God, and books were opened. And another book was opened, which is the Book of Life. And the dead were judged according to their works, by the things which were written in the books. The sea gave up the dead who were in it, and Death and Hades delivered up the dead who were in them. And they were judged, each one according to his works. Then Death and Hades were cast into the lake of fire. This is the second death. And anyone not found written in the Book of Life was cast into the lake of fire (Rev. 20:11-15).

Here is the ultimate end of all sin and rebellion against the authority and holiness of almighty God: to be cast forever into the lake of everlasting fire. Only those whose names are written in the Book of Life will escape this final judgement. The names recorded in this book are of those who during their life on earth availed themselves, through faith, of God's mercy and grace. These fall into various categories.

All those who put their faith in Christ's atoning sacrifice on behalf of mankind will already have been resurrected at the commencement of the millennium. They will have passed through their own appropriate judgement before the judgement seat of Christ – not for condemnation, but to assess their reward.

It seems certain that the majority of those who appear before the great white throne will not have fulfilled the conditions for receiving God's mercy and will therefore be condemned to the lake of fire. Nevertheless, as was pointed out in chapter 46, there will definitely be at least two categories of people before the great white throne who will escape condemnation and enter into eternal life.

The first category will consist of people such as the queen of the South and the men of Nineveh, who availed themselves of the mercy which God offered to them in one brief but decisive revelation of

Himself. Scripture does not indicate how many others there may have been in the course of history who were given a similar opportunity.

The second category will consist of all those who died in faith during the millennium.

Can we anticipate that there will be others to whom God will extend mercy from His great white throne? The answer to this is locked up within the omniscience of God. For us, with our limited knowledge and narrow perspective, it is foolish to speculate.

Let us rather adopt the attitude expressed by Abraham.

> Shall not the Judge of all the earth do right? (Gen. 18:25).

Those who have tasted God's measureless mercy are assured that He will never withhold His mercy from any who qualify for it.

Let us beware, however, of assuming that we can ever fully comprehend all that is included in the outworking of God's judgements. The studies in this book have merely touched on certain aspects which God has seen fit to record in Scripture. There remain many other areas of this vast subject which are totally beyond our powers of comprehension.

In the last resort, we can only share the awe and wonder expressed by Paul.

> Oh, the depth of the riches both of the wisdom and knowledge of God! How unsearchable are His judgements and His ways past finding out! (Rom. 11:33).

This appropriately concludes the systematic study of the six foundation doctrines of the Christian faith which have been the theme of this book.

By means of systematic study, we have thoroughly laid that scriptural foundation of doctrine upon which the faith of every Christian may be firmly built. With this foundation laid, it then becomes possible to obey the further exhortation of Hebrews 6:1.

> Let us go on to perfection.

Let us continue to build upon this foundation until we have achieved in our lives a completed edifice of Christian doctrine and practice. The same Word of God which provides the needed foundation also shows us how we may go on to the perfection of the completed edifice. Therefore, to all those who have followed with me in these studies, I will offer this final word of exhortation, taken from the life of Paul.

And now, brethren, I commend you to God and to the word of His grace, which is able to build you up and give you an inheritance among all those who are sanctified (Acts 20:32).

SCRIPTURE INDEX

1 Corinthians

TOPICAL INDEX

CHRISTIAN FOUNDATIONS COURSE

If you have enjoyed reading *Foundations for Christian Living* and would like to process and apply the teaching – why not enrol on Derek Prince's *Christian Foundations Course*?

Building on the Foundations of God's Word

A detailed study of the six essential doctrines of Christianity found in Hebrews 6:1–2

- Scripture-based curriculum
- Advanced learning techniques
- Practical, personal application
- Systematic Scripture memorisation
- Opportunity for questions and feedback from course tutor
- Certificate upon completion
- Modular based syllabus
- Set your own pace
- Affordable

Based on *Foundations for Christian Living*

Available by correspondence or online.

For a prospectus, application form and pricing information, please visit: www.dpmuk.org/biblecourse or contact:

DPM-UK • Kingsfield • Hadrian Way • Baldock SG7 6AN
Tel: + 44 (0)1462 492100 • Fax + 44 (0)1462 492102
Email: cfc@dpmuk.org • www.dpmuk.org

Books
by Derek Prince

Appointment in Jerusalem

The remarkable account of Lydia Prince, a Danish school teacher who had a life-changing encounter with the Holy Spirit, became the wife of Derek Prince and the mother of nine adopted daughters.

30th Anniversary expanded edition

Order Code: B26	Size: 234x156
ISBN: 978-1901144321	No Pages 234

Price: £9.99 Study Level 🎓

Atonement – Your Appointment with God

In this powerful and life-changing book, you will discover how repentance, faith, and a relationship with the Holy Spirit can make the realities of Christ's sacrifice present and active in your life.

Order Code: B47	Size: 216x135
ISBN: 978-1901144194	No Pages 222

Price: £6.99 Study Level 🎓🎓

DPM Bestseller

Blessing or Curse: You Can Choose

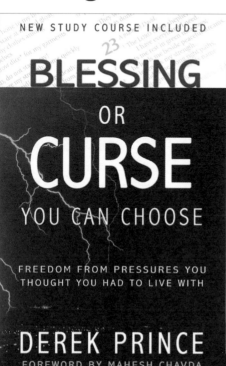

Are you continually frustrated by sickness, financial pressure, strained relationships or other struggles that just won't go away? In *Blessing or Curse: You Can Choose,* Derek Prince draws on real-life experiences of people who were astonished to discover that they were not the victims of blind chance or heredity, but a generational curse. Learn that a curse is not a superstition from the Dark Ages - but a very real force from which you can find freedom.

Order Code: B56	Size: 198x130
ISBN: 978-1901144406	No Pages 302

Price: £7.99 Study Level 🎓🎓

Declaring God's Word

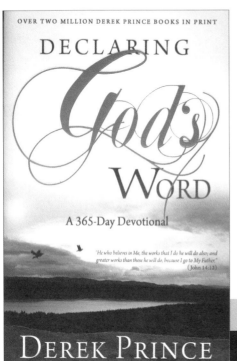

OVER TWO MILLION DEREK PRINCE BOOKS IN PRINT

DECLARING *God's* WORD

A 365-Day Devotional

'He who believes in Me, the works that I do he will do also; and greater works than these he will do, because I go to My Father.'
(John 14:12)

DEREK PRINCE

God expects us to speak Jesus' words and experience the same results that He did! For the first time, the world-renowned Bible teaching of Derek Prince has been condensed into a daily devotional.

Begin your day in the presence of the creator, rest on the truth of God's word, and you will experience the joy of seeing Him perform miracles, signs, and wonders in your life!

Order Code: B97
ISBN: 978-1603740678

Size: 230x153
No Pages 425

Price: £8.99   Study Level 🎓

The Choice of a Partner

In this simple, yet powerful, message, Derek Prince examines the choice of a spouse and shares insight into God's perspective in the matter.

Order Code: B75
ISBN: 978-089228328X

Size: 184x102
No Pages 16

Price: £1.50   Study Level 🎓

Complete Salvation

Salvation: one grand, all-inclusive word for everything Jesus obtained for us by His sacrificial death. This book introduces the first four steps for entering in.

Order Code: C83
ISBN: 978-1901144437

Size: 210x149
No Pages 76

Price: £3.99   Study Level 🎓

Derek Prince - A Biography

Hardcover

Derek Prince (1915-2003) is one of the most prominent Bible teachers of the 20th century. This biography is as gritty a book as you will ever read about a religious figure.

Order Code: B63
ISBN: 978-1901144291

Size: 241x162
No Pages 286

Price: £12.99 Study Level ☕

The Destiny of Israel and the Church

One of the most exciting features of the period in which we now live is that the destinies of Israel and the Church are once again beginning to converge.

Order Code: B40
ISBN: 978-1901144046

Size: 178x110
No Pages 151

Price: £5.99 Study Level ☕☕

Derek Prince: On Experiencing God's Power

God's Word holds power for every Christian. In this book, you will learn how to avail yourself of that power in every area of life - health, relationships, finances, prayer, and more.

A Compilation of 9 titles:
The Holy Spirit in You • God's Medicine Bottle • God's Remedy For Rejection • Marriage Covenant • God's Plan For Your Money • Does Your Tongue Need Healing? • How To Fast Successfully • Shaping History Through Prayer And Fasting • Spiritual Warfare.

Order Code: B43
ISBN: 978-0883685515

Size: 228x153
No Pages 527

Price: £9.99 Study Level ☕

The Divine Exchange

The entire message of the Gospel revolves around one historical event: the sacrificial death of Jesus on the Cross. Learn how this sacrifice provides so much more than simply an escape from Hell - but the supply of all your needs in life.

Order Code: B83
ISBN: 978-1901144011

Size: 210x148
No Pages 19

Price: £1.25 Study Level ☕

Does Your Tongue Need Healing?

The Bible tells us "life and death are in the power of the tongue." What we say - and how we say it - does matter. Learn how to control your tongue and use it to bless others.

Order Code: T85
ISBN: 978-0883682397

Size: 174x106
No Pages 102

Price: £3.50 Study Level ☕☕

The End of Life's Journey

Hardcover

In *The End of Life's Journey,* Derek Prince says that our appointment with death is inevitable. The wisdom and encouragement contained in *The End of Life's Journey* will help you face death with security and confidence.

Order Code: B62
ISBN: 978-1901144267

Size: 183x129
No Pages 190

Price: £6.99   **Study Level** 🎓🎓

Entering the Presence of God

Derek Prince shows the way to victorious intimacy with God. He explains how you can enter into the very presence of God to receive the spiritual, physical, and emotional blessings of true worship.

Order Code: B67
ISBN: 978-1901144420

Size: 178x110
No Pages 159

Price: £5.99   **Study Level** 🎓

Expelling Demons

We hear very little today about the casting out of demons, but Jesus Himself said "those who believe" would do it. It's time for the church to overcome the "spooky" extremes and devote prayerful, open-minded study to the subject.

Order Code: B70
ISBN: 978-0934920184

Size: 185x102
No Pages 23

Price: £1.50   **Study Level** 🎓

Extravagant Love

God's love is vast, boundless, extravagant! How shall we measure it? How shall we respond?

Order Code: T123
ISBN: 978-190114402X

Size: 178x110
No Pages 41

Price: £2.99   **Study Level** 🎓🎓

Explaining Blessings and Curses

Are you continually frustrated by sickness, financial pressure, strained relationships or other struggles that just won't go away? Derek suggests that two forces are at work in every life: blessings and curses.

Learn how to recognise a curse at work in your life and how to find release and God's blessings.

Order Code: BC36
ISBN: 978-1852403287

Size: 215x140
No Pages 63

Price: £3.99   **Study Level** 🎓

Foundations for Christian Living

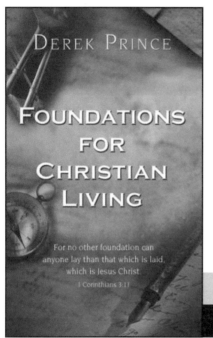

Using Hebrews 6:1-2 as a guide, Derek Prince unfolds in clear, simple language the six basic doctrines on which you must build. Revised and updated from the original *Foundation Series*.

This is the required texbook for the Christian Foundations Course. See page 527 for details.

Order Code: B54	Size: 216x135
ISBN: 978-1901144259	No Pages 526

Price: £9.99   Study Level 🎓

Faith to Live By

What is faith? How can I live my life in faith? How can my faith grow stronger? A resource for every Christian who purposes to obey Scripture and receive the promises of a faith-filled life.

Order Code: B29	Size: 210x131
ISBN: 978-0883685198	No Pages 187

Price: £4.99   Study Level 🎓

Fasting

God requires His people to humble themselves before Him, and has revealed a simple, practical way to accomplish this.

Order Code: T66	Size: 175x106
ISBN: 978-0883682583	No Pages 61

Price: £2.99   Study Level 🎓

The First Mile

Jesus challenged His disciples to go the extra mile. In this insightful booklet, Derek Prince challenges modern Christians to start by going the first mile. This perspective on servanthood could change your life.

Order Code: B78	Size: 184x101
ISBN: 978-0934920966	No Pages 17

Price: £1.50 **Study Level** 🎓

Freedom from the Past and Freedom for the Future

A compilation of:
God's Remedy for Rejection, God's Will for Your Life, and
The Holy Spirit in You.

Order Code: C86	Size: 216x135
ISBN: 978-1903725955	No Pages 153

Price: £7.99 **Study Level** 🎓

Gateway to God's Blessing

Getting the most out of life. Within the pages of this book is a plan to follow in order to live the life that you have always wanted: a life of blessing that God has made available, but you never knew how to obtain.

Order Code: B96	Size: 310x209
ISBN: 978-1603740525	No Pages 176

Price: £5.99 **Study Level** 🎓🎓

The Gifts of the Spirit

Every believer has been given at least one supernatural gift of the Holy Spirit. Do you know which one you have and how to operate in it?

Order Code: B92	Size: 229x152
ISBN: 978-0883682913	No Pages 253

Price: £6.99 **Study Level** 🎓🎓

God is a Matchmaker

Choosing your mate is one of the most important decisions you will ever make. The down-to-earth advice offered in *God is a Matchmaker* can help you avoid heartbreak and prepare you for marriage.

Order Code: B35	Size: 216x135
ISBN: 978-1901144161	No Pages 191

Price: £5.99 **Study Level** 🎓

God's Medicine Bottle

For those willing to follow its directions, God's 'medicine bottle' contains healing and health for all our flesh.

Order Code: T93	Size: 175x105
ISBN: 978-0883683323	No Pages 62

Price: £2.99 **Study Level** 🎓

God's Plan for Your Money

Your attitude towards money reveals your attitude to God. The right attitude produces the right results.

Order Code: T117
ISBN: 978-0883687070

Size: 209x131
No Pages 95

Price: £3.99

Study Level 🎓

God's Remedy for Rejection

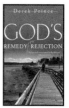

Many of our generation's greatest problems - depression, broken relationships, substance abuse - are rooted in rejection. Discover how to heal the wounds of rejection and enter into God's acceptance.

Order Code: B41
ISBN: 978-0883688646

Size: 209x131
No Pages 109

Price: £3.99

Study Level 🎓

God's Will for Your Life

There is a distinct difference between someone living a life of purpose and someone who wanders from one set of circumstances to the next. God has planned a unique destiny for each of us. Learn how to discover yours.

Order Code: T96
ISBN: 978-088368408X

Size: 209x131
No Pages 57

Price: £3.50

Study Level 🎓

The Grace of Yielding

Is the prospect of surrendering your entire life to God daunting or exciting? Discover the secret, hidden wisdom that comes from yielding to Him - and how to take hold of His grace to do it.

Order Code: B30
ISBN: 978-1901144119

Size: 178x110
No Pages 45

Price: £2.99

Study Level 🎓

The Holy Spirit in You

Discover how you can be filled with the Holy Spirit to enable you to walk as Christ walked - in love, in grace, and in the power of God.

As Christians, we have access to God's riches through the Holy Spirit - but only when we recognize Him as the sole administrator.

Order Code: T60
ISBN: 978-0883689618

Size: 210x132
No Pages 108

Price: £3.99

Study Level 🎓🎓

How to Fast Successfully

How long should I fast? How often? Should I abstain from food only, or also from fluids? How to obtain the greatest benefits from fasting, both spiritual and physical.

Order Code: B28
ISBN: 978-0883683453

Size: 173x103
No Pages 76

Price: £3.99   Study Level ☕

Husbands and Fathers

Nothing a man does at work - or at church – makes up for what he doesn't do at home. Derek Prince presents definitive guidelines for every man who wants to be a godly husband and father.

Order Code: B45
ISBN: 978-1852402733

Size: 198x130
No Pages 158

Price: £6.99   Study Level ☕

I Forgive You

Forgiveness centres in the cross vertically from God to man, horizontally toward our fellow-man. Experience the lifting of a burden when you say, "I forgive you!"

Order Code: T56
ISBN: 978-1901144376

Size: 178x110
No Pages 47

Price: £2.99   Study Level ☕

Judging

One of the most sensitive areas of our walk is to know the intricacies of judging. With this book, you will learn what you need to exercise judgment with wisdom, discernment and understanding.

Order Code: B49
ISBN: 978-0883686959

Size: 210x132
No Pages 128

Price: £3.99   Study Level ☕☕

Life's Bitter Pool

Often man's disappointments are God's appointments - but we can only discover His purposes in them as we respond in faith.

Order Code: T84
ISBN: 978-1901144100

Size: 178x110
No Pages 44

Price: £2.99   Study Level ☕

Lucifer Exposed

The fall of Lucifer set up "the battle of the ages." You are positioned right in the midst of this historic struggle. In this revealing book Derek exposes Satan's greatest weapon in enslaving the average human into bondage.

Order Code: B66
ISBN: 978-1901144383

Size: 216x135
No Pages 143

Price: £6.99   Study Level ☕☕

Marriage Covenant

Covenant is the divine key to a successful marriage and the only basis for true and lasting unity in all personal relationships.

Order Code: B31
ISBN: 978-0883687819

Size: 174x111
No Pages 173

Price: £3.99   **Study Level** 🎓

Orphans, Widows, the Poor and Oppressed

Care for the needy is identified as one of God's highest priorities throughout the entire Bible. Take a fresh look at an issue that goes much deeper than simply social concern.

Order Code: B46
ISBN: 978-1901144305

Size: 210x146
No Pages 45

Price: £1.99   **Study Level** 🎓🎓

Our Debt to Israel

Without the Jews, Christians would have no Bible and no Saviour! Discover the unique role played by the Jewish people in God's plans for the salvation of the world.

Order Code: B72
ISBN: 978-1901144185

Size: 178x110
No Pages 15

Price: £1.50   **Study Level** 🎓

Pages from My Life's Book

Derek Prince shares his personal search for truth as a young man and his life-changing discovery that truth is a Person.

Order Code: T30
ISBN: 978-1901144097

Size: 178x110
No Pages 64

Price: £2.99   **Study Level** 🎓

Partners for Life

Do you have a successful marriage - one that brings you genuine happiness and satisfaction? In this book, Derek Prince reveals that it truly is possible to have a successful marriage.

Order Code: T01
ISBN: 978-1901144314

Size: 210x148
No Pages 27

Price: £1.99   **Study Level** 🎓

Philosophy, the Bible and the Supernatural

"Listen in" as you read this transcript of Derek Prince's address to over 500 students and faculty of the University of British Columbia, making his case for Christianity and God's Word.

Order Code: B71
ISBN: 978-0934920222

Size: 183x101
No Pages 10

Price: £1.50   **Study Level** 🎓

The Power of Proclamation

Many Christians are not aware of this amazing potential that is available to them. The Word of God has powerful relevance in all situations, from personal needs to international crises.

Order Code: B69
ISBN: 978-1892283436

Size: 187x125
No Pages 103

Price: £4.99   Study Level ☞

The Power of the Sacrifice

In this powerful book, Derek Prince reveals the seven major ways the blood of Jesus impacts our lives. By understanding and embracing these truths, you too, can overcome Satan.

Order Code: B86
ISBN: 978-1901144305

Size: 210x148
No Pages 36

Price: £1.99   Study Level ☞☞

New Release

Prophetic Guide to the End Times

Even though God's "secret things" remain hidden, believers can study and act on the "revealed things" as He makes them known. Discover how acting on these assures our preservation and ultimate victory - and allows the Church to complete our mission to bring about the final sign of the end.

Order Code: B93
ISBN: 978-0800794453

Size: 216x135
No Pages 222

Price: £6.99   Study Level ☞☞

Prayers & Proclamations

These passages will remind you that God is the source of strength, healing, protection, victory, and more! Learn how to use the Bible as the authority over Satan in any situation.

Order Code: B59
ISBN: 978-0883682265

Size: 174x111
No Pages 75

Price: £6.99   Study Level 🎓

Praying for the Government

One of the most basic mandates for the Christian is to pray 'for kings and all who are in authority.' Now, perhaps more than ever before, we need to renew this commitment.

Order Code: B20
ISBN: 978-1901144123

Size: 178x110
No Pages 31

Price: £1.99   Study Level 🎓🎓

Protection from Deception

According to Scripture, supernatural signs and wonders will multiply as we approach the end times. In this book, Derek Prince shows how we can successfully navigate through this minefield. In *Protection from Deception,* renowned Bible scholar Derek Prince will equip you to:

- Test the source of signs and wonders
- Discern truth from falsehood
- Break free from the strongholds of Satan
- Resist the schemes of Satan
- Powerfully share the Gospel

You too can uncover the enemy's strategies, effectively engage in spiritual battles - and WIN!

Order Code: B94
ISBN: 978-0883682302

Size: 228x151
No Pages 240

Price: £5.99   Study Level 🎓🎓

Promised Land

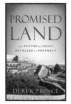

Now, more than ever, Israel is in the spotlight and we must understand God's purposes for this land and His chosen people. God will judge both individuals and nations by their response to the current re-gathering of Israel.

Order Code: B34
ISBN: 978-1892283220

Size: 208x136
No Pages 172

Price: £6.99   Study Level 🎓🎓

Receiving God's Best

Begin your journey today on the pathway of productive Christian living. Awaiting your discovery are keys to biblical success that can release God's very best for your life.

Order Code: T110
ISBN: 978-0883685930

Size: 175x105
No Pages 105

Price: £3.50   Study Level 🎓🎓

Rediscovering God's Church

How can you fulfil your calling for the 21st century? Where's your place in the church? In this comprehensive look at God's design for His church, you will discover how you can experience:

- The powerful, productive New Testament life
- Victory in spiritual warfare
- True fellowship with others
- God's will for your life

Order Code: B65   Size: 216x135
ISBN: 978-1901144345   No Pages 423

Price: £9.99   **Study Level** 🎓🎓

New Release

Secrets of a Prayer Warrior

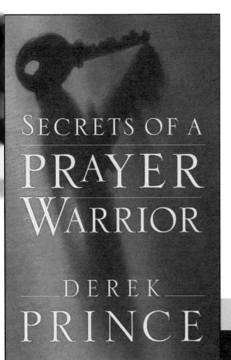

One of the most personal and powerful acts a Christian can engage in is prayer, yet many believers struggle with their prayer lives. Delving deep into the biblical understanding of prayer, Derek Prince shows readers the secret to leading a dynamic prayer life, how to receive what they ask for, and how to align themselves with the heart of God. Practical strategies like fasting, biblical study, discipline, and consistency are extensively explained and illustrated by powerful testimonies. This is a life-changing book.

Order Code: B95   Size: 216x140
ISBN: 978-0800794651   No Pages 224

Price: £7.99   **Study Level** 🎓🎓

Rules of Engagement

 With superb biblical exposition and practical application, Derek Prince offers you guidance to take your place in this monumental conflict. As you build the character of a warrior, you will become more like Jesus Christ, your commanding officer.

Order Code: B64
ISBN: 978-1901144338

Size: 216x135
No Pages 230

Price: £6.99   Study Level 🎓

Self-Study Bible Course

 The *Self-Study Bible Course* is an easy-to-use exploration of the foundations of the Christian faith. Discover the scriptural keys to understanding salvation, healing, prayer, and receiving guidance from God.

Order Code: B91
ISBN: 978-088368755

Size: 279x215
No Pages 211

Price: £8.99   Study Level 🎓

Shaping History through Prayer and Fasting

 You can make a difference in these volatile times. In *Shaping History through Prayer and Fasting,* you will discover the simple, yet powerful tools you need to have an impact on the destinies of nations.

Order Code: B25
ISBN: 978-0883687739

Size: 209x131
No Pages 189

Price: £5.99   Study Level 🎓🎓

Spiritual Warfare

 Headquarters - the heavenlies, the battlefield - our minds! All Bible believing Christians are involved in this battle whether they realise it or not!

Order Code: T36
ISBN: 978-0883686708

Size: 210x132
No Pages 138

Price: £5.99   Study Level 🎓🎓

Surviving the Last Days

 In this powerful booklet, you will learn about the great, basic problem humanity faces, the essential key to approaching the last days, and Jesus' role in the end of the age.

Order Code: B85
ISBN: 978-1892283328

Size: 185x101
No Pages 43

Price: £1.50   Study Level 🎓🎓

Through the Psalms with Derek Prince

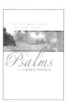 The Bible says that David - despite his glaring humanness - was a man after God's own heart. In this insightful devotional, Derek Prince teaches from David's psalms on pressing in closer to God.

Hardcover

Order Code: B33
ISBN: 978-1901144275

Size: 182x129
No Pages 221

Price: £6.99   Study Level 🎓

They Shall Expel Demons

In this readable, biblically based book, Derek Prince answers many vital questions. If you are struggling with problems that never seem to go away, has it ever occured to you that demons may be at work? In this practical comprehensive handbook on deliverance, Prince shares his own struggle with demons and addresses the fears and misconceptions often associated with deliverance.

| **Order Code: B42** | Size: 216x135 |
| ISBN:978-1901144062 | No Pages 283 |

Price: £7.99   Study Level ☗ ☗

Transformed for Life

Learn how to know God better and love Him more. Derek Prince reveals keys to understanding God's extravagant love and the completeness of Christ's sacrifice on the cross.

A Compilation of 6 titles:
- *Extravagant Love*
- *The Divine Exchange*
- *Who is the Holy Spirit?*
- *Life's Bitter Pool*
- *Fatherhood*
- *From Curse to Blessing*

| **Order Code: B48** | Size: 215x140 |
| ISBN: 978-0800793072 | No Pages 223 |

Price: £6.99   Study Level ☗

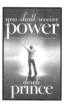